Sufficient Provision for Seekers of the Path of Truth

[Al-Ghunya li-Ṭālibī Ṭarīq al-Ḥaqq]

VOLUME TWO

Sufficient Provision for Seekers of The Path of Truth

[Al Ghunya li-Ṭālibī Ṭarīq al-Ḥaqq]

A COMPLETE RESOURCE ON THE INNER AND OUTER ASPECTS OF ISLAM

VOLUME TWO

SHAIKH 'ABD AL-QĀDIR AL-JĪLĀNĪ

TRANSLATED FROM THE ARABIC BY MUHTAR HOLLAND

AL-BAZ PUBLISHING, INC.
HOLLYWOOD, FLORIDA

"He [Allāh] is the Truth." Qur'ān (22:6)

Cover Design: Rohana Filippi

Using watercolor and wax to combine the beauty of Arabic script with the Qur'ānic message on paper, Italian artist Rohana Filippi has developed her own artistic style through personal research and inner inspiration. Her art is entirely devoted to "expressing Allāh's presence everywhere."
Ms. Filippi, who currently resides in Colombia, has lived and worked in Italy, England, Mexico, and the United States.

Cover Design: Dryden Design, Houston, Texas
Cover Preparation: Susan Lee Graphic Design, Ft. Lauderdale, Florida

Body text set in Jilani and Ghazali fonts by Al-Baz Publishing, Inc.

Printed on acid-free paper.

Library of Congress
Catalog Card Number: 95–75589

ISBN: 1–882216–08–3
Sufficient Provision for Seekers of the path of Truth, Vol. 2
ISBN: 1–882216–12–1
Sufficient Provision for Seekers of the path of Truth, set of 5 volumes

Published by Al-Baz Publishing, Inc.

4401 Sheridan Street, Suite 226, Hollywood, Florida 33021
Phone: (954) 964-5227 Fax: (954) 981-7304 E-mail: albaz@bellsouth.net

Printed and bound in the United States of America by McNaughton and Gunn, Inc.

Contents

Sufficient Provision for Seekers of the Path of Truth

[Al-Ghunya li-Ṭālibī Ṭarīq al-Ḥaqq]

VOLUME TWO

بِسْمِ ٱللَّهِ ٱلرَّحْمَٰنِ ٱلرَّحِيمِ

So remember Me,
and I will remember you…
(Qur'ān 2:152)

CHAPTER FIVE

A series of discourses *[majālis]* concerning the valuable lessons to be learned from the Qur᾿ān and the sayings of the Prophet (Allāh bless him and give him peace).

The First Discourse

Concerning the words of Allāh (Almighty and Glorious is He): When you recite the Qur᾽ān, seek refuge with Allāh from Satan the accursed.[1]

You should know that this verse *[āya]* occurs in *Sūrat an-Naḥl* [The Bee], which is a Sūra belonging to the Meccan period, except for three verses at the end of it, which were revealed at Medina. Its verses add up to a total of one hundred and twenty-eight. It contains one thousand eight hundred and forty-one [Arabic] words, and exactly seven thousand seven hundred and nine letters [of the Arabic alphabet].

According to scholars well versed in Qur᾽ānic exegesis *[ahl at-tafsīr]*,[2] the occasion of the revelation of this verse was as follows:

The Prophet (Allāh bless him and give him peace) recited *Sūrat an-Najm* [The Star], and he also recited [the Sūra[3] that begins:] "By the night when it enshrouds *[wa'l-laili idhā yaghshā]*," in the early morning ritual prayer *[ṣalāt al-fajr]* at Mecca. He therefore performed the recitation of both these Sūras in a voice that was audible to the people present.[4]

When [in the course of reciting Sūrat an-Najm] he reached the verse in which Allāh says:

> Have you thought of *al-Lāt* and *al-ʿUzzā*—and *Manāt* the third, the other? (53:19–20)[5]

—the Prophet (Allāh bless him and give him peace) experienced a moment of drowsiness *[naʿasa]*, whereupon Satan interjected into his

[1] *fa-idhā qara᾽ta'l-qur᾽āna fa-'staʿidh bi'llāhi mina'sh-shaiṭāni'r-rajīm*. (16:98)

[2] As defined by the Arabic lexicographers, the term *tafsīr* signifies "expounding, explaining, or interpreting the narratives *[qiṣaṣ]* that occur within the Qur᾽ān, and making known the significations of the strange words or expressions, and explaining the occasions on which the verses *[āyāt]* were revealed."

[3] *Sūrat al-Lail* [The Night]. This became Sūra 92 in the eventual compilation of the whole Qur᾽ān, the revelation of which was still at an early stage, of course, at the time of the incident described here.

[4] When conducting the early morning ritual prayer *[ṣalāt al-fajr]*, which consists of two cycles *[rakʿatān]*, the Imām recites *Sūrat al-Fātiḥa*, followed by another short Sūra, in each of the two cycles, and in a voice that is audible to the congregation.

recitation: "These are the exalted *gharānīq* (meaning the idols *[aṣnām]*); their intercession can be hoped for."[6]

The idolatrous polytheists *[mushrikūn]* were delighted to hear this, because they were firmly convinced that those idols of theirs were endowed with the power of intercession. They used to say: "These are our intercessors *[shufaʿāʾ]* in the presence of Allāh."

As Allāh (Almighty and Glorious is He) has said:

> [And those who choose protecting friends apart from Him, (say):] "We only serve them so that they may bring us close in nearness to Allāh." (39:3)[7]

They also used to maintain that they were pure bodies *[ajsām ṭāhira]*, free from any sins, and were therefore more worthy to be treated as objects of worshipful service *[ʿibāda]* than others, such as kings *[mulūk]* and angels *[malāʾika]*, since the latter are tainted with sins, and [cannot be pure bodies because] they are the possessors of souls or spirits *[dhawu'l-arwāḥ]*. Thus they likened the idols to the *gharānīq*—which are male birds (a single member of the species is called a *ghurnūq* or a *ghurnaiq*)—because they rise up and fly very high in the sky.

According to some authorities, the *ghurnūq* or *ghurnaiq* is a white bird, belonging to the aquatic family of birds. According to others, it is the crane *[kurkī]*. A very good-looking young man may also be referred to as a *ghurnūq*. The term occurs in this last sense in a traditional saying attributed to ʿAlī (may Allāh be well pleased with him): "So I seem to be looking at a *ghurnūq* (i.e., at a young man)[8] of [the tribe of] Quraish, who is wallowing in his blood."

According to Muqātil, the term *gharānīq* means the angels. He said: "They hoped that the angels would have a power of intercession *[shafāʿa]*, because a certain group among the unbelievers *[kuffār]* used to worship the angels."

[5] *a-fa-raʾaitumu'l-Lāta wa'l-ʿUzzā—wa Manāta'th-thālithata'l-ukhrā.*

[6] *tilka'l-gharānīqu'l-ʿulā—ʿindaha'sh-shafāʿatu turtajā.*

[7] *[wa'lladhīna 'ttakhadhū min dūnihi awliyāʾ]: mā naʿbuduhum illā li-yuqarribūnā ila'llāhi zulfā.*

[8] According to the Arabic lexicographers, the singular form corresponding to the plural *gharānīq*, as applied to the bird, may be *ghurnaiq*, *ghurnūq*, or *ghirnawq*. These, as well as several other forms *[ghirnīq, ghirnāq, gharawnaq and ghurāniq]*, may also be applied to "a tender youth; a youth white or fair, tender, having beautiful hair, and comely."

As far as the bird is concerned, it is variously described as: "a certain aquatic bird, long in the neck and in the legs, white [presumably the white stork, *ardea ciconia*] or black [presumably the black stork, *ardea nigra*]; or the bird also known as the *kurkī* [Numidian crane, *ardea virgo*], or a certain bird resembling this." (See: E.W. Lane, *Arabic-English Lexicon*, art. GH–R–N–Q.)

Well, to continue the story, when Allāh's Messenger (Allāh bless him and give him peace) had come to the end of *[Sūrat] an-Najm*, he bowed down in prostration *[sajada]*, and all who were present prostrated themselves, Muslim and idol-worshipper *[mushrik]* alike. The only exception was al-Walīd ibn al-Mughīra; he was a very old man, so he picked up a handful of dust, raised it to his forehead and made his act of prostration upon it, saying: "We bend as the mother of Aiman bends, she and her female companions [in mourning]." (Aiman was a servant of the Prophet—Allāh bless him and give him peace—who was slain on the day of [the battle of] Ḥunain.)

These two sentences went straight to the heart of every polytheistic idol-worshipper *[mushrik]*, although they represented nothing but the rhyming prose *[saj‘]* of Satan and his mischief,[9] interjected by him into the recitation of the Prophet (Allāh bless him and give him peace) at the point immediately following the reference to the false gods *[ṭawāghīth]* and the idols *[aṣnām]*. Both the two parties were amazed and delighted at their having performed the prostration all together, and at their having followed the lead of the Prophet (Allāh bless him and give him peace) in so doing.

As far as the Muslims were concerned, it came as a surprise to them to see the polytheistic idolaters *[mushrikūn]* performing the prostration *[sujūd]* in spite of their lack of faith *[īmān]* and certitude *[yaqīn]*.

As for the polytheistic idolaters, their feelings toward the Prophet (Allāh bless him and give him peace) and his companions became very amicable. On hearing from him what Satan had interjected into his longing, they were overjoyed and said: "Muḥammad has now come back to his first religion, the religion of his people." So they bowed in prostration to show their veneration for their gods *[āliha]*.

The two sentences soon spread far and wide among the people through Satan's broadcasting technique, until they reached as far as Abyssinia. This was a very serious problem for the Prophet (Allāh bless him and give him peace), so Gabriel (peace be upon him) came to him one evening and said: "May Allāh grant you protection from those two sentences. My Lord (Almighty and Glorious is He) did not reveal them, nor did He instruct me to communicate them."

[9] In Arabic, the two sentences—"These are the exalted *gharānīq [tilka'l-gharānīqu'l-‘ulā]*," and "Their intercession can be hoped for *[‘indaha'sh-shafā‘atu turtajā]*"—are constructed in rhyming prose *[saj‘]*.

As soon as Allāh's Messenger (Allāh bless him and give him peace) became aware of this, he was sorely troubled by it, and he said: "I have obeyed Satan. I have uttered his speech, and I have treated him as a partner in the business of Allāh (Almighty and Glorious is He)." Allāh then annulled what Satan had interjected, and He revealed to His Messenger (Allāh bless him and give him peace):

> We have not sent a Messenger or a Prophet before you without it happening that, when he experienced a longing, Satan cast suggestions into his longing. (22:52)[10]

That is to say, he interjected them into his reading and recitation.

> But Allāh will annul what Satan has suggested. Then Allāh will establish His revelations. Allāh is All-Knowing, All-Wise. (22:52)[11]

Now that Allāh (Almighty and Glorious is He) had absolved His Prophet (Allāh bless him and give him peace) of all culpability for the rhyming prose *[saj']* of Satan and his mischief, the polytheistic idolaters *[mushrikūn]* reverted to their errant ways and to their hostility toward the Prophet (Allāh bless him and give him peace) and his companions. Then the Prophet (Allāh bless him and give him peace) was commanded to make a practice of offering the prayer for Divine protection *[isti'ādha]*, for Allāh (Almighty and Glorious is He) sent down to him the revelation:

> When you recite the Qur'ān, seek refuge with Allāh from Satan the accursed. (16:98)

According to 'Abdu'llāh ibn 'Abbās (may Allāh be well pleased with him and with his father): "What this signifies is that, whenever you propose to recite the Qur'ān, you must say: 'I take refuge with Allāh from Satan the accursed *[a'ūdhu bi'llāhi mina'sh-shaiṭāni'r-rajīm]*.' In other words: 'I take precautions *[aḥtarizu]* with Allāh against Satan the accursed,' i.e., against Iblīs the damned *[la'īn]*, meaning the one who is cursed with damnation *[marjūm bi'l-la'na]*." For, as he also said, nothing is harder on Iblīs the damned than taking refuge *[ta'awwudh]* from him with Allāh:

> Surely he has no authority *[innahu laisa lahu sulṭānun]*

—in other words, no power of control *[mulk]*—

[10] *wa mā arsalnā min qablika min rasūlin wa lā nabiyyin illā idhā tamannā alqa'sh-shaiṭānu fī umniyyatih.*

[11] *fa-yansakhu'llāhu mā yulqi'sh-shaiṭānu thumma yuḥkimu'llāhu āyātih: wa'llāhu 'Alīmun Ḥakīm.*

> over those who believe and put all their trust in their Lord [*ʿala'lladhīna āmanū wa ʿalā Rabbihim yatawakkalūn*]. (16:99)

—in other words, those who place their full confidence in Allāh.

> His authority [*innamā sulṭānuhu*]

—meaning his power of control [*mulk*]—

> is only over those who take him for their friend [*ʿala'lladhīna yatawallawnahu*]

—that is to say, those who take Iblīs the damned for their friend, so that they follow him in what he commands, and thus he leads them astray from their religion, from Islām—

> and those who ascribe partners to Him [*wa'lladhīna hum bihi mushrikūn*]. (16:100)

—that is to say, those who ascribe partners to Allāh on Satan's behalf.

Concerning the meaning of the expression "I take refuge" *[aʿūdhu]*.[12]

What is signified by the expression "I take refuge" *[aʿūdhu]* may be explained as the act of seeking refuge *[istiʿādha]*,[13] asking for protection *[al-istijāra]*, and having recourse to a place of sanctuary or asylum *[iltijāʾ]*.[14] The corresponding noun *maʿādh* [place of refuge] is a synonym of *maljaʾ* [place of retreat or refuge; shelter; sanctuary; asylum].

When using the third person masculine singular of the verb in the past tense, one says [in Arabic]: *ʿādha bihi* [he took refuge with Him]. In the case of the third person masculine singular in the present/future tense, the verb takes the form *yaʿūdhu* [he takes/is taking/will take refuge]. The forms *ʿiyādh* and *ʿawdh* both occur as the corresponding verbal noun or infinitive.

[12] In order to grasp the full significance of many of the points discussed by Shaikh ʿAbd al-Qādir (may Allāh be well pleased with him) in this subsection, it is necessary to be aware of the basic structures of the Arabic language, especially the derivation of nouns, verbs and other parts of speech from 'roots' consisting (in the great majority of cases) of three consonants. The first such root to be considered here is made up of the consonant letters called *ʿain*, *wāw* and *dhāl*, which are represented in the system of transliteration employed in this English rendering of the text by: 1. the sign ʿ ; 2. *w* ; 3. the combination *dh*.

Since the Arabic letter *wāw* is a so-called 'weak' letter, it disappears from certain derived forms of any root of which it is one of the three elements. Thus, in some of the words derived from the root *ʿ–w–dh*, the central element may be 'hidden' in a long <ā> (represented by an *alif* in the Arabic script), a long <ū> (in which case the *wāw* is disguised in the transliteration, although it does appear in the original Arabic script), or it may have acquired the sound <y> or that of the long vowel <ī> (both represented by the Arabic letter *yāy*).

This should be borne in mind while reading this subsection, so that the reader will understand the linguistic and semantic connections between linking various terms discussed by the author, such as *aʿūdhu, istiʿādha, maʿādh, ʿādha, yaʿūdhu, ʿiyādh, ʿawdh, ʿawadh and uʿīdhu*—all of which are derivatives of the root *ʿ–w–dh*. (For a detailed listing of these and other words, phrases and sayings derived from this root, see E.W. Lane, *Arabic-English Lexicon*, art. *ʿ–W–DH*.)

[13] Under the heading *al-istiʿādha*, traditional collections of Islamic prayers of supplication include many invocations of Divine protection from specific as well as general evils.

[14] Shaikh ʿAbd al-Qādir (may Allāh be well pleased with him) has supplied numerous traditional prayers for the invocation of Divine refuge and protection.
(See pp. 42–43 below, also Vol. 1, pp. 15, 88–9, 338, 347–49, 358, 373 and 385–86.)

As for the expression *maʿādha'llāh,* which is also often used, it is another way of saying: "I resort to Him for protection *[aljaʾu ilaihi]* and I take refuge with Him *[aʿūdhu bihi]*."[15] Another related word is used when one says: "May this be a refuge *[ʿawadh]* for me from what I am afraid of." In other words: "May this be my protector *[mujīrī]* and my defender *[ad-dāfiʿ ʿannī]*."

The point of all this is that the servant [of the Lord] should take refuge with Allāh, so that He may keep him safe from the evil of Satan. To make a practice of taking refuge *[taʿawwudh]* in the Qurʾān[16] is to place oneself under its healing influence.

According to some authorities, the meaning of *istiʿādha* [seeking refuge] is *iḥtirāz* [taking precautions] with Allāh (Almighty and Glorious is He). As Allāh (Exalted is He) has said, when relating the words spoken by the mother of Mary:

> [She said...:] "I place her under Your protection, and her offspring *[uʿīdhuhā bika wa dhurriyyatahā]*,

—referring to Mary and [her son] Jesus—

> against Satan the accursed *[mina'sh-shaiṭāni'r-rajīm]*. (3:36)

[15] According to the Arabic lexicographers, the expressions *maʿādha 'llāh* and *maʿādhata'llāh* and *maʿādha wajhi'llāh* and *maʿādhata wajhi'llāh* and *ʿiyādha'llāh* all convey the same meaning, namely, *aʿūdhu bi'llāhi maʿādhan* [I take refuge with Allāh], which is equivalent to the saying: "May Allāh protect me," or "May Allāh preserve me." The exclamation *maʿādha'llāh* may often be heard in circumstances where an English speaker would be likely to say "God forbid!"

[16] Sūra 113 ('The Daybreak' *[al-Falaq]*) and Sūra 114 ('Mankind' *[an-Nās]*), the last two Sūras in the Qurʾān, are known as *al-Muʿawwidhatān* [the Two Pleas for Divine Refuge]. They read as follows:

In the Name of Allāh, All-Merciful and Compassionate.	*Bismi'llāhi'r-Raḥmāni'r- Raḥīm.*
Say: "I take refuge with the Lord of the Daybreak from the evil of what He has created, from the evil of the darkness when it is intense, from the evil of the witches who blow on knots, and from the evil of the envier when he envies."	*qul aʿūdhu bi-Rabbi'l-falaq— min sharri mā khalaq— wa min sharri ghāsiqin idhā waqab— wa min sharri'n-naffāthāti fi'l-ʿuqad— wa min sharri ḥāsidin idhā ḥasad.*
In the Name of Allāh, All-Merciful and Compassionate.	*Bismi'llāhi'r-Raḥmāni'r- Raḥīm.*
Say: "I take refuge with the Lord of mankind, the King of mankind, the God of mankind, from the evil of the slinking whisperer, who whispers in the breasts of mankind, of the jinn and of mankind."	*qul aʿūdhu bi-Rabbi'n-nās— Maliki'n-nās— Ilāhi'n-nās— min sharri'l- waswāsi'l-khannās— alladhī yuwaswisu fī ṣudūri'n-nās— mina'l-jinnati wa'n-nās.*

—in other words: "I take the precaution of looking to Allāh on behalf of the pair of them for protection from Satan the accursed."

As for the etymology of *ash-Shaiṭān* [Satan; the Devil], the name is derived from the same root, *sh-ṭ-n*, as the common noun *shaṭan*, meaning a long and strongly twisted rope. The corresponding verbal noun or infinitive, *shaṭn*, is a synonym for *buʿd* [to be remote; to keep one's distance]. The linguistic implication, therefore, is that he keeps himself at a very great distance from all that is good, while he stretches far into all that is evil and is intensely involved in it.

Then again, a human being may sometimes be referred to as a devil *[shaiṭān]*; that is to say, as someone who is like the Devil *[ash-Shaiṭān]* in his conduct and behavior. As a matter of fact, everything that is *mustaqbaḥ* [that is considered ugly, repugnant, repulsive, ignominious, infamous, shameful, disgraceful, foul, vile, base, mean, etc.] can be likened to the Devil. One may say, for instance: "So and so has a face like the face of the Devil, and his head is like the Devil's head." One such comparison is made in the words of Allāh (Almighty and Glorious is He), when He says:

> [It is a tree that comes forth in the root of Hell;] its spathes are as it were the heads of devils *[ruʾūsu'sh-shayāṭīn]*. (37:65)

The reference here is probably to the well-known [image people have of the] Devil's head *[raʾs ash-shaiṭān al-maʿrūf]*.[17] According to some authorities, however, it applies to certain snakes, which have repulsive heads and manes *[aʿrāf]*, while others have pointed out that "Devils' heads" *[ruʾūsu'sh-shayāṭīn]* is the name of a common plant.

As for the epithet *ar-rajīm* [the accursed], this is applied to the Devil because he is the one who has been cursed with damnation *[marjūm bi'l-laʿna]*. That is to say, Allāh (Exalted is He) has cursed him with damnation and has driven him into exile, far from the Divine Presence *[Ḥaḍra]*, as a punishment for his sinful disobedience in refusing to bow down in prostration before Adam (peace be upon him). The angels also cursed him by pelting him with gravestones *[rijām]*, with which they then proceeded to chase him out of heaven and down to the earth

[17] As noted by the Arabic lexicographers, "though the *shaiṭān* is not seen, he is conceived in the mind as the foulest, or ugliest, of things." (See E.W. Lane, *Arabic-English Lexicon*, art. *SH–Ṭ–N*.)

below. Then the stars *[kawākib]* were provided as missiles *[rujūm]* to be thrown at him.

So he and his offspring will be pelted with the stars and cursed with damnation until the Final Hour is at hand. As Allāh (Almighty and Glorious is He) has said:

> [And we have adorned the lower heaven with lamps] and We have made them missiles to be thrown at the devils *[wa ja'alnāhā rujūman li'sh-shayāṭīn]*. (65:7)

Concerning the remoteness of Satan from Allāh and from all that is good.

Satan *[ash-Shaiṭān]* is far removed from Allāh, distant from all that is good, remote from the Garden of Paradise and close to the Fire of Hell. This is why Allāh has commanded His Prophet (Allāh bless him and give him peace) and all decent members of his Community to make a practice of praying for refuge *[taʿawwudh]* from Satan the accursed, who is far from the All-Merciful One *[ar-Raḥmān]*, so that they may keep their distance from the Fires of Hell and draw close to the Gardens of Paradise, and so that they may look upon the Face of the King and Judge *[al-Malik ad-Dayyān]*.[18]

Allāh (Almighty and Glorious is He) is saying, in effect: "O my servant, Satan is far removed from Me, while you are close to Me. You must therefore be on your best behavior in order to preserve the right spiritual state *[ḥāl]*, so that Satan will not gain access to you by any means at all."

To be on our best behavior means that we must carry out the Divine commandments and observe the Divine prohibitions, and that we must be content to accept the course of destiny *[jarayān al-maqdūr]* as it affects us personally and as it affects our property, our family, our children and all the creatures in the universe.

Provided that the servant [of Allāh] can keep this up, that he can stick to it, persevere in it with diligence, and hold on to it with a firm embrace, he will enjoy salvation from the mischievous temptations

[18] In his *Ṣaḥīḥ*, Imām al-Bukhārī has recorded a traditional report, complete with its chain of transmitting authorities *[isnād]*, according to which ʿAbdullāh ibn Anas (may Allāh be well pleased with him) stated that he once heard Allāh's Messenger (Allāh bless him and give him peace) say:

> Allāh (Glory be to Him) will gather all His servants at the Resurrection, when He will summon them by calling out, in a voice that will be heard by those who are far away, just as clearly as it is heard by those who are close at hand: "I am the King *[Ana'l-Malik]*! I am the Judge *[Ana'd-Dayyān]*!"

[fitan] of the Devil and his insinuations *[waswās]*, as well as from the unworthy promptings and destructive tendencies of the lower self *[nafs]*, from the torment of the tomb and its suffocating pressure, from the terror and violence of the Resurrection, and from the agony and the groaning distress *[zafra]*[19] of the Fire of Hell. He will be in the vicinity of Allāh in the Garden of the Safe Resort *[Jannat al-Maʾwā]*,[20] in the company of "the Prophets, the champions of truth, the martyrs and the righteous—and the best of company are they!"[21] There he will have the bountiful blessings of Allāh at his disposal under every circumstance, and there he will abide for ever and ever. As Allāh (Exalted is He) has said:

> As for My servants, you shall have no authority over any of them, [except those who follow you, being perverse]. (15:42)[22]

It must follow, therefore, that when the servant is wearing the badge of servitude *[simat al-ʿubūdiyya]* to the King Most High *[al-Malik al-Aʿlā]*, it will not be possible for Satan the weak, the vile and the most inferior, to gain the upper hand over him and subject him to trial and tribulation—neither in a public setting nor when he is alone in private, and neither by influencing his heart toward committing an act of sinful disobedience when he is considering some course of action, nor by affecting the limbs of his physical body when they are on the verge of stumbling and falling to their ruin. At that very moment of peril, he will hear the cry: "This is how We treat someone who refuses to give in to his whims and passions *[hawā]*, and who follows the Truth *[Ḥaqq]* and is guided by it." The Assembly [of Angels] on High *[al-Malʾa al-Aʿlā]* will be engaged in a heated debate about him, as he is summoned by the Almighty *[al-ʿAẓīm]* to the Kingdom Most High *[al-Malakūt al-Aʿlā]*, and the King Most High *[al-Malik al-Aʿlā]* will speak of him in glowing terms—upon the

[19] According to the Arabic lexicographers, the word *zafra* means: A drawing in of the breath to the utmost, by reason of distress; a drawing-back of the breath so vehemently that the ribs become swollen out; or, an emission of the breath with a prolonged sigh or groan. (See E.W. Lane, *Arabic-English Lexicon*, art. *Z–F–R*.)

[20] An allusion to Qurʾān (53:15). According to various authors of Qurʾānic commentaries, the meaning of *Jannat al-Maʾwā* is: "The paradise to which repair the souls of the martyrs, or the pious, or the angels; or that in which the night is passed." (See E.W. Lane, *Arabic-English Lexicon*, art. *ʾ–W–Y*.)

[21] The words within inverted commas are from the Qurʾān (4:69): *an-nabiyyīna waʾṣ-ṣiddīqīna waʾsh-shuhadāʾi waʾṣ-ṣāliḥīn: wa ḥasuna ulāʾika rafīqā.*

[22] *inna ʿibādī laisa laka ʿalaihim sulṭānun [illā maniʾttabaʿaka minaʾl-ghāwīn].*

Throne *[ʿArsh]*, for He has firmly established Himself thereon[23]—in His Eternally Pre-Existent Speech *[bi-Kalāmihi'l-Qadīm]*, safeguarded from the rhyming prose *[sajʿ]* of Satan and all falsehood in the recitation of the reciter when he recites *[ʿinda qirāʾati'l-qāriʾi idhā qaraʾa]*:

> Thus it was, that We might ward off from him evil and foul abomination; he was surely one of Our devoted servants. (12:24)[24]

For such a servant is surely most righteously devoted to his duty, both in secret and in public.

To flee from Satan the accursed and from his beckoning call is therefore by far the better and more preferable course, since the warning has come down from the All-High, the Most High *[al-ʿAliyy al-ʿAlā]*, inasmuch as He has said:

> Surely Satan is an enemy to you; so treat him as an enemy. He summons his party only that they may be among the inhabitants of the blazing inferno. (35:6)[25]
>
> And yet he has led a great multitude of you astray; so did you not have any sense [of what you were getting yourselves into]? (36:62)[26]

For obedience to Satan is the root of all trouble and distress, whereas opposition to him is the basis of good fortune and bliss, of comfort and right guidance, and of eternal life in the abode of perpetuity *[dār al-baqāʾ]*.

[23] An allusion to the verse *[āya]* of the Qurʾān in which Allāh (Almighty and Glorious is He) has declared:

> The All-Merciful has firmly established Himself upon the Throne *[ar-Raḥmānu ʿala'l-ʿarshi'stawā]*. (20:5)

[24] *ka-dhālika li-naṣrifa ʿanhu's-sūʾa wa'l-faḥshāʾ: innahu min ʿibādina'l-mukhlaṣīn.*

[25] *inna'sh-shaiṭāna lakum ʿaduwwun fa-'ttakhidhūhu ʿaduwwā: innamā yadʿū ḥizbahu li-yakūnū min aṣḥābi's-saʿīr.*

[26] *wa-la-qad aḍalla minkum jibillan kathīrā: a-fa-lam takūnū taʿqilūn.*

Concerning the five benefits that accrue to the servant of Allāh from seeking refuge *[isti'ādha]* with Him.

Five benefits accrue to the servant of Allāh from seeking refuge *[isti'ādha]* with Him, namely the following:

1. Firm and constant adherence to the true religion and to right guidance *[ath-thabāt 'alā'd-dīn wa'l-hudā]*.
2. Salvation from the evil of [Satan] the damned and from trouble and distress *[as-salāma mina'l-la'īn wa'l-'anā']*.
3. Gaining admittance to the impregnable fortress and access to the nearness [of the Divine Protector] *[ad-dukhūl fi'l-ḥiṣn al-ḥaṣīn wa'z-zulfā]*.[27]
4. Attaining to the secure station[28] in the company of the Prophets, the champions of truth, the martyrs and the righteous *[al-wuṣūl ila'l-maqāmi'l-amīni ma'a'n-nabiyyīna wa'ṣ-ṣiddīqīna wa'sh-shuhadā'i wa'ṣ-ṣāliḥīn]*.
5. Obtaining the help and support of the Lord of the earth and the heaven *[nail ma'ūnati Rabbi'l-arḍ wa's-samā']*.

As the story is told in some of the previous [pre-Qur'ānic] Books of Scripture, when Iblīs the damned, addressing his words to Allāh (Almighty and Glorious is He), said:

> Then I shall come upon them from in front of them and from behind them, from their right hands and from their left hands. (7:17)[29]

[27] According to at least one Arabic lexicographer, *zulfā* may be a plural of *zulfa*, when the latter is used adjectivally in the sense of *qarīb* [near, close]. It is more commonly regarded, however, as a quasi-infinitive noun, meaning either "station, rank, degree" or "bringing very near." (See: E.W. Lane, *Arabic-English Lexicon*, art. *Z–L–F*.) The word occurs in several verses *[āyāt]* of the Qur'ān, including:

> And those who choose protecting friends apart from Him, (say): "We only serve them so that they may bring us close in nearness to Allāh" *[wa'lladhīna'ttakhadhū min dūnihi awliyā': mā na'buduhum illā li-yuqarribūnā ila'llāhi zulfā]*. (39:3)

[28] An allusion to the Qur'ānic verse *[āya]*:

> Surely those who were devoted to their duty shall be in a station secure *[inna'l-muttaqīna fī maqāmin amīn]*. (44:51)

[29] *thumma la-ātiyannahum min baini aidīhim wa min khalfihim wa 'an aimānihim wa 'an shamā'ilihim*.

—Allāh (Almighty and Glorious is He) said in reply:

> By My Might and My Majesty, I shall surely command them to appeal [to Me] for refuge, and then, when they seek refuge with Me, I shall protect them from the right with guidance, from the left with providential care, from behind with invulnerability, and from in front with invincible support, so that your devilish insinuation can never harm them, O damned one![30]

Among the traditional sayings *[aḥādīth]* handed down to us from Allāh's Messenger (Allāh bless him and give him peace), there is one in which the following words are attributed to him:

> If someone prays just once for refuge with Allāh, Allāh (Exalted is He) will keep him safe throughout the whole of the day in which he makes that plea.[31]

He also said (blessing and peace be upon him):

> Lock the doors of sinful disobedience by offering the prayer for refuge with Allāh *[bi'l-isti'ādha]*, and open the doors of worshipful obedience by invoking the Name of Allāh *[bi't-tasmiya]*.[32]

It has been said that Iblīs[33] sends out three hundred and sixty soldiers, on a daily basis, with the mission of leading the believer *[mu'min]* astray. But then, if the believer seeks refuge with Allāh, Allāh casts three hundred and sixty glances into his heart, and every one of those glances of His results in a fatal casualty for one of the soldiers of the Devil, may Allāh doom him to damnation!

[30] *wa 'Izzatī wa Jalālī la-āmurannahum bi'l-isti'ādha: fa-idha'sta'ādhū bī ḥafiẓtuhum 'ani'l-yamīni bi'l-hidāyati wa 'ani'sh-shimāli bi'l-'ināyati wa 'ani'l-khalfi bi'l-'iṣmati wa 'ani'l-quddāmi bi'n-nuṣra: ḥattā lā taḍurrahum waswatuka yā mal'ūn.*

[31] *mani'sta'ādha bi'llāhi marratan ḥafiẓahu'llāhu—ta'ālā—fī yamihi dhālik.*

[32] In other words, by saying: "*Bismi'llāh* [In the Name of Allāh]."

[33] Iblīs is the personal name of the Devil. Some Western scholars consider it to be an arabicized version of the Greek *diabolos*, but the Arab philologists derive it from the root *b–l–s*, on the grounds that Iblīs "has nothing to expect *[ublisa]* from the mercy of Allāh (Almighty and Glorious is He)." He is also called *ash-Shaiṭān* [Satan, the Devil], *'aduww Allāh* [the enemy of God] or simply *al-'aduww* [the Enemy]. Unlike the English word Satan, however, *ash-Shaiṭān* is not strictly speaking a proper name, as A.J. Wensinck points out in his article IBLĪS in the *SEI*. (See also: T.P. Hughes, *Dictionary of Islam*, art. DEVIL).

Concerning the things which Satan dreads, and against which he is always on his guard.

The things which Satan dreads, and against which he is ever on his guard, are: The prayer for Divine refuge *[isti'ādha]* and the rays of the light of intimate knowledge in the hearts of those who know through direct spiritual experience *[shu'ā' nūr ma'rifa qulūb al-'ārifīn]*.

So, if you are not yet one of those who are spiritually aware, you must make it your practice to offer the prayer for Divine refuge, following the example of those who are devout in the performance of their religious duties, until you progress to the stage of development attained by those who know through direct spiritual experience.

From that point on, the rays of the light of your heart will shatter his offensive power and put his troops to flight. They will destroy all his flourishing tentacles and extirpate his malignant tumor, as far as you personally are concerned. It may also happen that you will be put in charge of his imprisonment, for the sake of your brothers *[ikhwān]* and your followers, just as it happened in the case of 'Umar ibn al-Khaṭṭāb (may Allāh be well pleased with him). The Prophet (Allāh bless him and give him peace) is reported as having said:

> The Devil runs away from your shadow, O 'Umar!

and:

> Whenever 'Umar travels along a particular valley, the Devil always chooses a different valley for his own journey!

It has been said that the Devil used to suffer an epileptic fit whenever he caught sight of 'Umar (may Allāh be well pleased with him). It is safe to assume, therefore, that when the Devil recognizes sincerity *[ṣidq]* on the part of a servant [of the Lord] in his hostility toward him and in his opposition to his summons, he will despair of that individual, treat him as a lost cause, and focus his attention on somebody else. He will still approach him from time to time, however, sneaking up on him in disguise like a furtive thief, so the servant [of the Lord] must stick to his sincerity; he must remain vigilant and be ever on the watch in order to detect the approach of Satan and his cunning devices, for his probing instrument *[mithqab]* is very subtle, his animosity is primeval and fundamental, and he makes inroads through the skin and the flesh as blood flows through the veins.

We know of a traditional report to the effect that Abū Huraira (may Allāh be well pleased with him) used to say, after he had reached his senior years: "O Allāh, I take refuge with You from the possibility that I might perpetrate an unlawful sexual act or murder." When people asked him if he could really be afraid of that kind of thing, he would reply: "How can I not be afraid, as long as Iblīs is still alive?"

Concerning the most effective ways of seeking help in order to combat the Devil and keep him at bay.

For the purpose of waging war against the Devil and keeping him at bay, the most effective ways of seeking help are: (1) to utter the statement of sincere devotion *[kalimat al-ikhlāṣ]*,[34] and (2) for a man to remember his Lord (Almighty and Glorious is He).

As the Prophet (Allāh bless him and give him peace) has reported the words of his Lord (Almighty and Glorious is He):[35]

> "*Lā ilāha illa'llāh* [There is no god but Allāh]" is My fortress, so anyone who says these words will enter My fortress. And anyone who enters My fortress is surely safe from My torment.

The Prophet (blessings and peace be upon him) has also said:

> Anyone who says "*Lā ilāha illa'llāh* [There is no god but Allāh]," and who says it sincerely, will enter the Garden of Paradise.

The Devil is the cause of the torment [inflicted by Allāh], so when the servant [of the Lord] pronounces the statement [of sincere belief], and when he clothes himself with its necessary consequences by observing the Divine commandments and prohibitions, the Devil, seeing him wrapped up in all that, will keep his distance from him and will not approach him. The servant will thus be saved from Satan's mischievous temptation, just as he would be saved from the weapons of his enemy by a coat of armor worn in battle.

Similar protection is afforded by frequent invocation of the Name of Allāh, as we know from the traditional account of the following incident: The Prophet (Allāh bless him and give him peace) once

[34] The affirmation of Divine Unity: "*Lā ilāha illa'llāh* [There is no god but Allāh]."

[35] That is to say, in a Sacred Tradition *[Ḥadīth Qudsī]*, not a verse *[āya]* of the Qur'ān.

heard a man say: "May the Devil stumble and fall flat on his face *[taʿasa'sh-Shaiṭān]*!"[36] So he told the man:

> Do not say that kind of thing, for it will only serve to make Satan the damned feel more and more important, and he will say: "By my might I have gained the upperhand over you!" What you should say instead is "*Bismi'llāh* [In the Name of Allāh]," for that will make the Devil feel less and less important, till he is reduced to something no bigger than a speck of dust.

Equally effective, as a means of seeking help against the Devil, is the giving up of greedy ambition to acquire anything apart from the gracious favor of Allāh (Almighty and Glorious is He), such as the influential support of worldly people, their goods, their praise and their applause, their accumulated wealth, their conspicuous affluence and their gifts. For this world and its sons are the property of Satan, his soldiers and his party *[ḥizb]*. A man goes the way of the model he aspires to, and a king goes the way of his army.[37]

The servant [of the Lord] must therefore give up all interest in achieving such ambitions. He must be completely satisfied with Allāh (Almighty and Glorious is He). In Him he must place all his confidence *[thiqa]* and all his trust *[tawakkul]*. He must become accustomed to consulting Him in all his affairs and all his circumstances. He must practice pious caution *[waraʿ]*, by taking care to abstain from things that are merely dubious *[shubha]* as well as those that are clearly unlawful *[ḥarām]*. He must give up creature comforts and reduce to the minimum his consumption of worldly goods, be they lawful *[ḥalāl]* or merely permissible *[mubāḥ]*. He must refrain from taking his food with a ravenous appetite and gluttonous voracity, like the proverbial idiot who gathers wood at night *[ḥāṭib al-lail]* without careful examination and inspection. If someone does not care to notice where his food and drink come from, Allāh (Almighty and Glorious is He) will not care to notice by which of its gates He causes him to enter the Fire of Hell.

The servant [of the Lord] must therefore make it his regular practice to follow every piece of this advice, until Satan gives up all hope of controlling him, for then he will be safe through the mercy of Allāh and with His help. But if he does not act accordingly, then the Devil will be his comrade, within his heart and within his breast.

[36] As the Arabic lexicographers point out, the import of this vivid expression is: "May he perish; may he be destroyed!" (See: E.W. Lane, *Arabic-English Lexicon*, art. *T–ʿ–S*.)

[37] *al-mar'u maʿa mithālihi wa'l-maliku maʿa jundih.*

As Allāh (Almighty and Glorious is He) has said:

> And he whose sight is dim to the remembrance of the All-Merciful, to him We assign a devil who becomes his comrade. (43:36)[38]

There will be times when that devil whispers his evil suggestions to him during his ritual prayer *[ṣalāt]*. At other times he will excite him with futile desires, arousing all the appetites of the lower self, those that are strictly unlawful as well as those that are ordinarily permissible. There will also be times when he persuades him to hold back from prompt participation in good causes, from performing the customary and necessary religious duties *[as-sunan wa'l-wājibāt]*, from acts of worship and righteous deeds *[al-ʿibādāt wa'l-qurubāt]*. Thus he will lose both this world and the hereafter, and will eventually be resurrected in his [devil's] company.

It may happen that his devil-comrade will deprive him of his faith *[īmān]* at the very end of his life, so that he will be doomed on the Day of Resurrection to dwell with him for all eternity in the Fire of Hell, in the company of Pharaoh and Hārūn and Qārūn.

We take refuge with Allāh from the deprivation of faith, and from obediently following the Devil both in secret and in public.[39]

[38] *wa man yaʿshu ʿan dhikri'r-Raḥmāni nuqayyiḍ lahu shaiṭānan fa-huwa lahu qarīn.*

[39] *naʿūdhu bi'llāhi min salbi'l-īmān wa matābaʿati'sh-shaiṭāni fi's-sirri wa'l-iʿlān.*

The sons of Satan who oversee the sons of Adam [mankind], according to a traditional report handed down from the Prophet (Allāh bless him and give him peace).

According to a traditional report handed down to us from Muqātil, on the authority of az-Zuhrī, who transmitted it on the authority of ʿUrwa, the following account was originally given by ʿĀʾisha (may Allāh be well pleased with her):

The Companions of Allāh's Messenger (Allāh bless him and give him peace) set out one evening, hoping to spend some time together with Allāh's Messenger (Allāh bless him and give him peace). Included in their group were Abū Bakr, ʿUmar, ʿUthmān, ʿAlī, Salmān and ʿAmmār ibn Yāsir (may Allāh the Exalted be well pleased with each and every one of them). Allāh's Messenger (Allāh bless him and give him peace) did step out of doors to meet them, despite the fact that he was suffering from a bad case of *ar-ruḥaḍāʾ* (i.e., the heavy sweat caused by the fever). The beads of sweat were dripping from him like *jumān* (another word for *luʾluʾ* [pearls]). Then, when he had wiped his brow, he said:

> May Allāh damn the accursed one *[laʿana'llāhu'l-malʿūn]*!

He said this three times over, then he lowered his head and fell silent, so ʿAlī (may Allāh be well pleased with him) said to him: "Let my father be your ransom, and my mother too! Whom were you damning just a moment ago?" The Prophet (Allāh bless him and give him peace) said in reply:

> The wicked Iblīs, the enemy of Allāh, inserted his tail into his own backside, and then laid seven eggs. Such was the origin of his sons, who have been charged with the task of overseeing the sons of Adam. Their names and their particular areas of responsibility are as follows:
>
> 1. *al-Mudhish*. He is the one who has been entrusted with the task of overseeing the learned scholars *[ʿulamāʾ]*, whose attention he diverts into whimsical excursions of various kinds.

2. *Ḥadīth*. He is the one entrusted with the disruption of the ritual prayer *[ṣalāt]*, so he goes about his work by making worshippers forgetful of their duty to remember Allāh. By catching their wandering glances, he gets them involved in frivolous occupations. He causes them to experience bouts of yawning and moments of nodding off, so that one of them may actually fall asleep. Yet when that person is told that he has been sleeping, he will insist: "I did not go to sleep!" As a result, he will go ahead and start doing the ritual prayer without first performing the necessary ablution *[wuḍū']*.

By the One who holds the soul of Muḥammad in His hand, a person like that is quite likely to come away from his ritual prayer with no credit for even one half of it, or not even a quarter of it, or not even a tenth of it, and the burden of sin incurred in the process will be greater than the reward for doing the prayer.

3. *az-Zalbanūn*. He is the one in charge of the market places. His job is to instruct a person doing business there in the arts of giving short measure *[taṭfīf]*, telling lies in the course of his transactions, making his wares look more attractive than they really are, and advertising them in glowing terms when he offers them for sale, until he can find a buyer to take them off his hands.

4. *Batr*. He is the master of the beating of breasts and the scratching of faces [as a display of grief and dismay], of the crying of woe and total disaster whenever a misfortune falls to someone's lot, so that the spiritual reward which that person might have earned [by enduring the affliction with patience] will all be wasted and lost.

5. *Manshūṭ*. He is the master of false reports, slanderous gossip, sneers and jeers and taunts and gibes *[al-hamz wa'l-ghamz]*, and he uses his skill to lead the servants [of Allāh] into sin.

6. *Wāsim*. He is the one in charge of the posterior anatomy. He blows into the duct of the man's penis *[iḥlīl]* and into the buttocks *['ajuz]* of the woman, until each of them commits an unlawful sexual act with the other.[40]

7. *al-A'war*. He is the master of larceny *[sariqa]*. He says to the thief: "You will simply be using what you steal to provide for your basic needs, to settle your debts, and to keep yourself modestly clothed. You can always repent later on."

What is therefore required of every believer *[mu'min]* is that he should never let down his guard against the Devil under any circumstances, and that he should never feel safe from him in any of his affairs.

The tradition *[ḥadīth]* of the Prophet (Allāh bless him and give him peace) also includes this saying of his:

> The ritual ablution *[wuḍū']* has a devil of its own, who goes by the name of *al-Walhān*, so from him you must seek refuge with Allāh.

We have also learned from our traditional sources that the Prophet (Allāh bless him and give him peace) once said:

[40] *ḥattā yazniya kullu wāḥidin minhumā bi-ṣāḥibih.*

> You must keep very close to one another in the ranks [when you line up to pray in congregation], so that the Devil cannot find a gap through which to slip in between you. You must stick as closely together as the daughters of *jadaf*.

When people asked, "And what are the 'daughters of *jadaf*'?" Abū Ḥudhaifa said that, according to Abū ʿUbaida, they are those little sheep from the region of the Ḥijāz. One of them by itself is called a *jadafa*.[41] They are also known as *naqad*.[42] Some say that they have neither tails nor ears, and that they are imported from Jarash, a town in the Yemen.

According to a traditional report, it was ʿUthmān ibn Abu'l-ʿĀṣ (may Allāh be well pleased with him) who made the following statement: "I said: 'O Messenger of Allāh, what is he like, the devil who intervenes between me and my ritual prayer *[ṣālāt]* and my recitation of the Qurʾān?' He responded (Allāh bless him and give him peace) by saying:

> That particular devil is called *Khanzab*. When you feel aware of his presence, you must take refuge *[taʿawwadh]* from him with Allāh. You should also spit three times to your left."

ʿUthmān ibn Abu'l-ʿĀṣ (may Allāh be well pleased with him) went on to say: "I acted on this advice, and Allāh did cause that devil to go away and leave me."

In the well-known tradition *[ḥadīth mashhūr]*, the Prophet (Allāh bless him and give him peace) said:

> There is not a single one amongst you who does not have a devil of his own.[43]

People asked: "Not even you, O Messenger of Allāh?", so he responded (Allāh bless him and give him peace) by saying:

> Not even I. The only difference is that Allāh (Hallowed and Exalted is He) has helped me against him, and so I am safe.[44]

In yet another traditional account, the Prophet (Allāh bless him and give him peace) is reported as having said:

> There is not a single one of you who does not have a comrade from among the jinn, assigned to oversee him personally.[45]

[41] Or perhaps it should be read as *jadfa*. Since this meaning of the word is not listed in the dictionaries, it is impossible to be certain of the correct vowelling. The Arabic text shows only the consonantal outline: *j–d–f* for the plural or collective form, with the addition of *tāʾ marbūṭa* in the case of the singular.

[42] According to the Arabic lexicographers, *naqad* is a collective term for "a kind of sheep, of ugly form; a kind of sheep of al-Baḥrain, having short legs and ugly faces; or a kind of small sheep of al-Ḥijāz; or, simply, lambs." (See: E.W. Lane, *Arabic-English Lexicon*, art. *N–Q–D*.)

People asked: "Not even you, O Messenger of Allāh?", so he responded (Allāh bless him and give him peace) by saying:

> Not even I. The only difference is that Allāh (Hallowed and Exalted is He) has helped me against him, and so I am safe, for he never tells me to do anything but good.

It has been said that, when Allāh damned Iblīs, He brought his wife into existence from him. The She-Devil *[Shaiṭāna]* was created from his left rib, just as Eve *[Ḥawwā᾿]* was created from Adam (peace be upon him). Then Iblīs had sexual intercourse with her, as the result of which she became pregnant by him and produced thirty-one eggs. Such was the origin of his offspring, the starting point from which they dispersed in all directions, until they were eventually spread out far and wide, over the land and over the sea.

It has actually been said that the number of males and females hatched out of each and every one of those thirty-one eggs came to no fewer than ten thousand. Once they had been hatched, meaning once they had emerged from their eggs, they spread all over the globe to inhabit the mountains, the islands, the desolate ruins and barren wastes, the oceans, the desert sands, the forests *[adghāl]* and the jungles *[ājām]*, the wells, the junctions of the roads, the public steam baths *[ḥammāmāt]*, the toilets *[kunuf]*, the dunghills and garbage dumps *[mazābil]*, the air in the atmosphere, the battlefields, the bell-towers of the churches *[nawāqīs]*, the graveyards, the houses, the castles and palaces, the tents of the nomadic Arabs *[khiyām al-Aʿrāb]*, and every single plot of land.

[43] *mā minkum min aḥadin illā wa lahu shaiṭān.*

[44] *wa lā anā: illā anna'llāha—tabāraka wa taʿālā—qad aʿānanī ʿalaihi fa-aslamu.* According to a similar account, reported by Imām al-Ghazālī in Book 12 of his *Iḥyā' ʿUlūm ad-Dīn*, the Prophet (Allāh bless him and give him peace) said:

> Do not visit women whose husbands are away, for each of you has Satan in his bloodstream.

When asked if this was true even of himself, he responded by saying:

> I am no exception, though Allāh has helped me against him, so I am safe.

Sufyān ibn ʿUyaina points out that the [unvowelled] Arabic word must be *aslamu* ['I am safe'], since the reading *aslama* would mean that Satan had 'submitted' or 'become a Muslim.'

[45] *mā minkum min aḥadin illā wa-qad wukkila bihi qarīnuhu min al-jinn.*

Allāh (Exalted is He) has said:

> What, do you choose him and his offspring to be your protecting friends, instead of Me, when they are an enemy to you? How bad an exchange is that for the evildoers! (18:50)[46]

Woe, therefore to anyone who would try to substitute obedience to Satan and his offspring for the worshipful service *[ʿibāda]* of Allāh (Almighty and Glorious is He)! Anyone who does this will most certainly find himself in company with them in the Fire of Hell, doomed to dwell in it for all eternity, if he does not repent and if he does not come to his senses in time. So he needs to recover consciousness and make serious efforts to achieve redemption and to emancipate himself [from bondage to the Devil].

In order to accomplish this, he must part company with his evil comrades, and he must desist forthwith from his wicked behavior. He must refuse to have anything more to do with those who invite him to follow them down the path of error, or with the soldiers of Satan. For he must turn again toward Allāh and practice constant obedience to Him. He must frequent the company of the learned scholars *[ʿulamāʾ]* among His servants, of those who really know Him well, of those who put their knowledge into practice for His sake, of those who summon their fellow creatures to Him, of those who long to be close to Him, of those who hope to receive His gracious favor and are afraid of his terrifying onslaught, of those who dread His reproach, of those who abstain from this world, of those who yearn for the hereafter, of those who keep vigil during the night, of those who fast in the daytime, of those who shed many a tear of remorse over days that have been spent in idle and futile pastimes, of those who are now firmly determined to devote the hours that lie ahead to the best of causes, of those who are turning in repentance from all their sins and misdeeds, of those who are humbling themselves in worship throughout the night and throughout the day.

Such people can feel safe from the chains and shackles, from the plagues of this world, and from the terrors of the Fires of Hell, because they have refused to give obedience to the Devil, and have obeyed the All-Merciful *[Raḥmān]* both in secret and in the open. The Judge *[Dayyān]* has therefore granted them audience with Him, and the

[46] *a-fa-tattakhidhūnahu wa dhurriyyatahu awliyāʾa min dūnī wa hum lakum ʿaduww: biʾsa li-'z-ẓālimīna badalā.*

Benefactor *[Mannān]* has rewarded them in accordance with the declaration He has made in the Qur'ān:

> Therefore Allāh has warded off from them the evil of that day, and He has caused them to find radiance and gladness. And He has recompensed them for all that they have patiently endured, with a Garden and with garments of silk. (76:11,12)[47]

And in His words (Exalted is He):

> Surely the righteous shall dwell amid gardens and a river, in a sure abode, in the presence of a King All-Powerful. (54:54,55)[48]

He has also said (Exalted is He):

> But for him who fears the standing before his Lord there shall be two gardens. (55:46)[49]

What is more, Allāh (Almighty and Glorious is He) has made mention in this Book of His of the servant who is exposed to temptation *[maftūn]* after his conversion to pious devotion *[taqwā]*, for He has said (Exalted is He):

> As for the righteous, when a visitation from the devil disturbs them, they have only to remember [the guidance of their Lord], and then they see clearly. (7:201)[50]

Thus He (Almighty and Glorious is He) has given us to understand that the way to polish our hearts *[jalā' al-qulūb]* is through the remembrance of Allāh, for this is how they lose their coating of darkness, rust and neglect, and this is how troubles and cares are cleared away. Remembrance *[dhikr]* is the key to pious devotion *[taqwā]* and cautious restraint *[wara']*, and pious devotion is the gateway to the hereafter, just as passionate desire *[hawā]* is the gateway to this world. As Allāh (Exalted is He) has said:

> [Hold fast to that which We have given you] and remember what is in it, for then you may do your duty well. (2:63)[51]

Thus Allāh (Hallowed and Exalted is He) has given us to understand that, through remembrance *[dhikr]*, the human being will come to be devoted to his duty.

[47] *fa-waqāhumu'llāhu sharra dhālika'l-yawmi wa laqqāhum naḍratan wa surūrā—wa jazāhum bi-mā ṣabarū jannatan was ḥarīrā.*

[48] *inna'l-muttaqīna fī jannātin wa nahar—fī maq'adi ṣidqin 'inda Malīkin Muqtadir.*

[49] *wa li-man khāfa maqāma Rabbihi jannatān.*

[50] *inna'lladhīna'ttaqaw idhā massahum ṭā'ifun mina'sh-shaiṭāni tadhakkarū fa-idhāhum mubṣirūn.*

[51] *[khudhū mā ātainākum bi-quwwatin] wa'dhkurū mā fīhi la'allakum tattaqūn.*

Concerning the two tremors *[lammatān]* that are felt within the heart.

Two tremors *[lammatān]* are experienced within the heart. One tremor, which comes from the King *[Malik]*, is the promise of all that is good and the confirmation of the truth. The other tremor, which comes from the enemy [i.e., from Satan] is the threat of all that is evil, the denial of the truth, and the rejection of all that is good.

This version of this traditional report has been handed down to us on the authority of ʿAbdullāh ibn Masʿūd (may Allāh be well pleased with him).

As explained in the words of al-Ḥasan al-Baṣrī (may Allāh bestow His mercy upon him):

"These two [tremors] are actually two feelings of concern *[hammān]* which preoccupy the attention of the heart. One of these feelings of concern comes from Allāh, while the other comes from the Enemy. So Allāh bestows His mercy on a servant who concentrates on His concern, who gives effect to that which comes from Allāh, and who struggles to combat whatever comes from His enemy."

Mujāhid (may Allāh bestow His mercy upon him) offered an interpretation of the words of Allāh (Exalted is He):

> [Say: "I take refuge with the Lord of mankind, the King of mankind, the God of mankind] from the evil of the slinking whisperer." (114:1–4)[52]

According to Mujāhid (may Allāh bestow His mercy upon him):

"This means that Satan likes to make himself comfortably at home in the heart of the human being. When someone remembers Allāh, he slinks away and feels ill at ease, but whenever a person becomes forgetful, he stretches himself out in comfort over his heart."

[50] *innaʾlladhīnaʾttaqaw idhā massahum ṭāʾifun minaʾsh-shaiṭāni tadhakkarū fa-idhāhum mubṣirūn.*

[51] *[khudhū mā ātainākum bi-quwwatin] waʾdhkurū mā fīhi laʿallakum tattaqūn.*

[52] *[qul: aʿūdhu bi-Rabbiʾn-nās—Malikiʾn-nās—Ilāhiʾn-nās]—min sharriʾl-waswāsiʾl-khannās.*

In the words of Muqātil (may Allāh bestow His mercy upon him): "He [the slinking whisperer] is the Devil in the shape of a pig *[khinzīr]*, attached to the heart within the physical body of the son of Adam [i.e., the human being], where he infiltrates himself as smoothly as the flow of the blood. Allāh has given him control over that human being. Such is the import of His words (Exalted is He):

> [The slinking whisperer] who whispers in the breasts of men. (114:5)[53]

Thus, when the son of Adam becomes absentminded, the Devil insinuates his suggestions into his heart, until he swallows up his heart completely. He is called the Slinker *[khannās]* because, when the son of Adam remembers Allāh (Almighty and Glorious is He), he slinks away *[khanasa]* from his heart, leaves it and makes his exit from that person's physical body."

According to ʿIkrima (may Allāh bestow His mercy upon him): "In the case of a man, the Whisperer *[waswās]* has his place of lodging in his pericardium *[fuʾād]* and his eyes. In the case of a woman, however, his place of lodging is in her eyes when she is moving forward, and in her buttocks when she turns her back."

[53] *alladhī yuwaswisu fī ṣudūri'n-nāsi.*

Concerning the six 'notions' *[khawāṭir]* that may arise within the human heart.

The 'notions' *[khawāṭir]* that may arise within the human heart are six in number, namely:

1. The notion of the lower self *[khāṭir an-nafs]*.
2. The notion of the Devil *[khāṭir ash-Shaiṭān]*.
3. The notion of the spirit *[khāṭir ar-rūḥ]*.
4. The notion of the angel *[khāṭir al-malak]*.
5. The notion of the mind/intellect *[khāṭir al-ʿaql]*.
6. The notion of certainty *[khāṭir al-yaqīn]*.

Let us now proceed to consider the rôle and *modus operandi* of each of these six notions:

• The rôle of the notion of the lower self *[khāṭir an-nafs]* is to instruct the person in whom it arises to accept the demands of the carnal appetites *[shahawāt]* and to follow the promptings of passionate desire *[hawā]*, regardless of whether the objects of such desire are classed [in Islamic law] as indifferently permissible *[mubāḥ]* or as sinful and strictly prohibited *[ḥaraj]*.

• The rôle of the notion of the Devil *[khāṭir ash-Shaiṭān]* is primarily to instruct the person in whom it arises to commit the fundamental sins of *kufr* [unbelief] and *shirk* [associating partners with Allāh], of casting suspicion and doubt on Allāh (Exalted is He) in respect of His promise. In the fulfillment of its secondary task, it promotes the commission of various acts of sinful disobedience and the postponement of repentance, as well as anything that is conducive to the destruction of the soul in this world and the hereafter.

Both of these two notions are blameworthy and to be condemned as evil. They are characteristic of the general mass of the believers *[ʿumūm al-muʾminīn]*.

• The notion of the spirit *[khāṭir ar-rūḥ]* and the notion of the angel *[khāṭir al-malak]* have a shared rôle and purpose, since both of them communicate the truth, encourage obedience to Allāh (Almighty and Glorious is He), as well as promote everything that is conducive to salvation *[salāma]* in this world and the hereafter, and everything that is in conformity with true knowledge *[ʿilm]*.

• As for the notion of the mind/intellect *[khāṭir al-ʿaql]*, there are times when it gives the same instructions as the lower self and the Devil, while on other occasions it gives the same instructions as the spirit and the angel. Here we have a special wisdom *[ḥikma]* from Allāh and a skillful application of His handiwork *[itqān li-ṣanʿihi]*, with the purpose of ensuring that His servant will be dealing with matters of good and evil in the presence of a rational understanding *[bi-wujūd maʿqūl]*, and with a soundness of perception and power of discrimination *[ṣiḥḥat shuhūd wa tamyīz]*.

The consequences of his actions, in terms of reward and punishment, will thus be duly assigned to his own credit or debit, because Allāh (Exalted is He) has made the human body a setting for the application of His laws *[aḥkām]*, a site for the execution of His will *[mashīʾa]* within the structures of His wisdom *[mabānī ḥikmatihi]*. He has likewise made the rational mind *[ʿaql]* the vehicle *[maṭiyya]* of good and evil. It conveys them both into the storehouse of the human body, since this is a situation for the imposition of duties *[taklīf]* and an opportunity for the exercise of management *[taṣrīf]*, as well as a means of ascertaining the balance of profit or loss, in terms of blissful delight or painful torment.

• As for the notion of certainty *[khāṭir al-yaqīn]*, this is the spirit of faith *[rūḥ al-īmān]* and the source of true knowledge *[mawrid al-ʿilm]*, for it comes from Allāh (Exalted is He) and from Him it originates *[yaṣduru]*. It is peculiar to a special few *[makhṣūṣ bi-khawāṣṣ]* among the saints of sure conviction who are champions of the truth *[min al-awliyāʾ al-mūqinīn aṣ-ṣiddīqīn]*, the martyrs *[shuhadāʾ]* and the spiritual deputies *[abdāl]*.[54] It never communicates anything but truth *[ḥaqq]*, even if its

[54] *Abdāl* is the plural of *Badal*. In the Sixth Discourse of Revelations of the Unseen, Shaikh ʿAbd al-Qādir (may Allāh be well pleased with him) gives the following explanation: "Annihilation *[fanāʾ]* is the aim and object, the final destination of the journey of the saints. This was the direction sought by all previous saints and *Abdāl*: to become extinct to their own will, and let the Will of the Almighty and Glorious Truth take its place, as a permanent transformation, lasting until death. That is why they came to be called *Abdāl* [lit: 'substitutes'] (may Allāh be well pleased with them all)."

communication is in a secret code and delivered by very subtle means. It cannot be deciphered except by intuitive knowledge *[ʿilm ladunī]* and access to esoteric sources and secret information *[akhbār al-ghuyūb wa asrār al-umūr]*.

It comes only to those who are loved *[maḥbūbīn]*, to those who are sought *[murādīn]*, to those who are specially selected *[mukhtārīn]*, to those who pass beyond their own existence because of Allāh—into Him, out of them *[fānīn bi'llāh—fīhi ʿanhum]*, to those who are absent from their outer beings *[ghāʾibīn ʿan ẓawāhirihim]*, to those whose outer worship *[ʿibāda ẓāhira]* has been transformed into the inner kind *[bāṭina]*, apart from [the observance of] the obligatory duties *[farāʾiḍ]* and those customs [based on the exemplary practice of the Prophet (Allāh bless him and give him peace)] that are firmly established *[sunan muʾakkida]*.

Such people are always in a state of vigilant awareness of their inner beings *[bawāṭin]*, while Allāh (Exalted is He) is taking care of the development of their outer beings *[ẓawāhir]*. As He (Almighty and Glorious is He) has said in His Splendid Book:

> My Protecting Friend is Allāh who has sent down the Book, and He befriends and protects the righteous. (7:196)[55]

He befriends them and He provides for all their needs *[tawallāhum wa kafāhum]*. He keeps their hearts occupied with the study of the secrets of the invisible realms *[asrār al-ghuyūb]*, and He enlightens them through the [Divine] manifestation *[tajallī]* in everything that is near. For He has chosen them to enjoy His conversation *[muḥādatha]*, and granted them the special favor of His intimate friendship *[uns]*, of being at ease *[sukūn]* with Him, and of calm repose *[ṭumaʾnīna]* in His presence.

Every day brings them a greater store of knowledge *[ʿilm]*, a further growth of intuition *[maʿrifa]*, an abundance of illumination, and a closeness to the One they love and worship. All the while they are enjoying a bliss that knows no exhaustion, bounties that have no expiration, happiness that has no ultimate boundary and no termination, for when the script of destiny *[kitāb]* has come to its appointed conclusion, and there must be an end to what He has decreed for them as far as continued existence in the realm of the transitory *[dār al-fanāʾ]* is concerned, He will then transfer them from it by way of the most

[55] *inna waliyyiya'llāhu'lladhī nazzala'l-Kitāba wa Huwa yatawalla'ṣ-ṣāliḥīn.*

excellent transition—just as the bride or bridegroom is transferred from a small room to a house—from the lower to the higher.

This means that for them this world is a Garden of Paradise, and in the hereafter there will be a refreshing comfort for their eyes— namely, the vision of His Noble Countenance—without any veil or screen, without any door, without any chamberlain *[ḥājib]*, without any door-keeper, without any obstacle and without any hindrance, without any indebtedness and without any obligation, without any detriment and without any harm, without any severance and without any exhaustion. As Allāh (Almighty and Glorious is He) has said:

> Surely the righteous shall dwell amidst gardens and a river, in a sure abode, in the presence of a King All-Powerful. (54:54,55)[56]

And as He has also said (Exalted is He):

> For those who do good is the reward most fair and a surplus too. (10:26)[57]

They have done good in this world through obedience for His sake, so He has rewarded them in the hereafter with the Garden of Paradise and nobility, and He has granted them blessed favor and salvation. They have done even more for His sake through the purification of their hearts and the abandonment of work for the sake of anything apart from Him, so He has rewarded them (Glory be to Him and Exalted is He) with an extra blessing in the abode of perpetuity and grace *[dār al-baqā' wa'l-minna]*, namely, with the everlasting contemplation of His Noble Countenance, just as He has made it known in His lucid Book to those of His servants who are endowed with understanding hearts and minds.

[56] *inna'l-muttaqīna fī jannātin wa nahar—fī maqʿadi ṣidqin ʿinda Malīkin Muqtadir.*

[57] *li'lladhina aḥsanu'l-ḥusnā wa ziyāda.*

Supplementary Subsection[58]

Passages from other works by Shaikh ʿAbd al-Qādir al-Jīlānī (may Allāh be well pleased with him), in which further light is shed on the important subject of 'notions' *[khawāṭir]*.[59]

1. From the Fourth Discourse of *The Sublime Revelation [al-Fatḥ ar-Rabbānī]*, pp. 41 and 42:

If your luck *[bakht]* is good, the hand of [divine] jealousy will save you from the hand of everyone apart from the Lord of Truth (Almighty and Glorious is He), and it will take you to the gate of nearness to the Lord of Truth (Almighty and Glorious is He), for:

> There, protection belongs only to Allāh, the True. (18:44)

When you have achieved this completely, both this world and the hereafter will come to you as servants *[khādimatain]*, with no trouble or inconvenience. Knock on the door of the Lord of Truth (Almighty and Glorious is He), and stand fast at His door, because if you stay there you will learn to distinguish the various notions *[khawāṭir]* that arise in you: The selfish notion *[khāṭir an-nafs]*; the notion prompted by passion *[khāṭir al-hawā]*; the notion arising from the heart *[khāṭir al-qalb]*; the diabolical notion *[khāṭir Iblīs]*; and the angelic notion *[khāṭir al-malak]*.

You will be told: "This notion is valid *[ḥaqq]*, and this one is false *[bāṭil]*." You will learn to recognize each one by its distinguishing

[58] Supplied for the benefit of readers who do not have ready access to other works by Shaikh ʿAbd al-Qādir al-Jīlānī (may Allāh be well pleased with him)—and for the convenience of those who do.

[59] These passages are excerpted from the following works: (1) Shaikh ʿAbd al-Qādir al-Jīlānī. *The Sublime Revelation (Al-Fatḥ ar-Rabbānī)*. Translated from the Arabic by Muhtar Holland. Houston, Texas: Al-Baz Publishing, Inc., 1992. (2) Shaikh ʿAbd al-Qādir al-Jīlānī. *Utterances of Shaikh ʿAbd al-Qādir al-Jīlānī (Malfūẓāt)*. Translated from the Arabic by Muhtar Holland. Houston, Texas: Al-Baz Publishing, Inc., 1992.

characteristic. When you have reached this stage *[maqām]*, you will receive a notion from the Lord of Truth *[khāṭir mina'l-Ḥaqq]* (Almighty and Glorious is He), which will train you, stabilize you, make you stand up and make you sit down, set you in motion and bring you to rest, and tell you what you must and must not do.

2. From the Fifty-Sixth Discourse of *The Sublime Revelation [al-Fatḥ ar-Rabbānī]*, p. 386:

The believer *[mu'min]* has all his notions *[khawāṭir]* and aspirations *[himam]* united as one. He has nothing left except a notion *[khāṭir]* that occurs *[yakhṭuru]* to his heart from the Lord of Truth (Almighty and Glorious is He), while he is waiting at the door of his nearness to his Lord (Almighty and Glorious is He). Then, when his knowledge *[ma'rifa]* of Him is well established, the door is opened in front of him and he passes beyond it, to see that which he could never describe. A notion is for the heart, while an indication *[ishāra]* is secret speech *[kalām khafī]* to the innermost being *[sirr]*, when it has transcended one's lower self *[nafs]*, passions *[hawā]*, blameworthy characteristics *[akhlāq madhmūma]* and all creatures, into well-being, goodness and bliss. One is turned and moved about therein, like the Companions of the Cave *[aṣḥāb al-kahf]*, concerning whom Allāh (Almighty and Glorious is He) has said:

> And we turned them over to the right, then over to the left. (18:18)

3. From the Sixty-First Discourse of *The Sublime Revelation [al-Fatḥ ar-Rabbānī]*, pp. 417 and 418:

It was in the schoolhouse, on the 20th of Rajab, A.H. 546, that the Shaikh (may Allāh be well pleased with him) said, after some discussion and in response to a question someone put to him about notions *[khawāṭir]*:

How to explain to you what notions are? Your notions come from the devil *[shaiṭān]*, natural impulses *[ṭab']*, the passions *[hawā]* and this world. Your interest or concern *[hamm]* is whatever is most important to you *[ahammaka]*. Your notions correspond in kind to your interest while it is active. A notion *[khāṭir]* inspired by the Lord of Truth

(Almighty and Glorious is He) comes only to the heart, free from anything apart from Him. As He has said:

> Allāh forbid that we should seize anyone except him with whom we found our property. (12:79)

If Allāh (Almighty and Glorious is He) and His remembrance *[dhikr]* are present with you, your heart will certainly be filled with His nearness, and the notions suggested by the devil, the passions and this world will all avoid your company. There is a kind of notion belonging to this world, and a notion belonging to the hereafter. There is a notion belonging to the angels, a notion belonging to the lower self *[nafs]*, and a notion belonging to the heart. There is also a notion belonging to the Lord of Truth (Almighty and Glorious is He). It is therefore necessary for you, O truthful one *[ṣādiq]*, to get rid of all those other notions and to rely on the notion of the Lord of Truth (Almighty and Glorious is He).

If you reject the notion of the lower self, the notion of the passions, the devil's notion and the notion of this world, the notion of the hereafter will come to you. Then you will receive the angel's notion, then finally the notion of the Lord of Truth (Almighty and Glorious is He). This is the ultimate stage.

When your heart is sound, it will pause to ask each notion as it arises: "What kind of notion are you? From what source do you come?" So it will tell him: "I am the notion of such and such." "I am a true notion from the Truth *[khāṭir ḥaqq min al-Ḥaqq]*." "I am a loving counselor; the Lord of Truth (Almighty and Glorious is He) loves you, so I love you too." "I am the ambassador *[safīr]*." "I am your portion of the spiritual state *[ḥāl]* of Prophethood *[nubuwwa]*."

O young man! You must devote your attention to real knowledge *[maʿrifa]* of Allāh (Almighty and Glorious is He), for it is the root of all that is good. If you are constant in obedience to Him, He will grant you real knowledge of Himself. This is why the Prophet (Allāh bless him and give him peace) has said:

> When the servant obeys his Lord (Almighty and Glorious is He), He grants him real knowledge of Himself. Even if he then ceases to obey Him, He will not deprive him of it. Rather will He let it remain in his heart, so that He may bring it in evidence against him on the Day of Resurrection, when He will say to him: 'I honored you with real knowledge of Me, and I granted it to you as a privilege, so why did you not put into practice what you learned?'

4. From *Utterances [Malfūẓāt]*, p. 14:

I once entered the presence of a certain Shaikh while he was speaking about notions *[khawāṭir]*. "Do you like this business I am in?" he asked. "Yes," I replied. Then he said: "I fast all the year round *[aṣūmu'd-dahr]* and I break my fast every morning before dawn *[ufṭiru waqta kulli saḥar]*." He also remarked: "The food in this town is not good, so try to avoid it."

5. From *Utterances [Malfūẓāt]*, pp. 15 and 16:

The angel's notion *[khāṭir al-malak]* will come and make its presence felt in the heart of the believer *[mu'min]*, so he must pause beside it and ask it: "Who are you and where do you come from?" Then it will say: "I am your portion of Prophethood *[nubuwwa]* from the Truth *[Ḥaqq]*. I am the Truth. I come from the Friend *[Ḥabīb]*, I come from the Companion *[Rafīq]*." This notion will fill his inner being *[bāṭin]*, his hearing and his sight. You will see him becoming fond of solitude, emigrating from his native land. Then another command will come to him, to make him somewhat disturbed. Then yet another command will come to him, also causing disturbance, until calm eventually arrives. When calm has arrived, conversation will go on constantly. You will see him apparently lending his ear to someone at his side, as if someone is engaging him in conversation.

6. From *Utterances [Malfūẓāt]*, p. 46:

Among the companions of al-Junaid there was a man who was having doubts about the spontaneously arising notion *[khāṭir]*. Al-Junaid was made aware of this, so he asked the man: "What they are saying about you, is it true?" He said, "Yes," [so al-Junaid said:] "Let an utterance come through your heart." The man said, "Very well," and when asked what he had uttered [inwardly], he replied: "I uttered such and such." But [al-Junaid] said: "No, [that wasn't it]!" Then the man tried again, and when he reported [what he had uttered inwardly], he was again told: "No!" He then let one more utterance come to him through his heart, and reported to al-Junaid, who yet again said: "No!" So the man said: "O Shaikh, my experience is genuine, so you had better check your own!" To this al-Junaid replied: "I knew that everything you told me was true. I simply wanted to test the purity of your heart and its steadfastness."

7. From Utterances *[Malfūẓāt]*, pp. 59 and 60:

Our predecessors would learn to distinguish between different kinds of notions *[khawāṭir]*, before withdrawing into secluded retreats *[zawāyā]*. O you who cannot tell the difference between the notion *[khāṭir]* of the lower self *[nafs]*, that of the devil *[shaiṭān]* and that of the heart *[qalb]*, how can you withdraw into seclusion? The satanic notion prompts one to commit sins of disobedience and to make mistakes; it implants the root of unbelief *[kufr]*, then encourages the sins of disobedience that branch out from it. As for the angelic notion *[khāṭir al-malak]*, it prompts one to practice worshipful obedience and to perform righteous deeds.

Concerning the lower self *[nafs]* and the spirit *[rūḥ]* as focal points for the conflicting influences of the angel and the devil.

The lower self *[nafs]* and the spirit *[rūḥ]* are two focal points for the conflicting influences of the angel *[malak]* and the devil *[shaiṭān]*. On the one hand, the angel is inculcating pious devotion *[taqwā]* in the heart. The devil, on the other hand, is busy instilling moral depravity *[fujūr]* into the lower self. As a result, the lower self tries to persuade the heart to use the limbs and organs of the body for impious and immoral purposes.

Within the physical constitution *[binya]* there are also two target areas: the mind *[ʿaql]* and the passionate instinct *[hawā]*. The functioning of each of these is subject to the will of a controlling influence *[mash,ʾa ḥākim]*, namely, that of helpful [divine] guidance *[tawfīq]* and that of seductive [satanic] temptation *[ighwāʾ]*.

Within the heart there are two radiant lights, namely, knowledge *[ʿilm]* and faith *[īmān]*.

All of these elements are the instruments of the heart, its sensory faculties and its tools. The heart is right in the middle of these instruments, as if it were the king and these were his troops reporting to him for duty. Or, to take a different analogy, it is like the woman who is unveiled for the bridegroom's inspection *[al-marʾat al-majluwwa]*; with these pieces of equipment all around her she is exposed to view, so that he can see her, make a critical examination of her, and test her mettle.[60]

[60] As Shaikh ʿAbd al-Qādir (may Allāh be well pleased with him) has explained in an earlier chapter of al-Ghunya (Vol.1, p. 115): It is appropriate for the would-be husband to make an effort to catch a glimpse of the face and hands of his prospective bride, without actually being alone with her in private, before the marriage is contracted *[qabla'l-ʿaqd]*. [This is recommended as a precaution,] in case he should experience a change of heart and find her repugnant to him. [If this happened after the marriage contract,] it could result in his divorcing her by repudiation *[ṭalāq]* and separating from her in a short space of time. Such an outcome would be subject to stern disapproval in the sight of Allāh (Almighty and Glorious is He), because the Prophet (Allāh bless him and give him peace) has said:

> Nothing that is legally permissible is more hateful to Allāh (Exalted is He) than divorce by repudiation.

A series of invocations, by which the author (may Allāh be well pleased with him) seeks refuge with Allāh (Almighty and Glorious is He) from the Devil and from a wide range of specific evils and temptations.

I take refuge with the Lord of the Throne and the Pedestal
from Satan the misguided,
and evil notions, and the
promptings of the lower self;

a'ūdhu bi-Rabbi'l-
Arshi wa'l-Kursiyyi
mina'sh-Shaiṭāni'l-ghawiyyi
wa khawāṭiri's-sū'i
wa hawājisi'n-nafs—

and from the temptation
of every jinnī and human being;

wa min fitnati
kulli jinniyyin wa insiyy—

and from ostentation, hypocrisy,
vanity, arrogant pride,
associating partners with Allāh,
and the evil disorders that
can arise within the heart;

wa min riyā'in wa nifāqin
wa 'ujbin wa kibrin
wa shirkin
wa khilāli's-sū'i'n-nāshi'ati
fi'l-qalb—

and from every lust and
indulgence that may result
in mortal dangers for the soul;

wa min kulli shahwatin
wa ladhdhatin mu'addiyatin
ila'l-mahāliki li'n-nafs—

and from heretical innovations,
and wandering astray,
and passions that inflict
the Fires of Hell
upon the human body;

wa mina'l-bida'i
wa'ḍ-ḍalāli
wa'l-ahwiyati'l-musalliṭa
li'n-nīrāni
'ala'l-jism—

and from every word and deed
and aspiration that may bar
access to the unseen realms
around the Heavenly Throne;

wa min kulli qawlin wa fi'lin
wa himmatin taḥjubu
mina'l-ghuyūbi'l-
'arshiyya—

and from following misleading
whims and selfish inclinations,
and morals that are
depraved.

wa mina'ttibā'i'l-ahwiyati'l-
muḍillati wa'ṭ-ṭabā'i'i'n-
nafsiyyati wa'l-akhlāqi'r-
radiyya.

I take refuge with the Praise-
worthy and Illustrious King

wa a'ūdhu bi'l-Maliki'l-
Ḥamīdi'l-Majīdi

from the wicked and rebellious Satan.	*mina'sh-Shaiṭāni'l-* *khabīthi'l-marīd.*
I take refuge with the Ever-Loving Lord from His vengeance, lest I ever neglect to obey Him.	*wa aʿūdhu* *bi'r-Rabbi'l-Wadūdi* *min niqmatihi idhā* *ghafaltu ʿan ṭāʿatih—*
He is indeed nearer to me than my jugular vein.[61]	*idh Huwa aqrabu* *layya min ḥabli'l-warīd.*
I take refuge with Allāh from His terrible onslaught when He is angry with those who are guilty of disobedience.	*wa aʿūdhu bi'llāhi* *min saṭwatihi* *dhā ghaḍaba ʿalā* *ahli'l-maʿṣiya.*
I take refuge with Him from His awe-inspiring aspect, when the shock of His impact on the Day of Resurrection is felt by the wrongdoers among His creatures.	*wa aʿūdhu bihi* *min haibatihi* *ʿinda shiddati baṭshihi* *fī yawmi'l-qiyāmati* *li'ṭ-ṭāghīna* *min barriyyatih.*
I take refuge with Him from the removal of the covering and the veil;	*wa aʿūdhu bihi* *min kashfi'l-ghiṭāʾi* *wa's-satr—*
and wandering perplexed in disobedience to Him by land and by sea;	*wa't-tayhāni* *fī maʿṣiyatihi* *fi'l-barri wa'l-baḥr—*
and forgetting both the root and the branch;	*wa nisyāni'l-* *ṣli wa'l-farʿ—*
and tending to swerve in the wrong direction;	*wa'l-maili* *ila'z-zaigh—*
and thoughtlessness, arrogance and pride;	*wa'r-ruʿūnati* *wa'l-khuyalāʾi wa'l-kibr—*
and forsaking obedience, righteous deeds and piety;	*wa tarki'ṭ-ṭāʿati* *wa'l-qurbati wa'l-birr—*
and falling short in my duty to Him;	*wa't-taʾallī* *ʿalaih—*
and committing perjury and breaking an oath without due consideration;	*wa'l-aimāni'l-kādhiba* *wa'l-ḥinthi* *dūna'l-birr—*
and coming to a bad end, being bankrupt of everything good, and receiving bad news at the moment of death.	*wa khātimati's-sūʾi* *wa'l-iflāsi min kulli khairin* *wa'l-muwāfāti ʿinda ḥuḍūri'l-* *maniyyati bi'sh-sharr.*

[61] An allusion to the words of Allāh (Exalted is He) in the Qurʾān (50:16):

> We indeed created the human being, and We know what his lower self whispers within him, and We are nearer to him than the jugular vein.

Concerning the inner nature of the struggle with Satan *[mujāhadat ash-Shaiṭān]*.

The struggle with Satan is an inner struggle *[mujāhada bāṭina]*, for it is waged by the heart and the core of one's being, and by faith *[bi'l-qalb wa'l-janān wa'l-īmān]*. When you struggle with him, therefore, your help and support is the All-Merciful *[ar-Raḥmān]*, your mainstay is the King and Judge *[al-Malik ad-Dayyān]*, and your hope is the vision of the Face of the Majestic Benefactor *[al-Jalīl al-Mannān]*.

The holy war against the unbelievers *[jihād al-kuffār]* is the outer battle *[jihād aẓ-ẓāhir]* with the sword and the spear, in which your support is provided by the ruler and the armed forces, and in which your hope is to enter the Gardens of Paradise. If you are slain in the struggle with the unbelievers, your reward will be life everlasting in the abode of perpetuity *[khulūd fī dār al-baqā']*. But if you are killed in the course of waging war on Satan and while you are committed to opposing him, due to the expiration of your appointed term *[ajal]* and because your moment to die *[maniyya]* has arrived, your reward will be the vision of the Face of the Lord of All the Worlds *[Rabb al-'ālamīn]* at the meeting [with Him]. If you are slain by an unbeliever *[kāfir]*, you will be a martyr *[shahīd]*. But if you are killed by the Devil through following him obediently and carrying out his orders, you will be an outcast *[ṭarīd]*, banished from the nearness of the All-Compelling King *[al-Malik al-Jabbār]*.

The holy war against the unbelievers *[jihād al-kuffār]* has an end and there comes a point when it is over. But the holy war against the Devil and the lower self *[jihād ash-Shaiṭān wa'n-nafs]* is one that has no final limit and no point of termination. As Allāh (Glorious and Exalted is He) has said:

> And serve your Lord, till the Certainty comes to you. (15:99)[62]

[62] *wa' 'bud Rabbaka ḥattā ya'tiyaka'l-yaqīn.*

—that is to say, till death and the meeting [with Him], for worshipful service *[ʿibāda]* is performed by offering opposition to Satan and to passionate desire *[hawā]*.

Allāh (Almighty and Glorious is He) has said:

> Then they shall be pitched into it [the Fire of Hell]—they and the perverse, and the hosts of Iblīs, all together. (26:94,95)[63]

The Prophet (Allāh bless him and give him peace) said, when he came home from the military expedition [ghazwa] of Tabūk:

> We have come home from the minor holy war *[al-jihād al-aṣghar]* to fight the major holy war *[al-jihād al-akbar]*.

What he meant by "the major holy war" (Allāh bless him and give him peace) was the struggle with Satan, the lower self and passionate desire *[mujāhadat ash-Shaiṭān wa'n-nafs wa'l-hawā]*, and he referred to it as such because of its constant duration, the extent of the exertion it demands, the danger it entails, and the fear that it might turn out badly at the very end.

May Allāh bless Muḥammad and every chosen servant in all the universe *[wa ṣalla'llāhu ʿalā Muḥammadin wa ʿalā kulli ʿabdin muṣṭafā min kulli'l-ʿālamīn]*. Āmīn.

[63] *fa-kubkibū fīhā hum wa'l-ghāwūn—wa junūdu Iblīsa ajmaʿūn.*

The Second Discourse

Concerning the words of Allāh (Almighty and Glorious is He):

It is from Solomon, and it is "In the Name of Allāh, the All-Merciful, the All-Compassionate."

You should know that this noble verse *[āya]* occurs in *Sūrat an-Naml* [The Ant], which is a Sūra belonging to the Meccan period. Its verses adds up to a total of ninety-three. It contains a total of one thousand one hundred and forty-nine [Arabic] words and exactly four thousand seven hundred and ninety-nine letters [of the Arabic alphabet].

It concerns an episode in the life of the Prophet Solomon, the son of David (peace be upon him, upon our own Chosen Prophet *[Nabiyyuna'l-Muṣṭafā]*, and upon all the other Prophets *[anbiyā᾿]*, the true believers *[mu᾿minīn]* and all the righteous servants *[ʿibād ṣāliḥīn]* of Allāh, and the angels brought near [to Him] *[malā᾿ika muqarrabīn]*).

As Allāh (Almighty and Glorious is He) has told us in the Qur᾿ān:[65]

> And We gave David and Solomon knowledge, and they said: "Praise be to Allāh, who has preferred us over many of His believing servants." (27:15)
>
> And Solomon was David's heir, and he said: "O mankind, we have been taught the language of the birds,[66] and we have been given [an abundance] of all things; this surely is evident favor." (27:16)
>
> And mustered unto Solomon were his armies of the jinn and humankind, and of the birds; and they were drawn up in good array, till, when they came to the Valley of Ants, an ant said: "Ants, enter your dwelling places, lest Solomon and his armies crush you, being unaware!" (27:17,18)

[65] The translator has taken the liberty of inserting the following verses *[āyāt]* from *Sūrat an-Naml* (27:15–20) at this point in the text, since a familiarity with them is clearly presupposed by the author (may Allāh be well pleased with him).

[66] *Manṭiq aṭ-Ṭair* [The Language of the Birds] is the title of a celebrated work, an allegory of the spiritual path, by the Persian author Farīd ad-Dīn ʿAṭṭār (d. ca. A.H. 627/1229 C.E.).

> But he smiled, laughing at its words, and he said: "My Lord, dispose me to be thankful for Your blessing, with which You have blessed me and my parents, and to do righteous work that shall be well-pleasing unto You; and include me, through Your mercy, in [the company of] Your righteous servants." (27:19)
>
> And he reviewed the birds; then he said: "How is it that I do not see the hoopoe? Or is he among the absentees?" (27:20)

When Solomon (peace be upon him) had moved on from the Valley of the Ants, in the course of his journey from Jerusalem *[Bait al-Maqdis]* to the Yemen, he led his people into a barren desert, where they were soon afflicted by thirst and started begging for water. In response to this need, he looked all around in search of the hoopoe *[hudhud]*, inquiring if anyone had seen him. He summoned the Captain of the Birds *[Amīr aṭ-Ṭuyūr]*, who happened to be the Numidian crane *[kurkī]*, and asked him if he knew where he was. Knowing that there was only one hoopoe in his company, the Numidian crane replied: "I have no idea where he went off to; he did not get his orders from me."[67]

Solomon (peace be upon him) had a very good reason for trying to find the hoopoe, since he wanted the bird to probe the ground with his beak, in order to let him know the depth at which water could be found, whether close to the surface or far beneath it, as measured by the fathom *[qāma]* or the parasang *[farsakh]*.[68]

The hoopoe was uniquely well equipped for this task, endowed as he was with a special expertise that none of the other birds possessed. Whenever he was required to perform this operation, he would fly up to a great height in the atmosphere, till he reached a vantage point from which to scan the earth below. Then, having spotted a plot of land containing water, he would swoop down upon it, sticking his beak into the ground in order to mark the spot for excavation.

At this point the devils *[shayāṭīn]* would waste no time in playing their part, by digging a well on that same plot of land. The water would soon come gushing forth, and they would direct it into basins, ponds and watering troughs. Flasks and water skins and other vessels could now

[67] In the First Discourse (p. 6 above), the author (may Allāh be well pleased with him) states that some traditional authorities equate the Numidian crane *[kurkī]* with the bird called *ghurnūq* or *ghurnaiq*. This may have some bearing on its status as Captain of the Birds *[Amīr aṭ-Ṭuyūr]*.

[68] The *qāma* [fathom] is equal to six feet, while the *farsakh* [parasang, or league] is three miles of the Hāshimī measure.

be filled, and there would be plenty for all to drink, for beasts and human beings and jinn alike. Then they would be ready to set off on the next stage of their journey.

It should therefore come as no surprise to us that Solomon (peace be upon him) reacted as he did on that occasion, when he discovered that the hoopoe was nowhere to be found. His anger over the situation amounted to a furious rage, and he blurted out:

> "I will surely chastise him with a terrible chastisement, or I will go so far as to slaughter him, or else he will have to bring me a clear legitimation." (27:21)

By saying, "I will surely chastise him with a terrible chastisement," he meant: "I will surely pluck his feathers, so that he cannot fly with the other birds for the space of one whole year!" But then, after threatening to "go so far as to slaughter him," he did offer him a loophole, by adding: "or else he will have to bring me a clear legitimation." He was saying, in effect: "or else he had better bring me a good excuse, and a clear and convincing explanation." The harshest form of punishment he ever inflicted on any of the birds, when he saw fit to chastise one of them, was to pluck its feathers until he had left it completely bald, without a single feather on its body. [As for the missing hoopoe, however,] Allāh (Almighty and Glorious is He) has told us:

> But he did not tarry long, and he said, "I have comprehended that which you have not comprehended, and I have come from Sheba to you with a sure tiding." (27:22)

In other words, he did not stay away for an extended period of time. Then, when he did come back, the hoopoe was told: "Solomon has threatened to punish you!" So he asked: "Did he leave me any loophole?" Since the answer was "Yes," he approached [his master] until he stood before him, then he bowed down in prostration and said: "May your kingdom endure for all eternity, and may you live for ever and ever!"

He started pecking with his beak and nodding his head toward Solomon, as he said to the latter: "I have comprehended that which you have not comprehended." He was saying, in effect: "I reached a certain place and I learned certain things—a place you had not reached, and things of which you had no knowledge," meaning: "I have brought you news of a matter about which the jinn have neither informed you nor advised you, and concerning which no human being has notified you." When he went on to say: "And I have come to you from Sheba," he meant: "from the land of Sheba," and by "with a sure tiding" he meant: "with an amazing piece of information, the accuracy of which is beyond the slightest doubt."

"Well, what is this amazing piece of information you have brought me?" Solomon asked. So the hoopoe told him:

> "I found a woman ruling over them, and she has been given [an abundance] of everything, and she possesses a mighty throne. (27:23)
>
> "I found her and her people prostrating themselves in worship to the sun, instead of to Allāh; Satan has made their deeds seem comely to them, and he has barred them from the way, and therefore they are not guided aright. (27:24)
>
> "So they do not prostrate themselves in worship to Allāh, who brings forth what is hidden in the heavens and the earth, and who knows what you conceal and what you publish. (27:25)
>
> "Allāh, there is no god but He, the Lord of the Mighty Throne." (27:26)

When he says, "I found a woman ruling over them," he is referring to the lady called Bilqīs the Ḥimyarite, the daughter of Abū Sarḥ.[69]

[69] Early in 1980, while he was working as Senior Research Fellow at the Islamic Foundation in Leicester, England, the translator was asked to provide an English version of an article published in the Arabic-language journal *The Family Today [al-Usra al-Yawm]*.

This article, by a writer called Aḥmad Muḥammad Jamāl, was entitled "Bilqīs: Ruler of Resolve." It is interesting to note that the story discussed in this Discourse by Shaikh ʿAbd al-Qādir al-Jīlānī (may Allāh be well pleased with him) may still be regarded as highly relevant and instructive to contemporary Muslim society:

"The lady of whom we are speaking was both a noble specimen of womanhood and a splendid model of social and political action, which she not only undertook, but carried to success...."

The article is also useful in that it provides us with some interesting background information that explains how Bilqīs came to ascend the throne as Queen of Sheba:

"She was the daughter of the King of Sheba. When her father died, her cousin mounted the throne, but he was neither good nor just; indeed, he was a wicked man, who had no respect for people, who violated everything sacred, and who abused his authority in order to assault the women of Sheba, both married women and virgins. Eventually, tempted by his own power, he got the devilish idea of presuming to approach his cousin, the daughter of the previous King, whose throne he had seized, with a suggestion offensive to pure and modest women.

"Now Bilqīs was wise and clever—the Qurʾān tells us about her keen intelligence. She therefore pretended to agree to what he wanted. She invited him to her palace at night, intending to kill him and to rid the country and its folk of his oppression and corruption. Unsuspecting, he came in disguise to Bilqīs's palace, congratulating himself on the great happiness he would experience on meeting Bilqīs. Little did he know that he was rushing to his death—'hastening to his doom.'

"Bilqīs said to the people of Sheba: 'I did what I have done because I found no man among you defending the honor of his daughter or his wife. I have killed him because he defiled my father's throne, and tried to defile the honor of my father's daughter. It is now up to you to choose yourselves a good king to govern your affairs.'

"But the people of the Yemen declined to have anyone rule over them except Bilqīs, who had done what the men were incapable of doing, and had rid the land and its folk of the tyranny, corruption and disaster of the former King. Thus Bilqīs became Queen of the Yemen, promising to govern its people with justice and by consultation."

By saying, "and she has been given [an abundance] of everything," he means: "She has been gifted with everything in her country of the Yemen and its neighboring territories, including knowledge, political authority, material wealth, military forces, and horses of all breeds and varieties."

In mentioning that "she possesses a mighty throne," the hoopoe is describing her splendid elevated couch *[sarīr]*. This throne of hers was in fact raised heavenwards to a height of thirty cubits, or of eighty cubits according to some accounts, and in width it measured eighty cubits. It was richly adorned with all kinds of jewels, gems and pearls.

The hoopoe "found her and her people prostrating themselves in worship to the sun, instead of to Allāh," which means that they must have been practicing the religion of the Magians[70] *[dīn al-Majūs]*. Then he reported that "Satan has made their deeds seem comely to them," which is a way of saying that he caused them to see their evil deeds in a favorable light, and that "he has barred them from the way." In other words, Satan had been keeping Bilqīs and her soldiers from the path of Islām [submission to the Will of Allāh] and right guidance.

As a result, the hoopoe continues, "they are not guided aright," since they do not recognize Islām, and so, of course, "they do not prostrate themselves in worship to Allāh, who brings forth what is hidden (i.e., the unseen *[ghaib]* and the secret *[sirr]*) in the heavens and the earth, and who knows what you conceal and what you publish (with your tongues)." [At this point, the hoopoe concludes his report to Solomon with the affirmation:] "Allāh, there is no god but He, the Lord of the Mighty Throne."[71]

[70] Otherwise known as the Zoroastrians.

[71] At this point in the Arabic text, the author (may Allāh be well pleased with him) finds it necessary to add a note of explanation, hardly translatable into English, in order to emphasize the correctness of an interpretation based on the grammatical assumption that, in this instance, the noun qualified by the adjective *al-ʿAẓīm* [the Mighty] is *ʿArsh* [Throne], rather than *Rabb* [Lord]. Without this explanation, the phrase *Rabbu'l-ʿArshi'l-ʿAẓīm* might be taken to mean "The Mighty Lord of the Throne," rather than "The Lord of the Mighty Throne."

(The possibility of confusion arises because the adjective *[a]l-ʿAẓīm* occurs here in a pausal position in the Qurʾānic text, and its final vowel is therefore omitted. In a non-pausal situation, the form *[a]l-ʿAẓīmi*, with final vowel *-i*, would indicate grammatical agreement with *[a]l-ʿArshi*, whereas the form *[a]l-ʿAẓīmu*, with final vowel *-u*, would indicate grammatical agreement with *Rabbu*.)

Then Solomon said to the hoopoe: "Show us where we can find water!"

> [Solomon] said: "Now we shall see whether you have spoken truly, or whether you are among those who lie." (27:27)

After the bird had led them to water, and when they had drunk enough of it to satisfy their thirst, as well as filling up their containers, Solomon summoned the hoopoe once again. He wrote a letter in his presence, sealed it with his personal seal, and handed it over to him, then said:

> "Take this letter of mine, and deliver it to them (i.e., to the people of Sheba), then turn away from them (i.e., come back here) and see what they return (i.e., what kind of a reply they send back with you)." (27:28)

What he wrote in the letter was: "In the Name of Allāh, the All-Merciful, the All-Compassionate *[Bismi'llāhi'r-Raḥmāni'r-Raḥīm]*.

It is from Solomon (the son of David). Do not exalt yourselves against me (i.e., do not be too proud to obey me), but come to me as those who surrender *[muslimīn]* (i.e., as those who are ready to make peace *[muṣāliḥīn]*, for either you are from among the jinn, in which case you have already been rendered subservient to me, or else you are members of the human race, in which case it is your duty to hear and to obey)."[72]

The hoopoe then set off on his long flight, carrying the letter with him until he finally reached his destination in the land of Sheba. He arrived there in the middle of the day, at the very time when Bilqīs was enjoying her siesta inside the walls of her palace. In order to ensure her absolute privacy, all the gates and doors had been locked shut, so that nothing whatever could get in to disturb her, and sentries had also been posted all around her castle.

From among her own people, Queen Bilqīs had twelve thousand warriors at her command, each and every one of these being himself the commander *[amīr]* of one hundred thousand fighting men, not to mention all their wives and offspring. On a certain day in every week, she would go out to meet her people, giving them the benefit of her judgment in settling their affairs and concerns. On these occasions, her

[72] In presenting this version of Solomon's letter, the author (may Allāh be well pleased with him) has slightly rearranged the elements of it as they occur in the Qur'ān (27:30,31), as well as adding his own explanations or interpretations, which appear within parentheses in this translation.

throne would be mounted on four pillars of gold, then she would take her seat upon it, in a position from which she could see the people without their being able to see her.

If any man wished to apply to her for help with some problem or matter of business, he could present her with his request. In order to do so, he had to stand there in her presence, showing respect for her by keeping his head bowed low and not looking in her direction, then by prostrating himself without raising his head, until she gave him permission to speak. When she had dealt with their concerns and delivered her instructions, she would withdraw into her palace, and they would not see her again until the same day of the following week.

Her authority was a mighty authority indeed, so when the hoopoe arrived with the letter, he found that all the gates and doors had been locked to ensure her privacy, while the guards were on duty all around the castle, patrolling the entire perimeter. In the face of these formidable obstacles, he nevertheless kept searching for some way of getting through to Queen Bilqīs, until he finally succeeded—through a skylight in the roof of the palace.

Once he had discovered this opening, he went from one royal suite to the next, until he finally came to the far end of seven suites, where her throne towered thirty cubits high. It was there that he saw her, lying sound asleep upon her throne. She was wearing nothing at all, except for a piece of cloth to cover her most private part *[ʿawra]*, this being her usual habit whenever she lay down to sleep. He therefore placed the letter beside her on the elevated couch, then flew up and perched in a skylight, expecting that she would soon wake up from her slumber and read the letter.

As it turned out, however, he stayed there waiting for a very long time, while she was still not showing any sign of waking up. The moment came when he could tolerate no further delay, so he swooped down and pecked her. She came to her senses immediately, and the first thing she caught sight of was the letter, lying right there beside her on the couch. She picked it up, rubbed her eyes, and started to examine the condition of the letter. How could such a letter have reached her anyway, she wondered, what with the doors all locked....

She went outside to check, and finding that the guards were still on patrol around the palace, she inquired of them: "Did you notice anybody opening a door and entering my private apartment?"

"No," they assured her, "the doors have all remained as firmly locked as ever they were, and we have been constantly on guard around the outside of the palace."

It was at this point that Bilqīs finally opened the letter and read it, she being a lady who knew how to read and write.[73] She noticed at once that it contained the words: "In the Name of Allāh, the All-Merciful, the All-Compassionate *[Bismi'llāhi'r-Raḥmāni'r-Raḥīm]*." Then, when she had read it through, she sent for her people and they assembled in response to her summons.

> She said: "O Council, see, a noble letter has been delivered unto me." (27:29)

She described the letter as "noble" because it was properly composed and stamped with the personal seal of the sender.

> "It is from Solomon, and it is: 'In the Name of Allāh, the All-Merciful, the All-Compassionate. Do not exalt yourselves against me, but come to me as those who surrender.'" (27:30, 31)

[As explained above] the expression "those who surrender *[muslimīn]*" means "those who are ready to make peace *[muṣāliḥīn]*."

> She said: "O Council, give me your formal opinion concerning my affair; I am not used to deciding an affair until you are present to bear me witness." (27:32)

In other words: "Let me know what I ought to do about this affair of mine, for I am not used to taking action until you are present to be informed and ready to participate in the process of consultation."

> They said: "We are lords of might and lords of great prowess, but the affair rests with you; so consider what you will command." (27:33)

They were saying, in effect: "We possess invincible force *[manaʿa]*. No enemy has ever achieved supremacy over us, whether in active combat, in defensive capacity, or in sheer numbers, and we have never conceded the rôle of leadership to anyone else." And yet, according her the respect she deserved, they insisted: "But you know best when it comes to your own affair, so give us your command and we shall follow it."

[73] A rare accomplishment, no doubt, in the distant age of Bilqīs herself, and the comment would seem to suggest that female literacy was also far from common in the time of Shaikh ʿAbd al-Qādir al-Jīlānī (may Allāh be well pleased with him).

She then made a knowledgeable statement and announced her decision:

> She said: "Kings, when they enter a township, despoil it and cause the dignified people among its inhabitants to be humiliated. This is just what they too will do. But I am going to send them a present, and then see what the envoys bring back." (27:34, 35)

When kings went to war, they could indeed be expected to bring ruin and devastation to the cities they conquered, and to reduce their honorable dignitaries to a state of abysmal degradation. They could be expected to seize their possessions, kill their fighting men, and abuse their offspring. Bilqīs had therefore decided to send a present to Solomon, in order to see what her envoys would bring back to her, and what they would report to her about him.

As one part of her present to Solomon, Bilqīs sent him twelve young servants who were actually males, but who were rather effeminate in their appearance. Their hands were dyed with henna, and she had them comb their hair and dress in the kind of clothing normally worn by young women. She came forward to interview them, and gave them their instructions. If they were questioned in the presence of Solomon, or if he should actually speak to them himself, they were to use an effeminate manner of speaking when giving their replies.

As another part of her present, she also sent him twelve young servants who were actually females, in spite of their rough and tough appearance, which was due to the fact that she had all the hair plucked from their heads, and made them wear masculine-style pants and shoes. To them she said: "If Solomon happens to speak to you, you must respond by giving him an honest answer."

Bilqīs sent Solomon many other gifts along with these, including aloes-wood [*ʿūd yalanjūj*],[74] musk [*misk*],[75] ambergris [*ʿanbar*],[76] and silk

[74] The word *yalanjūj* is the Persian term for aloes-wood. The Arabic word *ʿūd* may sometimes mean the same (according to the Arabic lexicographers: "a well-known odiferous substance," or "a certain aromatized wood, with which one fumigates oneself"), but it may also have the more general meaning: "wood; timber; any slender piece of wood or timber," and in some contexts it refers specifically to the musical instrument called the lute (the English term being derived from the Arabic *al-ʿūd*.) See: E.W. Lane, *Arabic-English Lexicon*, art. *ʿ–W–D*.

[75] The Arabic word *misk* may be derived from the Persian *mushk*. According to *Webster's Ninth New Collegiate Dictionary*, the English form "musk" has the following derivation: "ME *muske*, fr. MF *musc*, fr. LL *muscus*, fr. Gk *moschos*, fr. Pers. *mushk*, fr. Skt *muṣka* testicle, fr. dim. of *mūṣ* mouse; akin to OE *mūs* mouse."

[76] The English word "amber" is derived from the Arabic *ʿanbar*.

[ḥarīr], which were carried by the maidservants in covered trays. She sent twelve Bactrian camels *[bukhtiyya]*,[77] valuable for the quantity of milk they could yield. She also sent him a pair of *kharaz* [gem stones of the kind that are often pierced and strung to make a necklace], one of which had been pierced with a crooked drill hole, while the other was left unpierced, and she sent him an empty goblet.

Bilqīs sent a woman emissary to accompany this collection of gifts. She instructed her to commit to memory every single detail that might be important in relation to Solomon, as well as everything he said, so that she could bring back a full report of it all to her mistress.

To all those who were being sent on the mission, she said: "Once you have come into the presence of Solomon, you must maintain an upright posture. Do not sit down until he commands you to do so. If he happens to be a cruel tyrant *[jabbār]*, he will not command you to be seated. Should this be the case, I am going to placate him with material wealth, so that he will leave us in peace. If he is actually a tolerant person, learned and wise, then of course he will command you to be seated."

Then, turning to the woman emissary, she instructed her to tell Solomon that he must cause a thread to be inserted into the pierced gem stone, but without employing the skill of any human being or member of the jinn. She instructed her to tell him that he must drill a hole through the other precious stone, but without using an iron tool, and without employing the skill of any human being or member of the jinn. He must also be able to tell the difference between the male and the female servants. She went on to instruct her to tell him that he must fill the goblet with an overflowing quantity of thirst-quenching water, which must be drawn neither from the earth nor from the sky.

Bilqīs also wrote Solomon a letter, in which she asked him questions concerning one thousand chapters of knowledge. Then her envoys set out on the road with her collection of presents. When their journey had finally brought them all the way to Solomon, and they had laid the gifts before him, they remained standing on their feet and were careful not to sit down.

[77] According to the Arabic lexicographers, the *bukhtiyya*, a member of the species of camels for which *bukht* is the collective term, is "the Khurāsānī or Bactrian camel, begot between an Arabian she-camel and a *fālij* [a large two-humped camel brought from Sind for the purpose of covering]." See: E.W. Lane, *Arabic-English Lexicon*, art. *B–KH–T*.

Solomon glanced at them, but not for one instant did he make the slightest movement of hand or foot, nor did he show any sign of being excited or pleased by the gifts they had brought him. The envoys had no idea that such behavior might be encountered from him, and they had never experienced it from anyone else in a comparable situation.

When he did eventually lift his head and look directly at the messengers of Bilqīs, he said: "The earth belongs to Allāh, and the sky belongs to Allāh. He has raised the sky aloft, and He has set the earth down here below, so those who wish to do so may stand, and those who wish to do so may sit." Thus did he give them permission to be seated.

At this point the woman emissary stepped forward and presented Solomon with the pair of gem stones, as she told him: "Bilqīs says that you must cause a thread to be inserted into the pierced gem stone, so that it goes right through the drill hole and comes out on the other side, but without employing the skill of any human being or member of the jinn. You must also drill a hole through the second precious stone, all the way through to the other side, but without using an iron tool, and without employing the skill of any human being or member of the jinn." She then presented him with the goblet, telling him as she did so: "Bilqīs says that you must fill the goblet with an overflowing quantity of thirst-quenching water, which must be drawn neither from the earth nor from the sky." Then she presented the menservants and the maidservants, and she told him: "Bilqīs says that you must be able to tell the difference between the male and the female servants."

Faced with this series of challenging demands, Solomon immediately summoned the people of his kingdom, and they gathered promptly in response to his call. He then produced the pair of gem stones, and asked: "Who is prepared to help me out with this first gem stone, by inserting a thread so that it goes right through the drill hole and comes out on the other side?"

Up spoke a worm, a red worm to be precise, who happened to be in the midst of the green trefoil *[fiṣfiṣa]*, i.e., the fresh clover *[raṭba]*.

"O king," said the worm, "I am ready to do what you need to have done in this case, on condition that you will grant me a plentiful supply of fresh clover, which is my favorite food."

Solomon said yes, he would agree to these terms. He then proceeded to tie a piece of thread to the worm's head, and she poked herself into the gem stone, wriggling through the crooked drill hole until she came out on the other side. As he had promised, Solomon rewarded the worm by granting her a plentiful supply of fresh clover, her favorite food.

Then, having put the second gem stone on display, Solomon asked: "Who is prepared to help me out by drilling a hole through this gem stone here, without using an iron tool?"

Up spoke another worm who happened to be present, this one being a woodworm or termite *[arḍa]*. "O king," said she, "I am ready to do what you need to have done in this case, on condition that you will grant me a plentiful supply of my favorite food, which is dry timber."

"That you may have," said Solomon, whereupon the termite hopped on top of the gem stone and drilled a hole right through to the other side of it. As he had promised, Solomon rewarded the creature by granting her a plentiful supply of her favorite food, dry timber.

Next, having set the goblet in front of him, Solomon ordered a roundup of the purebred Arabian horses *[khail ʿirāb]*. Once they had been rounded up, these animals were made to gallop around and around until they were getting weary and close to exhaustion, and their sweat was flowing profusely. At this point Solomon filled the goblet with the horses' sweat, which constituted "an overflowing quantity of thirst-quenching water, drawn neither from the earth nor from the sky."

Solomon then gave the command for some ordinary water to be made available, and as soon as it had been set before him, he said to the servants: "Now let me see how you go about washing your hands *[tawaḍḍaʾū]*!"[78]

His purpose in making this demand was to distinguish the menservants from the maidservants. What would happen in the case of those who were actually young women, when they set about pouring water onto the palms of their hands, was that each of them would start by taking some water in the palm of her left hand, from which she would

[78] In a strictly Islāmic context, the verb *tawaḍḍaʾa* (from which the plural imperative form *tawaḍḍaʾū* is derived) would usually mean "to perform the minor ablution *[wuḍūʾ]* for, or preparatory to, the ritual prayer *[ṣalāt]*." As noted by the Arabic lexicographers, however, this verb is by no means always used in this precisely technical sense. It can also convey the more general meaning: "to make oneself fair, beautiful, neat, or clean," and it sometimes signifies: "to wash one or more of the members of the body; to purify one's hand or hands, and one's mouth, by washing to remove the unpleasant odor of fat or greasy food." (The Islāmic ablutions are discussed at length in Vol. 1 of *al-Ghunya*, pp. 8–10 and 338–50.)

let it trickle over her left forearm, then her next move would be to wet her right hand and wash it clean. By following this procedure, she was therefore announcing the fact that she was a female.

Solomon was thus able to check them out one by one, until he had accounted for twelve young women, identified as female servants. In the case of those who were actually young men, on the other hand, each manservant would start by taking some water in the palm of his right hand, using that same water to wash his right forearm, then he would repeat the process with his left hand. Solomon could thereby identify him as a male, and so he checked them out one by one, until he had accounted for all twelve of the young men.

Now that these tricky problems had been dealt with satisfactorily, Solomon could turn his attention to the list of scientific questions posed by Bilqīs in her letter, so he composed his own list of a thousand answers, and placed it in the hands of her messenger. Then he sent her entire collection of presents back home to Bilqīs.

> He said: "What, would you bolster me with material wealth? But what Allāh has given me is better than what He has given you. Oh no, it is you [and not I] who exult in your gift!" (27:36)

He was addressing these words to her emissary, stating in no uncertain terms that "what Allāh has given me," i.e., Prophethood *[nubuwwa]* and kingship, "is better than what He has given you," i.e., material wealth. In this context, the expression "it is you who exult in your gift" means "it is you who think your gift is so wonderful."

Then he wrote Bilqīs a letter, handed it to the hoopoe, and said:

> "Return to them; we shall assuredly come against them with hosts they have not the power to resist, and we shall drive them out from there, abased and utterly humbled." (27:37)

That is to say: "We shall attack them with troops they are powerless to resist, and expel them from the town of Sheba...."

Once again the hoopoe flew off to the land of Sheba, where Bilqīs immediately read the letter he brought her from Solomon. As soon as her messengers had also returned, they recounted to her in detail the whole story of their experience with Solomon. They described how he had dealt with each of those challenging riddles she had sent to him, and they reported what he had sent back to her by way of a response.

Bilqīs then said to her people: "This whole affair has descended upon us from heaven above. It would not make sense to treat it as none of our business, and it is simply not within our power to dismiss it."

Next, she turned her attention to ensuring the safe storage of her throne, arranging for it to be installed in the farthest of seven apartments in her palace, and instructing the sentries to stand guard over it during her absence. Then, after taking these precautionary measures, Bilqīs set out on her journey to visit Solomon.

At this point the hoopoe flew back to Solomon, in order to give him the news that Bilqīs was already on her way to meet him. Solomon promptly assembled the experts of his kingdom, then:

> He said: "O Council, which one of you will bring me her throne, before they come to me as those who surrender?" (27:38)

Her "throne" *[ʿarsh]* refers to her elevated couch *[sarīr]*, while the expression "as those who surrender" *[muslimīn]* means "as those who are ready to make peace" *[muṣāliḥīn]*. Solomon was therefore saying in effect: "Because it will no longer be lawful for us to seize it once the peace treaty *[ṣulḥ]* has been concluded."

> An *ʿifrīt*[79] from among the jinn said: "I will bring it to you, before you can rise from your place; I have the strength for it and I am an agent worthy of trust." (27:39)

This particular *ʿifrīt* was called ʿUmarrad, an appropriate name for a member of the jinn who was so energetic and tough.[80] When he said,"before you can rise from your place," he meant: "from your seat in the court of justice," which would be in session until midday. When he said, "I have the strength for it," he meant that he was strong enough to carry the throne of Bilqīs, and in claiming to be "an agent worthy of trust," he was maintaining that he could be trusted with the extremely

[79] The term *ʿifrīt* may be applied in general to anything that exceeds the ordinary bounds. When applied to a jinnī, or metaphorically to a human being, *ʿifrīt* means "one who is sharp, vigorous, and effective in an affair, exceeding the ordinary bounds therein with craftiness or cunning and wickedness or malignity." Some say that it is properly applied to "an evil jinnī that is powerful, but inferior to the type called *marid*." (See: E.W. Lane, *Arabic-English Lexicon*, art. *ʿ–F–R–T*.)

[80] The adjective *ʿumarrad* is often applied to a horse that is "evil in disposition, very perverse, and strong." It may also be used to describe a wolf as "malignant and very cunning." (See: E.W. Lane, *Arabic-English Lexicon*, art. *ʿ–M–R–D*.)

valuable items embedded in it: the pearls, the jewels, the chrysolite or peridot *[zabarjad]*,[81] and all that gold and silver.

The strength of this *ʿifrīt* is said to have been such that he could plant his foot wherever his glance could reach, in other words, at the farthest point within his range of vision. He was therefore telling Solomon: "In a single stride, I can plant my foot at the most distant point my eyes can see, so it will not take me long to fetch you the throne of Bilqīs." But Solomon said: "I want it brought here even more quickly than that!"

> Said he who possessed a [special item of] knowledge from the Book: "I will bring it to you, even before your glance returns to you." (27:40)

This means that the person concerned had knowledge of the Mightiest Name[82] of Allāh *[Ismu'llāhi'l-Aʿẓam]*, which is: "O Ever-Living One *[yā Ḥayy]*, O Eternally Self-Sustaining One *[yā Qayyūm]*!"[83] He was therefore saying by implication: "I shall offer a prayer of supplication to my Lord, then I shall focus my attention, look into the Book of my Lord, and bring you the throne of Bilqīs."

According to one traditional account, this person was Āṣaf ibn Barakhiyyā ibn Shaʿiyyāʾ, and his mother's name was Bāṭūrā. He was one of the Children of Israel *[banī Isrāʾīl]*, and he had come to know the Mightiest Name of Allāh.

When he said to Solomon: "I will bring it to you, even before your glance returns to you," he meant: "before your glance—your eyesight, that is—has time to register an impression of the thing it is reaching out to see."

[81] The principal Arabic-English dictionaries give chrysolite as the meaning of *zabarjad*. According to *Webster's Ninth New Collegiate Dictionary*, the chrysolite or olivine is "a usually greenish mineral, that is a complex silicate of magnesium and iron, used esp. in refractories," while the peridot is "a deep yellowish green transparent olivine used as a gem."

[82] It is likely to strike the English-speaking reader as rather strange, that the Mightiest Name is said here to be not one Name but two, and that each of the two is preceded by the vocative particle: "O" in English, corresponding to the Arabic *yā*. We should therefore explain that the Arabic word *ism*, for which "name" is in most instances a perfectly satisfactory translation, can sometimes mean "the act of calling by a name." The term "appellation" conveyed this latter meaning in archaic English usage, but in the modern language it almost always means "an identifying name or title." In any case, the translation "Mightiest Appellation of Allāh" would hardly commend itself on esthetic grounds.

For the sake of consistency, and to avoid inflicting cumbersome circumlocutions on the poor reader, the translator has decided to stick to the rendering "Mightiest Name" in all contexts, trusting that this note of explanation will suffice.

[83] At the beginning of the third Sūra of the Qurʾān, the Book of Allāh, we read:

> *Alif–Lām–Mīm.* Allāh! There is no god but He, the Ever-Living, the Eternally Self-Sustaining *[Allāhu lā ilāha illā Huwa'l-Ḥayyu'l-Qayyūm]*. (3:1,2)

Solomon then told him: "I shall triumph if you can do what you say you can do for me, but if you cannot do it, I shall be the object of scorn among the jinn, regardless of the fact that I am the overlord *[sayyid]* of human beings and jinn alike."

Āṣaf proceeded to make himself ready by performing an act of ablution *[tawaḍḍaʾa]*,[84] then he bowed down in prostration *[sajada]* to Allāh (Almighty and Glorious is He), invoking Allāh by His Mightiest Name, as he cried: "O Ever-Living One *[yā Ḥayy]*, O Eternally Self-Sustaining One *[yā Qayyūm]* !"[85]

No sooner had Āṣaf uttered this invocation than the throne of Bilqīs disappeared beneath the surface of the earth, where it remained out of sight until it reemerged next to Solomon's chair of state.[86] When they noticed that the throne had emerged from the ground, the jinn said to Solomon: "Āṣaf is obviously capable of fetching the elevated couch *[sarīr]*, but he may not be equal to the task of fetching Bilqīs herself." Āṣaf responded to this by telling Solomon: "Oh yes, I am going to bring Bilqīs here as well!"

Solomon now gave orders to his builders, who complied by constructing an elegant pavilion *[ṣarḥ]* for him, using building materials made entirely of pieces of glass. As soon as this edifice had been erected, he arranged to have water flowing underneath it, and to have the water stocked with fish. The glass structure was so transparent that the fish in the pond were clearly visible from the very top of the lofty pavilion. Then Solomon ordered his servants to move his chair of state, which was now to be placed in the center of the newly built pavilion. He also commanded a special set of chairs to be installed for the use of his companions, and then, once all the chairs had been set in place, he seated himself upon his own chair while his companions occupied those assigned to them.

[84] See note [78] on p. 58 above. Although we can hardly know for certain, it seems fair to assume that the ablution Āṣaf performed on this occasion was at least very similar to the *wuḍūʾ* [minor ritual ablution] as it has been practiced by Muslims since the time of the Prophet Muḥammad (Allāh bless him and give him peace), in accordance with the prescriptions of Islāmic law.

[85] ***Author's note:*** According to another traditional account, however, ʿAlī ibn Abī Ṭālib (may Allāh be well pleased with him) is reported as having said:

> "[The Mightiest Name of Allāh] is the Name to which, whenever it is used in a prayer of supplication addressed to Him, He always responds, and in answer to which, whenever it is used in asking Him for something, He always gives. And this [Mightiest Nameof Allāh] is: "O Lord of Majesty and Honor *[yā Dha'l-Jalāli wa'l-Ikrām]*."

[86] ***Author's note:*** According to some traditional authorities, it actually surfaced beneath a stool on which Solomon used to rest his feet, when he was seated upon his great chair of state *[kursī kabīr]*.

As for the order of precedence among the holders of the chairs, those sitting nearest to Solomon (peace be upon him) were the human beings, followed by the jinn and then by the devils *[shayāṭīn]*. This was the regular procedure he adopted (peace be upon him) for all purposes, so that, whenever he wished to travel about the country, he would sit upon his chair of state and they would sit on their chairs, then he would command the wind to transport them between the sky above and the earth below. If a moment came when he wished to travel on the ground, he had only to give the command for the wind to stop blowing, then he could alight and travel on the surface of the earth.

Solomon (peace be upon him) had a council of ministers *[majlis]*, his practice in this respect being no different from that of kings in our own day and age. It was only when his council had reconvened, therefore, that he summoned Āṣaf to present himself once again.

Āṣaf duly returned, bowed down in prostration, and invoked Allāh (Almighty and Glorious is He) by His Mightiest Name:
"O Ever-Living One *[yā Ḥayy]*, O Eternally Self-Sustaining One *[yā Qayyūm]* !" At that very moment, lo and behold, he had Bilqīs firmly seated right there beside him![87]

> Then, when he saw it settled in his presence, he [Solomon] said: "This is from the bounty of my Lord that He may try me, whether I am thankful or ungrateful. Whenever someone gives thanks, he is giving thanks only for the good of his own soul, and whoever is ungrateful—my Lord is surely Self-Sufficing, All-Generous." (27:40)

In other words, Solomon was saying: "that He may put me to the test of experience, to see whether I am thankful for the royal status that has

[87] ***Author's note:*** It is maintained by some traditional authorities that the person referred to in the Qur'ān (27:40) as "he who possessed a [special item of] knowledge from the Book" was not Āṣaf but a man called Ṣubba ibn Add, the officer in charge of Solomon's horses. Yet others insist that al-Khiḍr* (peace be upon him) is actually the one "who possessed a [special item of] knowledge from the Book."

****Translator's note:*** The alternative spelling *al-Khaḍir* means "the Green Man." By either name, he is a popular figure, who plays a prominent part in Islāmic legends. According to some, he became green through diving into the spring of life. There is no agreement among the traditional authorities as to whether or not he should be counted as a Prophet *[Nabī]*. Some say that he lived in the time of Abraham (peace be upon him), some in the time of Noah (peace be upon him).

His name does not actually appear in the Qur'ān, but nearly all the commentators agree that the mysterious person referred to in Q.18:59–81 is indeed al-Khiḍr. He is represented in those verses *[āyāt]* as the companion of Moses (peace be upon him). It is usually believed that he is still alive in the flesh and still to be seen in sacred places, such as Mecca and Jerusalem, and some maintain that he flies through the air and meets Elias (peace be upon him) at the dam of Alexandria and makes the pilgrimage with him every year. (See: T.P. Hughes, *Dictionary of Islam*, pp. 272–73, and A.J. Wensinck's article AL-KHAḌIR in *SEI*.)

been conferred upon me, or ungrateful for all the blessings I have received, since I have now seen that someone, though inferior to me in rank, may nevertheless be superior to me in knowledge." He was thus stating his determination to be thankful to Allāh (Almighty and Glorious is He), while acknowledging that his Lord would not be in a hurry to punish someone who proved to be ungrateful for His blessings.

When the jinn heard of this, they started making disparaging remarks about Bilqīs in the presence of Solomon, with the intention of getting him to dislike her. They were afraid that he might decide to marry her, and that she would then be in a position to inform him about their private affairs. She was in fact quite knowledgeable in this area, since her own mother was a jinniyya, known by the name of ʿUmaira, the daughter of ʿAmr.[88]

It was this that prompted the jinn to say: "May Allāh prevent the king from making a serious mistake! There is something wrong with her mind, and her legs are like the shanks of a donkey." Bilqīs was in fact decidedly hirsute *[halbāʾ]*, or hairy *[shaʿrāʾ]*, to use a more common word.

When Solomon heard them say these things about her, he conceived a plan that would enable him to examine her mental capacity, and which would also let him see her legs for himself. In order to put this plan into effect, he had some water channeled into a pond, then caused the pond to be stocked with frogs and fish. He also gave orders for certain alterations to be made to the throne of Bilqīs, by adding some new features to it and subtracting some of the existing elements from it, so that he could examine her mental faculty of recognition. As Allāh (Exalted is He) has told us:

> [Solomon] said: "Disguise her throne for her, so that we may see whether she will be guided aright, or if she is one of those that are not rightly guided." (27:41)

In other words, he was saying: "Make her elevated couch *[sarīr]* look different to her, so we may see whether she can still recognize it, or if she is one of those who cannot recognize the truth."

Bilqīs then approached until she eventually reached the pavilion, at which point:

> It was said to her: "Enter the pavilion." (27:44)

We understand this pavilion *[ṣarḥ]* to have been a palatial building *[qaṣr]*, but there are some who maintain that *ṣarḥ* is the word for an

[88] ***Author's note:*** Some say that her name was Rawwāḥa, and that she was the daughter of as-Sakan, the king of the jinn.

ordinary house *[bait]* in the dialect of Ḥimyar.

> But when she saw it, she supposed it was a fathomless pool. (27:44)

Since she reckoned that the pool of water was very deep indeed, Bilqīs said to herself: "He must be intending to drown me. What I shall have to do now may be unfortunate, but isn't it surely a lot better than that?"

> And she bared her legs. (27:44)

Lo and behold, two hairy legs were thus exposed to view. She was nevertheless a very fine person indeed, and as far removed as could possibly be from what Solomon had been told about her.

> [Solomon] said: "It is a pavilion, made smooth." (27:44)

In other words: "It is a sleekly constructed palace, the surface of which is perfectly smooth and bristle-free, so that it may be compared to a beardless youth *[amrad]* who has yet to grow any hair on his face. It appears that each building block has been seamlessly fixed to its neighbor, since all the blocks consist of crystal glass."

When Bilqīs moved over toward Solomon, he noticed that her legs had been exposed, and then he also noticed that the hair on her legs had been neatly trimmed. He was very pleasantly surprised by the sight he saw!

> So, when she came, it was said: "Is your throne like this?" (27:42)

That is to say, when she came to Solomon she was asked: "Is your throne like this?" So she looked at it, then began to react with acknowledgment and disavowal simultaneously. But then she said to herself: "How can this elevated couch have come to be here with me now, if it is indeed the one I left behind in the innermost of seven apartments, with my palace guards on duty all around it?" She would therefore neither acknowledge nor disown it directly.

> She said: "It seems as though it were the very same." And [Solomon said]: "We were given the knowledge before her, and we had already surrendered [to Allāh]." (27:42)

In other words: "We were given the knowledge before Bilqīs, for she was still a Magian *[Majūsiyya]* when we had already surrendered [to Allāh]." But now:

> She said: "My Lord, indeed I have wronged myself, and I surrender along with Solomon to Allāh, the Lord of All the Worlds." (27:44)

Her confession may be understood to mean: "I have wronged myself by thinking so badly of Solomon that I imagined he actually wanted to drown me." Some commentators, however, prefer to interpret the expression "I have wronged myself" as meaning: "I have brought injury upon myself through the practice of sun worship *[ʿibādat ash-shams]*." As for her declaration: "and I surrender with Solomon...," this may be taken to mean: "and with Solomon I now pay obedience to Allāh *[aṭaʿtu'llāh]*." Another possible interpretation is: "I now devote myself sincerely *[akhlāṣtu]*, with Solomon, to the worship of Allāh, the Lord of All the Worlds."

Thus it came to pass that Bilqīs surrendered [to Allāh].

> And [Solomon] turned her away from what she had been worshipping instead of Allāh,[89] for she came of a people who were unbelievers. (27:43)

Solomon did in fact make her his wife. Once they were married, he ordered the preparation of the depilatory paste called *nūra*, which Solomon and Bilqīs then adopted for their personal use. He was actually the very first person ever to use *nūra* as a means of removing hair from the body.[90]

It is said that Solomon would ask Bilqīs about various things, and that she would ask him questions in her turn.

Solomon consummated his marriage with Bilqīs, and so she came to bear him a son, to whom he gave the name of David *[Dāwūd]*. This David died during his father's lifetime, then Solomon died, and Bilqīs died one month after the death of her husband. According to one traditional account, Solomon granted her a village in Syria, from which she then continued to collect the revenues *[kharāj]*[91] until she died.

According to another version of the story, however, once Solomon had consummated his marriage with her, he released her, let her resume command of her armies, and sent her back to her own kingdom. He would come to visit her once every month, so he was often on that journey from Jerusalem *[Bait al-Maqdis]* to the Yemen—the journey we mentioned earlier [near the beginning of this discourse].[92]

[89] Some commentators, and the translators who follow them, prefer to treat "what she had been worshipping instead of Allāh" as the subject of the verb-plus-object-pronoun *ṣaddahā* ["turned her away"]. Thus Pickthall gives the translation:

> But all that she served, apart from Allāh, barred her, for she was of a people of unbelievers.

[90] According to E.W. Lane (*Arabic-English Lexicon*, art. *N–W–R*), *nūra* is "a depilatory composed of quick lime with a small proportion (about an eighth part) of orpiment [trisulphide of arsenic]; it is made into a paste with water, before application, and loosens the hair in about two minutes, after which it is immediately washed off."

[91] At a later period in history, the term *kharāj* would come to have a special significance in the technical vocabulary of Islāmic jurisprudence, meaning "the poll-tax paid by the *ahl adh-dhimma*, i.e., the Jewish, Christian or Sabean subjects of an Islamic state, who, in return for the payment of this special tax, are entitled under Islamic law to security of their persons and their property."

[92] See p. 48 above.

Shaikh ʿAbd al-Qādir al-Jīlānī (may Allāh be well pleased with him) explains that he chose to tell this story at length, because it is so very instructive for every intelligent believer.

If I have devoted much of this discourse to recounting this story at length and in detail, I have chosen to do so because the lessons it contains are of seriously instructive value to every intelligent believer *[muʾmin ʿāqil]*. The intelligent believer is one who keeps his attention focused on the ultimate consequences *[ʿawāqib]*. As a student of history, he is interested in learning about the lives of our ancient predecessors *[siyar as-salaf]*, both the righteous *[ṣāliḥ]* and the wicked *[ṭāliḥ]*, and about the influence exerted by the Power of Allāh to affect the development of nations *[umam]* that are now long past and gone.

What does the intelligent believer learn from these studies? They teach him that Allāh (Almighty and Glorious is He) bestows His gracious favor on people who practice worshipful obedience to Him, and that He makes those who rebel against Him subservient to those who obey Him, in that He authorizes the latter to exercise control over the former and to treat them as their inferior subjects.

These studies also teach him that Allāh (Almighty and Glorious is He) grants dominion over the rest of His creatures to members of that special group whose relationship with Him is one of close friendship *[walāya]* and loving affection *[maḥabba]*. In the case of Solomon, for instance, we have seen how his Lord (Almighty and Glorious is He) rewarded his worshipful obedience by granting him dominion over Bilqīs and her kingdom.

This is all the more amazing when we learn that the population of her kingdom included twelve thousand warriors, each and every one of whom was himself the commander of a further hundred thousand, whereas the total strength of Solomon's army consisted of four hundred thousand soldiers, two hundred thousand being members of the human race, while the other two hundred thousand were drawn from the ranks of the jinn. The disparity between the two armies was clearly enormous, yet the king with his smaller army was enabled to be victorious, on account of his worshipful obedience, while the queen with her vastly larger army was vanquished, on account of her unbelief *[kufr]* and her sinful disobedience.

You must therefore acknowledge the fact, O human being, that Islām will surely prevail, and that it will not be overcome.

> And Allāh will not grant the unbelievers any way [by which to triumph] over the believers. (4:141)

Likewise in your case, O you who have access to the help and guidance of Allāh, as long as you truly believe *[āmanta]*, you will be safe *[aminta]*, not only from your enemies in this world, but also from Allāh's blazing fire in the world of the hereafter. The Fire of Hell will put itself at your service. It will bow its head silently before you, and it will show you the way [to pass through in safety], treating you with honor and respect in obedience to the commandment of its Master *[Mawlā]* and in compliance with His instructions. It will actually say to you: "Pass on through, O believer, since your light has extinguished my flame!"[93]

If you have earned the right to be addressed with such courtesy and politeness by the Fire of Hell, it must mean that you are a truly dignified and enlightened person. Since you are clad in the robe of honor conferred by the King, and since you bear the distinctive mark of the kind of dignity that always commands respect, it is incumbent upon all the royal attendants and slaves to treat you with the utmost reverence and solemnity, and to put themselves at your service.

As for the unbeliever *[kāfir]* and the rebellious sinner, the Fire of Hell will fly into a furious rage against them. It will wreak vengeance on them with all the vindictiveness of a cruel tyrant, when he takes his revenge on the enemy he has just defeated in battle.

[93] Although he does not mention the attribution here, Shaikh ʿAbd al-Qādir al-Jīlānī (may Allāh be well-pleased with him) has told us elsewhere, notably in the Thirteenth Discourse of *Revelations of the Unseen [Futūḥ al-Ghaib]*, that this saying can be found in "traditions reliably ascribed to the best of humankind, the best of those ever carried by the earth and sheltered by the sky, Muḥammad the Chosen (Allāh bless him and give him peace)."

As Allāh (Almighty and Glorious is He) has told us:

> When it sees them from a far-off place, they shall hear what a raging and a roaring it can make. (25:12)

It follows therefore, that if you wish for glory *[ʿizza]* in this world and the hereafter, you must practice worshipful obedience to Allāh, and you must be very careful to refrain from sinful disobedience to Allāh, for then, through the mercy of Allāh (Exalted is He), you may find the glory you seek. As Allāh (Exalted is He) has told us in His own words:

> Whoever may wish for glory, the glory belongs entirely to Allāh. (35:10)

He has also said (Exalted is He):

> Yet glory belongs to Allāh, and to His Messenger and the believers, but the hypocrites do not know it. (63:8)

This means that your hypocrisy *[nifāq]*, O you who claim to have true faith *[īmān]*, and your associating partners with Allāh *[shirk]*, O you who lay claim to sincere devotion *[ikhlāṣ]*, are the obstacles that have prevented you from seeing the glory of the All-Compelling One *[al-Jabbār]*, of His chosen Prophet *[nabiyyihi'l-mukhtār]*, and of the most excellent believers *[al-muʾminīna'l-akhyār]*.

If only you would conduct yourself in accordance with the demands of true faith *[īmān]*, and if only you could feel the genuine conviction that is needed in order to fulfill the prerequisites of sincere devotion *[ikhlāṣ]*, you would enjoy in this world a guarantee of safety from every influence that causes harm, and from every devil *[shaiṭān]* among both humankind and the species of the jinn. You would also enjoy a guarantee of safety in the hereafter from the torment of the Fires of Hell. The divine help that brings victory *[nuṣra]* would be yours, while your enemies would suffer the shame of defeat. As Allāh (Almighty and Glorious is He) has told us:

> If you help Allāh, He will help you, and He will make your foothold firm. (47:7)

He has also said (Exalted is He):

> So do not falter and cry out for peace, when you are the ones who will prevail, and Allāh is with you, and He will not grudge you [the reward you have earned by] your deeds. (47:35)

In your case, unfortunately, the effects of heedless negligence have piled up to form a thick coating that covers your heart. Layers of rust have accumulated all over it, and darkness and gloom have gathered around it. Serious indeed will be the consequences, in terms of sorrow and remorse:

> On the day when the innermost beings shall be put to the test. (86:9)

That is to say, on the Day of the Resurrection *[Yawm al-Qiyāma]*, the Day of the Stark Reality *[al-Ḥāqqa]*,[94] the Day of the Great Catastrophe *[aṭ-Ṭāmmat al-Kubrā]*,[95] the Day of the Sudden Disaster *[al-Qāriʿa]*,[96] the Day of the Deafening Cry *[aṣ-Ṣākhkha]*.[97]

> On that day you will be exposed; not a secret of yours will be concealed. (69:18)
>
> Upon that day mankind will issue forth in scattered groups to be shown their works, and anyone who has ever done an atom's weight of good will see it then, and anyone who has ever done an atom's weight of evil will see it then. (99:6–8)

According to some authorities on the subject, the term *dharra* ["atom" in the English translation of the Qurʾānic quotation immediately above] is properly applied to one of those tiny particles of dust that appear like pinheads in the rays of the sun. Others maintain that four *dharrāt* are equal to the weight of a mustard seed. Still others insist that *dharra* signifies the small red ant, which is almost invisible when it crawls about. The *dharra* is also said to be one thousandth part of a single pearl of barley. ʿAbdu'llāh ibn ʿAbbās (may Allāh be well pleased with him and with his father) once said: "When you spread the palm of your hand and place it on the dusty ground, then raise it back up, every particle of dust that sticks to it can be referred to as a *dharra*."[98]

[94] The Arabic word *ḥāqqa* is derived from the same triliteral root—*ḥ–q–q*—as *ḥaqīqa* [reality, actual fact] and *al-Ḥaqq* [the (Divine) Truth]. Where *al-Ḥāqqa* occurs in the Qurʾān (69:1,2,3; also in the traditional title of that Sūra), the commentators understand it to mean the Resurrection, "because in it shall be manifest the true natures of things or actions," or "because in it things that are denied shall be surely known; namely the raising of the dead, and the reckoning, and the recompensing." (See E.W. Lane, *Arabic-English Lexicon*, art. Ḥ–Q–Q.)

[95] The expression occurs in Qurʾān 79:34.

[96] The term *al-Qāriʿa* occurs in each of the first three verses *[āyāt]* of the 101st Sūra of the Qurʾān (traditionally entitled *Sūrat al-Qāriʿa*), where it is understood by the commentators to mean the Resurrection. It also occurs in the above-mentioned *Sūrat al-Ḥāqqa*

[97] Also interpreted as "the Deafening Blast [of the Trumpet]." See Q. 80:33.

[98] After perusing this passage, the reader will understand that the appropriate English equivalent of the Arabic word *dharra* (of which *dharr* is the collective form and *dharrāt* the plural) will usually be "atom" or "tiny particle" or "mote" or "speck"—although the context may call for the rendering "tiny ant" or "grub."

Well then, the important question is: Where do you stand in relation to the day when deeds will be weighed in the balance, and when some will prove to be heavy enough, but some will prove to be too light? That is the day of which Allāh (Exalted is He) is speaking when He says:

> On the day when We shall gather the righteous unto the All-Merciful, a goodly company, and We shall drive the guilty culprits into Hell, a weary herd.[99] (19:85,86)

At this point the veil will be drawn aside, and the face that was hidden behind the veil will be revealed. The true believer *[mu'min]* will be clearly distinguishable from the unbeliever *[kāfir]*, the champion of truth *[ṣiddīq]* from the hypocrite *[munāfiq]*, the one who affirms the Divine Unity *[muwaḥḥid]* from the one who associates partners with Allāh *[mushrik]*, the friend *[waliyy]* from the foe *['aduww]*, and the one who is really telling the truth *[muḥiqq]* from the one who is merely pretending *[mudda'ī]*.

You must therefore be on your guard, O miserable wretch, against the terror of that day. You must take a good look, and see which of the two parties you belong to. If you are working for the sake of Allāh, the Almighty *[al-'Aẓīm]*, if you are dedicated in all your work to performing your duty to the One who is All-Aware *[al-Khabīr]*, and if you keep your work free from any impurity that would offend the All-Seeing Examiner *[an-Nāqid al-Baṣīr]*, then you belong to the party *[ḥizb]* of the righteous *[muttaqīn]*, as a member of the goodly company that will be gathered unto the All-Merciful *[ar-Raḥmān]* on the Day of Resurrection.

If such be the case, then you deserve respect, O honorable one! And you deserve congratulations and glad tidings, O wise one! But if this description does not fit, you must realize that you are attached to the other party, and therefore doomed along with all those who are doomed to perish in the Fire of Hell, following in the footsteps of Pharaoh and Hāman and Qārūn. As Allāh (Almighty and Glorious is He) has told us:

> So whoever hopes for the meeting with his Lord, let him do righteous work, and let him give no one any share at all in the worship due unto his Lord. (18:110)

You have thus been given notice that nothing will come to your rescue on that Day, apart from righteous work.

[99] ***Author's note:*** That is to say, a thirsty herd.

Concerning the special merit of "In the Name of Allāh, the All-Merciful, the All-Compassionate *[Bismi'llāhi'r-Raḥmāni'r-Raḥīm]*."

From a traditional report that has been transmitted on the authority of ʿAṭāʾ, we learn that Jābir ibn ʿAbdi'llāh (may Allāh be well pleased with him and with his father) once said:

"When the expression 'In the Name of Allāh, the All-Merciful, the All-Compassionate *[Bismi'llāhi'r-Raḥmāni'r-Raḥīm]*' was first sent down [by divine revelation to mankind], the clouds fled away to the East, the winds died down, the waves of the ocean heaved in a tempestuous storm, the beasts pricked up their ears to listen, the devils *[shayāṭīn]* were pelted with stones *[rujimat]* [100] to drive them from the sky, and Allāh (Almighty and Glorious is He) swore by His Almighty Glory that His Name would never be uttered over an illness without His healing that illness, that His Name would never be pronounced over anything without His blessing it, and that anyone who ever recited 'In the Name of Allāh, the All-Merciful, the All-Compassionate *[Bismi'llāhi'r-Raḥmāni'r-Raḥīm]*' would surely enter the Garden of Paradise."

We have it on the authority of Abū Wāʾil that it was ʿAbdu'llāh ibn Masʿūd (may Allāh be well pleased with him) who said:

"If anyone wishes to have Allāh rescue him from the clutches of the nineteen *zabāniya* [tormenting angels within the Fire of Hell], he has only to say: 'In the Name of Allāh, the All-Merciful, the All-Compassionate *[Bismi'llāhi'r-Raḥmāni'r-Raḥīm]*,' for these words are spelled with nineteen letters [of the Arabic script],[101] and Allāh

[100] The Arabic verb *rujimat* is formed from the three root letters *r-j-m*, from which the adjective *rajīm* [accursed], the passive participle *marjūm* [cursed] and the nouns *rijām* [gravestones] and *rujūm* [missiles] are also derived. The connections are fully explained in the preceding Discourse (see pp. 10–13 above).

[101] Namely, the Arabic letters: *bāʾ, sīn, mīm, alif, lām, lām, hāʾ, alif, lām, rāʾ, ḥāʾ, mīm, nūn, alif, lām, rāʾ, ḥā, yāy, mīm*. (As used in the text of this translation, the romanized transliteration of Arabic words and phrases is designed to represent the pronunciation, rather than the Arabic spelling.)

(Exalted is He) will respond to each letter in turn by substituting a Garden of Paradise for one of the *zabāniya*."[102]

According to another traditional account, this one transmitted by Ṭāwūs on the authority of Ibn ʿAbbās (may Allāh be well pleased with him and with his father), ʿUthmān ibn ʿAffān (may Allāh be well pleased with him) once asked the Prophet (Allāh bless him and give him peace) about "In the Name of Allāh, the All-Merciful, the All-Compassionate *[Bismi'llāhi'r-Raḥmāni'r-Raḥīm]*," and he replied:

> It is one of the Names *[Ism min Asmāʾ]* of Allāh (Almighty and Glorious is He), and the closeness between it and the Mightiest Name[103] of Allāh is just like the closeness that exists between the iris and the white of the eye.

It is on the authority of Anas ibn Mālik (may Allāh be well pleased with him) that this next saying is attributed to Allāh's Messenger (Allāh bless him and give him peace):

> If someone picks up from the ground a piece of paper with "*Bismi'llāhi'r-Raḥmāni'r-Raḥīm*" upon it, because he regards Allāh as far too Exalted to have His Name trampled underfoot, that person will be recorded in His presence as one of the champions of truth *[ṣiddīqīn]*, and his parents will be granted an alleviation [of their punishment], even if they are guilty of associating partners with Allāh *[mushrikīn]*.

It has been said that Iblīs[104] the Damned was never heard to utter a plaintive cry, except on three occasions. The first time he uttered a plaintive cry was when he was damned and expelled from the Kingdom of Heaven. He emitted another such cry when the Prophet (Allāh bless him and give him peace) was born, and he uttered his third lament

[102] In a verse *[āya]* of the Qurʾān (96:18), Allāh (Exalted is He) declares: "We shall summon the *zabāniya*." Since the triliteral Arabic root *z-b-n* conveys the idea of "shoving" or "thrusting", the commentators have understood the term to mean "certain angels, so called because they are charged with the task of thrusting the damned into the Fire of Hell."

In the Fifth Discourse of *The Removal of Cares [Jalāʾ al-Khāwaṭir]* Shaikh ʿAbd al-Qādir al-Jīlānī (may Allāh be well pleased with him) tells us that the Prophet (Allāh bless him and give him peace) is reported as having said:

> Allāh (Almighty and Glorious is He) has created tormenting angels *[zabāniya]* within the Fire of Hell. They serve Allāh by inflicting vengeance on His enemies, the unbelievers. So, when He wishes to chastise an unbeliever *[kāfir]*, He says to them: "Seize him!" Seventy thousand of them immediately rush toward that unbeliever, and as soon as he falls into the hands of one of them, he melts like fat in the fire, so that nothing is left on his body but the dripping *[wadak]*. Then Allāh (Almighty and Glorious is He) restores his normal constitution to him, whereupon they proceed to bind him with shackles and chains of fire, tying his head and his feet together. Then they hurl him unto the Fire of Hell.

[103] For more on the Mightiest Name *[al-Ism al-Aʿẓam]*, see p. 61 above.

[104] See note 33 above.

when the Opening Sūra of the Qur'ān *[Fātiḥatu'l-Kitāb]* was revealed, because it began with the words:
"In the Name of Allāh, the All-Merciful, the All-Compassionate *[Bismi'llāhi'r-Raḥmāni'r-Raḥīm]*."

According to a report transmitted on the authority of Sālim ibn al-Ja'd, it was 'Alī [ibn Abī Ṭālib] (may Allāh be well pleased with him) who said that, soon after "In the Name of Allāh, the All-Merciful, the All-Compassionate *[Bismi'llāhi'r-Raḥmāni'r-Raḥīm]*" had been revealed, Allāh's Messenger (Allāh bless him and give him peace) had this to say about it:

> When this *āya* [verse of Scripture] was first sent down to Adam, he said: "My offspring will be safe from punishment, as long as they continue to recite it!" Then it was taken away, until it was sent down again to Abraham, the Special Friend of Allāh *[Ibrāhīm al-Khalīl]*, who recited it while he was held in the sling of the catapult, whereupon Allāh made the fire [of the furnace into which he was about to be hurled] become coolness and peace for his sake.[105]
>
> Then it was taken away after Abraham's time, not to be sent down again until it was revealed to Solomon, whereupon the angels exclaimed: "Now, by Allāh, your dominion is finally complete!" Then it was taken away once again, but Allāh (Almighty and Glorious is He) has now sent it down to me.
>
> Eventually, when they come to the Day of Resurrection, the members of my Community will be saying: "In the Name of Allāh, the All-Merciful, the All-Compassionate *[Bismi'llāhi'r-Raḥmāni'r-Raḥīm]*," and so, when their deeds are placed in the balance, their good deeds will outweigh [their bad deeds].

Allāh's Messenger (Allāh bless him and give him peace) has left us with this instruction concerning *Bismi'llāhi'r-Raḥmāni'r-Raḥīm*:

> Write it in your books, and, when you set it down in writing, pronounce it aloud!

[105] An allusion to Qur'ān 21:69.

Further discussion concerning the special merit of "In the Name of Allāh, the All-Merciful, the All-Compassionate [*Bismi'llāhi'r-Raḥmāni'r-Raḥīm*]."

ʿIkrima (may Allāh bestow His mercy upon him) is reported as having said:

"The very first objects to be created by Allāh were the Tablet *[Lawḥ]* and the Pen *[Qalam]*. Allāh then commanded the Pen to move across the Tablet, setting down upon it the record of all that was to be until the Day of Resurrection *[Yawm al-Qiyāma]*. The very first inscription to be written upon the Tablet was: 'In the Name of Allāh, the All-Merciful, the All-Compassionate *[Bismi'llāhi'r-Raḥmāni'r-Raḥīm]*.'

"Then Allāh decreed that this *āya* [verse of Scripture] would serve as an assurance of protection *[amān]* for His creatures, as long as they made a regular practice of reciting it. The recitation of it thus became the regular practice of the inhabitants of the Seven Heavens, the inhabitants of the Highest Plane, the inhabitants of the Canopies of Glory *[Surādiqāt al-Majd]*, and the Archangels *[Karūbiyyūn]*,[106] as well as of all pure beings and those who constantly proclaim the absolute glory of the Lord *[musabbiḥūn]*.[107]

"The first time 'In the Name of Allāh, the All-Merciful, the All-Compassionate *[Bismi'llāhi'r-Raḥmāni'r-Raḥīm]*' was revealed to mankind was when it was sent down to Adam (peace be upon him), and when he received it he said: 'My offspring will be safe from punishment, as long as they continue to recite it!'

[106] The Archangels *[Karūbiyyūn]* (called Cherubim in the Hebrew Bible) are said to be the chiefs or princes of the angels, included among whom are Gabriel *[Jabra'īl* or *Jibrīl]*, Michael *[Mīkā'īl]* and Isrāfīl. They are sometimes referred to as *al-Muqarrabūn* [those brought near], because they are the nearest of the angels to the Bearers of the Divine Throne *[Ḥamalat al-ʿArsh]*. (See: E.W. Lane, *Arabic-English Lexicon*, art. *K–R–B*.)

[107] During the Islāmic ritual prayer *[ṣalāt]*, the glorification of the Lord *[tasbīḥ]* is uttered each time the worshipper adopts the postures of bowing *[rukūʿ]* and prostration *[sujūd]*. While adopting the bowing posture, one says: "*Subḥāna Rabbiya'l-ʿAẓīm* [Glory to my Lord, the Almighty!]" and when in prostration: "*Subḥāna Rabbiya'l-Aʿlā* [Glory to my Lord, the Most High!]"

"But then it was taken away [from mankind, the Children of Adam], until it was sent down again to Abraham, the Special Friend of Allāh *[Ibrāhīm al-Khalīl]* (peace be upon him), when it was revealed to him in the Sūra of Praise *[Sūrat al-Ḥamd]*.[108] He recited it while he was held inside the sling of the catapult *[manjanīq]*, whereupon Allāh made the fire [of the furnace into which he was about to be hurled] become coolness and peace for his sake.

"Then it was taken away after Abraham's time, not to be sent down again until it was revealed to Moses (peace be upon him) in the Scrolls *[Ṣuḥuf]*,[109] enabling him to triumph over Pharaoh and his sorcerers, Hāmān and his soldiers, and Qārūn and his followers.

"After the time of Moses (peace be upon him), it was taken away once more, but it was later sent down to Solomon the son of David (peace be upon them both). This prompted the angels to exclaim: 'Today, by Allāh, your dominion is finally complete, O son of David!' It was indeed the case that Solomon had only to recite it over something he needed to control, and that thing would at once be rendered subject to his bidding.

"On the very same day on which Allāh sent down that revelation to him, He commanded Solomon to issue the following invitation to all the tribes *[asbāṭ]* of the Children of Israel: 'Is there anyone amongst you who would like to hear the verse of Scripture *[āya]* that guarantees the protection *[amān]* of Allāh? If such there be, let him come and present himself to Solomon in the temple *[miḥrāb]*[110] of David, for Solomon intends to deliver a sermon there.'

"There was in fact not a single devotee, whether pious recluse *[maḥbūs]* or wandering ascetic *[sā'iḥ]*, who chose to ignore this invitation. They all came to him as fast as they possibly could, so it was not long

[108] Another name for *Sūrat al-Fātiḥa*, the Opening Sūra of the Noble Qur'ān.

[109] The term *Ṣuḥuf* is traditionally applied to the Scrolls, meaning texts of revealed Scripture, that were sent down to Abraham and Moses (peace be upon them), as mentioned in the Qur'ān:

> Surely this is in the ancient Scrolls, the Scrolls of Abraham and Moses *[inna hādha la-fi'ṣ-Ṣuḥufi'l-ūlā—Ṣuḥufi Ibrāhīma wa Mūsā]*. (87:18,19)

[110] The term *miḥrāb* has come to mean the niche in a mosque that indicates the *Qibla* [direction of prayer]. To explain the fact that *miḥrāb* (of which *maḥārīb* is the plural form) is derived from the triliteral root *ḥ-r-b*, which normally has a warlike connotation, the Arabic lexicographers define *maḥārīb Banī Isrā'īl* as meaning: "The places of worship of the Children of Israel, in which they used to assemble for prayer, or in which they used to sit, as though they sat therein to consult respecting war." (See: E.W. Lane, *Arabic-English Lexicon*, art. *Ḥ–R–B*.)

before all the rabbis *[aḥbār]*, devotees *[ʿibād]* and ascetics *[zuhhād]* from all the tribes were assembled in his presence.

"Solomon then arose and mounted the pulpit *[minbar]* of the Special Friend of Allāh *[al-Khalīl]*, and so it was from the pulpit of Abraham that he recited to them the verse of Scripture that guarantees protection *[āyatu'l-amān]*: 'In the Name of Allāh, the All-Merciful, the All-Compassionate *[Bismi'llāhi'r-Raḥmāni'r-Raḥīm]*.' No one heard these words without being filled with joy. They all said: 'We now bear witness that you are indeed the Messenger of Allāh, really and truly *[ḥaqqan]*!'

"It thus enabled Solomon to vanquish the kings of the earth, and it was to be the means by which Allāh would effect the conquest *[iftataḥa]*[111] of Mecca for the sake of His Prophet Muḥammad (Allāh bless him and give him peace).

"After the time of Solomon, however, it was again taken away from mankind, until it was sent down to the Messiah *[Masīḥ]*, Jesus the son of Mary (peace be upon him), who received it with great joy, and whose Disciples *[Ḥawāriyyūn]*[112] welcomed the glad tidings it represented. Allāh (Exalted is He) conveyed to him by way of inspiration: 'O son of the Virgin *[ʿAdhrāʾ]*, do you realize what kind of *āya* it is that I have just revealed to you? It is actually the verse of Scripture that guarantees protection *[āyatu'l-amān]*, that is to say, My words: "In the Name of Allāh, the All-Merciful, the All-Compassionate *[Bismi'llāhi'r-Raḥmāni'r-Raḥīm]*." You must therefore recite it very frequently, in your standing and your sitting and your lying down, in your coming and your going, in your climbing uphill and in your climbing down.'

"[Allāh (Exalted is He) continued:] 'If anyone shows up on the Day of Resurrection with "In the Name of Allāh, the All-Merciful, the All-Compassionate *[Bismi'llāhi'r-Raḥmāni'r-Raḥīm]*" inscribed eighty times in his record book, and if he is one who truly believes *[muʾmin]* in Me and in My Lordship *[Rubūbiyyatī]*, I will grant him immunity

[111] The verb *iftataḥa* is derived from the triliteral root *f–t–ḥ*, which conveys the basic idea of "openness." For a full account of many important ramifications of this Arabic root, see the Translator's Introduction to *The Sublime Revelation [al-Fatḥ ar-Rabbānī]*, another volume in the Al-Baz series of English translations of the works of Shaikh ʿAbd al-Qādir al-Jīlānī (may Allāh be well pleased with him).

[112] Several authorities assign to the singular form *ḥawārī* the meaning: 'A person who whitens clothes by washing and beating them,' and then explain that its plural form is applied to the disciples of Jesus (peace be upon him) because their trade was to do this. Others trace the application to meanings like: 'One who is freed and cleared from every vice, fault or defect.' (For yet other explanations, see E.W. Lane, *Arabic-English Lexicon*, art. *Ḥ–W–R*.)

from the Fire of Hell and I will cause him to enter the Garden of Paradise. It must therefore be pronounced as the preface to your recitation of the Scriptures, and as the introduction to your performance of the ritual prayer *[ṣalāt]*, for if anyone should die in the course of a recitation or prayer begun with these words, [the pair of angels called] Munkar and Nakīr will not subject him to their usual post-mortem interrogation, the agonies of death *[sakarāt al-mawt]* and the crushing pressure of the grave will be alleviated in his case, and My mercy *[raḥma]* will be upon him. I shall allow him to have plenty of space inside his grave. I shall give him plenty of light within his grave. I shall let him have light therein to the full extent of his faculty of sight.

"'When I bring him forth from his grave [on the Day of Resurrection], it will be with his body perfectly clean and his face most radiant, shining with a brilliant glow. When I call him to account, I shall make it an easy reckoning for him to pass, and I shall tip the scale of the balance in his favor. I shall provide him with perfect illumination on the Bridge *[Ṣirāṭ]*, so that he can cross over safely and enter the Garden of Paradise. I shall also command the herald to announce him, when he is ushered onto the Fields of the Resurrection *['Araṣāt al-Qiyāma]*, as one who is worthy of bliss and forgiveness.'

"Jesus (peace be upon him) then responded with the question: 'O Allāh! O my Lord! Can this be specially for me?' So the Lord told him: 'For you in particular, as well as for those who follow you, who conduct themselves in keeping with your example, and who speak as you speak. It is also for Aḥmad and his Community *[Umma]*, after you.'

"Jesus (peace be upon him) conveyed this news to his followers, to whom he said:

> I am also bringing good tidings of a Messenger who shall come after me, whose name shall be Aḥmad [Praiseworthy]. (61:6)[113]

"When he had explained to them that the name Aḥmad [Praiseworthy] would be in keeping with the excellence of his nature, his character, his refinement, and so on and so forth, Jesus (peace be upon him) accepted from his followers their solemn covenant to believe in this coming Messenger. Later, when Allāh (Exalted is He) raised him up to heaven, he reemphasized the importance of this covenant to his companions. In the course of time, however, when all the Disciples and all the other

[113] *wa mubashshiran bi-Rasūlin ya'tī min ba'di'smuhu Aḥmad.*

followers who had known him during his lifetime had passed away, along came the more recent generations, who began to go astray and to lead other people astray. They pursued their worldly interests instead of the interests of their religion *[dīn]*, and they encouraged other people to do the same. As this tendency continued, the verse of Scripture that guarantees protection *[āyat al-amān]* was withdrawn from the breasts of the Christians *[Naṣāra]*, although it did remain intact within the breasts of those People of the Gospel who had truly submitted to Allāh *[muslimī ahl al-Injīl]*, such as the monk *[rāhib]* Baḥīrā[114] and others like him.

"The time came at last when Allāh sent forth the Prophet (Allāh bless him and give him peace) to carry out his mission, and so *'Bismi'llāhi'r-Raḥmāni'r-Raḥīm'* was once again sent down, for it was revealed to him in Mecca as part of the Sūra of Praise *[Sūrat al-Ḥamd]*.[115] In accordance with the instructions which were then issued by Allāh's Messenger (Allāh bless him and give him peace), this was to be inscribed at the head of the various Chapters[116] in which the text of the Qur'ān was compiled, as well as on the front pages of official dispatches *[rasā'il]* and registers *[dafātir]*.

"The fact that this *āya* had been sent down to Allāh's Messenger (Allāh bless him and give him peace) was indeed a mighty triumph *[fatḥ]*.[117] The Lord of Almighty Glory *[Rabb al-'Izza]* swore by His Almighty Glory that no truly convinced believer *[mu'min mūqin]* would ever preface an undertaking with this invocation of His Name, without His granting that person His blessing for the success of the undertaking concerned, and that no believer would ever recite it without the Garden of Paradise saying to Him: 'I wait intent upon Your service, time and time again, and upon aiding Your cause, time and time again

[114] According to traditional accounts, Baḥīrā was a Nestorian monk whose dwelling in Syria lay along the route followed by the Meccan caravans. One of the caravans that stopped there was accompanied by the Prophet Muḥammad (Allāh bless him and give him peace), who was only twelve years of age at the time, and who was traveling with his uncle Abū Ṭālib on the return journey from Syria to Mecca. Baḥīrā is said to have realized, through witnessing various signs and portents, that the young traveler in his presence was indeed the Messenger foretold by Jesus (peace be upon him).

[115] This is another name for the Opening Sūra *[Sūrat al-Fātiḥa]* of the Qur'ān.

[116] *Suwar*, plural of *Sūra*.

[117] For the derivation and range of meaning of the term *fatḥ*, see note [111] above.

[labbaika wa sa'daik].[118] O Allāh, allow this servant of Yours to enter me, on the strength of "In the Name of Allāh, the All-Merciful, the All-Compassionate *[Bismi'llāhi'r-Raḥmāni'r-Raḥīm].*""

The significant point is that, when the Garden of Paradise makes such a plea on behalf of a servant [of Allāh], it is a foregone conclusion that he will be considered worthy to enter therein, for the Prophet (Allāh bless him and give him peace) has said:

> No supplication *[du'ā]* will ever be rejected if it is prefaced with "*Bismi'llāhi'r-Raḥmāni'r-Raḥīm* [In the Name of Allāh, the All-Merciful, the All-Compassionate]."

He has also told us:

> When they come at last to the Day of Resurrection, the members of my Community will be saying: "In the Name of Allāh, the All-Merciful, the All-Compassionate *[Bismi'llāhi'r-Raḥmāni'r-Raḥīm],*" and so, when their deeds are placed in the balance, their good deeds will outweigh [their bad deeds].
>
> The other religious communities will then of course ask: "What can have caused the scales to weigh so heavily in favor of the Community of Muḥammad (Allāh bless him and give him peace)?"
>
> So their Prophets *[anbiyā']* will tell them: "Whenever they had something important to say, the members of the Community of Muḥammad (Allāh bless him and give him peace) would always begin by invoking three of the Noble Names of Allāh (Exalted is He),[119] knowing the gravity of those Names to be such that if they were placed in one scale of the balance, even if all the bad deeds of their fellow creatures in their entirety were placed in the other scale, their good deeds would certainly weigh heavier [than the bad]."

Finally, he has given us this assurance:

> Allāh (Exalted is He) has caused this *āya* to be effective as a cure for every sickness, an aid to every kind of healing treatment, a relief from every form of poverty, a shield against the Fire of Hell, and a guarantee of security from degradation *[khasf]*, misrepresentation *[maskh]* and slanderous accusation *[qadhf]*, as long as they [His believing servants] keep up the practice of reciting it.

[118] This expression occurs in the formula pronounced, as a recommended practice, before the recitation of *Sūrat al-Fātiḥa* in the Islāmic ritual prayer *[ṣalāt]*:

> *Labbaika wa sa'daika wa'l-khairu baina yadaika wa'sh-sharru laisa ilaik* [I wait intent upon Your service, time and time again, and upon aiding Your cause, time and time again; and all that is good is in Your presence, while evil cannot be imputed to You].

[119] The whole expression "In the Name of Allāh, the All-Merciful, the All-Compassionate *[Bismi'llāhi'r-Raḥmāni'r-Raḥīm]*" is sometimes referred to as a Name *[Ism]*. In this instance, however, the reference is to the three Noble Names contained within it, viz., (1) Allāh, (2) the All-Merciful *[ar-Raḥmān]* and (3) the All-Compassionate *[ar-Raḥīm]*.

Some interpretative commentary *[tafsīr]* on His words: "In the Name of Allāh, the All-Merciful, the All-Compassionate *[Bismi'llāhi'r-Raḥmāni'r-Raḥīm]*."

On the subject of His words (Exalted is He): "In the Name of Allāh *[Bismi'llāh]*," the following story has come down to us from ʿAṭiyya al-ʿAwfī, according to whom Abū Saʿīd al-Khudrī (may Allāh be well pleased with him)[120] reported that Allāh's Messenger (Allāh bless him and give him peace) once said:

> Jesus (peace be upon him) was sent by his mother (may Allāh be well pleased with her) to take lessons at the elementary school *[kuttāb]*. When the teacher told him to say: "In the Name of Allāh, the All-Merciful, the All-Compassionate *[Bismi'llāhi'r-Raḥmāni'r-Raḥīm]*," Jesus (peace be upon him) said: "Do you know what *Bismi'llāh* stands for?"
>
> "I have no idea," the teacher replied, so the child went on to explain: "The letter *B* stands for *Bahā' Allāh* [the Beautiful Majesty of Allāh], the letter *S* stands for *Sanā' Allāh* [the Splendid Exaltation of Allāh], and the letter M stands for *Mamlakatuhu* [His Mighty Kingdom]."

Let us now compare the commentary of Abū Bakr al-Warrāq, who had this to say on the subject:

"'In the Name of Allāh *[Bismi'llāhi]*,' is one of the meadows *[riyāḍ]* of the Garden of Paradise. For every letter of the Arabic alphabet with which it is spelled, there is a separate interpretation *[tafsīr]*.

"As for the letter *Bā'*, its significance is sixfold:

"First of all, it points to the fact that Allāh is the *Bāri'* [Maker] of His entire creation, from the Heavenly Throne to the earth below. To cite the Qur'ānic proof *[bayān]* of this:

> He is Allāh, the Creator, the Maker [of everything from the Heavenly Throne to the earth below]. (59:24)[121]

[120] Saʿīd Saʿd ibn Mālik ibn Sinān al-Khudrī al-Anṣārī (may Allāh be well pleased with him) was a Companion of the Prophet (Allāh bless him and give him peace) and a famous narrator of Tradition. He died in A.H. 74 or, according to some reports, in A.H. 63–4.

[121] *Huwa'llāhu'l-Khāliqu'l-Bāri'*.

"Secondly, it points to the fact that Allāh is the *Baṣīr* [All-Seeing], meaning that He sees every detail of His entire creation, from the Heavenly Throne to the earth below. Consider the Qur'ānic text:

> And Allāh is All-Seeing over what you do. (49:18)[122]

"Thirdly, it points to the fact that Allāh is the *Bāsiṭ ar-rizq* [Ample Provider] for all His creatures, from the Heavenly Throne to the earth below. The evidence is in the following Qur'ānic text:

> Allāh provides the means of livelihood in ample measure for whomever He will, and He limits the measure [thereof for whomever He will]. (13:26)

"Fourthly, it points to the fact that Allāh is *Bāqin* [Everlasting] after the passing away *[fanā']* of all and everything in His creation, from the Heavenly Throne to the earth below. In evidence of this, let me cite the Qur'ānic text:

> All those who are upon it [upon the earth] shall pass away, yet still abides the Face of your Lord, in majesty and splendor. (55:26,27)[123]

"Fifthly, it points to the fact that Allāh is the *Bā'ith* [Resurrector] of all His creatures after death, from the Heavenly Throne to the earth below, in order to apportion the reward and the punishment they have deserved. To cite the relevant Qur'ānic text:

> And because Allāh will raise up those who are in the graves. (22:7)

"Sixthly, it points to the fact that Allāh is *Bārr* [Benign] toward all true believers *[mu'minīn]*, from the Heavenly Throne to the earth below. Here again, we find our evidence in the Qur'ān:

> He is the All-Benign, the All-Compassionate. (52:28)[124]

"Let us now turn our attention to the letter *Sīn*, the significance of which is fivefold:

"Firstly, it points to the fact that Allāh is the *Samī'* [All-Hearing], meaning that He hears all the sounds and voices of His creatures, from the Heavenly Throne to the earth below. To cite the relevant text of the Qur'ān:

> Or do they reckon that We cannot hear their secret thoughts and their private confidences? (43:80)

122 *wa'llāhu Baṣīrun bi-mā ta'malūn.*

123 *kullu man 'alaihā fān—wa yabqā wajhu Rabbika Dhu'l-Jalāli wa'l-Ikrām.*

124 *Huwa'l-Barru'r-Raḥīm.*

"Secondly, it points to the fact that Allāh is a *Sayyid* [Sovereign Lord] whose sovereignty *[su'dad]* holds absolute sway over all, from the Heavenly Throne to the earth below. To cite the Qur'ānic authority for this assertion:

> Allāh, the Everlasting Lord. (112:2)[125]

"Thirdly, it points to the fact that Allāh is *Sarī'u'l-ḥisāb* [Swift at reckoning] with all His creatures, from the Heavenly Throne to the earth below. As we read in the Qur'ān:

> And Allāh is Swift at reckoning. (2:202)[126]

"Fourthly, it points to the fact that Allāh is the *Salām* [Source of Peace], who keeps His creatures safe from the dark forces of oppression, from the Heavenly Throne to the earth below. This we know from the Qur'ānic text:

> The Source of Peace, the Safekeeper. (59:23)[127]

"Fifthly, it points to the fact that Allāh is the *Sātir* [Veiler] of the sins committed by His servants, from the Heavenly Throne to the earth below. To quote the relevant text of the Qur'ān:

> The Forgiver of sin, the Accepter of repentance.... (40:3)[128]

"In the case of the letter *Mīm*, there are twelve distinct aspects:

"Firstly, it points to the fact that Allāh is the *Malik* [King] of His entire creation, from the Heavenly Throne to the earth below. We know this from the Qur'ānic text:

> The King, the Holy One. (59:23)[129]

"Secondly, it points to the fact that Allāh is the *Mālik* [Owner of Dominion] over His entire creation, from the Heavenly Throne to the earth below. The evidence is in the Qur'ānic text:

> Say: "O Allāh, Owner of Dominion!" (3:26)[130]

[125] *Allāhu'ṣ-Ṣamad.*

[126] *wa'llāhu Sarī'u'l-ḥisāb.*

[127] *as-Salāmu 'l-Mu'min.*

[128] *Ghāfiri'dh-dhanbi wa Qābili't-tawb....*

[129] *al-Maliku'l-Quddūs.*

[130] *quli'llāhumma Mālika'l-Mulk.*

"Thirdly, it points to the fact that Allāh is the *Mannān* [Generous Benefactor] to all His creatures, from the Heavenly Throne to the earth below. We know this from the Qur'ānic text:

> Oh no, it is rather that Allāh confers a favor upon you. (49:17)

"Fourthly, it points to the fact that Allāh is the *Majīd* [Gloriously Exalted Lord] of all His creatures, from the Heavenly Throne to the earth below. To cite the relevant Qur'ānic text:

> Lord of the Throne of Glory. (85:15)[131]

"Fifthly, it points to the fact that Allāh is the *Mu'min* [Safekeeper], the One who keeps all of His creatures safe, from the Heavenly Throne to the earth below. Consider the Qur'ānic text:

> And [the Lord who] has made them safe from fear. (106:4)

"Sixthly, it points to the fact that Allāh is the *Muhaimin* [Guardian] who watches over all His creatures, from the Heavenly Throne to the earth below. The evidence is in the Qur'ānic text:

> The Safekeeper, the Guardian. (59:23)[132]

"In the seventh place, it points to the fact that Allāh is the *Muqtadir* [Omnipotent Ruler] of His entire creation, from the Heavenly Throne to the earth below. Consider the Qur'ānic text:

> In a secure abode, in the presence of a King Omnipotent. (54:55)[133]

"In the eighth place, it points to the fact that Allāh is the *Muqīt* [Supervisor] of His entire creation, from the Heavenly Throne to the earth below. We know this from the Qur'ānic text:

> And Allāh is supervising all things. (4:85)[134]

"In the ninth place, it points to the fact that Allāh is the *Mukarrim* [Ennobler] of His protégés *[awliyā']*, from the Heavenly Throne to the earth below. To cite the relevant Qur'ānic text:

> And We have indeed honored the Children of Adam. (17:70)

131 *Dhu'l-'Arshi'l Majīd.*

132 *al-Mu'minu'l-Muhaimin.*

133 *fī maq'adi ṣidqin 'inda Malīkin Muqtadir.*

134 *wa kāna'llāhu 'alā kulli shai'in Muqītā.*

"In the tenth place, it points to the fact that Allāh is the *Mun*ʿ*im* [Source of Gracious Favors] to His creatures, from the Heavenly Throne to the earth below. To cite the relevant text of the Qurʾān:

> And He has lavished His favors upon you, both outwardly and inwardly. (31:20)

"In the eleventh place, it points to the fact that Allāh is the *Mufḍil* [Bountiful Donor] to His creatures, from the Heavenly Throne to the earth below. To cite the relevant Qurʾānic text:

> Allāh is truly Bountiful toward mankind. (10:60)

"In the twelfth place, it points to the fact that Allāh is the *Muṣawwir* [Shaper] of all and everything in His entire creation, from the Heavenly Throne to the earth below. Let me cite the Qurʾānic authority for this final assertion:

> The Creator, the Maker, the Shaper. (59:24)[135]"

According to those who concentrate on the essential facts of actual experience *[ahl al-ḥaqāʾiq]*, the significance of "In the Name of Allāh, the All-Merciful, the All-Compassionate *[Bismi'llāhi'r-Raḥmāni'r-Raḥīm]*" can be stated in quite simple terms. They value it as the key to attracting favorable influences and receiving positive blessings, and they encourage people to preface anything they intend to say or do with "In the Name of Allāh *[Bismi'llāh]*," just as Allāh (Glory be to Him and Exalted is He) has made it the introduction[136] to His Mighty and Splendid Book.

[135] *al-Khāliqu'l-Bāriʾu'l-Muṣawwir*.

[136] The author uses the verb *iftataḥa* at this point. For the important connotations of this and of other terms derived from the triliteral root *f–t–ḥ*, see note [111] above.

Concerning the opinions offered by various experts in the field of Arabic lexicology to explain the linguistic origin of the Name "Allāh" and the meaning thereof.

The reader should be aware that people have held many different opinions concerning this Name. According to Khalīl ibn Aḥmad,[189] whose view is shared by one group of experts in the field of Arabic lexicology *[ahl al-ʿarabiyya]*, it is a Name that applies only to Allāh (Almighty and Glorious is He), and absolutely no one is entitled to share it with Him.

Allāh (Exalted is He) has said:

> Do you know anyone who can be named as a namesake of His? (19:65)[137]

What this signifies is that every Name that applies to Allāh (Exalted is He) is applicable not only to Him but to others as well—to Him in the real sense *[ʿala'l-ḥaqīqa]* and to others in a figurative or metaphorical sense *[majāz]*—with the exception of this one Name, for the Name "Allāh" belongs exclusively to Him, since it contains the meaning of Supreme Lordship *[Rubūbiyya]* and all the implications *[maʿānī]* thereof are covered by it.

It is very interesting to see what happens when you drop the letters one by one from the Name "Allāh" as it is spelled in the Arabic script *[alif–lām–lām–hā']*: When you drop the *alif*, you are left with *lām–lām–hā'*, which is the way we spell *li'llāh* [to, or for, Allāh]. When you drop the first of the two *lām's*, you are left with *lām–hā'*, which is the way we spell *lahu* [to, or for, Him]. Then, when you also drop the *lām* in *lahu*, you are left with the letter *hā'*, representing the syllable *hu*, which is here pronounced as *Hū [He]*.[138]

[137] Khalīl ibn Aḥmad (d. A.H. 160 or 170 or 175) is credited with the composition of the first general lexicon of the Arabic language, or at least with having begun the composition of that work, under the title *Kitāb al-ʿAin* (because the first words listed in it were those beginning with the letter *ʿain*).

[138] When "Allāh" is grammatically in the nominative case, the vowel *-u* is added at the end. The prolonged sound *-ū* is heard in the actual pronunciation, although the vowel-sign (when supplied, as in the text of the Qur'ān) is that which normally indicates the short vowel *-u*.

As far as its lexical derivation *[ishtiqāq]* is concerned, the linguistic experts have suggested a wide range of possibilities. According to an-Naḍir ibn Shumail, the Name "Allāh" may be derived from *ta'alluh*, which is a synonym for *tanassuk* [devotion to religious exercises] and *ta'abbud* [devotion to services of worship], or from the expression *alaha ilāhatan*, which has the same meaning as *'abada 'ibādatan* [to serve, worship, adore].[139]

Others maintain that it is derived from *ilāh*, in the sense of *i'timād* [reliance upon someone for protection], for if a person is heard to say: "I sought asylum *[alihtu alahan]* with so-and-so," he will be understood to mean: "I felt myself to be in grave danger, so I took refuge with him and relied on him for protection."

To explain how this relates to Allāh, and the possible derivation of His Name, the point is that when His creatures find themselves in disastrous situations and in dire need of help, they seek refuge with Him and implore Him to give them protection. Since He does indeed grant them asylum *[ya'lahuhum]*, the term *Ilāh* is properly applied to Him, just as the person who is accepted as a leader *[yu'tammu bih]* is properly referred to as an Imām.

As for His human servants, they are *mu'allahūn* in relation to Him; that is to say, they are compelled to accept their utter dependence upon Him, whether it be to secure things that are beneficial or to avoid things that cause harm. In this respect, their condition is just like that of the lovelorn fool *[wālih]*, who is totally subject to compulsion and completely overwhelmed by a force beyond his control.

According to Abū 'Amr ibn al-'Alā', the Name "Allāh" is actually derived from the expression you might use if you found something utterly bewildering *[alihta'sh-shai']*, in the sense that you were so perplexed by it that you could not figure out the right approach toward it. The point he is making is that our human minds become hopelessly confused when they try to grasp the very essence *[kunh]* of His divine quality *[ṣifa]* and His sublime majesty *['aẓama]*, and when they try to grasp His unique mode of being *[kaifiyya]*. If we accept this derivation,

139 In this and similar cases, for the sake of clarity and simplicity, the translator has given the English infinitive ("to serve," etc.) instead of the literal equivalent ("he served a service," etc.) The structure of the Arabic language makes it convenient for traditional grammarians and lexicographers to use a verb in the third person masculine singular, followed by the corresponding verbal noun as its object, as their basic unit of reference.

the term *Ilāh* is properly applied to Him because it is equivalent in meaning to *Ma'lūh* [One who is Held in Awe], just as *kitāb* is equivalent in meaning to *maktūb* [set down in writing; a letter, book, manuscript] and *ḥisāb* to *maḥsūb* [reckoned or counted; a reckoning or account].[140]

According to al-Mubarrad, the Name "Allāh" is derived from an idiomatic expression, peculiar to the pure speech of the Arabs of the desert *[qawl al-ʿArab]*,[141] whereby one of them would use the word *alihtu*, rather than *sakantu*, if he had reason to say: "I felt really at home with so-and-so." It would seem that when he came to propose this derivation, al-Mubarrad must have been considering the sense of comfort and peaceful repose that is felt by Allāh's creatures when they remember Him. As Allāh (Almighty and Glorious is He) has told us:

> It is truly in the remembrance of Allāh that hearts feel comfortably at rest. (13:28)[142]

There are some who maintain that the Name "Allāh" is derived from *walah*, which is the Arabic term for the loss of reason that one may experience through being bereaved of someone very dear and precious. In proposing this derivation, they would seem to be suggesting that He came to be called "Allāh" because human hearts are thrown off balance *[tawlahu]* by the feeling of love for Him, and because they become unsettled and filled with yearning when they experience what it means to remember Him.

Others maintain that the meaning of "Allāh" is "the One who veils Himself *[Muḥtajib]*," because if something has once been visible to the Arabs of the desert, but has then come to be veiled from their sight, they

[140] The nouns *Ilāh*, *kitāb* and *ḥisāb* are all formed after the generic pattern called *fiʿāl* by the Arab grammarians, who use the root consonants *fāʾ–ʿain–lām* as a kind of algebraic *x–y–z*. Thus each of the three nouns mentioned here is formed by inserting the vowels *-i-* and *-ā-* within the framework of its particular triliteral root (*ʾ–l–h*, *k–t–b* and *ḥ–s–b*, respectively).

By a similar process, *Ma'lūh*, *maktūb* and *maḥsūb* are all formed after the generic pattern called *mafʿūl*, which indicates a passive particle. It should be noted that a word of the pattern *fiʿāl* is only exceptionally equivalent in meaning to the *mafʿūl* formed from the same root.

[141] According to the authorities cited by E.W. Lane in his *Arabic-English Lexicon*, art. *ʿ–R–B*, the term *al-ʿArab* is generally used as "an appellation of common application [to the whole nation]," but where it occurs in the lexicons and lexicological works, it is "applied to the desert Arabs of pure speech." Since al-Mubarrad was a celebrated lexicologist, the translator has therefore taken his expression *qawl al-ʿArab* to mean "the pure speech of the Arabs of the desert," rather than simply "the speech of the Arabs."

[142] *a-lā bi-dhikri'llāhi taṭmaʾinnu'l-qulūb.*

refer to it as a *lāh* [mirage]. When the bride conceals herself behind a veil, she is sometimes said to have disappeared like a mirage *[lāhati'l-ʿarūs; talūhu lawhā]*. In the case of Allāh (Exalted is He), He is Manifest *[Ẓāhir]* as far as His Supreme Lordship *[Rubūbiyya]* is concerned, through signs and indications, but He is also the One who veils Himself *[Muḥtajib]* with regard to His unique mode of being, in order to deter illusory speculations.

Yet others maintain that "Allāh" means "the Exalted One *[Mutaʿālī]*." Their view is based on the assumption that it must be derived from the Arabic verb *lāha*, which can mean "to rise; to ascend." A similar derivation may account for the term *ilāha* [goddess], as it used to be applied to the sun *[shams]*.[143]

It has also been suggested that "Allāh" means "the One who is Capable of Original Creation, without instrument or preexisting model *[al-Qādir ʿala'l-ikhtirāʿ]*," while some say that it means "the Lord and Master *[as-Sayyid]*."

[143] Since the Arabic word *shams* is grammatically feminine, the sun was referred to by its worshippers as a goddess *[ilāha]*, rather than a god *[ilāh]*.

Various interpretations of "the All-Merciful, the All-Compassionate *[ar-Raḥmān ar-Raḥīm]*."

According to one group, the meaning of both *ar-Raḥmān* and *ar-Raḥīm* is one and the same, namely, "the Owner of Mercy *[Dhu'r-Raḥma]*," and they are both included among the attributes of the Divine Essence *[ṣifāt adh-Dhāt]*.

Some authorities, however, while they agree that the two words are identical in meaning, maintain that they refer specifically to the nonimposition of punishment on those who deserve to be punished, and the conferring of goodness upon those who do not deserve it. According to those who take this view, both *ar-Raḥmān* and *ar-Raḥīm* should rather be counted among the attributes of the Divine Action *[ṣifāt al-Fiʿl]*.

All the other interpreters have drawn some kind of distinction between the two terms. They generally maintain that *ar-Raḥmān* has the form of an intensive epithet, and that its meaning must therefore be "the One whose Mercy extends to cover everything," whereas *ar-Raḥīm* is not quite so all-embracing in degree.

In order to clarify this distinction, some of them explain that *ar-Raḥmān* means "the One who is Kindly Disposed *[ʿĀṭif]* toward each and every one of His creatures—not only toward the believer *[muʾmin]* amongst them but also toward the unbeliever *[kāfir]*, not only toward the righteous *[barr]* amongst them but also toward the sinful transgressor *[fājir]*, inasmuch as He has created them and provided them with their sustenance." As they point out, Allāh (Exalted is He) has told us:

> And My Mercy embraces all things. (7:156)

They say that what is meant by *ar-Raḥīm*, on the other hand, is that He is All-Compassionate toward the believers *[muʾminīn]* in particular, inasmuch as He blesses them with right guidance *[hidāya]* and helpful direction *[tawfīq]* in this world, and with the Garden of Paradise *[Janna]* and the Beatific Vision *[Ruʾya]* in the hereafter.

As Allāh (Exalted is He) has told us:

> And to the believers He is All-Compassionate. (33:43)

This whole explanation is based on the understanding that *ar-Raḥmān* is specific when considered strictly as a unit of vocabulary *[khāṣṣ al-lafẓ]*, but universal with respect to its meaning *[ʿāmm al-maʿnā]*, whereas *ar-Raḥīm* is universal when considered simply as a unit of vocabulary *[ʿāmm al-lafẓ]*, but specific with respect to its meaning *[khāṣṣ al-maʿnā]*.

In the case of *ar-Raḥmān*, it is specific inasmuch as it cannot be used to name anyone other than Allāh, and universal inasmuch as its meaning embraces all entities that exist *[mawjūdāt]* by virtue of His creation, sustenance, beneficence and protection.

In the case of *ar-Raḥīm*, it is universal in the sense that mere creatures are entitled to share its use as an epithet among their own kind,[144] but it is specific in terms of its meaning, since it refers to treating certain people with tender kindness *[luṭf]* and helping them to succeed *[tawfīq]*.

Ibn ʿAbbās (may Allāh be well pleased with him and with his father) once said: "Two subtle Names *[Ismān daqīqān]*, one of them more subtle than the other!"

It was Mujāhid (may Allāh bestow His mercy upon him) who said: "He is *ar-Raḥmān* in dealing with the people of this world, and *ar-Raḥīm* in dealing with the people of the hereafter. This is why we should appeal to Him by saying: 'O All-Merciful Lord of this world! O All-Compassionate Lord of the hereafter! *[yā Raḥmāna'd-dunyā, yā Raḥīma'l-ākhira]*.'"

The order appears to be reversed in this saying of aḍ-Ḍaḥḥāk (may Allāh bestow His mercy upon him): "He is *ar-Raḥmān* in relation to the people of Heaven, inasmuch as He has allowed them to reside in the heavens, has made it easy for them to practice all forms of worshipful obedience, has rendered them immune to all painful misfortunes, and has kept them from being influenced by desires and temptations. And He is *ar-Raḥīm* in relation to the people of the earth, inasmuch as He has sent the Messengers *[Rusul]* to them, and has revealed to them the Books of Scripture."

[144] In other words, it is permissible to refer to a fellow human being as *ar-raḥīm*, if one has reason to describe that person as compassionate or sympathetic. (It should be noted that there is no corresponding distinction, in the Arabic script itself, to the spelling device conventionally adopted in transliteration, where the contrast between an upper-case and a lower-case initial is used to distinguish a Divine Name like *ar-Raḥīm* from the ordinary adjective *ar-raḥīm*.)

To quote the words of ʿIkrima (may Allāh bestow His mercy upon him): "He is *ar-Raḥmān* by virtue of one single Mercy, and *ar-Raḥīm* by virtue of a hundred mercies."

According to a traditional report that has been handed down to us from Abū Huraira (may Allāh be well pleased with him), the Prophet (Allāh bless him and give him peace) once said:

> Allāh (Almighty and Glorious is He) has no fewer than a hundred mercies. One of these mercies He has already sent down to the earth, where He has distributed it among His creatures, and this is what enables them to treat one another with considerate kindness *[yataʿāṭafūn]* and to feel sympathy for one another *[yatarāḥamūn]*. The other ninety-nine He has kept back for His own eventual use, His purpose being to use them for the merciful treatment of His servants on the Day of Resurrection.

In a slightly different version, part of the wording is as follows:

> Allāh (Exalted is He) will add this [one] to those [ninety-nine], so they will make a total of one hundred, and He will use them for the merciful treatment of His servants on the Day of Resurrection.

The All-Merciful *[ar-Raḥmān]* is the One who gives when He is asked, while the All-Compassionate *[ar-Raḥīm]* is the One who gets angry when He is not asked. In a saying *[ḥadīth]* attributed to him by Abū Huraira (may Allāh be well pleased with him), the Prophet (Allāh bless him and give him peace) has told us:

> If someone never asks Allāh for anything, He becomes angry toward that person.

And in the words of the poet:

> Allāh gets vexed if you stop asking Him for things,
> whereas being asked has that effect on human beings.

He is *ar-Raḥmān* from the standpoint of blissful well-being, for blissful well-being is what the All-Merciful grants and bestows, and He is *ar-Raḥīm* from the standpoint of all forms of painful suffering, for painful suffering is what the All-Compassionate dispels and takes away.

He is *ar-Raḥmān* from the standpoint of deliverance from the Fires of Hell, the deliverance mentioned in His glorious words:

> And you were on the brink of a pit of fire, and He did save you from it. (3:103)[200]

And He is *ar-Raḥīm* from the standpoint of admission to the Gardens of Paradise, as He has said:

> Enter them [the Gardens of Paradise] in peace and security! (15:46)

He is *ar-Raḥmān* from the standpoint of His merciful treatment of our lower selves *[nufūs]*, and He is *ar-Raḥīm* from the standpoint of His compassionate way of dealing with our hearts *[qulūb]*. He is *ar-Raḥmān* from the standpoint of dispelling grief and woe *[kurūb]*, and *ar-Raḥīm* from the standpoint of forgiving sins *[dhunūb]*. He is *ar-Raḥmān* from the standpoint of clearly marking out the path *[ṭarīq]*, and He is *ar-Raḥīm* from the standpoint of providing safeguards and helpful direction *[tawfīq]*. He is *ar-Raḥmān* from the standpoint of forgiving bad deeds, even if they happen to be major offenses *[ʿaẓīmāt]*, and He is *ar-Raḥīm* from the standpoint of accepting acts of worshipful obedience, even if they happen to be less than pure *[ghair ṣāfiyāt]*. He is *ar-Raḥmān* from the standpoint of promoting His servants' best interests in the life of this world *[maʿāsh]*, and He is *ar-Raḥīm* from the standpoint of promoting their best interests in the life of the hereafter *[maʿād]*.

As the All-Merciful *[ar-Raḥmān]*, He is the One who always acts mercifully, and can use His power to remove all that is harmful and to drive away everything bad. As the All-Compassionate *[ar-Raḥīm]*, He provides His creatures with sustenance and supplies them with food, although He has no need of food for Himself.

> He is indeed Allāh. He is the All-Provider, the Lord of Mighty Strength, the Ever-Firm. (51:58)

He is *ar-Raḥmān* in His treatment of those who refuse to believe in Him *[jaḥadah]*, and He is *ar-Raḥīm* in His treatment of those who affirm His Oneness *[waḥḥadah]*. He is *ar-Raḥmān* in His treatment of those who are ungrateful toward Him *[kafarah]*, and He is *ar-Raḥīm* in His treatment of those who give thanks to Him *[shakarah]*. He is *ar-Raḥmān* in His treatment of those who say that He has a partner or peer *[nidd]*, and He is *ar-Raḥīm* in His treatment of those who say that He is Unique *[Fard]*.[145]

[145] In the original text of this passage, we have an example of the style of Arabic composition known as *sajʿ* or *kalām musajjaʿ*, which is a kind of rhymed prose. (According to the Arabic lexicographers, the term *sajʿ* refers, in its primary signification, to the modulated cooing of the pigeon.)

The sentences are not metrical, as they are in poetry, although they are characterized by a certain rhythm. The rhyming quality of the two words that end two corresponding clauses may be obvious, as in the case of *jaḥadah*... *waḥḥadah*, and then *kafarah*... *shakarah*, in the passage above. In some instances, however, the rhyming element is no more than the repetition of a final consonant, like the *-d* that enables *nidd* to "rhyme" with *Fard* in the two clauses of the last sentence in the passage here discussed.

After giving the advice: "Say: 'In the Name of Allāh *[Bismi'llāh]*,' for then you will find Allāh's forgiveness," the author (may Allāh be well pleased with him) pauses to interject some profound questions concerning the quality of our hearing.[146]

Say: "In the Name of Allāh *[Bismi'llāh]*," for then you will find Allāh's forgiveness.

This is the way you listen to the human reciter *[qāri']*, so how are you going to listen to the Maker *[Bāri']*? This is the nature of your hearing now, while sorrow is still prevalent *[bāq]*, so how will your hearing be in the presence of the Lord, when He is offering a refreshing drink *[sāq]*? This is the way you hear when you listen to an intermediary *[bi-wāsiṭa]*, so how are you going to hear directly from the source *[bi-lā wāsiṭa]*? This is the way you hear in this abode of delusion *[ghurūr]*, so how are you going to hear in the abode of joy and delight *[surūr]*? This is the way you hear in this abode of the Devil *[Shaiṭān]*, so how are you going to hear in the vicinity of the All-Merciful *[ar-Raḥmān]*? This is the way you listen to a lowly servant *['abd dhalīl]*, so how are you going to listen to the Majestic King *[al-Malik al-Jalīl]*?

This is the thrill of learning by hearsay *[khabar]*, so how about the thrill of seeing for oneself *[naẓar]*? This is the thrill of studious endeavor *[mujāhada]*, so how about the thrill of direct witnessing *[mushāhada]*? This is the thrill of obtaining a secondhand explanation *[bayān]*, so how about the thrill of enjoying an unfiltered view *['iyān]*? This is the thrill of communicating in the absence of personal contact *[mughāyaba]*, so how about the thrill of communicating face to face *[mu'āyana]*?

[146] Apart from the opening sentence, the entire text of this subsection is composed in the rhymed and rhythmic, but nonmetrical prose called *saj'*. (See note [145] above.)

A series of invocations, each of them beginning with: "In the Name of Allāh, who... *[Bismi'llāhi'lladhī...]*." [147]

Say: "In the Name of Allāh, who utterly transcends any attribution of counterparts *[aḍdād]*. In the Name of Allāh, who is absolutely exempt from any attribution of partners or peers *[andād]*. In the Name of Allāh, who is far removed in His Holiness from the begetting of children *[awlād]*.

"In the Name of Allāh, who causes all lights to shine *[nawwara'l-anwār]*. In the Name of Allāh, who honors those who are righteous and fine *[abrār]*. In the Name of Allāh, who has predetermined all destinies *[aqdār]*, and who has enlightened human hearts and eyes *[abṣār]*. In the Name of Allāh, who manifests Himself to the hearts of the righteous *[abrār]* in those moments just before the break of day *[asḥār]*.

"In the Name of Allāh, who allows dear friends to gain knowledge of the mysteries *[asrār]*, for He floods them with rays of light *[anwār]* and entrusts them with the keeping of those secrets *[asrār]*. From them He banishes all dangers *[akhṭār]*. He preserves them from being enslaved by jealous rivals *[aghyār]*, and He relieves them of all burdens, shackles, bonds *[āṣār]* and heavy loads *[awzār]*. For indeed, He has been characterized from all eternity by the attributes of beneficence, abundant grace, and readiness to forgive the sins of those who seek forgiveness *[ahl al-istighfār]*."

Say: "In the Name of Allāh, the Name of the One who causes the flowing of the rivers *[anhār]* and the sprouting of the trees *[ashjār]*."

[Say: "In the Name of Allāh," for that is] the Name of the One who brings prosperity to countries and towns by populating them with truly obedient folk from among His servants *[ʿibād]*. Such people serve as mainstays *[awtād]*, as mountain-like pillars of support, so that, for those

[147] This subsection is also composed entirely in *sajʿ* (and, as readers will surely notice in due course, if they compare the transliterated Arabic words in brackets, so are all the remaining subsections in this Second Discourse).

who dwell upon it, the earth comes to be as safe and as cozy as the cradle *[mihād]*. They are the Forty, the pick of the spiritual deputies *[abdāl]*, the ones who never let it be forgotten that the Lord is totally exempt from any attribution of partners and peers *[andād]*. They are kings in this world, and they will be intercessors on behalf of humankind upon the Day of the Final Summoning *[Yawm at-Tanād]*. My Lord has indeed created them as a benefit to all the world, and as a gift of mercy to His servants *[ʿibād]*.

On some of the many precious blessings conferred by "In the Name of Allāh *[Bismi'llāh]*."

"In the Name of Allāh *[Bismi'llāh]*" is a treasure for those who remember, a mighty resource for the strong, a protective talisman for the weak, a radiant light for lovers, and a joyful delight for those who are filled with yearning.

"In the Name of Allāh *[Bismi'llāh]*" is the consolation of our spiritual natures *[arwāḥ]*. "In the Name of Allāh *[Bismi'llāh]*" is the salvation of our bodily forms *[ashbāḥ]*.

"In the Name of Allāh *[Bismi'llāh]*" is the light that illuminates our breasts *[ṣudūr]*. "In the Name of Allāh *[Bismi'llāh]*" is the organizing principle that regulates our affairs *[umūr]*.

"In the Name of Allāh *[Bismi'llāh]*" is the crown of the truly confident *[tāj al-wāthiqīn]*. "In the Name of Allāh *[Bismi'llāh]*" is the lamp of those who reach their destination *[sirāj al-wāṣilīn]*. "In the Name of Allāh *[Bismi'llāh]*" is that which satisfies the needs of ardent lovers *[mughni'l-ʿāshiqīn]*.

"In the Name of Allāh *[Bismi'llāh]*" is the Name of the One who honors certain servants and humiliates certain servants *[ʿibād]*.

"In the Name of Allāh *[Bismi'llāh]*" is the Name of the One who keeps the Fire of Hell in store for His enemies as an ambush *[mirṣād]*, and who keeps the Beatific Vision in store for His friends as a promised rendezvous *[mīʿād]*.

"In the Name of Allāh *[Bismi'llāh]*" is the Name of the Single One without number *[Wāḥid bi-lā ʿadad]*. "In the Name of Allāh *[Bismi'llāh]*" is the Name of the One who endures forever without end *[al-Bāqī bi-lā amad]*. "In the Name of Allāh *[Bismi'llāh]*" is the Name of the One who stands firm without supporting props *[Qāʾim bi-lā ʿamad]*.

"In the Name of Allāh *[Bismi'llāh]*" is the invocation that serves as an introduction *[iftitāḥ]* to every Sūra [of the Qurʾān].

It is the Name of the One who brings good cheer to those who practice solitary retreats *[khalawāt]*. It is the Name of the One who brings a sense of completeness to those who perform the ritual prayers *[ṣalawāt]*.

It is the Name of the One who inspires us to improve our minds by thinking better thoughts *[ẓunūn]*. It is the Name of the One for whose sake we spend the night with sleepless eyes *[ʿuyūn]*. It is the Name of the One who has only to say to something, "Be!" and there it is *[yakūn]*.[148]

It is the Name of the One who is far beyond description in terms of physical touch *[misās]*. It is the Name of the One who can dispense entirely with human beings *[unās]*. It is the Name of the One who rises majestically above all comparison *[qiyās]*.

Say: "In the Name of Allāh *[Bismi'llāh]*" letter by letter *[ḥarfan ḥarfā]*, for then you will receive the recompense in multiples of a thousand *[alfan alfā]*, and the burdens of sin will be scooped away from you by the shovelful *[jarfan jarfā]*.

If someone says it with his tongue, that person will witness all that is offered by this world *[dunyā]*. If someone says it with his heart, that person will witness all that is offered by the world hereafter *[ʿuqbā]*. And if someone says it with his innermost being, that person will actually witness the Master *[Mawlā]*.

"In the Name of Allāh *[Bismi'llāh]*" is a phrase that brings a pleasant sensation to the mouth *[fam]*. "In the Name of Allāh *[Bismi'llāh]*" is a phrase with which no feeling of unhappiness *[ghamm]* can coexist.

It is a phrase that brings about the perfection of good fortune *[niʿma]*. It is a phrase that brings about the abolition of misfortune *[niqma]*. It is a phrase that accounts for the special privileges enjoyed by this [the Islamic] Community *[Umma]*.

To utter the whole phrase, "In the Name of Allāh, the All-Merciful, the All-Compassionate *[Bismi'llāhi'r-Raḥmāni'r-Raḥīm]*," is to pronounce a simultaneous invocation of Divine Majesty *[Jalāl]* and Divine Beauty *[Jamāl]*, for "In the Name of Allāh *[Bismi'llāh]*" is an invocation of Divine Majesty within an expression of majesty *[Jalāl fī jalāl]*, while "the All-Merciful, the All-Compassionate *[ar-Raḥmāni'r-Raḥīm]*" is an invocation of Divine Beauty within an expression of beauty *[Jamāl fī jamāl]*.

[148] An allusion to the Qur'ān, where Allāh says of Himself (Exalted is He):

> To Him belongs all that is in the heavens and the earth; all obey His will—the Creator of the heavens and the earth; and when He decrees a thing, He but says to it "Be," and it is *[kun fa-yakūn]*. (2:116,117)

Those who witness His Majesty are likely to lose their wits *[ṭāsha]*; whereas those who witness His Beauty are sure to prosper *[ʿāsha]*.

The whole phrase represents a simultaneous invocation of Divine Power *[Qudra]* and Divine Mercy *[Raḥma]*, whereby the Divine Power adds together all the acts of obedience performed by the obedient *[muṭīʿīn]*, while the Divine Mercy erases all the sins committed by the sinners *[mudhnibīn]*.

Concerning the progressive stages of spiritual development that stem from the invocation: "In the Name of Allāh *[Bismi'llāh]*."

Say: "In the Name of Allāh *[Bismi'llāh]*," for [when you pronounce these words of His] it is as if He is saying:

"With My help, a person arrives at the stage where he is capable of performing meaningful acts of worshipful obedience. Then, by the light of those acts of worshipful obedience, he moves on until he reaches the stage of direct witnessing *[ʿiyān]*, at which point he is able to dispense with secondhand explanation *[bayān]*. His heart has now become a vessel worthy of containing both the esoteric mysteries and the exoteric branches of religious knowledge *[ʿulūm al-adyān]*.

"When someone attains to the Loving Friend *[Ḥabīb]*, he is safely delivered from woe and lamentation *[naḥīb]*. When someone attains to unfiltered vision *[naẓar]*, he has no further use for hearsay information *[khabar]*. When someone attains to the Everlasting Lord *[aṣ-Ṣamad]*, he is safely delivered from grief and sorrow *[kamad]*. When someone attains to close companionship *[rifāq]*, he is safely delivered from lonely separation *[firāq]*. When someone attains to noble dignity *[majd]*, he ceases to be affected by emotional upheaval *[wajd]*. And when someone attains to the Ultimate Meeting *[Liqāʾ]*, he is rendered immune to painful suffering *[shaqāʾ]*."

Some further interpretations of the Arabic letters and words that occur in: *"Bismi'llāhi'r-Raḥmāni'r-Raḥīm* [In the Name of Allāh, the All-Merciful, the All-Compassionate]."

Say: "*Bismi'llāh* [In the Name of Allāh]." According to one interpretation, the letter *bā'* stands for *Bāri' al-barāyā* [the Maker of all creatures], while the letter *sīn* stands for *Sattār al-khaṭāyā* [the Veiler of faults], and the letter *mīm* stands for *al-Mannān bi'l-'aṭāyā* [the Bestower of gifts].

There are some who maintain that the letter *bā'* stands for *Barī' min al-awlād* [the One who is Exempt from begetting children], while the letter *sīn* stands for *Samī' al-aṣwāt* [the Hearer of the voices (that appeal to Him)], and the letter *mīm* stands for *Mujīb ad-da'awāt* [the One who responds to prayers of supplication].

According to another interpretation, the significance of these three letters [in reverse order] is expressed by the following commands of the Lord: "Offer food to your fellow creatures, for I am the One who provides you with food *[Muṭ'imukum]*. Offer them water to drink, for I am the One who quenches your thirst *[Sāqīkum]*. Pay attention to Me, for I am your Eternal Lord *[Bāqīkum]*."

Still others maintain that the letter *bā'* stands for *bukā' at-tā'ibīn* [the weeping of those who repent], while the letter *sīn* stands for *sujūd al-'ābidīn* [the act of prostration made by worshippers (in their ritual prayer)], and the letter *mīm* stands for *ma'dhirat al-mudhnibīn* [the pardoning of sinners].

Turning from letter-by-letter to word-by-word interpretations, we find that some have explained the nuances of meaning as follows:

Allāh is the Remover of trials and tribulations *[Allāhu Kāshif al-balāyā]*. The All-Merciful is the Giver of gifts *[ar-Raḥmānu Mu'ṭi'l-'aṭāyā]*. The All-Compassionate is the Forgiver of faults *[ar-Raḥīmu Ghāfir al-khaṭāyā]*.

"Allāh" is for those who know by intuition *[Allāhu li'l-'ārifīn]*. "The All-Merciful" is for devout worshippers *[ar-Raḥmānu li'l-'ābidīn]*.

"The All-Compassionate" is for sinners *[ar-Raḥīmu li'l-mudhnibīn]*.

Allāh is the One who created you all, and He is the Most Excellent of Creators *[Aḥsan al-Khāliqīn]*. The All-Merciful *[ar-Raḥmān]* is the One who provides for you all, and He is the Best of Providers *[Khair ar-Rāziqīn]*. The All-Compassionate *[ar-Raḥīm]* is the One who is ready to forgive you all, and He is the Best of Forgivers *[Khair al-Ghāfirīn]*.

We also encounter this alternative explanation:

He is "Allāh" from the standpoint of the actual process of bestowing lavish blessings *[Allāhu bi-isbāgh an-niʿam]*, and He is "the All-Merciful, the All-Compassionate" with regard to the qualities of magnanimity and generosity *[ar-Raḥmān ar-Raḥīm bi'l-jūd wa'l-karam]*. He is "Allāh" by virtue of the fact that He brings us forth from our mothers' wombs *[buṭūn]*. He is "the All-Merciful *[ar-Raḥmān]*" by virtue of the fact that He brings us forth from our graves *[qubūr]*. He is "the All-Compassionate *[ar-Raḥīm]*" by virtue of the fact that He brings us forth from the depths of darkness into the light *[nūr]*.

Concerning some particular benefits obtained by those who invoke the Divine Mercy by saying: "In the Name of Allāh *[Bismi'llāh]*."

Allāh will surely bestow His mercy upon those who refuse to follow Satan *[Shaiṭān]*, who turn away from sinful disobedience *[ʿiṣyān]*, who take good care to avoid the Fires of Hell *[nīrān]*, who make it their regular practice to perform works of charity *[iḥsān]*, and who constantly remember the All-Merciful *[ar-Raḥmān]*, for they never fail to invoke His Mercy by saying: "In the Name of Allāh *[Bismi'llāh]*."

Allāh will surely bestow His Mercy upon those who take refuge with Allāh, who turn in repentance to Allāh, who put their absolute trust in Allāh, and who actively practice the remembrance of Allāh, for they never fail to invoke His Mercy by saying: "In the Name of Allāh *[Bismi'llāh]*."

Allāh will surely bestow His Mercy upon those who abstain from this world *[dunyā]*, who long for the hereafter, who endure with patience when they must suffer pain *[adhā]*, who give thanks for blessed well-being *[naʿmā']*, and who actively practice the remembrance of the Master *[Mawlā]*, for they never fail to invoke His Mercy by saying: "In the Name of Allāh *[Bismi'llāh]*."

Congratulations to any servant [of Allāh] who is steering well clear of the Tempter *[Ṭāghūt]*, who is expecting nothing more from this world than his basic nourishment *[qūt]*, and who is actively practicing the remembrance of the Living One who never dies *[al-Ḥayy alladhī lā yamūt]*, for that servant is surely saying right now:

"In the Name of Allāh *[Bismi'llāh]*."

The Third Discourse

Concerning the words of Allāh (Almighty and Glorious is He):

And repent unto Allāh all together, O believers, for then you may be able to succeed.[149]

Here we have an exhortation to repentance *[tawba]* addressed in general terms to the community at large.

As a term in the nontechnical vocabulary of classical Arabic, the verbal noun *tawba* is actually a synonym of *rujūʿ* [returning; going back; coming back]. The same applies to the corresponding verbs, as in the expression: "So-and-so has returned *[tāba]* from such and such," where the meaning would be identical if we substituted *rajaʿa* for *tāba*.[150]

This accounts for the special significance acquired by the term *tawba* in a religious context [where it is usually translated "repentance"], because it has come to mean: "the act of returning *[rujūʿ]* from that which is blameworthy according to the sacred law *[sharʿ]* to that which is praiseworthy according to the sacred law, in acknowledgment of the fact that sins and acts of disobedience are causes of perdition, distancing those who commit them from Allāh (Almighty and Glorious is He) and from His Garden of Paradise, while the abandonment of such offenses brings one near to Allāh (Almighty and Glorious is He) and to His Garden of Paradise."

[149] *wa tūbū ila'llāhi jamīʿan ayyuha'l-muʾminūna laʿallakum tufliḥūn*. (24:31)

[150] Both *tawba* and *tāba* are derived from the tri-consonantal root *t–w–b*, while the root of *rujūʿ* and *rajaʿa* is *r–j–ʿ*. Since the Arabic letters *rāʾ*, *jīm* and *ʿain* are all "strong" consonants, they appear not only in *rujūʿ* and *rajaʿa*, but in all other words derived from the same root. The letter *wāw* is a "weak" consonant, however, and it therefore disappears from certain derivatives of any root in which it occurs. Thus the hypothetical form *tawaba* is actually pronounced *tāba*, and since it is written as it is pronounced, the root connection with the noun *tawba* is slightly disguised.

He is saying in effect (Almighty and Glorious is He): "Come back *[irjiʿū]* to Me, instead of following the whims and passions of your own lower selves *[nufūs]*, and instead of indulging in the satisfaction of your carnal desires, for then you may well succeed in obtaining your dearest wish in My presence, in the life hereafter *[maʿād]*. You may enjoy My gracious favor forever, dwelling in the abode of perpetual rest and permanent repose *[dār al-baqāʾ wa'l-qarār]*. You may prosper and triumph and attain salvation, and, through My mercy, you may be admitted to the Highest Garden of Paradise, which has been made ready to receive the righteous."

He has also addressed the believers in more specific and more exacting terms, for He has said (Exalted is He):

> O you who believe, turn to Allāh in repentance—in sincere repentance! It may be that your Lord will acquit you of your evil deeds, and will admit you into Gardens beneath which rivers flow. (66:8)

What is meant by sincere repentance *[tawba naṣūḥ]* is the kind of repentance that is wholly and purely for the sake of Allāh (Exalted is He), entirely devoid of any ulterior motive whatsoever. The adjective *naṣūḥ* is derived from the same root as the noun *niṣāḥ*, which is the Arabic word for a plain thread used in sewing. This kind of repentance is therefore quite simple and straightforward, without complications and free from attachments.

With such a thread to guide him, the servant will keep to the straight path of worshipful obedience, without veering off toward sinful disobedience. He will not indulge in furtive maneuvers like the sly tricks of the fox. He will not persuade himself to lapse back into behaving like a rebel and committing the odd sin now and then. He is committed to abstaining from all sins for the sake of Allāh, purely and simply, just as he used to commit them purely and simply to satisfy his whims and passions, in order that He may bring him to a good end.

Repentance *[tawba]* of every kind of sin must be regarded as a necessary duty *[wājiba]*, for it is classed as such by the consensus of the entire Islāmic community *[ijmāʿ al-umma]*.[151]

[151] In the technical vocabulary of Islāmic jurisprudence *[fiqh]*, the term *wājib* (or *wājiba*, when it refers to a grammatically feminine word like *tawba*) is applied to a religious duty that is "necessary," but which cannot be classed as "absolutely obligatory" *[farḍ]*. It is not permissible to accuse an unrepentant sinner of being an unbeliever *[kāfir]*, as Shaikh ʿAbd al-Qādir al-Jīlānī (may Allāh has stated most emphatically in an earlier chapter (Vol. 1, p. 216).

In the Qur'ān, Allāh (Glorified and Exalted is He) has made more than one mention of those who repent *[at-tā'ibīn]*. Let us consider, for instance, His glorious words:

> Truly, Allāh loves those who repent, and He loves those who keep themselves clean. (2:222)

Thus He has let us know that He loves them on account of their repentance, and because they keep themselves clean, meaning free from the contamination of sins that would set them far apart from Him (Almighty and Glorious is He).

Allāh (Exalted is He) has also said:

> [Triumphant are] those who repent [to Allāh], those who serve [Him], those who praise [Him], those who fast, those who bow, those who fall prostrate [in worship], those who enjoin what is right and fair and forbid what is wrong and unfair, and those who keep the limits of Allāh. And give good tidings to the believers! (9:112)

In this case, He begins with a specific reference to a particular set of people, namely, those who repent, then He goes on to qualify them with all those other praiseworthy attributes. In so doing, He is giving us to understand that the penitent *[tā'ib]* is the kind of person who fits this description. From this it follows naturally that such a person must be worthy of the good tidings conveyed to those who possess true faith *[īmān]*, in accordance with His words: "And give good tidings to the believers!"

Various opinions of the scholars concerning the number and nature of the major sins *[kabā'ir]*.

As we have been made aware by the One who has summoned us to repentance *[tawba]*, a distinction does exist between major sins *[kabā'ir]* and minor sins *[ṣaghā'ir]*. Among the religious scholars *['ulāmā']*, however, there is considerable disagreement concerning the number and nature of the major sins.

Certain scholars maintain that there are no more than three major sins, while others set the number at four, seven, nine, or eleven. Ibn 'Umar (may Allāh be well pleased with him and with his father) once said: "The major sins are seven in number." But whenever this was mentioned in the hearing of Ibn 'Abbās (may Allāh be well pleased with him and with his father), he would say: "Their true number is much closer to seventy than to seven!" Then he would go on to say: "Anything that Allāh has forbidden constitutes a major sin."

According to some authorities, the exact number of the major sins is something that cannot be stated with certainty, since this is one of those matters that have been kept deliberately vague, like the date of the Night of Power *[Lailat al-Qadr]* and the moment of the Day of Resurrection *[Yawm al-Jam']*.[152] Where these two events are concerned, the ambiguity serves the purpose of encouraging people to make the effort to discover the timing for themselves. Similarly, in the case of the major sins, the ambiguity is intended to make people extra cautious, to the point of giving up all sins of any kind.

Some say that anything which Allāh has threatened to punish with the Fire of Hell must constitute a major sin. For others, the definition of a major sin is "anything for which the penalty, here in this world, is a punishment specifically prescribed by Islāmic law *[ḥadd]*."[153]

[152] Literally, the Day of the [Final] Congregation.

[153] The specific punishments prescribed by Islāmic law *[ḥudūd*, pl. of *ḥadd]* are: (1) For *zinā* in the sense of adultery: stoning *[rajm]*. (2) For *zinā* in the sense of fornication: one hundred lashes. (3) For *qadhf* [false accusation of adultery]: eighty lashes. (4) For apostasy *[irtidād]*: death. (5) For drinking intoxicating liquor *[shurb]*: eighty lashes. (6) For theft *[sariqa]*: amputation of the right hand. (7) For highway robbery *[qaṭ' aṭ-ṭarīq]*: (a) amputation of hands and feet (for robbery only); (b) death by the sword or crucifixion (for robbery with murder).

A certain learned man, one of those well versed in the knowledge of Allāh (Almighty and Glorious is He), has given us the following account of his research concerning the number and nature of the major sins:

"They add up to a total of seventeen. Four of them are committed within the heart, namely:

1. Associating partners with Allāh *[shirk bi'llāh]*.
2. Stubborn persistence in disobedience toward Allāh.
3. Despairing of the mercy *[raḥma]* of Allāh.
4. Daring to consider one's deceitfulness safe from detection by the ingenious devices *[makr]* of Allāh.

The next four are committed by the tongue, namely:

5. Bearing false witness *[shahādat az-zūr]*.
6. An unsubstantiated accusation of adultery against a married person of unblemished reputation *[qadhf al-muḥṣan]*.[154]
7. Deliberately premeditated perjury *[yamīn ghamūs]*, i.e., making a statement—under oath—which results in a false claim being established as true, and a rightful claim being dismissed as unfounded, or in the wrongful seizure of the property of a Muslim—be it no more than a piece of tooth stick *[siwāk]*[154] from the thorny tree called *arāk*.[217]
8. Uttering the incantations of sorcery and witchcraft *[siḥr]*.

Three are committed in the belly, namely:

9. The drinking of wine *[khamr]* and any other beverage that causes intoxication *[muskir]*.
10. Wrongfully consuming the property of an orphan.
11. Knowingly consuming unjustified profit *[ribā]*.

154 In order to escape the penalty of eighty lashes incurred under Islāmic law by a person making such an accusation, the accuser would have to produce four male witnesses of impeccable character, each of whom would be required to testify that he had actually seen "the pen in the pen-holder."

155 The *siwāk* is a small stick, softened at the tip by chewing or beating to form a kind of toothbrush, the use of which is a traditionally recommended practice *[sunna]* for anyone performing the Islāmic ritual ablution *[wuḍū']*.

156 According to the Arabic lexicographers, the *arāk* is not only the best tree for tooth sticks (made from its branches, and more especially from its roots); it is also "the best of all the trees upon which camels and other beasts feed, with respect to the odor of the milk produced by those animals." (See: E.W. Lane, *Arabic-English Lexicon*, art. ʾ–R–K.)

Two are committed in the genital region *[farj]*, namely:

12. Adultery and fornication *[zinā]*.

13. Sodomy and pederasty *[liwāṭa]*.[157]

The next two are committed by the using the hands:

14. Murder *[qatl]*.

15. Theft *[sariqa]*.

One is committed by means of the feet, namely,

16. Desertion from a Muslim army on the march against an army of unbelievers *[firār min az-zaḥf]*, no matter what the odds may be.

Finally, there is one major sin in which all parts of the body are involved:

17. Undutiful treatment of one's parents *[ʿuqūq al-wālidain]*, which may mean any or all of the following: failing to respect their solemn warnings, striking them when they speak to you reproachfully, refusing to give them something when they ask you for it, or refusing to feed them when they are hungry and begging you to give them some food."

[157] The noun *liwāṭa* is derived from the triliteral root *l–w–ṭ*, which indicates that it refers to the homosexual vices of the people of Lot *[Lūṭ]*, whose name is spelled *l–w–ṭ* in the Arabic script.

Concerning the minor sins *[ṣaghā'ir]*, which are innumerable.

As far as the minor sins *[ṣaghā'ir]* are concerned, there are far too many of them to be counted. We have no means by which to identify them all with absolute precision, and no list of them can ever be regarded as fully comprehensive. Nevertheless, we do know how to recognize them through the indications provided by the sacred law *[shar']*, as well as by the light of our perceptive faculties, for the aim of the sacred law is to advance the spiritual progress of the heart, so that it may draw nearer and nearer to Allāh (Almighty and Glorious is He) by refraining from the commission of sins. As He has told us (Exalted is He):

> Forsake the outer aspect of sin, and the inner aspect of it as well. (6:121)

A list of typical minor sins would include the following:

1. Eyeing, kissing, and lying in bed with a person one finds physically attractive, but without engaging in sexual intercourse.
2. Insulting and abusing a Muslim brother, but without going so far as to smear his character with a false accusation of sexual misconduct *[qadhf]*,[158] and without subjecting him to a physical beating.
3. Backbiting *[ghība]*.[159]
4. Malicious and mischievous misrepresentation *[namīma]*.
5. Telling outright lies.

The list could go on and on, but it would need a very lengthy commentary.

When the believer *[mu'min]* turns in repentance from the major sins *[kabā'ir]*, the minor sins *[ṣaghā'ir]* are implicitly covered by his act of repentance, because Allāh (Exalted is He) has told us:

> If you avoid the major sins that you are forbidden to commit, We will acquit you of your evil deeds, and We will admit you by a gate of honor. (4:31)

[158] See note [153] above.

[159] Backbiting *[ghība]*, i.e., saying bad things about someone in the absence of the person concerned, is considered extremely reprehensible, regardless of whether those things happen to be true or false.

Rather than taking this for granted, however, the penitent believer should make a serious effort to be conscious of all the sins he is giving up, the minor as well as the major, when he comes to the point of declaring his repentance *[tawba]*.

In the words of the poet:

You must forsake all kinds of sin, the great and the small alike,
for such is the pious duty of the righteous and devout.
You must advance as you would when treading over thorny ground,
avoiding the prickly spots and casting warily about.
Do not rule out a little sin as trivial in itself;
since mountains are made of pebbles,
they can never be ruled out.

Anas ibn Mālik (may Allāh be well pleased with him) is reported as having said:

"Allāh's Messenger (Allāh bless him and give him peace) once stopped to make camp, he and his Companions, in a dry river bed in which there was no firewood, and nothing else as far as they could see. Nevertheless, he told them to go and gather firewood. When they said: 'O Messenger of Allāh, we cannot see any firewood to collect,' he replied: 'Do not rule out anything you can get hold of, however insignificant it may seem at first glance.'

"So, the men set about collecting whatever odds and ends they could find, bit by bit, until they had eventually stacked up an enormous pile. He then said to his Companions: 'Don't you see? This is just how it happens with all those individual items of good and evil that are so readily dismissed as insignificant. One little sin gets piled on top of another little sin, one big sin on top of another big sin, something good on top of something else that is good, and something evil on top of something else that is evil.'"

Some say that when a sin appears tiny in the eyes of the servant [of the Lord], it becomes enormous in the sight of Allāh (Exalted is He), but then, if the servant comes to see it as enormous, it becomes tiny in the sight of Allāh (Exalted is He). It is actually because of the enormous strength of his faith *[īmān]*, and the high level of understanding he has attained through experience *[maʿrifa]*, that the believing servant comes to attach enormous importance to even a little sin.

As we know from one of the sayings *[ḥadīth]* traditionally ascribed to the Prophet (Allāh bless him and give him peace):

> The believer *[mu᾿min]* looks upon his sin as a mountain towering high above him, so he is afraid that it may topple down upon him, whereas the hypocrite *[munāfiq]* sees his sin as nothing more than a fly that comes buzzing around his nose, so he tries to flick it away.

A certain wise man said: "The unforgivable sin is the one that is perpetrated when a man dares to say: 'How I wish that every sin I committed could be as trivial as this!'"

The point of this remark is that he could not bring himself to say such a thing, if it were not for the incompleteness of his faith *[īmān]*, the weakness of his intuitive understanding *[ma῾rifa]*, and the woeful inadequacy of his knowledge *[῾ilm]* concerning the Majesty of Allāh (Almighty and Glorious is He). If he had any cognition of that Divine Majesty *[Jalāl]*, he would regard the little sin as a big one, and the insignificant offense as an enormous one. He would heed the following advice, which Allāh (Exalted is He) conveyed to one of His Prophets by way of inspiration:

> Pay no attention to the smallness of the gift, but do pay attention to the greatness of the One who gives it. Pay no attention to the paltry nature of the offense, but do pay attention to the grandeur of the One you are offending with it.

This explains why that wise man then went on to say: "When someone holds an illustrious rank and an exalted station in the sight of Allāh (Almighty and Glorious is He), for him there is no such thing as a minor sin *[ṣaghīra]*. As far as he is concerned, even the slightest misdemeanor represents the commission of a major sin *[kabīra]* against Allāh (Exalted is He)."

One of the Companions *[Ṣaḥāba]* of the Prophet (Allāh bless him and give him peace) once said to his friends among the Successors *[Tābi῾īn]*:[160] "Some of the misdeeds you people commit are obviously less significant, in your eyes, than a slender strand of hair, whereas we, during the lifetime of Allāh's Messenger (Allāh bless him and give him peace), would have counted them among the deadliest of sins *[mūbiqāt]*."

If he felt able to say such a thing, it was surely because of his closeness

[160] In his *Malfūẓāt [Utterances]*, Shaikh ῾Abd al-Qādir al-Jīlānī (may Allāh be well pleased with him) says: "Of them [the people of the Lord] He has made firm anchors for the religion *[dīn]*. The senior rank among them is that of the Prophet (Allāh bless him and give him peace); junior to this is the rank of the Companions *[ṣaḥāba]*, and below this again is the rank of the Successors *[tābi῾ūn]*. They always put what they say into practice, carrying it out in word and deed, in private and in public." (See p. 26 of the Al-Baz edition of this work in English translation.)

to the Prophet (Allāh bless him and give him peace) and to Allāh (Glorious is His Majesty). As far as the ignorant person *[jāhil]* is concerned, certain types of behavior may be quite inconsequential, but for someone who has acquired knowledge *[ʿālim]* they can assume enormous importance. The ordinary person may be allowed to get away with things that would not be tolerated in the case of a person with spiritual experience *[ʿārif]*, depending on the extent of the disparity that exists between them in knowledge *[ʿilm]*, experience *[maʿrifa]*, and stage of spiritual development *[manzila]*.

Repentance *[tawba]* is a personal religious obligation *[farḍ ʿain]*, incumbent upon every single individual.[161] It is inconceivable that any member of the human race could be exempt from the duty to repent. In the first place, it is highly unlikely that there is any human being who has never committed acts of sinful disobedience with the limbs and organs of his physical body. Even if such a person does exist, he will almost certainly be guilty of sins committed within his heart. In the improbable event that he is indeed innocent on that score too, he can hardly be impervious to the whispering *[waswās]* of the Devil, insinuating all manner of notions *[khawāṭir]*[162] that are calculated to distract him from the remembrance of Allāh (Exalted is He). Finally, if he does pass even that well-nigh impossible test, he will still be found guilty of some kind of negligence, and of leaving some gap in his knowledge of Allāh (Almighty and Glorious is He), with respect to His attributes *[ṣifāt]* and His actions *[afʿāl]*.

In all of this, there is an appropriate degree of strictness corresponding to each of the various stages experienced by the believers *[manāzil al-muʾminīn]* in the development of their spiritual states *[aḥwāl]* and stations *[maqāmāt]*. For every particular spiritual state *[ḥāl]*, there are particular acts of worshipful obedience *[ṭāʿāt]* to be performed, particular sins *[dhunūb]* to be avoided, and particular guidelines *[ḥudūd]* and conditions *[shurūṭ]* to be observed.

To observe these requirements is to be in a state of worshipful obedience, while any neglect or heedless omission is counted as a sin,

[161] In Islāmic jurisprudence *[fiqh]*, a distinction is drawn between *farḍ ʿain*, i.e., a religious duty that is incumbent on every individual Muslim, and *farḍ ʿala'l-kifāya*, meaning a collective duty, incumbent on the Islāmic community as a whole, though not on every individual Muslim.

[162] On the subject of 'notions' *[khawāṭir*, pl. of *khāṭir]*, see pp. 32–40 above.

and sin necessitates repentance *[tawba]*. Repentance means that the believer must abandon the devious course *[taʿwīj]* upon which he finds himself embarked, and return to the track of the straight path *[sanan aṭ-ṭarīq al-mustaqīm]* that has been clearly charted for him by the sacred law, leading to a situation that has been established for him, and to an honorable position that has been made accessible to him.

Everyone stands in need of repentance, so the difference between one set of people and another can only be a matter of degree. As far as the ordinary people *[ʿawāmm]* are concerned, repentance means turning away from sins *[dhunūb]*. For the élite *[khawāṣṣ]*, repentance means turning away from heedless negligence *[ghafla]*. In the case of the élite of the élite *[khāṣṣ al-khāṣṣ]*, repentance means turning away from letting the heart rely upon anything apart from Allāh (Almighty and Glorious is He).

It was actually Dhu'n-Nūn al-Miṣrī ["the Egyptian"][163] (may Allāh bestow His mercy upon him) who said: "As far as the ordinary people are concerned, repentance means turning away from sins. For the élite, repentance means turning away from heedless negligence." And it was Abu'l-Ḥusain an-Nūrī who said: "Repentance means that you are turning away from everything apart from Allāh (Almighty and Glorious is He)."

How vast is the difference between each person and the one mentioned after him in the following list:

1. The penitent who is turning in repentance from simple lapses and mistakes *[zallāt]*.
2. The penitent who is turning in repentance from sins of heedless negligence *[ghafalāt]*.
3. The penitent who is turning in repentance from thinking too highly of his own good deeds *[ruʾyat al-ḥasanāt]*.

[163] Dhu'n-Nūn Abu'l-Faiḍ (or Fayyāḍ) Thawbān ibn Ibrāhīm al-Miṣrī was born at Ikhmīm in Upper Egypt, ca. A.H. 180/796 C.E., the son of a Nubian father. His life is shrouded in obscurity, in spite of the many legends related about him in detailed biographies by later authors. It can be stated with a fair degree of certainty, however, that he lived in Cairo, and that he traveled extensively. We also know that he was arrested (like Imām Aḥmad ibn Ḥanbal) for upholding the traditional Islāmic doctrine that the Qurʾān is uncreated, in opposition to the Muʿtazilite thesis that was espoused by some of the ʿAbbāsid Caliphs. He was transported to Baghdād, released after a term of imprisonment, and returned to die at Gīza near Cairo in A.H. 245/859 C.E. According to A.J. Arberry (art. DHU 'L-NŪN in *SEI*):

> "His sayings display the same intensity of style and rich imagery which characterize such other [Islāmic saints] as Junaid and Abū Yazīd al-Bisṭāmī. His skill in epigrams is illustrated by the saying: 'Make yourself dead during the days of your lifetime, that you may live among the dead when you are gone.'"

4. The penitent who is turning in repentance from letting his heart feel at ease with anything other than the Creator of all creatures *[Khāliq al-bariyyāt]*.

The Prophets (peace be upon them) were certainly not beyond the need for repentance. Just consider the saying traditionally ascribed to our own Prophet Muḥammad (Allāh bless him and give him peace):

> A coating of rust is always threatening to cover my heart, so I beg forgiveness of Allāh (Almighty and Glorious is He) no less than seventy times every day and night.

As soon as Adam (peace be upon him) had eaten the fruit of the forbidden tree, all the clothes he had been wearing immediately stripped themselves off his body and scattered in every direction, leaving him with his private parts exposed to view. His head was still covered, however, because his crown and diadem felt too embarrassed to take themselves off and leave him bareheaded, so Gabriel (peace be upon him) had to come and take the crown *[tāj]* from his head and the diadem *[iklīl]* from his brow.

Adam and Eve then heard the voice of the Lord, as He told them: "Get yourselves down below, the pair of you, out of My vicinity, for no one who disobeys Me can be allowed to dwell in close proximity to Me."

So Adam turned to Eve in shame, as he said to her: "This first disastrous act of sinful disobedience has resulted in our expulsion from the vicinity of the Beloved, obliging us to accept the necessity of repentance *[tawba]*, humble entreaty *[taḍarruʿ]*, begging like a pauper *[iftiqār]*, submissive resignation *[istikāna]* and abasement *[dhilla]*—and all this after we had been so accustomed to a comfortably settled way of life *[ʿaish qārr]*."

They had in fact been accustomed to a way of life in which they enjoyed enormous power and wealth, great luxury, honor and dignity, gracious favor, and exalted rank in the noblest of situations— in those that are most pure, in those that are most secure, and in those that are nearest to Allāh (Exalted is He). So, if there had ever been anyone who could dispense with repentance, who could feel quite safe from any hostile force, be it the mischief of the lower self *[nafs]* or the whispered insinuations *[waswās]* and cunning machinations of the Devil *[Shaiṭān]*, and who could pride himself on the nobility and purity of his situation, on his nearness to Allāh and the closeness of his station, the person most obviously matching this description would surely have been Adam (peace be upon him). Yet he stood in need of repentance [and of having his repentance accepted], until Allāh relented toward him, as we know from His words (Almighty and Glorious is He):

> Then Adam received certain words [of revelation] from his Lord, and He relented toward him. He is indeed the Relenting One, the All-Compassionate. (2:37)

Al-Ḥasan the son of ʿAlī (may Allāh be well pleased with them both) is reported as having said:

"When Allāh relented toward Adam (peace be upon him), the angels offered him their congratulations. Gabriel (peace be upon him) came down from on high, along with Mīkāʾīl and Isrāfīl (peace be upon them both), and they all said: 'O Adam, be of good cheer, for Allāh has relented toward you!' Adam (peace be upon him) responded to this by saying: 'O Gabriel, if there is any question still to be asked after this acceptance of my repentance, it is: "Where do I stand now?"'

"Allāh therefore conveyed to him by way of inspiration: 'O Adam, you have bequeathed to your descendants a legacy of trouble and toil, while I have made them heirs to [the benefits of] repentance *[tawba]*. This means that, whenever any of them appeal to Me in prayer, I shall answer their call, just as I have answered your call, and whenever any of them beg Me to grant them forgiveness, I shall not give them a grudging response, for I am Ever-Near *[Qarīb]* and Ever-Ready-to-Respond *[Mujīb]*. O Adam, when the Day of Resurrection comes, I shall assemble in the Garden of Paradise all those who turn in repentance from their sins. I shall bring them forth happy, laughing and rejoicing from their graves, and their supplication *[duʿāʾ]* will receive a positive response.'"

The case of the Prophet Noah *[Nūḥ]* (peace be upon him) is essentially similar to this. In response to his plea, Allāh (Exalted is He) drowned all the inhabitants of the East and the West, in order to defend his honor, and to show the intensity of His anger toward them for having called him a liar. He is in fact the second Adam, because all surviving human creatures must be descended from his offspring, if we are to believe the statement that none of the people who were with him aboard the Ark succeeded in producing any children, apart from his own three sons, whose names were Ḥām, Sām and Japhet *[Yāfith]*.

This means that all subsequent branches of the human race can be traced back to Noah (peace be upon him) through these three sons of his. Yet in spite of this very special status, he said:

> My Lord, I take refuge with You, lest I should ask of You that whereof I have no knowledge; for unless You forgive me and have mercy on me, I shall be among the losers. (11:47)

Let us also consider the essential similarity of the case of Abraham, the Special Friend of Allāh *[Ibrāhīm al-Khalīl]* (peace be upon him), despite the loftiness of his rank, and the fact that Allāh chose him to be the recipient of His special friendship *[khulla]* and caused him to become the father and direct ancestor of so many of the Prophets *[anbiyā᾿]* and Messengers *[mursalīn]*. As we know from traditional reports, his own children and the offspring of his children account for no fewer than four thousand Prophets (peace be upon them all). Allāh (Exalted is He) has told us:

> And We made his offspring the survivors. (37:77)

Even our own Prophet Muḥammad (Allāh bless him and give him peace) is one of his direct descendants, as are Moses and Jesus and David and Solomon (peace be upon them all), to mention only a few by name. Nonetheless, Abraham (peace be upon him) was in no way exempt from the need to experience repentance *[tawba]*, submissive resignation *[istikāna]*, and the condition of abject poverty *[iftiqār]* in relation to Allāh (Almighty and Glorious is He). Indeed, it was he who said [as we are told in the Qur᾿ān]:

> They are all an enemy to me, except the Lord of All the Worlds, the One who created me, and Himself guides me, and Himself gives me to eat and drink, and, whenever I am sick, heals me, and who causes me to die, then brings me back to life, and who, I ardently hope, will forgive me my sin on the Day of Doom. (26:77–82)

And it was he, as Allāh (Almighty and Glorious is He) has also told us, who offered the prayer:

> And show us our rites of worship, and relent toward us. You, only You, are the Relenting One, the All-Compassionate. (2:128)

Moses (peace be upon him) was no exception to the general rule concerning the necessity of repentance, in spite of the loftiness of his rank and his many special privileges, which include the fact that Allāh selected him for the office of Messengership *[Risāla]*. Allāh (Almighty and Glorious is He) engaged in verbal conversation *[kalām]* with him, brought him up to be a servant and a spokesman for Himself,[164] and imbued him with His love.[165] He also helped him to substantiate his Prophetic claims by means of the spectacular miracles *[muʿjizāt]* performed with the hand and the staff, as well as the nine marvelous portents *[āyāt]* and all the things that happened to him in the wilderness, such as the pillars of light that appeared in the night, the manna *[mann]* and the quails *[salwā]*. Moses (peace be upon him) was blessed with these and other signs and wonders that had not been granted to any of the Prophets before him, and yet even he acknowledged the need for repentance. As Allāh (Almighty and Glorious is He) has told us:

> He said: "My Lord, forgive me and my brother, and enter us into Your mercy, for You are the Most Merciful of the merciful." (7:151)

The Prophet David (peace be upon him) is another case in point, despite the loftiness of his rank, and the fact that Allāh bestowed such a mighty kingship upon him. His royal guards were thirty-three thousand strong. Whenever he recited the Psalms *[Zabūr]*, the birds would alight in rows upon his head; the water would halt the flow of its restless current; human beings and jinn would line up in orderly ranks all around him, and the savage beasts and reptiles would do the same, without harming one another in any way; the mountains would resound with the proclamation of his glory; hard iron would turn soft and pliable to serve his needs.

He had all this at his disposal, to magnify his stature and preserve his authority, yet he wept incessantly for forty days while bowing in prostration, until green grass sprouted from the ground where his tears

[164] An allusion to the verse *[āya]* of the Qurʾān in which Allāh (Almighty and Glorious is He) says to Moses (peace be upon him):

> And I have reared you for Myself *[wa'ṣṭanaʿtuka li-Nafsī]*. (20:41)

Some of the traditional Qurʾānic commentators interpret this to mean: "I have reared you [or, I have chosen you] for Myself, to establish My evidence and to serve as My spokesman between Me and My creatures, in such a way that your doing it will be the same as My doing it Myself." According to others, the meaning is: "I have reared you [or, I have chosen you] for Myself, for a special affair which I require you to accomplish in a sufficient manner, concerning Pharaoh and his forces." (See: E.W. Lane, *Arabic-English Lexicon*, art. Ṣ–N–ʿ.)

[165] An allusion to the verse *[āya]* of the Qurʾān in which Allāh (Almighty and Glorious is He) says to Moses (peace be upon him):

> And I have imbued you with love from Me *[wa alqaitu ʿalaika maḥabbatan minnī]*. (20:39)

kept falling. It was then that Allāh (Exalted is He) had mercy on him and relented toward him. It was then that He (Almighty and Glorious is He) accepted his repentance and said:

> So We forgave him that, and he enjoyed access to Our presence and a happy journey's end. (38:25)

In the case of David's son Solomon (peace be upon them both), repentance proved to be a very painful experience indeed, in spite of his mighty kingship. He even had a wind at his beck and call, a wind that he could command to blow in one direction for a month, and then for a month in the opposite direction. So great was his sovereign power, as a matter of fact, that no one has ever wielded the like of it since his time. When he was condemned to suffer punishment for his sin, on account of the sculptured image he had worshipped in his palace for a period of forty days, he went wandering about for some time with a haughty expression on his face. He would ask for food by making a gesture with the palms of his hands, so he was not given anything to eat. When he tried saying: "You must give me something to eat, for I am Solomon, the son of David," he received a crack in the skull, a beating, and some very rude comments—apart from being simply dismissed as a liar.

One day, as he was being chased away from a house he had approached to ask for food, a woman spat in his face. According to one traditional report, an old woman once came out with a jar full of urine, which she proceeded to pour all over his head.

He continued to suffer this kind of degradation, until Allāh brought forth the signet ring *[khātam]* from the belly of a fish *[ḥūt]*, and gave it to him. He then wore the signet ring until the end of the forty days, that is to say, for the duration of his punishment. As soon as that period had expired, the birds came flocking to him, and the jinn, the devils and the wild beasts all came and gathered around him. Now that he was recognized by those who had despised him and beaten him, they offered him their apologies for all the bad treatment they had meted out to him, but he said: "I do not blame you for whatever you did before, nor do I praise you for what you are doing now. This whole business came from the presence of my Lord, so everything about it has been inevitable."

It was at this point that Allāh accepted his repentance and relented toward him, and so He restored his kingship to him, granting him even greater scope and authority than before (peace be upon him).

Well then, if such was the spiritual condition of all these great masters and leaders, these governors of the people and administrators of the sacred law *[sharʿ]*, these deputies *[khulafāʾ]* of Allāh among His creatures, what are we to say about your spiritual condition, about you and your state of delusion, O miserable wretch?

There you are, in the house of illusion *[dār al-ghurūr]*, within the territory allotted to the devils as their feudal estate *[iqṭāʿ ash-shayāṭīn]*, surrounded by all the hostile forces in the realm of creation, such as whims and passions *[hawā]*, the mischief of the lower self *[nafs]*, the lusts of the flesh *[shahawāt]*, willful desires *[irādāt]*, insidious temptations *[wasāwis]*, and the seductive and glamorized enticements of Satan *[Shaiṭān]*.

You beguile yourselves with the outer forms of worship *[ʿibādāt ẓāhira]*, such as fasting *[ṣawm]*, the ritual prayer *[ṣalāt]*, the alms-due *[zakāt]* and the pilgrimage *[ḥajj]*, and with physical abstinence from external acts of sinful disobedience, while your inner being *[bāṭin]* is utterly devoid of the inner forms of worship. There is nothing but an empty blank in the space that ought to be filled with the virtues of pious caution *[waraʿ]*, unhurried deliberation *[taʾannī]*, devotion to duty *[taqwā]*, detachment from worldly concerns *[zuhd]*, patience and perseverance *[ṣabr]*, contentment *[riḍā]*, frugal satisfaction *[qanāʿa]*, absolute trust *[tawakkul]*, commitment *[tafwīḍ]*, conviction *[yaqīn]*, a sense of integrity *[salāmat aṣ-ṣadr]*, personal generosity *[sakhāwat an-nafs]*, the cultivation of good grace *[minna]*, good intention *[niyya]*, active good will *[iḥsān]*, seeing things in a favorable light *[ḥusn aẓ-ẓann]*, goodness of character *[ḥusn al-khulq]*, a good approach to daily life *[ḥusn al-maʿāsh]*, good spiritual experience *[ḥusn al-maʿrifa]*, excellent obedience *[ḥusn aṭ-ṭāʿa]*, honesty *[ṣidq]*, sincerity *[ikhlāṣ]*, and many other such qualities, which could be listed at very great length.

As far as your content is concerned, you are stuffed to the full with disgustingly immoral traits of character. You are stuffed with the mothers of all sins *[ummahāt adh-dhunūb]*, from which all kinds of torment and catastrophe are spawned, including every lethal and soul-destroying affliction in this world and the hereafter: such as the fear of poverty, resentment of the destiny *[qadar]* decreed by Allāh (Almighty and Glorious is He), reluctance to accept His judgment concerning His creation, and harboring suspicions about Him in this regard, as well as doubting the fulfillment of His promise.

In listing these deadly vices we must also make mention of malicious spite *[ghill]*, rancor *[ḥiqd]*, envy *[ḥasad]*, and cheating *[ghishsh]*, along with the pursuit of high rank and status, the love of praise and approbation, the love of worldly prestige, being content with this world and feeling perfectly at home in it, overbearing pride and arrogance toward the servants of Allāh, and turning up one's nose in haughty disdain. As Allāh (Exalted is He) has said:

> And when he is told: "Be careful of your duty to Allāh," vainglory traps him in sin. (2:206)

The list continues with anger *[ghaḍab]*, fanaticism *[ḥamiyya]*, scornful contempt *[anafa]*, the love of political power *[riyāsa]*, animosity *[ʿadāwa]*, hatred *[baghḍāʾ]*, greedy ambition *[ṭamaʿ]*, avarice *[bukhl]*, tight-fistedness *[shuḥḥ]*, covetousness *[raghba]*, timidity *[rahba]*, excessive hilarity *[faraḥ]*, impertinence *[ashar]*, cockiness *[baṭar]*, aggrandizing the rich and belittling the poor, boastfulness *[fakhr]*, conceitedness *[khuyalāʾ]*, ruthless competition *[tanāfus]* and boastful rivalry *[mubāhāt]* in the advancement of your worldly interests, the pursuit of superficial notoriety *[riyāʾ]* and fame *[sumʿa]*, disregarding the truth in order to give yourself an air of importance *[istikbār]*, becoming engrossed in matters that are none of your business *[khawḍ fī mā lā yaʿnī]*, indulging in a lot of talk *[kathrat al-kalām]* for no good purpose, bragging *[tīh]* and showing off *[ṣalaf]*, prying *[ikhtibār]* into the affairs of other people (while neglecting your valid concerns and leaving your worship to chance), engaging in fawning *[tamalluq]* and trying to gain influence through flattery *[iqtidār]*, treating the commandment of Allāh as something of little or no importance *[tahāwun]*, treating mere creatures with veneration *[tawqīr]* and exaggerated respect *[mudāhana]*, taking conceited pride *[ʿujb]* in your accomplishments, loving the praise you receive for things you have not done, preoccupation with the faults of your fellow creatures and blindness to your own shortcomings, forgetting the blessings of Allāh and attributing them to yourself (or to your fellow creatures, who are merely the instruments and tools for the delivery of those blessings), confining your attention to the outer form *[ẓāhir]* and making no effort to examine the basic roots *[uṣūl]*, failing to observe the rules of law *[ḥudūd]* and to put each thing in its proper place, and having a predilection for happiness and an intense dislike of sorrow.

The absence of sorrow spells the ruination of the heart, and the departure therefrom of fearful apprehension. When sorrow is kept at a distance, the light of wisdom *[ḥikma]* is snuffed out, but when sorrow is experienced in ever increasing measure, it leads to the nearness of the Lord; to intimate friendship *[uns]* with Him; to hearing His voice and acquiring understanding from Him; to satisfaction with Him alone, so that one feels no need of anything in the entire creation; to eternal felicity *[sa'āda abadiyya]*; to everlasting salvation *[najāt sarmadiyya]*, and to universal bliss *[ni'ma kulliyya]*.

Your condition, unfortunately, is that of someone who is fully loaded with all the resources you need to ensure the triumph of the lower self *[nafs]*, in case it should ever have the opportunity to experience the abject humiliation *[dhilla]* that would actually contain its remedy, its true felicity, and the key to its admission into the company of the dearly beloved friends *[aḥbāb]* of Allāh (Exalted is He), His chosen ones *[aṣfiyā']*, His loyal followers *[khulaṣā']*, His martyrs *[shuhadā']*, His truly learned ones *['ulamā']*, those who are experienced *['ārifīn]* in the working out of His decrees of destiny *[aqdār]*, and the spiritual deputies *[abdāl]* of His Prophets *[anbiyā']* (peace be upon them all).

By the same token, you are poorly equipped with the kinds of resources required to support the cause of the Lord of Truth (Glorious is His Majesty), to ensure the triumph of the champions *[anṣār]* of His religion *[dīn]*—His saints *[awliyā']* who exist to bear witness on His behalf, who summon their fellow creatures to worship and obey Him, who warn them of His wrathful vengeance and His Fire of Hell by reminding them thereof every day of their lives, and who are always trying to awaken their desire for His mercy and His Garden of Paradise.

You delude yourself by taking pride in the fact that you treat your brothers *[ikhwān]* to a fine display of friendship in public, despite the hostility you actually feel toward them in private. You have shown no inclination to follow the good example set by those righteous individuals *[abrār]* who are brokenhearted and contrite *[munkasirīn al-qulūb wa'l-af'ida]*, although it is they who are the boon companions of the All-Merciful One *[julasā' ar-Raḥmān]* (Glorious is His Majesty).

They are the ones who put their trust in Him with quiet confidence, remaining steadfast through adversity and constantly diligent in service. They are the ones who enjoy the blessings of grace, who wear the robes of honor, and who bear the insignia that mark the loyal adherents *[khulaṣā᾿]* of the All-Merciful, the Lord of Glory. They are the ones who are safe in this world from the effects of political upheaval and civil strife, safe in their graves from the awful terror of the interrogation [by the angels Munkar and Nakīr] and the crushing pressure, and [they are the ones who will be] safe at the Resurrection from prolonged examination and desolate loneliness. They are the ones who will dwell forever in the abode of everlasting life, in a permanent state of bliss and happiness and joy and gladness. They are the ones who will be favored there with every kind of pleasant and refined delight, every hour, every moment and every single instant.

You are also lulled into a sense of false security by the worldly goods that have been placed at your disposal, by the free rein you have been granted in the pursuit of your worldly ambitions and desires, and by the extent to which you have been relieved of worldly cares.

You have therefore come to feel that you are in no danger of being deprived of the gifts, the favors and the benefits that once belonged to others, but which have since been handed down from them to you. They have been handed down from people long past and gone, from Pharaoh and Hāmān and Qārūn, from Shaddād and ʿĀd, from Caesar and Chosroes *[Kisrā]*,[166] from kings who reigned in ancient times, and from nations that have ceased to exist.

This world had its fun and games with those people. It encouraged them to entertain false hopes and aspirations, so that, when Allāh's commandment came, the illusion emboldened them to disobey Allāh, and they were prevented from obtaining what they most desired. They were gathered together and then scattered apart. They were separated from the goods they had once been allowed to call their own. They were driven from the beds they had made so comfortable for themselves. They were obliged to make their departure from the stately mansions they had erected. They were deprived of the power and glory they had so triumphantly acquired, and of the regal authority they claimed and imagined to be theirs by right. Then they were called to account for all

[166] Chosroes or Khosrau (*Kisrā* in Arabic) was the title of the ancient Kings of Persia.

the deposits that had been entrusted to their charge, and for all the loans they had been assigned to administer with responsible care.

What they were now receiving from Allāh was an experience they had not anticipated. They were brought face to face with the wickedness of their conduct, and interrogated in minute detail concerning the evil deeds they had perpetrated. They were locked up in the narrowest cells in the jails of this world, where they had once imprisoned their own victims, and made to suffer the harshest treatment they had ever imposed on those victims. They were sentenced to undergo the most extreme form of punishment they had ever inflicted on others. They were scorched by the Fire of Hell, into which they were thrust with their hands and feet shackled and chained. They were forced to eat the infernal diet called *zaqqūm*[167] and *ḍarī*ʿ,[168] and they were given boiling hot water to drink. They were also driven into a state of mental disorder by means of a certain slimy, poisonous substance *[min ṭīnati khabālin tuyyimū]*.[169]

You can surely learn some valuable lessons from these people of times gone by. If you pause to consider how many of them were taken into captivity and torn from their families, you will see this as a warning to

[167] Allāh (Almighty and Glorious is He) first mentioned *zaqqūm* when He said:

> The tree of *az-zaqqūm* is the food of the sinner. (44:43,44)

According to some Qurʾānic commentators, when the notorious Abū Jahl heard this revelation, he responded by saying: "Dates and fresh butter! We shall swallow it at our leisure." Allāh (Exalted is He) thereupon sent down the grim warning:

> We have assigned it as a torment for the evildoers. It is a tree that sprouts at the very bottom of Hell. The spathes thereof are like the heads of devils, and they must eat of it, and with it they must fill their bellies. (37:63–6)

[168] Like *zaqqūm*, the infernal food called *ḍarī*ʿ is mentioned in the Qurʾān, in the words of Allāh (Almighty and Glorious is He):

> There shall be no food for them except *aḍ-ḍarī*ʿ. (88:6)

According to the Arabic lexicographers, *aḍ-ḍarī*ʿ is "a certain plant in water that has become altered for the worse by long standing or the like, having roots that do not reach the ground," or "a certain thing in Hell, more bitter than aloes, and more stinking than the carcass, and hotter than the fire." See: E.W. Lane, *Arabic-English Lexicon*, art. *Ḍ–R–*ʿ. (Pickthall translates *aḍ-ḍarī*ʿ as "bitter thorn-fruit.")

[169] The meaning of this sentence is by no means crystal clear to the translator, who derives some comfort from the fact that it was evidently somewhat puzzling to the editor of the Damascus edition. In a footnote to the Arabic text, the latter suggests (with the wise qualification: "*Allāhu A*ʿ*lam* [Allāh knows best]") that it may refer to the drinking of wine, which has an intoxicating effect in this world and deadly consequences in the hereafter. (According to some lexicographers, one meaning of *khabāl* is "the fluid squeezed, or wrung, or flowing, from the inhabitants of Hell, or from their skins." See: E.W. Lane, *Arabic-English Lexicon*, art. *KH–B–L*.)

beware of claiming to possess what they have left behind. You will beware of settling down to live in the buildings they constructed, and from which they were eventually expelled, since they committed so many acts of tyranny and oppression in the places they built.

How many a side and back, how many a cheek and head, they must have injured and flogged! How often they must have caused the eye of some wretchedly poor and miserable beggar to weep and stream with tears! How many a rich man of good repute they must have degraded and reduced to poverty! How many times they must have given legal force to some heretical innovation *[bidʿa]*, and promulgated regulations to establish some bad practice! How often they must have broken and enraged the heart of someone who offered them nothing but wise and sensible advice! How often, in the shadow of the night, it must have been possible to hear a prayer of supplication *[duʿāʾ]*, a sad lament, or a mournful voice, as people of good heart cried out to the All-Merciful *[Raḥmān]* in protest against their tyranny, complaining to Him about them as a way of expressing their grief and pain.

Those plaintive cries were immediately brought to the notice of the One who is All-Aware *[Khabīr]*, for the noble angels have been appointed to discharge that very task. The victims of oppression went speeding toward Him, till they reached their destination and found themselves in the presence of the Almighty King *[al-Malīk al-ʿAẓīm]*, the One who is Just and Fair *[Munṣif]*, instead of being a cruel tyrant. The inner contents of their breasts were obvious to the One who is All-Glorious *[ʿAzīz]*, All-Wise *[Ḥakīm]*, and All-Knowing *[ʿAlīm]*, and nothing could be hidden from the One who is All-Aware *[Khabīr]*, whether they declared it openly or tried to keep it to themselves, as He examined every aspect of what they were complaining and clamoring about. Then the All-Glorious and Majestic One *[al-ʿAzīz al-Jalīl]* assured them:

> I will surely help you, even if only after a while *[la-anṣuranna-kum wa-law baʿda ḥīn]*.[170]

He has indeed appointed a time of harvest, when tyrannical and wrongdoing groups of people are bound to reap what they have sown. [In the Qurʾān, for instance, after mentioning the violent destruction

[170] A non-Qurʾānic Divine Saying *[Ḥadīth Qudsī]*.

of the tribes of Thamūd and ʿĀd,[171] He asks His Messenger (Allāh bless him and give him peace):]

> And now can you see any remnant of them? (69:8)

For one set of tyrants the harvest has been destruction by drowning in the ocean; for another, by sinking into the earth and being swallowed up beneath its surface; for another, by being used as the firewood of Hell; for another, by being put to the slaughter; and for another, by the transmutation of their outer forms *[maskh aṣ-ṣuwar]*. In the case of yet another group, destruction has taken the form of transmutation affecting their spiritual contents *[maʿānī]*, in that He has rendered their hearts as hard as deaf stones, then stamped them with the stamp of unbelief *[kufr]*, sealed them with the seal of idolatrous polytheism *[shirk]*, coated them with rust, and covered them with darkness, for neither submission *[islām]* nor faith *[īmān]* were ever going to take firm root in them. And then:

> He gripped them with an exceedingly tight grip. (69:10)

He seized them with all the force ever used by a tyrant *[jabbār]*,[172] then thrust them into the Abode of Ruin *[Dār al-Bawār]*.[173]

> As soon as their skins are well and truly burned, We shall exchange them for fresh skins, so that they may taste the torment. (4:56)

Thus they will be forever undergoing punishment, constantly exposed to infernal heat *[jaḥīm]*, struggling to swallow food that always sticks like a lump in the throat, and suffering excruciating agony. As Allāh (Almighty and Glorious is He) has told us:

> There they must abide as long as the heavens and the earth endure. (11:107)

They are in a place where they can never die, and which they can never leave. There is no end to their woe, nor is there any limit to their wailing. The life they must lead there is a narrow life of utter misery.[174]

171 As for Thamūd, they were destroyed by the thunderbolt; and as for ʿĀd, they were destroyed by a fierce roaring wind. (69:5,6)

172 An allusion to the verse *[āya]* of the Qurʾān:

> And when you seize by force, do you seize with the force of tyrants? (26:130)

173 An allusion to the words of Allāh (Almighty and Glorious is He):

> Have you not seen those who exchanged the bounty of Allāh for thanklessness, and caused their people to dwell in the Abode of Ruin? (14:28)

174 An allusion to the warning in the Qurʾān:

> But if anyone turns away from remembrance of Me, for him there will be a narrow life, and We shall bring him forth blind to the assembly on the Day of Resurrection. (20:124)

No spirit *[rūḥ]* can come to their rescue, and neither breath nor spirit can escape from them. Their hopes are at a standstill, and their voices have been stilled. Their hearts have been dissolved into tiny fragments in their gullets, and their tongues have been rendered incapable of speech. They have been told:

> Slink away into it, and do not speak to Me. (23:108)

Well then, you had better be on your guard, O miserable wretch, in case you do the things they used to do, or in case you develop the same bad habits. Once you start following in their footsteps, you may die without repentance *[tawba]*. You may be snatched away quite suddenly, being caught entirely unawares, before you have time to prepare an excuse for yourself, before you have time to get a good answer ready, or an explanation that could save you. Since it will then be too late for you to take the necessary precautions, all that torment and chastisement will be inflicted upon you, just as it was inflicted on those we have been describing.

Concerning the preconditions of repentance *[tawba]* and the manner in which it must be carried out.

As for the preconditions that must be satisfied before repentance *[tawba]* can be valid, they are three in number:

1. The penitent must feel remorse *[nadam]* for all the transgressions he has ever committed. This is based on the clear statement of the Prophet (Allāh bless him and give him peace):

> Remorse is a form of repentance *[an-nadam tawba]*.

The symptoms that most clearly indicate the genuine quality of remorse are: (a) the delicate sensitivity *[riqqa]* of the heart, and (b) the copious shedding of tears.

This explains the significance of the saying attributed to the Prophet (Allāh bless him and give him peace):

> You must sit in the company of those who repent *[at-tawwābīn]*, for they are very tenderhearted *[araqq af'ida]*.

2. The renunciation of all forms of misbehavior *[zallāt]* under all circumstances and at all times.

3. The strong determination never to repeat the acts of disobedience *[ma'āṣī]* and the sinful errors *[khaṭī'āt]* of which one has previously been guilty.

This is the import of the response given by Abū Bakr al-Wāsiṭī, when someone asked him a question about sincere repentance *[tawba naṣūḥ]*,[175] for he said: "It means that no trace of sinful disobedience remains attached to the person who is repenting, neither in private nor in public. When someone's repentance is sincere, he is not the least bit worried about anything that may lie in store for him that night or the morning after."

[175] The questioner was obviously alluding to the expression used by Allāh (Almighty and Glorious is He), when He says in the Qur'ān:

> O you who believe, turn to Allāh in repentance—in sincere repentance! (66:8)

Remorse does indeed give rise to a strong determination *[ʿazm]* and a clear sense of purpose *[qaṣd]*. The remorseful person acquires a strong determination never to repeat the acts of disobedience and sinful errors of which he has been guilty in the past, because with the experience of remorse comes the realization that sins create a barrier between him and his Lord, and that they make it impossible for him to enjoy the pleasurable aspects of life in this world without incurring grave consequences in the hereafter.

This is neatly expressed in the traditional saying *[khabar]* that has been handed down to us [and which may be attributed to the Prophet himself (Allāh bless him and give him peace)];[176]

> All because of just one sin he happens to have committed, the servant [of the Lord] must forfeit a great deal of the worldly benefit that would otherwise be his portion *[rizq]*.

Also relevant in this context is the traditional saying:

> Unlawful sexual intercourse *[zinā]*[177] brings poverty in its wake.

To quote the wise words of one of the few who are qualified to speak from real experience *[ʿārifīn]*:

"Whenever you notice a change for the worse, a narrowing tendency in your way of life, increasing difficulty in making ends meet, and growing disorder in your state of being, you need to realize that you must be ignoring the commandment of your Master *[Mawlā]* and following your personal whims and desires *[hawā]*. "Whenever you become aware that the hands and tongues of other people have gained control over you, and that you have succumbed to malignant influences affecting yourself, your wife, your property and your children, you need to realize that you must be guilty of violating the prohibitions established by the sacred law, failing to discharge your obligations *[ḥuqūq]*, transgressing the legal bounds *[ḥudūd]* and breaking the rules *[rusūm]*.

[176]As used by the relaters of tradition, the term *khabar* is sometimes synonymous with *ḥadīth*, meaning a report than can be traced all the way back to the Prophet Muḥammad himself (Allāh bless him and give him peace), whether the substance of that report be a saying of his or a description of his behavior in a certain situation. In some cases, however, the term *khabar* is applied to a tradition that may well have originated with the Prophet (Allāh bless him and give him peace), but which can only be traced with certainty to one of his Companions, or to some other reliable early source.

[177] In the vocabulary of Islāmic jurisprudence *[fiqh]*, the Arabic word *zinā* covers both adultery and fornication. For a precise technical definition, see J. Schacht, *An Introduction to Islamic Law* (Oxford University Press, 1979), p. 178.

"Whenever you notice that cares, worries and anxieties have piled up on a massive scale within your heart, you need to realize that you must be reluctant to accept what your Lord has destined and decreed for you, doubtful about the fulfillment of His promise, guilty of associating *[mushrik]* His creatures with Him as if they were partners in His business, unwilling to place your trust in Him, and unhappy with His management of you and the rest of His creation."

Once the penitent has come to recognize the truth of all this, through examining his spiritual condition and reflecting on it, he will experience a feeling of remorse. What is meant by remorse *[nadam]* is the kind of heartache *[tawajjuʿ al-qalb]* that a person feels on learning of the loss of someone very dear to him, so the penitent is bound to go through a long and painful process of sighing and sobbing, sorrowing and grieving, weeping and moaning, and pouring out all the feelings he needs to express in words. He will therefore be determined never to put himself through anything like that again, now that his own experience has taught him just how terrible are the consequences of sinful disobedience. He has learned that it is far more harmful than any deadly poison, than any beast of prey, than any blazing fire or the cutting edge of any sword. He has also learned that the true believer *[muʾmin]* must not let himself be stung twice by a scorpion from the same hole, so he flees out of sheer necessity from sinful disobedience in all its forms, just as he would flee from those physically obvious dangers and perils.

In all forms of sinful disobedience there lies the risk of absolute damnation *[halāk kullī]*, while eternal salvation *[salāma abadiyya]* means blissful well-being not only in this world but also in the life hereafter, so if only sins had never been created and had never come to be! Many a moment of passion has brought a long period of grief in its wake, has been the cause of a terrible disease, has brought a long life to a disastrous conclusion, and has even condemned an entire nation to the Fire of Hell.

As for the clear sense of purpose *[qaṣd]* that is generated by the experience of remorse, along with the strong determination *[ʿazm]* we have just been discussing, it may be defined as the wish and intention to make amends *[tadāruk]*. One aspect of this relates to the immediate present, inasmuch as the remorseful penitent feels obliged to desist forthwith from every forbidden thing *[maḥẓūr]* with which he has been and continues to be involved, and to discharge every religious duty that is incumbent upon him at the present moment. A second aspect of it relates to the past, since he also feels obliged to make amends for previous omissions. Then there is a third aspect, which relates to the future, for he recognizes that he must persevere henceforth until death in the practice of worshipful obedience, and in refraining from sinful disobedience.

As far as the aspect relating to the past is concerned, the following requirements must be met by the penitent who genuinely wishes to make amends: He must begin by casting his mind back to the day when he first reached the age of puberty and experienced proof of his sexual maturity *[iḥtilām]*.[178] Then he must make a thorough survey of his life from that time on, year by year, month by month, day by day, hour by hour, and breath by breath, checking to see where and when he failed to perform certain acts of worshipful obedience correctly, and where and when he was guilty of perpetrating certain sins of disobedience.

Let us start by considering some instances where acts of worshipful obedience *[ṭā'āt]* have either been omitted altogether or have been inadequately performed:

1. In the case of the Islāmic ritual prayer *[ṣalāt]*, the need to make amends may be due to the fact that a particular ritual prayer was totally omitted by the person concerned. It may also be due to his having performed the ritual prayer without observing its necessary preconditions *[sharā'iṭ]* and without including all its essential elements *[arkān]*.[179] For instance:

(a) He may have performed the ritual prayer without first performing the ritual ablution *[wuḍū']*.

(b) He may have performed the ritual ablution, but done so imperfectly, through neglecting either a basic prerequisite, like the formulation of the intention *[niyya]*, or some of the necessary elements *[wājibāt]*, such as rinsing out the mouth *[maḍmaḍa]*,[180] snuffing water up the nostrils *[istinshāq]*, and washing the face as well as certain other parts of the body.

[178] The term *iḥtilām* refers specifically to the involuntary emission of seminal fluid during a dream.

[179] The necessary preconditions *[sharā'iṭ]* and basic essentials *[arkān]* of the ritual prayer are listed and discussed in Vol. 1, pp. 8–13.

[180] The full definition of the term *maḍmaḍa* is "moving water all around inside the mouth, then spitting it out and ejecting it."

(c) He may have performed the ritual prayer in an article of clothing that was stained with a foul impurity *[najis]*, in one made of silk *[ḥarīr]*, or in one acquired by illegal means *[ghaṣb]*; or he may have performed it on land acquired by usurpation *[arḍ maghṣūba]*.

The penitent is required to make up for all the ritual prayers he ever omitted or performed defectively, from the time he reached puberty *[bulūgh]* right up to the moment of his repentance *[tawba]*. First of all, he must concentrate on making up for those that are classed as obligatory *[farā'iḍ]*. He must devote himself continuously to the performance of compensatory prayers, interrupting the process only when he would otherwise miss the period of time prescribed for one of the obligatory prayers of the current day. At this point he is obliged to perform the prayer in question as a present duty *[adā']*, but then he must immediately apply himself again to the task of making up for past omissions, continuing in this fashion until he has compensated for them all.

If other worshippers gather in his presence, he should join them when they pray as a congregation *[jamā'a]*, while formulating the intention that his own prayer is to be one of compensation *[qaḍā']*. He should then go on praying in his usual manner, until the period of time for praying together with the Imām has almost expired, at which point he should perform the currently due prayer on his own, as a present duty. The advantage of following this procedure is that it serves to ensure the correct sequence in the performance of compensatory worship.

This is a necessary requirement *[wājib]* according to our doctrine,[181] [rather than an absolute obligation], which means that if the penitent does formulate the intention, when joining the congregational prayer led by the Imām, to perform that prayer as a present duty, he will be treated with leniency and granted a dispensation from having to repeat that particular prayer. Nevertheless, the procedure first mentioned is really the proper course, especially for one who has previously been a mixer *[mukhliṭ]* in his religious life. Allāh (Exalted is He) is referring to such people when He tells us:

> And [there are] others who have acknowledged their faults. They mixed a righteous action with another that was bad. It may be that Allāh will relent toward them. Allāh is indeed All-Forgiving, All-Compassionate. (9:102)

[181] When he uses the expression *'indanā* [in our opinion; according to our doctrine], the author (may Allāh be well pleased with him) is no doubt referring to the doctrine of the Ḥanbalī school *[madhhab]* of Islāmic jurisprudence *[fiqh]*.

When a person is a mixer, he is sometimes influenced predominantly by faith *[īmān]*, and his behavior is quite excellent as long as that is the case. He is diligent in performing his ritual prayer *[ṣalāt]*, in keeping the fast, and in guarding against causes of defilement and things forbidden by the sacred law *[shar']*. He treats his religion *[dīn]* with the utmost care and respect. At other times, however, he gets carried away by mischief, with the result that Satan causes him to stumble and slip.

Whenever this happens, he is likely to perform his ritual prayer in a state of impurity, and to become quite lax in his attitude toward its preconditions *[sharā'iṭ]*, its basic essentials *[arkān]* and its necessary elements *[wājibāt]*.[182] He may attend to some of these requirements, while forgetting about the rest. He may perform the ritual prayer one day, and then skip it altogether for the next few days, or he may perform one or two of the daily prayers, and skip the rest of the five that are obligatory.

In order to make amends, therefore, the penitent who has been such a mixer must begin by making a very serious effort to examine his personal record in matters of this kind.

Provided that he can review his performance of a particular religious duty, and can feel certain beyond any doubt that he attended to every element of it—fully and completely—in a manner permitted by the sacred law *[shar']*, there will be one obligation at least for which he does not have to make up, although he will still have to make up for all the rest. If he is really looking after his own best interests, however, he will be committed to judging his own conduct by the most rigorous standards, and he will therefore decide to make up for absolutely everything.

This is indeed a wise precaution, a good investment for the benefit of his own soul in the life hereafter, an expiation *[kaffāra]* and atonement *[tarqī']* for all the offenses with which he will be charged on the Day of Resurrection, and a passport to high levels in the Garden of Paradise, assuming that he dies in a state of repentance *[tawba]*, true to Islām and faithful to the Sunna [the noble example set by the Prophet (Allāh bless him and give him peace)].

As we have explained, the remorseful penitent must first of all make up for omissions and shortcomings in the performance of those religious

[182] The nine necessary elements *[wājibāt]* of the ritual prayer *[ṣālāt]* are listed and discussed in Vol. 1, p. 14.

duties that are classed as obligatory *[farāʾiḍ]*. Once he has completed this task, he may find that Allāh has deferred his appointment with death and granted him a respite; that He has accepted him as fit for His service, approved him for His worshipful obedience, and established him therein; that He has included him among those worthy of His love; that He has delivered him from error; that He has extricated him from the companionship of Satan and from allegiance to him, as well as from addiction to his own whims and passions and the gratification of his lower self *[nafs]*, and that He has thereby caused him to turn his back on his interest in this world, and directed him toward his interest in the hereafter.

If such be the case, he must set about making up for omissions and shortcomings in the performance of those religious duties that are classed as firmly established customary practices *[sunan muʾakkada]*, including those that normally form part of every ritual prayer *[ṣalāt]*,[183] along the lines we have described in connection with the strictly obligatory duties *[farāʾiḍ]*.

Then, once he has dealt with the firmly established customary practices *[sunan muʾakkada]* connected with the obligatory ritual prayers, the penitent should devote the same kind of attention to recommended but noncompulsory observances, such as the prayers called *tahajjud*,[184] the prayer of night vigil *[ṣalāt al-lail]*, and the recitation of litanies *[awrād]*,[185] which we shall be discussing toward the end of this book, if Allāh (Exalted is He) so wills.

2. In the case of the Ramaḍān fast *[ṣawm]*, the need to make amends may be due to the fact that it was not kept during a period of travel or sickness.

Other possible reasons are that the person concerned once broke the fast for some deliberate purpose [before the normal time for breaking fast], even though he was in his place of residence at the time, or that

[183] See Vol. 1, pp. 14 and 15.

[184] The term *tahajjud* is sometimes synonymous with *ṣalāt al-lail* [the prayer of night vigil]. In the present context, however, since the latter is mentioned separately, *tahajjud* probably refers to the voluntary prayers performed after the compulsory prayer of late evening *[ʿishāʾ]*.

[185] Etymologically, the term *wird* [plural: *awrād*] means "to go down to a watering place." In the context of Islamic worship, it refers to a definite time of day or night devoted to private prayer (over and above the five daily prayers), as well as to the 'litany' recited on this occasion. In its simplest form, the *wird* consists of four cycles *[rakaʿāt]* of prayer, with the recitation of one seventh of the Qurʾān.

one night, whether deliberately or because of absentmindedness, he neglected to formulate the intention *[niyya]* to keep the fast during the following day.[186]

Whatever the reason may have been, the penitent is obliged to make up for all his omissions. If he is in any doubt, he must make a thorough review of his past performance in this area, in an effort to resolve the uncertainty. Then he should make up for any omission of which he is reasonably sure. He may assume that the rest of his fasting was properly performed, unless he prefers to take the most prudent and cautious approach, in which case it will be better for him to repeat all his previous fasts without exception.

He should reckon from the time when he reached puberty *[bulūgh]* right up until the moment of his repentance *[tawba]*. Then, if he counts ten years in the interval between those two events, he should fast for ten extra months. If twelve years have elapsed, he should fast for a whole extra year, treating every month of the year as if it were the month of Ramaḍān.

3. In the case of the alms-due *[zakāt]*, the penitent must base his reckoning on the total value of all his property assets.[187] He must also count however many years have elapsed since he first acquired ownership of any part of that property, not just since the time he reached puberty and came to be regarded as a person of sound mind, because payment of the alms-due *[zakāt]* is incumbent on the juvenile *[ṣabī]* and even on the insane [*majnūn]* according to our interpretation of Islāmic doctrine.[188] He will therefore be obliged to produce the whole of the amount for which he is liable, and to pay it over to those legally entitled to receive it, such as the destitute *[fuqarāʾ]* and the indigent *[masākīn]*, to mention only two of the eight classes of beneficiaries mentioned in the Qurʾān.[189]

If he has already paid the full amount due for certain years, although he is still behind with his payments for other years, he must do the necessary accounting and then pay whatever happens to be outstanding.

[186] This subject is treated at length in Vol. 1, pp. 21–23.

[187] For a detailed treatment of the alms-due *[zakāt]*, see Vol. 1, pp. 17–19.

[188] See note [181] above.

[189] The eight classes are mentioned in the following Qurʾānic verse *[āya]*:

> The alms are only for the poor and the needy, and those who work to collect them, and those whose hearts are to be reconciled, and to free the slaves and the debtors, and for the Cause of Allāh, and [for] the wayfarers: a duty imposed by Allāh. Allāh is All-Knowing, All-Wise. (9:60)

He is under no strict obligation to overcompensate for what he has properly discharged in the past, as we have explained above in connection with fasting *[ṣawm]* and ritual prayer *[ṣalāt]*.

4. In the case of the Pilgrimage *[Ḥajj]*, there may have been a point in the penitent's life when all the preconditions for its performance had been satisfactorily accounted for,[190] as far as his personal situation was concerned, so that it actually became his religious duty to prepare for the undertaking and embark upon it. Let us suppose, however, that he dillied and dallied, neglecting the opportunity until he became impoverished. For a short period of time, he found himself in a situation where the necessary preconditions could no longer be fulfilled, but now—since he has recovered his capacity—he must once again regard it as his duty to leave home and set out for Mecca in order to perform the Pilgrimage *[Ḥajj]*.

Even if he cannot find the money for the journey, he is under the obligation to embark upon it, penniless though he may be, as long as he is physically capable of traveling away from home. If he really cannot manage to do it without any money, he must find some lawful means *[ḥalāl]* by which to earn enough to pay for provisions and a camel to ride. If he cannot earn enough, he should ask people to treat him as a would-be pilgrim, and therefore as an appropriate recipient of part of their obligatory alms-due *[zakāt]* and their voluntary charitable donations *[ṣadaqāt]*, because the Pilgrimage *[Ḥajj]* comes under the heading of the Cause *[Sabīl]* according to our interpretation of the Islāmic doctrine. The Cause of Allāh is one of the eight categories [of beneficiaries entitled to this kind of support], as He Himself has told us (Almighty and Glorious is He).[191]

So, if he should die before discharging this obligation, our would-be penitent will die a disobedient sinner, because he failed to seize the opportunity to perform the Pilgrimage *[Ḥajj]*, which is a religious duty that must be performed at the earliest opportunity, according to our interpretation of the Islāmic doctrine,[192] based on the saying of the Prophet (Allāh bless him and give him peace):

> If a person can find provisions for the journey and a riding camel to transport him to the House [of Allāh], yet he does not perform the Pilgrimage, he may as well die as a Jew or a Christian.

[190] For a detailed treatment of the Pilgrimage *[Ḥajj]*, see Vol. 1, pp. 26–46.

[191] See note [181] above.

[192] See note [189] above.

All of the foregoing is intended to emphasize the importance of respect for the commandment of Allāh, to encourage the utmost care in observing it, and to inspire fear at the prospect of missing the opportunity to carry it out.

In addition to all that we have said about making amends for omissions and shortcomings in the basic religious duties of ritual prayer *[ṣalāt]*, fasting *[ṣawm]*, alms-due *[zakāt]* and Pilgrimage *[Ḥajj]*, we should also advise the penitent that he is obliged to settle any outstanding acts of atonement *[kaffārāt]* and solemn vows *[nudhūr]*, and that he should proceed with prudent caution in these matters, as we have explained elsewhere.[193]

Now that we have considered how the penitent needs to go about making amends for all the acts of worshipful obedience *[ṭāʿāt]* that he has either omitted altogether or performed inadequately, let us consider how he should make amends for all the acts of sinful disobedience *[maʿāṣī]* of which he has ever been guilty.

Where acts of sinful disobedience are concerned, what is required of the penitent is that he conduct a painstaking self-examination, starting from the time when he first reached puberty *[bulūgh]*, in the course of which he must review the behavior of his faculty of hearing, his faculty of sight, his tongue, his hands, his feet, his genitals, and all the other limbs and organs of his physical body. Then, once he has taken a really close look at every day and every moment he has lived through since that time, he must compile for his personal reference a detailed register *[dīwān]* of all the acts of sinful disobedience he has ever committed, so that he can study them all with care, taking stock of the minor transgressions *[ṣaghāʾir]* as well as the major offenses *[kabāʾir]* amongst them.

He must also make the effort to remember each and every one of them in context, by reminding himself of the companions who were with him at the time and who participated with him in the perpetration of those sinful acts, by recalling the places where he yielded to temptation, and by revisiting those situations in which he assumed that he would be concealed from prying eyes, forgetting about those eyes that never sleep

[193] For instance, in Vol. 1, p. 97, where we read:

> Obedience to parents cannot go so far as to include the abandonment of obligatory religious duties *[farāʾiḍ]*, such as the testimony of Islām *[ḥujjat al-islām]*, the five ritual prayers *[aṣ-ṣalāwāt al-khams]*, payment of the alms-due *[zakāt]*, an act of atonement *[kaffāra]* or the fulfillment of a solemn vow *[nadhr]*.

and never glance away from him, not even for the split second it takes for a human eye to blink:

> And yet over you there are watchers, Noble Recorders, who know whatever you do. (82:10–12) Not a word does he utter, without there being an observer at the ready by his side. (50:18)

He had obviously forgotten all about these noble guardian angels, but his heedlessness did not alter the fact that:

> He has attendant angels ranged before him and behind him, watching over him as instructed by the commandment of Allāh. (13:11)

It could not alter the fact that they are always there to record all the things that he does, even the breaths that he breathes, so that he can be called to account for them all [on the Day of Resurrection]. Needless to say, he had also forgotten about the One who knows the secret and that which is more deeply hidden still,[194] who knows the inner content of His servants' breasts,[195] and is All-Aware *[Khabīr]* of what His creatures try to conceal and what they reveal in public.[196]

Next, the penitent must check through all the entries he has made in his register of sins, noting which of them represent violations of the right *[ḥaqq]* of Allāh (Exalted is He), and of His right alone, as distinct from those which also constitute acts of wrongdoing and injustice *[maẓālim]* in the sphere of human rights. The distinction between these two categories is very important, so let us now consider each of them in turn:

1. Sins that violate the right *[ḥaqq]* of Allāh (Exalted is He).

If sins belong in this category, making amends for them is entirely a matter between the sinner and Allāh (Exalted is He). Offenses of this kind include the following:

(a) Adultery and fornication *[zinā]*.

(b) Imbibing intoxicating liquor *[shurb al-khamr]*.

(c) Listening to distracting musical entertainments *[samāʿ al-malāhī]*.

(d) Staring at a person of the opposite sex who is neither one's spouse nor a relative within the prohibited degrees of marriage *[an-naẓar ilā ghairi maḥram]*.

194 In the Qur'ān, Allāh says of Himself (Almighty and Glorious is He):

> He surely knows the secret and that which is yet more deeply hidden *[fa-innahu yaʿlamu's-sirra wa akhfā]*. (20:7)

195 Allāh is indeed Aware of the hidden content of the breasts *[inna'llāha ʿAlīmun bi-dhāti'ṣ-ṣudūr]*. (3:119)

196 Allāh most certainly knows what they try to keep secret and what they publicly proclaim *[lā jarama anna'llāha yaʿlamu mā yusirrūna wa mā yuʿlinūn]*. (16:23)

(e) Sitting in the mosque *[masjid]* while one is in a state of ritual impurity *[junub]*.

(f) Touching a copy of the Qur'ān *[muṣḥaf]* without having cleansed oneself first by performing the ritual ablution *[wuḍū']*.

(g) Adopting any heretical innovation *[bid'a]* as if it were an article of faith.

In cases like these, repentance *[tawba]* is expressed through remorse *[nadam]* and regret *[taḥassur]*, and by offering apologies *[i'tidhār]* to Allāh (Almighty and Glorious is He). The penitent must make a careful assessment of the scale and scope of each offense, in terms of its frequency and duration. He must then endeavor to perform a good deed commensurate with each act of sinful disobedience, until the good deeds added to his credit are sufficient in every respect to cancel out all the bad deeds in his account. This is based on the words of Allāh (Exalted is He):

> Surely the good deeds will drive away the evil deeds. (11:114)

In order to emphasize the point, we may also quote the saying of the Prophet (Allāh bless him and give him peace):

> Be aware of your duty to Allāh wherever you may be, and always follow a bad deed with a good deed in order to cancel it out.

For each bad deed, therefore, the way to ensure atonement *[takfīr]* is by means of a good deed of approximately the same type. In other words, the closer the comparison between the act of expiation *[kaffāra]* and the corresponding act of sinful disobedience, the more appropriate the act of expiation will be. This point can best be made clear by providing a number of examples:

(i) For the sin of imbibing intoxicating liquor *[shurb al-khamr]*, the most appropriate atonement the penitent could make would be to offer, as a donation to some charitable cause *[taṣadduq]*, whatever lawful beverage *[sharāb ḥalāl]* he himself prefers, the one he personally considers to be the tastiest of them all.

(ii) For the sin of listening to distracting musical entertainments *[samā' al-malāhī]*, what atonement could be more appropriate than listening to the recitation of the Qur'ān, the traditions *[aḥādīth]* of Allāh's Messenger (Allāh bless him and give him peace), and the stories of the righteous *[ḥikāyāt aṣ-ṣāliḥīn]*?

(iii) For the sin of sitting in the mosque *[masjid]* while in a state of ritual impurity *[junub]*, the most suitable form of expiation would be to spend some time there in a state of seclusion *[iʿtikāf]*,[197] combined with concentrated devotion to various practices of religious worship *[ʿibāda]*.[198]

(iv) For the sin committed by touching a copy of the Qurʾān *[muṣḥaf]* while in a state of ritual uncleanliness, the penitent could make atonement by approaching the volume with veneration, by frequently reading the text of the Qurʾān recorded between its covers, by frequently studying what it teaches on the subject of ritual purity *[ṭahāra]*, by learning all the lessons it has to impart, by heeding all the advice it has to offer, by treating it with great respect, and by putting its teachings into practice. He would also do well to make a copy of the Qurʾān in his own handwriting, then present it to the mosque as a pious endowment *[waqf]*, so that it will always be available for his fellow Muslims to read.

(v) Under this same heading, we must also give examples of the forms of expiation required in order to atone for acts of wrongdoing and injustice *[maẓālim]* committed against one's fellow human beings. In offenses of this nature there is always an element of sinful disobedience and serious violation of the right *[ḥaqq]* of Allāh (Exalted is He), since He has forbidden His creatures to wrong one another, just as He has forbidden adultery and fornication *[zinā]* and the drinking of intoxicating liquor *[shurb al-khamr]*. To the extent that his misconduct has amounted to a violation of the right *[ḥaqq]* of Allāh (Exalted is He), the penitent must therefore make amends *[tadāruk]* through remorse *[nadam]* and regret *[taḥassur]*, by committing himself to refrain from any repetition of such misconduct in the future, and by performing good works in order to atone for his previous offenses.

When it comes to the matter of atonement *[takfīr]* for the injuries he has inflicted upon other people, the penitent must take steps to promote the welfare of his victims. He must also offer prayers of supplication *[duʿāʾ]* on their behalf. If it should be the case that one of his victims is no longer alive at the time of his repentance, he can still atone by begging Allāh to have mercy on his departed soul

197 Under normal circumstances, where expiation is not the main issue, the practice of seclusion *[iʿtikāf]*—in a place of worship *[masjid]* where there is room for ritual prayer in congregation *[jamāʿa]*—is recommended for one who is keeping the fast.

198 See Vol. 1, pp. 24 and 25.

[bi't-taraḥḥum ʿalaih],[199] as well as by making efforts to promote the welfare of his children and his other legal heirs.

The foregoing applies when the injuries were inflicted through direct verbal abuse or physical assault against the persons concerned. In order to atone for the wrongful seizure *[ghaṣb]* of other people's property, insofar as this also represents a violation of the right *[ḥaqq]* of Allāh (Exalted is He), the penitent must make donations to charitable causes *[taṣadduq]* from whatever possessions he has acquired by lawful means *[ḥalāl]*.

The penitent may be guilty of having damaged the good reputations *[aʿrāḍ]* of other people. For example, he may have spoken ill of them behind their backs, spread slanderous rumors about them, and defamed their characters. In cases of this sort, and assuming of course that the victims of his slanderous attacks are in fact devoutly religious people and faithful followers of the Sunna of the Prophet (Allāh bless him and give him peace) *[ahl ad-dīn wa's-sunna]*, the penitent should make atonement by seizing every opportunity, at gatherings and meetings attended by his colleagues and peers, to extol their virtues and proclaim the good qualities he knows them to possess.

For manslaughter and homicide *[qatl an-nufūs]*, insofar as the unlawful taking of human life represents a violation of the right *[ḥaqq]* of Allāh (Exalted is He), the form of atonement required is the emancipation of slaves *[ʿitāq ar-riqāb]*, because giving a slave his freedom is tantamount to restoring him to life. The slave is actually a missing person *[mafqūd]*, a nonentity *[maʿdūm]* as far as his own individuality is concerned. As Allāh (Almighty and Glorious is He) has said:

> Allāh has coined a similitude: [on the one hand] a slave possessed by his master, having no control over anything, and [on the other hand] someone upon whom We have bestowed a fair provision from Us, so that he now expends from it both secretly and openly. Are they equal? Praise be to Allāh! But then most of them do not know. (16:75)

The condition of the slave is such that his entire being is subject to his master's control, including all his actions, all his movements and all his situations. The sole purpose of his existence is to serve his owner, to whom he belongs absolutely. To emancipate him is therefore to give him a personal existence and a life of his own.

[199] That is to say, by offering the invocation "*Raḥimahu'llāh* [may Allāh have mercy upon him]" whenever he mentions the name of the deceased person, and whenever he hears it mentioned by someone else.

The point would seem to be that the murderer *[qātil]* has annihilated one slave, a servant of Allāh (Exalted is He) who would otherwise still be capable of worshipful obedience to Him, and since he has thereby violated a right *[ḥaqq]* of His, he has been commanded to effect the resurrection of another slave just like him, another servant of Allāh (Exalted is He).

For this to be realized in practice, the slave must be emancipated from the bondage of slavery *[riqq al-ʿubūdiyya]*, so that he can be free to function by and for himself, without let or hindrance. Thus the act of annihilation *[iʿdām]* is offset by the act of bringing into being *[ījād]*.

Before we move on to our next topic, let us bear in mind that we have thus far been discussing the subject of atonement only insofar as it relates to violation of the right *[ḥaqq]* of Allāh (Exalted is He).

2. Atonement for the violation of human rights *[ḥaqq al-ʿibād]*.

As far as violations of human rights *[ḥaqq al-ʿibād]* are concerned, we have only four categories to consider, namely: (a) cases involving persons *[nufūs]* who have been caused to suffer the loss of life or limb; (b) cases where pecuniary resources and property assets *[amwāl]* have been usurped; (c) cases where good reputations *[aʿrāḍ]* have been besmirched; and (d) cases where people have been badly affected in their hearts *[qulūb]*, but where the injury was strictly confined to the realm of the inner feelings.

(a) Within the category of cases involving persons who have been caused to suffer the loss of life or limb, the particular offense for which the penitent needs to atone may be an accidental homicide *[qatl khaṭaʾan]*. If such be the case, his penance can only be accomplished through payment of the blood money *[diya]*, which must be handed over directly to those relatives of the victim who are entitled to receive it, or to a trustee appointed to act on their behalf, or to the Imām [leader of the Islāmic Community].

Under normal circumstances, the responsibility will not be discharged until the blood money *[diya]* has actually reached the ultimate beneficiaries, whether the payment comes from the killer's clan *[ʿāqila]* [200] or from the [public treasury administered by] the Imām. Their claim may

[200] The term *ʿāqila* is applied to those relatives who are traditionally required to band together in order to raise the blood money *[diya]* on behalf of a clan member who has committed unintentional homicide. They must be relatives descended from one common father.

be rendered null and void, however, in a case where the killer has no clansmen [*ʿāqila*] to make the payment on his behalf, and where there are no funds available in the public treasury [*bait al-māl*], because even though the killer may be personally capable of paying the necessary sum, his legal obligation is limited, in the absence of an *ʿāqila*, to the emancipation of a believing slave [*ʿitq raqaba muʾmina*]. The better course would be for him to pay the blood money [*diya*] as a voluntary gesture, in which case he would definitely be acting of his own free will, since payment of the blood money [*diya*] is strictly incumbent upon no one apart from the *ʿāqila*. According to our interpretation of the Islāmic doctrine, which is undoubtedly the correct interpretation, it is not permissible to exact payment from the killer in person.[201]

If the penitent is guilty of intentional homicide [*qatl ʿamdan*], however, the only way for him to clear his conscience is by exposing himself to the possibility of retaliation [*qiṣāṣ*].[202] The same is also true in a case of intentional but less than fatal wounding, provided that the mutilation was inflicted on a part of the victim's body such that equal retaliation is a feasible operation.[203]

If the homicidal attack proved fatal to his victim, the repentant killer will have to discuss the consequences with the victim's closest legal heir

[201] ***Author's note:*** There are some, however, who maintain that payment of the blood money [*diya*] is actually incumbent on the killer in such a case [i.e., in a case where he is personally capable of paying the necessary sum] despite the fact that he has no clansmen to act as his *ʿāqila*, and they hold the view that legal action may be taken to exact it from him.

This is the doctrine adopted by the school [*madhhab*] of ash-Shāfiʿī (may Allāh bestow His mercy upon him), on the grounds that payment of the blood money [*diya*] is incumbent on the killer himself in the first instance, although some of the responsibility may subsequently be assumed by the *ʿāqila*, for the sake of lightening his burden, lending him their support and sharing his obligation to make reparation, as is quite proper in view of the relationship that exists between them in terms of mutual rights of inheritance [*tawāruth*].

In a case like this, where there is no *ʿāqila* to be taken into account, jurists of the Shāfiʿī school will argue that the full liability must rest with the killer himself, especially when he is supposed to be in a state of repentance [*tawba*], determined to separate himself from all forms of injustice [*maẓālim*], intent on leading a life of piety [*tawarruʿ*], and eager to atone for any offenses by which he may have violated the rights of his fellow human beings [*ḥuqūq al-ādamiyyīn*].

[202] The Islāmic law of retaliation [*qiṣāṣ*] is based on the verse [*āya*] of the Qurʾān in which Allāh (Almighty and Glorious is He) has told us:

> And We prescribed for them therein [in the Torah]: "A life for a life, an eye for an eye, a nose for a nose, an ear for an ear, a tooth for a tooth, and for wounds retaliation." But if anyone forgoes it as a freewill offering, that shall be an expiation for him. (5:45)

[203] Equal retaliation is a feasible operation if the assailant has caused the victim to lose a foot, for example, or his nose. Cases where retaliation is not a feasible operation include those that would involve the breaking of any bones apart from the teeth.

[wārith]. If it resulted in less than fatal injury, on the other hand, he must hold that discussion with his victim in person. Perhaps the parties concerned will be disposed to waive their right to exact retaliation, in which case, if they simply decide to grant him an outright pardon *[ʿafw]*, the case will be closed without further ado. If they offer him a pardon in exchange for a financial consideration, he will have acquitted himself of his liability as soon as he has paid them the stipulated amount.

In a case of intentional homicide where the identity of the murderer has hitherto been unknown to anyone but himself, the penitent killer is obliged to confess his guilt to the *walī ad-dam* [the guardian of the blood, i.e., the relative of the victim who is entitled to exact retaliation], and he must be prepared to let this person be the judge as to whether he should live or die. The *walī ad-dam* may then grant him an unconditional pardon, if he wishes to do so, or he may kill him, if he chooses to go to the other extreme, or he may prefer to take the middle course and accept a financial compensation from him in exchange for a pardon. It is not permissible, in a case like this, for the penitent killer to keep his identity concealed, because repentance in the abstract *[mujarrad at-tawba]* is not enough to relieve him of the burden of guilt.

A different approach is called for, however, if the penitent has killed a multitude of victims at various times and in widely scattered places, especially if it all happened long ago, so that he does not even know exactly how many people he has killed—let alone who their executors *[awliyāʾ]* might be. In a case like this, the penitent must make sure that his repentance is as good as it could possibly be, and that his conduct is correspondingly improved. He must impose upon his own lower self *[nafs]* the legal penalty *[ḥadd]* prescribed by Allāh, by subjecting it to a variety of strenuous exertions and punishing tasks. He must extend forgiveness to those who treat him unjustly and do him harm. He must pay for the emancipation of slaves. He must make financial contributions to charitable causes. He must perform many supererogatory acts of worship *[nawāfil]*. He must do all these good deeds so that, on the Day of Resurrection, he will be able to distribute among his victims the spiritual reward he has earned in the process, giving them all their shares in proportion to their various rightful claims *[ḥuqūq]* against him. His own salvation will thereby be secured, and he will be admitted into the Garden of Paradise through the mercy of Allāh (Exalted is He), whose mercy *[raḥma]* embraces all and everything, for He is the Most Merciful of the merciful *[Arḥam ar-rāḥimīn]*.

It is therefore quite pointless, in a case like this, to insist on a detailed discussion of all the crimes the penitent has ever committed. There is nothing to be gained by listing the various types of homicide, cases of wounding *[jirāḥāt]*, and acts of highway robbery *[qaṭʿ aṭ-ṭarīq]*, since he will never be able to trace the victims—or their authorized representatives—in order to satisfy their claims or to seek exoneration from them. His time and energy will be far more productively spent on the course of action we have outlined above.

The same principle should be applied in cases where the penitent has been guilty of adultery and fornication *[zinā]*; of drinking intoxicating liquor *[shurb al-khamr]*; of theft *[sariqa]* from an owner whose identity is unknown to him; of highway robbery *[qaṭʿ aṭ-ṭarīq]* committed against a victim whose identity is likewise unknown to him; or of unlawful contact with a woman—short of complete sexual intercourse *[dūna'l-farj]*, but sufficient to incur either the penalty *[ḥadd]* prescribed by Allāh or the discretionary punishment *[taʿzīr]* imposed by the court in less serious cases.

This statement is based on the fact that the penitent is under no obligation to prove the validity of his repentance by exposing himself to disgrace, discarding his cover, and inviting the Imām or the judge *[ḥākim]* to impose on him the legal penalties prescribed by Islāmic law *[ḥudūd]*.

Far from resorting to such inappropriate behavior, he should keep his faults modestly concealed from the eyes of his fellow creatures, by availing himself of the screen provided by Allāh (Exalted is He). Whenever the issue is one that needs to be resolved between himself and Allāh, it is only to Allāh (Almighty and Glorious is He) that he must turn in repentance. He should therefore keep himself fully occupied with strenuous exertions of various kinds, such as fasting during the hours of daylight, cutting back on his consumption of goods that are ordinarily permissible *[mubāḥ]* and reducing his enjoyment of worldly pleasures, keeping vigil by night *[qiyām al-lail]*, reading the Qurʾān, frequently repeating the glorification *[tasbīḥ]*[204] of Allāh, and

[204] By saying: "*Subḥāna'llāh* [Glory be to Allāh]."

generally cultivating a pious lifestyle *[tawarruʿ]*. As the Prophet (Allāh bless him and give him peace) has told us:

> If a person has committed any of these foul abominations, let him avail himself of the screen provided by Allāh (Exalted is He). Let him not disclose his record sheet *[ṣafḥa]* for us to see, for if anyone does reveal his record sheet to us, we shall have no choice but to impose upon him the penalties *[ḥudūd]* prescribed by Allāh.

If a particular penitent chooses to reject this good advice of ours, and decides to bring his own case to the notice of the relevant authority *[wālī]*, who must then impose the legal penalty *[ḥadd]* upon him, he will have brought the inevitable outcome upon himself. This will not affect the validity of his repentance, which will still be acceptable in the sight of Allāh. He will be relieved of any further liability for his offense. He will be cleansed of his sin, and the blot will have disappeared from his record.

(b) Cases where pecuniary resources and property assets *[amwāl]* have been usurped.

Cases of this type include the misappropriation of any item of material value *[māl]* belonging to a fellow human being, whether by extortion *[ghaṣb]*, theft *[sariqa]*, highway robbery *[qaṭʿ aṭ-ṭarīq]*, breach of trust *[khiyāna]* in connection with an asset held in the form of a deposit *[wadīʿa]* or a loan *[ʿāriya]*, or any transaction which involves some kind of deceptive misrepresentation *[talbīs]*. Examples of the latter include putting counterfeit money into circulation *[tarwīj zāʾif]*,[205] concealing a defect in an article offered for sale, and underpaying an employee—or even cheating him out of his wages altogether.

The penitent is obliged to undertake a thorough self-examination, with a view to detecting all such offenses of which he has been guilty at any time during his entire life, not only during the period since he reached puberty *[bulūgh]*. He is responsible, of course, for anything of the kind that may have occurred since he reached physical and mental maturity, or in other words, since he attained the age of discretion *[tamyīz]*, but he also bears responsibility in these matters for his conduct at an even earlier stage. He must therefore look back and review the period when he was still a minor in the care of his guardian *[walī]* and

[205] The term *zāʾif* is applied to gold or silver coins that contain an adulterating alloy. Some say that such coins are rejected by officers of the state treasury, but that they are less seriously defective than those termed *bahraj*, which are also rejected by merchants and traders. (See: E.W. Lane, *Arabic-English Lexicon*, art. Z–Y–F.)

custodian *[waṣī]*, with whose property his own estate may well have come to be mixed up. It may be that his guardian considered this a trivial matter, and that he never thought twice about it, for the simple reason that he lacked any sense of justice and viewed his religion *[dīn]* with reckless disdain. In a case like this, the property of the minor would inevitably become entangled in the unlawfulness *[ḥarām]* of the situation, sometimes due to the behavior of the minor himself, and at other times due to the misconduct of his custodian.

Now that he is an adult, the penitent must therefore reexamine the manner in which his property was handled while he was still a minor. Then, as soon as he has completed this review, he must restore whatever is due to the rightful owners, thereby ridding his personal estate of all those dubious assets *[shubuhāt]* and cleansing it of all those elements of illegality *[ḥarām]*.

In order to ensure that his repentance is complete, the penitent must call himself to account for all the smallest details, the tiniest grains and atoms, from the day when he first committed an offense right up to and including the day of his repentance *[tawba]*. He must do this in good time, before death comes and catches him unawares, without forewarning. He must do it before the Resurrection takes him by surprise, with no opportunity for gaining any merit or setting any record straight. If he leaves it too late, he may ask, but he will hear no answer; he may feel remorse, but remorse *[nadam]* will do him no good; he may beg for a second chance, but he will not be given a second chance;[206] he may try to apologize, but his apologies will not be accepted; he may ask for a respite, but he will not be granted a respite; and he may plead for intercession, but there will be no intercession on his behalf.

This is all he can expect, since he wasted his opportunities while he was still alive; since he behaved with reckless abandon while he was in a state of wakefulness and should have had his wits about him; since he was always on the lookout for some advantage in the affairs of his daily life; since he greedily pursued the satisfaction of his carnal appetites and

[206] An allusion to the Qur'ānic verse *[āya]*:

> And if they ask to be regarded with favor, they are not of those to whom favor can be shown *[wa in yasta'tibū fa-mā hum mina'l-mu'tabīn]*. (41:24)

According to some traditional commentators, this means: "If they ask [their Lord] to grant them the favor of restoring them to the world, He will not do so [for He knows that, if He did restore them to the world, they would return to that which they have been forbidden to do]."

lustful desires; since he followed his whims and passions *[hawā]* and the promptings of his devil *[shaiṭān]*; since he recoiled from obedience to his Lord and from the honor due to Him; since he neglected to heed His call; and since he was always quick to disobey Him and to violate His commandments.

For all these reasons, his reckoning at the Resurrection will be prolonged; his wailing and his lamentation will be very loud indeed; his back will be broken; his head will be bowed; his disgrace and his shame will be very intense; his evidence and his proof will be refuted; his good deeds will be subtracted from his record; his bad deeds will be multiplied; his deals will turn sour and his bankrupt state will become apparent; the wrath of his Lord will descend upon him with great fury and seize him in its grasp; and the guardians *[zabāniya]* of the Fire of Hell will drag him off to face the torment of his Lord, which he has made ready for himself, for he has in fact caused his own ruination and brought about his own destruction. He is thus on an equal footing with as such denizens of the Fire of Hell as Qārūn and Pharaoh and Hāmān.

This warning may sound very grim indeed, but grim it needs to be, since there is no room for easygoing compromise when it comes to making amends for violations of human rights, and to ignore such offenses altogether is entirely out of the question. This is vividly described in the traditional saying *[athar]*:[207]

> [On the Day of Resurrection] the servant [of the Lord] will surely be made to stand trial in the presence of Allāh (Exalted is He). When that moment comes, his good deeds may be of such mountainous proportions that, if they were credited to him in their entirety, he would certainly be numbered among the inhabitants of the Gardens of Paradise.
>
> But the victims of wrongdoing and injustice will also be there to bring their charges against him, and he may be found guilty on a variety of counts. He may have damaged this person's reputation by libel or slander, unlawfully seized that person's property, and subjected yet another person to physical beating.
>
> His good deeds will therefore be whittled away, until he ends up with nothing at all to his credit, at which point the angels will say: "O Lord, his good deeds have all disappeared, but many claimants are still awaiting satisfaction!"
>
> The Lord will then say: "Take some of their bad deeds and throw them into the scale on top of his bad deeds, then give him a slap that will send him reeling into the Fire of Hell." Thus he will go to his doom on account of the bad deeds of others, by way of retaliation.

[207] The term *athar* is often synonymous with *khabar* (see note [176] above). In some contexts, however, a traditional report will be classed as an *athar* if it is generally attributed to a righteous individual from the early period of Islām, but cannot be traced as far back as the Prophet himself (Allāh bless him and give him peace).

By the same token, the victim of wrongdoing *[maẓlūm]* may be saved by a good deed originally credited to the wrongdoer *[ẓālim]*, since the latter must transfer that good deed to his victim's account in compensation for the wrong he inflicted upon him.

According to his wife ʿĀʾisha (may Allāh be well pleased with her), Allāh's Messenger (Allāh bless him and give him peace) once said:

> There are three registers *[dawāwīn]*: (1) a register *[dīwān]* of that which is forgiven by Allāh (Exalted is He); (2) a register of that which Allāh (Exalted is He) does not forgive; and (3) a register from which nothing is ever omitted. As for the register of that which Allāh (Exalted is He) does not forgive, the only item listed therein is the sin of associating partners *[shirk]* with Allāh (Glorious is His Majesty). Allāh (Almighty and Glorious is He) has said:
>
> Whoever attributes partners to Allāh, for him Allāh will surely prohibit entrance to the Garden [of Paradise], and his final abode will be the Fire [of Hell]. (5:72)
>
> As for the register of that which is forgiven by Allāh (Exalted is He), it records the wrong done by the human being to himself, in cases that are strictly between him and his Lord. And as for the register from which nothing is ever omitted, it is the list of wrongs committed by His servants against their fellow human beings.

According to a traditional report that has been handed down to us on the authority of Abū Huraira (may Allāh be well pleased with him), the Prophet (Allāh bless him and give him peace) once asked his Companions: "Do you know which member of my Community will be the one who is bankrupt *[muflis]* on the Day of Resurrection?" To this they replied: "O Messenger of Allāh, according to our understanding, the bankrupt is someone who has neither money nor property to call his own." So the Prophet (Allāh bless him and give him peace) explained:

> The bankrupt member of my Community will be someone who brings his ritual prayer *[ṣalāt]* and his fasting with him on the Day of Resurrection, but who is guilty of defaming this person's reputation, of slanderously accusing this other person of sexual misconduct, of consuming the property that rightfully belonged to this third person, of shedding the blood of this fourth person, and of subjecting this fifth person to a physical beating.
>
> To each of these victims he will have to pay compensation from his stock of good deeds. If his stock of good deeds becomes exhausted, some of their sins will be taken from them and dumped on him, then he will be dumped into the Fire of Hell.

It is clearly most important for the sinner to waste no time in repenting! According to another traditional report, this one transmitted on the authority of Ibn ʿAbbās (may Allāh be well pleased with him and with his father), the Prophet (Allāh bless him and give him peace) once said:

> Doomed to perdition are the procrastinators *[musawwifūn]*, the people who keep saying: "We are going to repent *[sawfa natūbu]*."

Allāh (Almighty and Glorious is He) has told us:

> But the human being would rather press ahead with his wicked conduct.[208] (75:5)

According to the interpretation that has been reported on the authority of Ibn ʿAbbās (may Allāh be well pleased with him and with his father), this means that the human being gives immediate priority to his sins and keeps postponing his repentance.[209] He may go on saying, "I shall repent at some point in the future," until death catches up with him, in which case he will still be on the same wicked course when he has to die.

Luqmān the Wise *[al-Ḥakīm]* said to his son: "O my dear son, do not put off repentance till tomorrow, for death may come and catch you by surprise."

It is therefore necessary for each and everyone to repent when morning breaks and again when the day is done. To quote the saying of Mujāhid[210] (may Allāh bestow His mercy upon him): "If someone does not repent in the morning and then again when evening comes, he must be counted as one of the wrongdoers."

As we have indicated earlier on in this discourse, repentance must be considered from two different points of view.[211] One has to do with the penitent's duty toward his fellow human beings *[ḥaqq al-ʿibād]*, and this is the aspect we have just been discussing. The second has to do with cases where repentance is strictly between you and Allāh (Exalted is He).

[208] The translation given here has been chosen—from among several possible versions—in order to reflect the particular interpretation cited by the author (may Allāh be well pleased with him).

[209] According to some other traditional commentaries, however, this verse *[āya]* of the Qurʾān should be understood to mean: "But the human being prefers to disbelieve in that which is before him [namely the Resurrection, with the reckoning and retribution that must then be faced]." (This interpretation is reflected in Pickthall's translation: "But man would fain deny what is before him.")

[210] Abu 'l-Ḥajjāj Mujāhid ibn Jabr al-Makkī (may Allāh bestow His mercy upon him) was a *tābiʿī* [member of the generation following that of the Companions] and a disciple of Ibn ʿAbbās (may Allāh be well pleased with him and with his father). By the time of his death in A.H. 104, he had come to be regarded as one of the most outstanding scholars in the fields of Islāmic jurisprudence *[fiqh]* and Qurʾānic exegesis *[tafsīr]*.

[211] See pp. 139 and 143 above.

As viewed from this second perspective, repentance is a matter of pleading with the tongue for forgiveness from Allāh (Exalted is He), feeling remorse *[nadam]* in the heart, and conceiving a profound determination never to repeat the acts of sinful disobedience committed against Him in the past.

In the case we are now considering, the penitent must exert himself to even greater lengths, since he needs to make amends for wrongdoing *[ẓulm]* by which the rights of his fellow human beings were violated. He must make every conceivable effort to perform as many good deeds as he possibly can, in order to equip himself for the retaliation that will be inflicted upon him on the Day of Resurrection, for his good deeds will then be taken from him and placed in the scales of his victims. He must strive to ensure that his good deeds are at least equal in number to the acts of wrongdoing he has committed against his fellow human beings, otherwise he will be doomed to perdition because of the bad deeds of other people [from whom they will be taken and charged to his account].

This calls for nothing less than a total, lifelong commitment to the performance of good works, assuming that the time he has left to live is as long as the period spent in wrongdoing. But what if death has set an ambush for him? Perhaps his appointed hour *[ajal]* is near at hand, so that the fatal decree *[maniyya]* could easily snatch him away before the achievement of the aspiration *[umniyya]*, or even before the sincere commitment to the task, the formulation of a genuine intention *[taṣḥīḥ an-niyya]*, and the first step toward purification *[taṣfiyat al-luqma]*.[212] The penitent must therefore set to work without a moment's delay. In order to maximize his effort, he should make written notes of all that he has to attend to, listing the names of his victims one by one. Then he must embark on a tour that may take him through all the four quarters of the globe, through the regions and districts of all the various countries. He must seek out all his victims, and then, whenever he finds them alive, he must either ask for [and obtain] a waiver from them or else satisfy their claims in full. If he cannot find his actual victims, he must approach their legal heirs *[waratha]* and settle accounts with them.

In the course of this whole operation, the penitent must be in constant

[212]Literally, "the purification of the mouthful/morsel." The significance of this idiomatic expression is that a reformed way of life would have to begin with conversion to a pure diet, free from the slightest morsel of unlawful food.

fear of Allāh's punishment, in constant hope of His mercy, careful to refrain from everything of which his Master *[Mawlā]* would disapprove, vigorous in his efforts to obey Him and to earn His good pleasure. Then, if his predestined moment of death should overtake him while he is in this state, his reward will be incumbent upon Allāh, for as Allāh (Almighty and Glorious is He) has told us:

> And if someone goes away from his home, as one who is emigrating to Allāh and His Messenger, and then death overtakes him, his reward will be incumbent on Allāh. (4:100)

The following story is recorded in the collection known as the *Ṣaḥīḥ* as a tradition unanimously accepted as authentic *[muttafaq ʿalaih]*. It has been handed down to us on the authority of Abū Saʿīd al-Khudrī[213] (may Allāh be well pleased with him), according to whom the Prophet (Allāh bless him and give him peace) once said:

> In the days of your pre-Islāmic ancestors, there lived a man who had murdered no fewer than ninety-nine victims. He eventually felt the pangs of remorse, so he asked if anyone could tell him where he might find the most learned man in all the world. A certain monk *[rāhib]* was pointed out as fitting this description, so he approached him, confessed to him that he had murdered ninety-nine victims, and asked him whether there was any possibility of repentance being accepted in his case. "No," said the monk, so he killed him on the spot, thereby rounding his total up to one hundred.
>
> The murderer then renewed his inquiries. The person pointed out to him this time, as the most learned in the world, was a man of practical wisdom *[ʿāmil]*. So he approached him, confessed to him that he had murdered one hundred victims, and asked him whether there was any possibility of repentance being accepted in his case.
>
> "Yes," came the reply, "but you must avoid the company of those who stand as an obstacle between you and repentance. You must move far away, to the land I shall indicate to you, for in it there are people who worship Allāh. You must worship Allāh together with them, and never return to your own country, for it is the land of evil."
>
> The murderer set off toward the destination recommended by the man of practical wisdom, but he had barely covered half the distance along his path when death came upon him. As soon as this happened, the angels of mercy *[malāʾikat ar-raḥma]* and the angels of punishment *[malāʾikat al-ʿadhāb]* began to argue over him. In support of their claim to his soul, the angels of mercy said: "He came here as a penitent, on his way to meet Allāh!" But the angels of punishment objected, saying: "He never did any good at all!"
>
> At this point they were joined by another angel, this one in the shape of a human being *[ādamī]*, so they agreed to appoint him as an arbitrator. Having

[213] See note [120] above.

heard both sides of the argument, he said: "Measure the distance between this spot and each of the two countries [the one he had left behind and the one he was traveling toward]. Then treat him as belonging to whichever land is the closer of the two." They proceeded to measure the distance in either direction, and discovered that he was closer to the land he had been aiming to reach, so the angels of mercy bore him away with them.

In another traditionally accepted version *[riwāya]* of this story, the conclusion is slightly different, namely:

It turned out that he was nearer to the righteous township by a single inch, so he was counted as one of its inhabitants.

There is yet another traditionally accepted version, in which the story ends as follows:

Allāh (Almighty and Glorious is He) sent forth instructions by way of inspiration, ordering the country of the wicked to move further away, and commanding the country of the righteous to move closer to the spot. It was also He who told the angels: "Measure the two distances and see how they compare," and so they discovered that the spot where the body of the penitent lay was closer to the country of the righteous by a single inch, for He had indeed forgiven him.

This story provides us with clear evidence that the sinner is bound to gain by setting his sights on repentance and taking steps toward it, and that his intention *[niyya]* to repent is sure to stand him in good stead [even if he dies before he has time to accomplish it fully]. The story also serves to prove the point that there can be no salvation for anyone [on the Day of Resurrection] unless the balance shows an ultimate preponderance of good deeds in his favor, if only by the weight of a single speck of dust. It is therefore essential for the penitent to amass as many good deeds as possible, so that he can use them to compensate the plaintiffs on the Day of Resurrection. It is also vitally important for him to perform as many supererogatory acts of worship *[nawāfil]* as he possibly can, since these will be needed to patch the holes in his obligatory religious duties *[farā'iḍ]*. As the Prophet (Allāh bless him and give him peace) has said:

Perform as many supererogatory acts of worship *[nawāfil]* as you can, for these will serve to patch up the obligatory religious duties *[farā'iḍ]*.[214]

The penitent must enter into a valid and strictly binding contract with Allāh (Exalted is He), making a reliable commitment to the effect

[214] ***Author's note:*** This may be a slightly paraphrased version of the saying of the Prophet (Allāh bless him and give him peace), rather than a strict quotation.

that he will never go back to those former sins, and that he will never be guilty of any others like them. In order to fulfill this solemn pledge, he will need to have recourse to solitude *[ʿuzla]* and silence, to eating very little and sleeping very little, to maintaining a diet of strictly lawful food *[ḥalāl]*, and to abstaining from anything that is unlawful *[ḥarām]* or merely dubious *[shubha]*, whether it be something he has earned, something he has come to possess through inheritance, or something he has obtained by other lawful means. If there is any dubious or unlawful element in the property he has acquired by way of inheritance, he must get rid of it all, refrain from making any use of it, and avoid entanglement with any part of it.

The principal cause of all forms of sinful disobedience is the consumption of unlawful sustenance *[ḥarām]*, while the essential prerequisite of the religious life *[dīn]* is the consumption of lawful sustenance *[ḥalāl]*. It is therefore necessary to adopt an attitude of pious caution *[tawarruʿ]*, and to keep one's diet absolutely pure *[taṣfiyat al-luqma]*.[215] Every aspect of the way a human being develops, the good and the bad alike, is fundamentally affected by the diet consumed. Lawful sustenance gives rise to good characteristics in the person who consumes it, while unlawful sustenance gives rise to bad characteristics in the individual concerned.

In this respect, we may compare the human being to a pot on the stove. As soon as the cooking process has reached the point where the stuff in the pot is well done, the pot emits the fragrant aroma (or the unpleasant odor) of its contents. In the words of the proverbial saying: "Every porous vessel gives off the smell of its own contents."

The penitent will also need to spend much of his time as a student of the experts in Islāmic jurisprudence *[fuqahāʾ]* and the scholars *[ʿulamāʾ]* who have knowledge of Allāh. What he learns from them will prove extremely useful to him in the practice of his religion *[dīn]*. They will teach him how to find his way along the path toward Allāh (Exalted is He), how to conduct himself properly in obedience to Him, and how to manage his affairs correctly. They will make him aware of many facts concerning the course he needs to follow, important facts of which he would otherwise be unaware.

Like any traveler whose destination lies at the end of an unfamiliar road, the penitent simply cannot do without a guide *[dalīl]* to show him

[215] See note [212] above.

the way, a director *[murshid]* to give him directions, a pilot *[hādī]* to keep him on course, and a leader *[qā'id]* to set an example for him to follow.

At every stage of his progress, the penitent must prove by his actions that he is truly capable of honesty *[ṣidq]*, sincerity *[ikhlāṣ]*, and serious dedication to the cause for which he is supposed to be striving *[jidd fi'l-mujāhada]*.

Allāh (Exalted is He) has told us:

> As for those who strive in Our cause, surely We shall guide them to Our paths. (29:69)

This means that He has guaranteed right guidance *[hidāya]* to anyone who is genuinely and earnestly committed to following His path. As long as the penitent is true to that commitment, we can therefore say for certain that he will never be deprived of guidance, because Allāh does not fail to keep His promise,[216] and He is never tyrannical toward His servants.[217] He is in fact the Most Merciful of the merciful *[Arḥamu'r-rāḥimīn]*, Kind and Compassionate *[Ra'ūfun Raḥīm]*, Gentle *[Laṭīf]* and Beneficent *[Bārr]* toward His creatures. He is Helpful *[Mu'īn]* and Supportive *[Muwaffiq]* in dealing with those who seek to approach Him. As for those who turn their backs and move away from Him, He invites them with gentle kindness to return. The delight He takes in their repentance *[tawba]* is like the joy experienced by a tenderhearted mother, when her son comes home at long last from a journey to faraway places.

The Prophet (Allāh bless him and give him peace) has said:

> Great indeed is the delight that Allāh takes in the repentance *[tawba]* of any one of you. It is even greater than the happiness felt by a man at the outcome of the following experience:
>
> The man is traveling across a stretch of country fraught with pestilence and deadly peril, accompanied by a camel that is laden with his supplies of food and drink and everything else that he needs in order to survive the journey. But somehow he lets the camel go astray, so he searches for it high and low, until he is on the verge of giving up the ghost.
>
> At this point he says to himself: "I may as well go back to the spot where I first noticed that my camel had wandered off. That is where I shall die." No sooner

[216] Allāh (Almighty and Glorious is He) has told us:

> Allāh does not fail to keep the tryst *[inna'llāha lā yukhlifu'l-mī'ād]*. (3:9 and 13:31)

[217] An allusion to several verses *[āyāt]* of the Qur'ān, including:

> And [you must know] that Allāh is never tyrannical toward His servants *[wa anna'llāha laisa bi-ẓallāmin li'l-'abīd]*. (8:51)

> has he found his way back to the place, however, than a fit of drowsiness overwhelms him. He closes his eyes for one brief moment, but then he is suddenly wide-awake once more—and lo and behold, his camel is right there beside him, still laden with all his supplies of food and drink!

ʿAlī (may Allāh ennoble his countenance) said that he heard from the ever-truthful Abū Bakr (may Allāh be well pleased with him) that Allāh's Messenger (Allāh bless him and give him peace) had said:

> In no case will it ever happen that a servant [of Allāh] commits a sin, but then gets up and washes himself clean *[tawaḍḍaʾa]*, performs the ritual prayer *[ṣallā]*, and begs Allāh to forgive his sin, without it being incumbent upon Allāh to forgive him.

In His own words (Glorious and Exalted is He):

> And whenever someone does something evil, or wrongs himself, then begs forgiveness of Allāh, he will find that Allāh is All-Forgiving, All-Compassionate. (4:110)

If it happens to be a simple matter for the penitent to sort out the assets in his possession that have been wrongfully acquired *[maghṣūba]*, his next step will depend on whether or not the identity of the rightful owner can be ascertained. Whenever such identification is possible, he must make immediate restitution to the rightful owner in person, or else to his legal heirs *[waratha]*, as explained in an earlier passage.[218] If the identity of the rightful owner is unknown, on the other hand, the penitent is obliged to dispose of the assets in the form of charitable donations made on behalf of the person concerned.

It may not be so easy, however, to sort out the unlawful element *[ḥarām]* from that which is lawful *[ḥalāl]*. For example, the wrongfully acquired property may have been woven into an otherwise lawful inheritance. In a case like this, the penitent must take careful stock of the situation. Once he has made a serious effort to quantify the unlawful element, and has distributed the amount concerned for the benefit of charitable causes, he is entitled to keep the remainder for himself and his dependents.

(c) What the penitent must do in order to make amends for offenses against the honor and good repute of his fellow human beings.

As far as people's reputations *[aʿrāḍ]* are concerned, the damage is sometimes done by making defamatory remarks *[sabb]* and casting aspersions *[shatm]* directly in their faces. In cases like this, the

[218] See p. 152 above.

transgression is committed against the hearts of the victims. The same kind of damage may also be done by slandering people in their absence, by speaking ill of them and saying unkind things about them when their backs are turned. To be guilty of backbiting *[ghība]* is to talk about someone in his absence *[ghaiba]*, saying things he would not like to have said to his face.

For the penitent who has slandered a certain individual behind his back *[ightābahu]*,[219] atonement can be a simple matter of confessing to the victim and asking him to pardon the offense. If he has slandered a whole group of people, however, he must seek out all the members of that group and approach them one by one. He may discover in the process that some of his victims have already died, in which case he will have to make amends by performing many good deeds, as we have previously explained.[220]

All of these statements are relevant if—and only if—the victims are actually aware that the backbiting has taken place. If it has not come to their notice, the penitent is not obliged to seek their pardon for the offense. More than that, it is not permissible for him to do so, because he would only be causing unnecessary pain to their hearts. Instead of confessing to his unwitting victims, he must approach the people in whose presence he uttered the slanderous remarks, denounce himself to them as having been a liar at the time, and then speak approvingly about those whom he had formerly slandered.

[219] Like the noun *ghība* [backbiting], the Arabic verb *ightāba* [to slander someone] is derived from *gh-y-b*, the triliteral root of which "invisibility" is the primary signification.

[220] See p. 152 above.

On the importance of disclosing to one's victim the full extent of each offense committed against him.

It is strictly necessary for the penitent to acquaint his victim with the full extent of each offense he has committed against him, and he must not give him an ambiguous description of any of the wrongs to which he is confessing. A vaguely worded plea for absolution *[istiḥlāl]* is not sufficient in such cases, because it is always possible that the injured party *[maẓlūm]*, if he came to know all the facts concerning the extent of his injury, would not feel disposed to waive his right to exact retribution. He might prefer to postpone that retribution to the Day of Resurrection, in order to receive his compensation by having good deeds transferred to his account from that of his malefactor, or by having some of his own bad deeds transferred to the debit scale of the latter.

This rule does not apply, however, if the victim would suffer further injury from the knowledge of every specific item in the whole catalog of offenses against him. For instance, the offender would only add to the harm he had already caused, if he told his victim that he was guilty of sexual misconduct *[zinā]* with his maidservant or his wife, or that he had spread rumors about some hidden defect in his character. In cases like this, the penitent has no alternative but to couch his plea for absolution in rather vague terms. Even if he succeeds in obtaining the pardon he seeks, he will still be in debt to his victim because of a certain element of unrequited wrong, so he must repair that wrong by performing good deeds, just as he would have to repair the wrong if his victim happened to be dead or otherwise absent beyond his reach.

When a person is actually a victim, but he is unaware that an offense has been perpetrated against him, and he only learns of it when the remorseful offender approaches him with a confession, he can hardly be expected to feel an immediate urge to grant an unqualified pardon *[iḥlāl]*! The initial instinct of the injured party is bound to be the feeling that he should insist on receiving full compensation. The offender must therefore be prepared to adopt the only right and sensible approach, which is to treat his victim with every courtesy and kindness, doing his utmost to further his interests and help him achieve his goals. With all the affection and sympathy he manifests toward him in the process, he may eventually win his heart over, for, as the saying goes, the human being takes kindly to kindness *[al-insān ʿabd al-iḥsān]*.[221] Just as surely as you can alienate people by treating them badly, you can win them back by treating them well.

If this is unfortunately beyond his capacity, the only form of expiation *[kaffāra]* left to the penitent will be the performance of many good deeds, with which to pay compensation on the Day of Resurrection to the victim of his criminal behavior. When that Day comes, Allāh (Exalted is He) will render judgment against him and in favor of his victim. Having given this verdict, He will make it obligatory for the victim to accept those good deeds from the offender as compensation for the offense committed against him, even if he happens to be reluctant to accept them. This is the same principle of justice that would be applied in an Islāmic court here in this world, if a person had damaged or destroyed an article of property belonging to another, and then offered its equivalent by way of compensation, only to hear the injured party reject this offer of restitution and refuse to release him from any further liability. In settling such a case, the judge would issue an order requiring the plaintiff to accept the compensation offered, whether he wished to do so or not. Allāh (Almighty and Glorious is He) will deliver the very same ruling in the courtyards of the Resurrection *[ʿaraṣāt al-Qiyāma]*, for He is the Fairest of all judges *[Aḥkam al-ḥākimīn]* and the Justest of the just *[Aʿdal al-ʿādilīn]*.

[221] Literally, "the human being is the slave [or servant] of beneficent treatment."

Concerning the pious restraint *[wara‘]* which must be observed by the penitent in every aspect of his future conduct.

Once he has acquitted himself of all liability for offenses committed against his fellow human beings, and has become free to devote himself exclusively to the worshipful service of Allāh (Exalted is He), the penitent must stick to the path of pious restraint *[wara‘]*. This is the path that a servant [of Allāh] must follow in order to avoid incurring obligations to his fellow servants, in this world and the hereafter, and to avoid incurring the punishment of Allāh (Almighty and Glorious is He). This is the path he must follow in order to be relieved of the reckoning *[ḥisāb]* he would otherwise have to undergo on the Day of Resurrection, because the reckoning on the Day of Resurrection will be about the rights and dues of human beings *[ḥuqūq al-‘ibād]*, and about all the transactions that have taken place between human beings in this world without regard for the sacred law *[shar‘]*.

Let us consider the case of a person who always holds himself accountable here in this world, who takes from his fellow creatures only that to which he has a rightful claim, who abstains from that which does not belong to him, and who dreads the prospect of a lengthy reckoning at the Resurrection. What will he need to account for [on that Day]? According to the traditional report *[khabar]*:[222]

> Allāh (Exalted is He) will regard it as unworthy of Him to subject those who practice pious restraint *[al-wari‘īn]* to reckoning at the Resurrection.

This is why the Prophet (Allāh bless him and give him peace) said:

> Call yourselves to account before you are called to account, and weigh your own selves before they are weighed.

He also said (Allāh bless him and give him peace):

> Part of the excellence of a man's Islām is paying no attention to that which does not concern him.

[222] See note [176] above.

This gives us a clear indication of how important it is to proceed with the utmost caution in everything we undertake, and to refrain from embarking on any course of action without the permission of the sacred law *[sharʿ]*. If a person can find enough evidence in the sacred law to justify the action he is contemplating, he may go ahead and do what he proposes. If not, he should hold back and wait till he sees a better alternative. In other words, he should follow the advice of Allāh's Messenger (Allāh bless him and give him peace):

> Leave whatever causes you to feel misgivings, in favor of that which does not make you feel misgivings.[311]

The following sayings of his (Allāh bless him and give him peace) are also highly relevant in this context:

> The believer is one who takes a stand on principle, while the hypocrite is a hasty opportunist.[312]
>
> Even if you went on performing the ritual prayer until you came to be permanently curved like bows *[ḥanāyā]*, and kept on fasting until you were as thin as bowstrings *[awtār]*, nothing would do you any good except a healthy dose of pious restraint *[waraʿ]*.
>
> The true believer is a very thorough investigator *[al-muʾmin fattāsh]*.
>
> If someone does not care about the source of his food and drink, Allāh (Exalted is He) will not care by which gate He causes him to enter the Fire of Hell.

According to a report transmitted on the authority of Jābir ibn ʿAbdi'llāh (may Allāh be well pleased with him and with his father),[223] Allāh's Messenger (Allāh bless him and give him peace) once said:

> O people, not one of you will die until he has received his full quota of worldly provisions *[rizq]*, so do not be in a hurry to obtain those provisions. Observe your duty to Allāh, and behave with decency as you go about your search. Take only what is lawful for you, and leave what has been declared unlawful for you.

According to another traditional report, transmitted on the authority of Ibn Masʿūd[224] (may Allāh be well pleased with him), Allāh's Messenger (Allāh bless him and give him peace) once said:

> If the servant [of Allāh] has acquired a certain amount of wealth by unlawful means, he cannot expect to be rewarded for giving some of it away as alms, nor to receive a blessing for spending some of it on charitable causes. He may try to leave it behind him as a legacy [when he dies], but it will go along with him in the form of provisions for his journey to the Fire of Hell.

[223] Abū ʿAbdi'llāh Jābir ibn ʿAbdi'llāh al-Anṣārī was a Companion of the Prophet (Allāh bless him and give him peace), from whom he transmitted a very considerable number of traditions *[ḥadīth]*. He died at Medina between A.H. 68 and 78.

He also said (Allāh bless him and give him peace):

> Allāh does not use evil to wipe out evil, but He does wipe out evil with goodness.

According to yet another traditional report, transmitted on the authority of ʿImrān ibn al-Ḥuṣain[225] (may Allāh be well pleased with him), Allāh's Messenger (Allāh bless him and give him peace) said:

> Allāh (Exalted is He) says: "My servant, fulfill the religious obligations I have imposed upon you, and you will be numbered among the most worshipful of all the people in the world. Avoid doing anything that I have forbidden you to do, and you will be numbered among the most pious of all the people in the world. Be well satisfied with the sustenance I have provided for you, and you will be numbered among the richest of all the people in the world."

The Prophet (Allāh bless him and give him peace) once said to Abū Huraira[226] (may Allāh be well pleased with him):

> Practice pious restraint *[kun wariʿan]* and you will be numbered among the most worshipful of all the people in the world.

It was al-Ḥasan al-Baṣrī[227] (may Allāh bestow His mercy upon him) who said: "The weight of one tiny atom of pious restraint *[waraʿ]* is better than a thousand measures of fasting and ritual prayer *[ṣalāt]*."

Allāh (Exalted is He) conveyed *[awḥā]* to Moses (peace be upon him) by way of inspiration:

> For those who seek to draw close, there is nothing to compare with pious restraint as a means of drawing close to Me.

[224] Abū ʿAbd ar-Raḥmān ʿAbduʾllāh ibn Masʿūd al-Hudhalī (d. A.H. 32 or 33). One of the earliest and closest Companions of the Prophet (Allāh bless him and give him peace). A man of lowly antecedents, he became an authority on the recitation and interpretation of the Qurʾān, as well as an expert on Islamic law and the Prophetic tradition.

[225] Abū Najīd ʿImrān ibn al-Ḥuṣain ibn ʿUbaid ibn Khalaf al-Khuzāʿī al-Kaʿbī (may Allāh be well pleased with him) embraced Islām in A.H. 7, the year of the expedition to Khaibar. He fought at the side of the Prophet (Allāh bless him and give him peace) during several later expeditions.

The Caliph ʿUmar ibn al-Khaṭṭāb (may Allāh be well pleased with him) sent him to Baṣra to provide the people of that city with instruction in the science of Islāmic jurisprudence *[fiqh]*, and he made such a favorable impression that Muḥammad ibn Sīrīn said of him: "Of all the Companions of the Prophet (Allāh bless him and give him peace), never did we in Baṣra see any who could surpass the excellence of ʿImrān ibn al-Ḥuṣain." He died in Baṣra in A.H. 52, leaving numerous descendants in that city.

[226] Abū Huraira ["Father of a Kitten"] is a nickname he acquired on account of his fondness for a little cat. His real name is uncertain, although some call him Abū Huraira ad-Dawsī al-Yamānī. He is famous for having related more traditions than any other Companion of the Prophet (Allāh bless him and give him peace). Having embraced Islām A.H. 7, the year of the expedition to Khaibar, he joined the special group of materially impoverished Muslims known as the Companions of the Bench *[Aṣḥāb aṣ-Ṣuffa]*. He died in Medina in A.H. 57 or 59, at the age of 78.

[227] Al-Ḥasan ibn Abi ʾl-Ḥasan al-Baṣrī is revered as one of the greatest saints of early Islām. Born in Medina in A.H. 21/642 C.E., he was brought up in Baṣra, where he met many Companions of the Prophet (Allāh bless him and give him peace.) He died in A.H. 110/728 C.E.

There is a saying to the effect that the act of repaying one *dānaq* [small coin][228] of silver is more meritorious in the sight of Allāh than six hundred pilgrimages, all of them blessed with acceptance *[ḥijja mabrūra]*. (According to another version: "than seventy pilgrimages, all of them worthy of acceptance.")

In the words of Abū Huraira (may Allāh be well pleased with him): "Tomorrow [in the life hereafter], those who sit at ease in the company of Allāh (Exalted is He) will be those who have practiced pious restraint and abstinence *[ahl al-wara' wa'z-zuhd]*."

It was Ibn al-Mubārak[229] (may Allāh bestow His mercy upon him) who said: "To decline the unlawful offer of a single penny *[fals]*[230] is more meritorious in the sight of Allāh than donating one hundred pennies to charitable causes."

The following story is told about Ibn al-Mubārak: He once spent some time in Syria, for the purpose of making a written record of the traditions *[ḥadīth]* of the Prophet (Allāh bless him and give him peace). While he was engaged in this activity, the pen he was using happened to break, so he borrowed another pen from one of the local residents. Then, when he had finished writing, he absentmindedly slipped the pen into his own pen case.

It was not till much later, by which time he had already returned to his home in Merv, that Ibn al-Mubārak set eyes on that pen again. He recognized it as the one he had borrowed, so he immediately set about making preparations for another long trip to Syria, for the sole purpose of giving the pen back to its owner.

According to traditional reports, an-Nu'mān ibn Bashīr[231] (may

228 The *dānaq* was valued at one sixth of a dirham.

229 Abū 'Abd ar-Raḥmān 'Abdu'llāh ibn al-Mubārak al-Ḥanẓali al-Marwazī was born in A.H. 118/736 C.E. The son of a Turkish father and a Persian mother, he studied under many teachers in Merv and elsewhere, and became erudite in many branches of learning, including grammar and literature. Although he was a wealthy merchant, he was renowned for the ascetic quality of his personal lifestyle, and he distributed much of his wealth in alms to the poor. Of his many learned works on the traditions of the Prophet (Allāh bless him and give him peace), the one that has survived is devoted to the theme of asceticism.

230 The *fals* (pronounced *fils* in colloquial Arabic) is a small copper coin.

231 Abū 'Abd'illāh an-Nu'mān ibn Bashīr ibn Sa'd al-Khazraji (d. A.H. 74). After having served as governor of Kūfa and Ḥimṣ, under the Umayyad Caliph Yazīd, he joined the revolt of 'Abd'ullāh ibn az-Zubair and was killed.

Allāh be well pleased with him) used to say: "I heard these words from Allāh's Messenger (Allāh bless him and give him peace):

> That which is lawful *[ḥalāl]* is clearly defined, and that which is unlawful *[ḥarām]* is likewise clearly defined. Between the two there are matters of ambiguity *[mushtabihāt]*, and not many people are adequately informed about these. In order to keep his religion *[dīn]* and his honor intact, a person must therefore be extremely wary of things that are of dubious legality *[shubuhāt]*.
>
> When someone fails to exercise the utmost caution in approaching things that are merely dubious, he is liable to stumble into something that is strictly unlawful. Just like the shepherd who pastures his flock around the perimeter of the forbidden zone, he is always on the verge of trespassing inside it. Every king maintains a forbidden zone *[ḥimā]*, and Allāh's forbidden zone is the area that contains His inviolable sanctuaries *[maḥārim]*.
>
> And what about the human body? Does it not contain a peculiar lump of flesh *[muḍgha]*, peculiar because the whole body is sound when it is sound, and because the whole body is unsound when it is unsound? Yes indeed, that lump of flesh is the heart!"

Abū Mūsā al-Ashʿarī[232] (may Allāh be well pleased with him) is reported as having said: "Everything has a defining statute *[ḥadd]*, and the defining statutes *[ḥudūd]* of Islām are pious restraint *[waraʿ]*, modest humility *[tawāḍuʿ]*, patience *[ṣabr]* and thankfulness *[shukr]*. Pious restraint is the essential mainstay *[malāk/milāk]* of all human affairs, while patience is the means of salvation from the Fire of Hell, and thankfulness is the passport to the Garden of Paradise."

Upon entering the city of Mecca, al-Ḥasan al-Baṣrī (may Allāh bestow His mercy upon him) noticed that a young man, one of the sons of ʿAlī ibn Abī Ṭālib (may Allāh be well pleased with him), was resting his back against the Kaʿba while preaching to the people. Al-Ḥasan went up to him and asked: "What is the essential mainstay of religion *[dīn]*?" "Pious restraint *[waraʿ]*," said the young preacher, to whom he then put the question: "What is the ruin of religion?" To this he received the answer: "Greedy ambition *[ṭamaʿ]*." Al-Ḥasan was quite amazed to hear such words of wisdom from one so young.

Ibrāhīm ibn Ad'ham[233] (may Allāh bestow His mercy upon him) had

[232] Abū Mūsā ʿAbd'ullāh ibn Qais ibn Sulaimān al-Ashʿarī (d. ca. A.H. 42) was a Companion of the Prophet (Allāh bless him and give him peace) who served as a general in many of the battles fought in the early days of Islām. In A.H. 37, he was appointed as an arbitrator to represent ʿAlī (may Allāh ennoble his countenance) at the Battle of Ṣiffīn. He was also a distinguished Qurānic scholar.

[233] Abū Isḥāq Ibrāhīm ibn Ad'ham ibn Manṣūr ibn Yazīd ibn Jābir at-Tamīmī al-ʿIjlī was born in Balkh of pure Arab descent. His life has often been compared to that of Buddha, since he is described in legend as the Prince of Balkh who renounced his kingdom and wandered westward to live a life of complete asceticism, earning his bread in Syria by honest manual labor until his death ca. A.H. 165/782 C.E.

this to say on the subject: "Pious restraint comes in two varieties *[al-wara' wara'ān]*: One form of pious restraint is an obligatory religious duty *[farḍ]*, while the other form of pious restraint is a measure of precaution *[ḥidhr]*. As an obligatory religious duty, pious restraint means abstaining from acts of outright disobedience against Allāh. As a measure of precaution, on the other hand, pious restraint means abstaining from things that are of dubious legality *[shubuhāt]*, just in case they are actually covered by the prohibitions of Allāh (Exalted is He)."

As far as ordinary people are concerned, pious restraint must therefore be a matter of abstinence not only from that which is definitely unlawful *[ḥarām]*, but also from that which is of dubious legality *[shubha]*. In other words, it requires the average person to abstain from anything by which he might incur some liability toward his fellow creatures, as well as from anything that would render him subject to a penalty prescribed by the sacred law *[shar']*.

As practiced by the élite *[khāṣṣ]*, pious restraint must also include abstinence from everything that is influenced by the passions, or motivated by the lower self *[nafs]* in its pursuit of carnal desires and worldly pleasures.

In the case of the élite of the élite *[khāṣṣ al-khāṣṣ]*, pious restraint must extend even further, to include abstinence from anything in which there is any trace of self-will *[irāda]* or ulterior motive *[ru'ya]*.

It can therefore be said that an ordinary person is exercising pious restraint *[yatawarra'u]* by giving up his attachment to this world, that a member of the élite is exercising pious restraint by giving up his attachment to the Garden of Paradise, and that a member of the élite of the élite is exercising pious restraint by giving up his attachment to everything apart from the One who has created and made [whatever exists in the entire universe].

According to Yaḥyā ibn Mu'ādh ar-Rāzī[234] (may Allāh bestow His mercy upon him): "There are two ways of looking at pious restraint *[wara']*: From the external point of view *[ẓāhir]*, it means that you do not make the slightest movement except for the sake of Allāh. From the perspective of the inner being *[bāṭin]*, it means that nothing apart from Him (Blessed and Exalted is He) is allowed to enter your heart."

[234] Abū Zakariyā' Yaḥyā ibn Mu'ādh ar-Rāzī was a disciple of Ibn Karrām. After leaving his native town of Rayy, he lived for a time in Balkh, then moved to Nīshāpūr where he died in A.H. 258/871 C.E.

Yaḥyā (may Allāh bestow His mercy upon him) also said: "If a person fails to pay attention to the subtle aspect of pious restraint, he will gain nothing from it, and he will not attain to the splendid gift he would otherwise receive."

It is the positive side of this equation that is emphasized in the saying: "If someone does pay meticulous attention to pious restraint, his status at the Resurrection will be glorious indeed!"

To quote yet another anonymous saying: "Pious restraint *[wara']* is much more difficult in relation to the faculty of speech than in relation to gold and silver. It is also true that voluntary detachment *[zuhd]* from political leadership is much more difficult than voluntary detachment from gold and silver, because you are willing to sacrifice these precious metals in pursuit of political leadership."

It was Abū Sulaimān ad-Dārānī[235] (may Allāh bestow His mercy upon him) who said: "Pious restraint *[wara']* is the first stage of voluntary detachment *[zuhd]*, just as frugal satisfaction *[qanā'a]* is the first stage of contentment *[riḍā]*."

Abū 'Uthmān[236] (may Allāh bestow His mercy upon him) once remarked: "The spiritual reward for pious restraint is the lightness of the reckoning [to be experienced at the Resurrection]."

We have already quoted one of the sayings of Yaḥyā ibn Mu'ādh ar-Rāzī (may Allāh bestow His mercy upon him), who also said: "Pious restraint is exercised by pausing at the boundary of knowledge *['ilm]*, without crossing over into fanciful interpretation *[ta'wīl]*."

According to a man of good repute (may Allāh bestow His mercy upon him): "If a person does not have pious restraint to keep him company while he is in a state of poverty, it is a foregone conclusion that he will consume unlawful food *[ḥarām]*."

Yūnus ibn 'Ubaidi'llāh[237] (may Allāh bestow His mercy upon him)

[235] Abū Sulaimān 'Abd ar-Raḥmān ibn Aḥmad ibn 'Aṭiyya ad-Dārānī (d. A.H. 205 or 215). A pious devotee whose inclination lay toward extreme asceticism. He is renowned for his many memorable sayings.

[236] Abū 'Uthmān Sa'īd ibn Ismā'īl al-Ḥīrī an-Nisābūrī (may Allāh bestow His mercy upon him) was one of the early Shaikhs of Khurāsān. He came originally from Rayy, where he knew Yaḥyā ibn Mu'ādh ar-Rāzī and Shāh ibn Shujā' al-Kirmānī. After moving to Nishapur he came under the influence of Abū Ḥafṣ al-Ḥaddād. He visited al-Junaid in Baghdād, and died at Nishapur in A.H. 298/911 C.E. "Even in the days of my childhood," he once said, "my heart was always seeking after something of reality. I was always convinced … that the Islāmic way of life held mysteries other than its external manifestations."

[237] Abū 'Abdi'llāh Yūnus ibn 'Ubaidi'llāh ibn Dīnār al-'Abdī al-Baṣrī (d. A.H. 139) was an expert in the traditions of the Prophet (Allāh bless him and give him peace) and a disciple of al-Ḥasan al-Baṣrī (may Allāh bestow His mercy upon him).

had this to say on the subject: "Pious restraint *[waraʿ]* means abstaining from everything that is of dubious legality *[shubha]*, and calling the lower self *[nafs]* to account with every passing moment."

Sufyān ath-Thawrī[238] (may Allāh bestow His mercy upon him) offered very straightforward advice: "As I see it," he said, "there is nothing simpler than pious restraint. If something grates on your nerves, just take the hint and have nothing to do with it."

This is almost an echo of the saying of the Prophet (Allāh bless him and give him peace):

> Sin is that which causes a feeling of irritation within your breast, and which you do not like other people to notice.

That is because it prevents the breast from expanding, and because it has a bad effect upon your heart, as indicated by another saying of his (Allāh bless him and give him peace):

> Sin is the disturber of hearts *[al-ithm ḥawwāz/ḥawāzz al-qulūb]*.[239]

In other words, it is that which cuts or notches *[ḥazza]* into your breast and causes a feeling of irritation *[ḥākka]*, a feeling so uncomfortable that the heart recoils from it.[240]

In this connection, we should remind ourselves of the *ḥadīth* [saying of the Prophet (Allāh bless him and give him peace)]:

> Beware of things that make you feel irritated, for such things are sins *[iyyākum wa'l-ḥakkākāt fa-innaha'l-maʾāthim]*.[241]

[238] Abū ʿAbdi'llāh Sufyān ibn Saʿīd ath-Thawrī was born in Kūfa in A.H. 97/715 C.E. He founded a school of Islāmic jurisprudence *[fiqh]* which survived for about two centuries after his death in Baṣra in A.H. 161/778 C.E.

[239] The reading *al-ithm ḥawwāz al-qulūb*, which is preferred by the editor of the Damascus edition of *al-Ghunya*, is explained as meaning: "Sin is what overcomes hearts, so that they commit that which is not incumbent." The reading more commonly adopted by the traditional lexicographers, however, is *al-ithm ḥawāzz al-qulūb*.

The form *ḥawāzz* is the plural of *ḥāzza*, meaning "a pain in the heart, arising from wrath and similar causes." Hence the interpretation: "Sin is those things that make an impression upon hearts, in much the same way as cutting or notching makes an impression on a material object, and cause one to suspect that they may be acts of disobedience, by reason of the uneasiness that is felt in relation to them." (See: E.W. Lane, *Arabic-English Lexicon*, art. *Ḥ–W–Z* and art. *Ḥ–Z–Z*.)

[240] In view of this explanation, it would seem that Shaikh ʿAbd al-Qādir al-Jīlānī (may Allāh be well pleased with him) preferred the second of the two readings mentioned in the preceding note.

[241] The term *ḥakkākāt* is derived from the triliteral root *ḥ–k–k*, which conveys the basic meaning: "to scratch, scrape, rub, grate, chafe, fret, abrade...." The meanings given by the traditional Arabic lexicographers are actually interpretations based on this saying of the Prophet (Allāh bless him and give him peace), e.g., "suggestions of the devil or of the mind, whereby the mind is disturbed; such as are termed *wasāwis* [evil insinuations]," and "things that make an abrasive impression *[taḥukku]* upon the heart, and are dubious to a man." (See: E.W. Lane, *Arabic-English Lexicon*, art. *Ḥ–K–K*.)

We should also remember his words (Allāh bless him and give him peace):

> Leave whatever causes you to feel misgivings, in favor of that which does not make you feel misgivings *[da' mā yurībuka ilā mā lā yurībuk]*.[242]

Ma'rūf al-Karkhī[243] (may Allāh bestow His mercy upon him) was recommending pious restraint *[wara']* when he said: "You must keep your tongue from expressing praise [of your fellow creatures], just as you would keep it from expressing blame."

According to Bishr ibn al-Ḥārith [al-Ḥāfī][244] (may Allāh bestow His mercy upon him): "The hardest things to practice are three, namely, generosity *[jūd]* in the midst of scarcity, pious restraint *[wara']* in one's private life, and speaking the truth *[kalimat al-ḥaqq]* in the presence of someone who is regarded with a mixture of fear and hope."

The following story is told about the sister of Bishr ibn al-Ḥārith al-Ḥāfī, and how she once came seeking the advice of Imām Aḥmad ibn Ḥanbal (may Allāh bestow His mercy upon all three of them): "O Imām," she said, "when we work at our spinning [after dark], we sit out on our roof terrace, so that we can see by the beams of light that shine from the lanterns in the neighborhood outside. Is it permissible for us to do our spinning by their beams of light?" On hearing this, the Imām exclaimed: "Who are you? May Allāh pardon and protect you!" When she said: "I am the sister of Bishr ibn al-Ḥārith," Imām Aḥmad (may Allāh bestow His mercy upon him) immediately burst into tears. "Pious restraint is sadly making its departure from your household," he said with a sigh, then he answered her question by telling her: "You must not work at your spinning by the light of their lanterns!"

[242] This saying of the Prophet (Allāh bless him and give him peace) was quoted earlier in this Discourse (see p. 162 above).

[243] Abū Maḥfūẓ Ma'rūf ibn Fīrūz al-Karkhī (d. A.H. 200/815 C.E.) is said to have been born to Christian parents. After his conversion to Islām, he acquired a saintly reputation as a teacher in Baghdād, noted for his emphasis on the spiritual content of the religion, and especially for his personal generosity and sincere devotion. One of his pupils was Sarī as-Saqaṭī (may Allāh bestow His mercy upon him), who became in turn the teacher of al-Junaid (may Allāh bestow His mercy upon him).

[244] Abū Naṣr Bishr ibn al-Ḥārith al-Ḥāfī ["the Barefoot"] was born near Merv ca. A.H. 150/767 C.E. After an early life of wanton dissipation, he settled in Baghdād and became a serious student of the traditions of the Prophet (Allāh bless him and give him peace), but then abandoned formal learning for the life of a wandering beggar. Destitute, starving and barefoot, he acquired the nickname al-Ḥāfī, yet he won the admiration of Imām Aḥmad ibn Ḥanbal and the respect of the Caliph al-Ma'mun. He died in Baghdād in A.H. 227/841 C.E. May Allāh bestow His mercy upon him.

We owe this next story to ʿAlī al-ʿAṭṭār[245] (may Allāh bestow His mercy upon him): "I was passing through one of the streets of Baṣra," he tells us, "when I noticed that some boys were playing games, without showing the slightest respect toward several old men who happened to be sitting nearby. I protested, saying: 'Have you no sense of shame in the presence of these elders?' Then one of the lads replied: 'These old men know little of pious restraint, so they hardly deserve much respect!'"

Mālik ibn Dīnār[246] (may Allāh bestow His mercy upon him) is said to have been a resident of Baṣra for a period of forty years, yet in all that time he never once saw fit to eat the dates of Baṣra, and he died without having tasted either the dried dates *[tamr]* or the fresh dates *[ruṭab]* of the region. On one occasion, when the season of fresh dates had drawn to a close, he said: "O people of Baṣra, this stomach of mine is none the worse for having gone without them, and they have not left you any better off than you were before."

Somebody once said to Ibrāhīm ibn Ad'ham (may Allāh bestow His mercy upon him): "Is it true that you do not drink water that is somewhat brackish *[zamzam]*?" To this he replied: "If I had a leather bucket I would drink some!"[247]

According to what they say about al-Ḥārith al-Muḥāsibī[248] (may Allāh bestow His mercy upon him), if he ever stretched out his hand toward a dish of food that happened to contain some dubious ingredient *[shubha]*, a vein would start to throb in the tip of his finger, letting him know that it was not lawful food.

[245] Not to be confused with the more famous Farīd ad-Dīn al-ʿAṭṭār (may Allāh bestow His mercy upon them both).

[246] Abū Yaḥyā Mālik ibn Dīnār as-Sāmī an-Nājī was a disciple of al-Ḥasan al-Bāṣrī (may Allāh bestow His mercy upon them). He is often noted as a reliable narrator of traditions of the Prophet (Allāh bless him and give him peace) and as an early calligrapher of the Qurʾān. He died ca. A.H. 130/748 C.E.

[247] Meaning, presumably: "I would go and draw water to drink from the Zamzam well." (This famous well, adjacent to the Kaʿba in Mecca, is said to be so called because its water is somewhat brackish *[zamzam]*.)

[248] Abū ʿAbdi'llāh al-Ḥārith ibn Asad al-Baṣrī al-Muḥāsibī (may Allāh bestow His mercy upon him) was born in Baṣra in A.H. 165/781 C.E. He was still at an early age when he moved to Baghdād, where he studied the traditions of the Prophet (Allāh bless him and give him peace) and became an expert in Islāmic theology *[kalām]*. He died in A.H. 243/857 C.E., but his teachings and writings continued to exert a profound and far-reaching influence, notably on the famous Abū Ḥāmid al-Ghazālī (the author of *Iḥyāʾ ʿUlūm ad-Dīn*).

In the case of Bishr [ibn al-Ḥārith] al-Ḥāfī (may Allāh bestow His mercy upon him), we are told that if a dish of food containing some dubious ingredient was served in front of him, his hand would simply refuse to reach out toward it.

As for the mother of Abū Yazīd al-Bisṭāmī[249] (may Allāh bestow His mercy upon them both), they say that if she was about to stretch out her hand toward a dish of food containing some dubious ingredient, she would feel herself losing the spiritual state she had known since she became pregnant with Abū Yazīd, and she would therefore refrain from stretching out her hand toward that dish of food.

In the case of one saintly individual, if there was any dubious ingredient in the food served to him, the emergence of an unpleasant odor would give him warning, and he would then refuse to eat the tainted food.

We have also been told how one such person would find it impossible to chew on a morsel of food that contained some dubious ingredient, because it would turn into a substance like sand as soon as he put it inside his mouth.

Allāh (Exalted is He) makes all of these things happen for the benefit of such people, for the sake of easing their task, treating them with mercy and compassion, and granting them a protective shield. Once they have resolved to keep their diet pure, and have made a very serious effort to seek out lawful food *[ḥalāl]*, as well as to abstain from anything unlawful *[ḥārām]* or dubious *[shubha]*, Allāh (Exalted is He) will see fit to supply them with the means to guard against consuming any of those foodstuffs that they now regard with distaste.

He will then provide them with a fail-safe device for the detection of unlawful or dubious ingredients. He will also save them the trouble of having to conduct investigations and inquiries concerning the livelihood and lifestyle of the food merchant, the price he paid for the produce he is trying to sell, where it came from and whether he obtained it by lawful means, and so on and so forth. By equipping them with a simple warning device, Allāh (Exalted is He) has made all of that redundant, so, while they must keep their hands off the food whenever

[249] Abū Yazīd Ṭaifūr ibn ʿĪsā ibn Sorushān al-Bisṭāmī (may Allāh bestow His mercy upon him) was born in the district of Bisṭām in northeastern Persia, and it was there that he died in A.H. 261 or 264/874 or 877 C.E. He is famous for the boldness of his utterances.

they notice the alarm signal, they can safely assume that it is lawful if they see that the alarm has not been triggered. This only applies, of course, to those noble masters *[sāda kirām]* who have already been blessed with providential care *[ʿināya]*, and have been assured of comprehensive safekeeping *[riʿāya]*.

As for the meaning of "lawful conduct *[ḥalāl]*"[250] in relation to the ordinary folk who make up the great majority of the believers *[muʾminīn]*, it can be defined as "every kind of behavior that does not cause a person to incur some liability toward his fellow creatures, and that does not render him subject to a penalty prescribed by the sacred law *[sharʿ]*."

Sahl ibn ʿAbdi'llāh at-Tustarī[251] (may Allāh bestow His mercy upon him) was asked more than once to explain the meaning of lawful conduct *[ḥalāl]*. He replied on one occasion by saying: "Lawful conduct *[ḥalāl]* is conduct in which one commits no sinful act of disobedience against Allāh." On another occasion he said: "Pure lawful conduct *[al-ḥalāl aṣ-ṣāfī]* is conduct in which one does not forget about Allāh."

As it is normally used, the term *ḥalāl* refers to something that is lawful as a matter of actual legal practice *[ḥalāl ḥukm]*, not to something that is lawful in essence or substance *[ḥalāl ʿain]*.

If *ḥalāl* could only mean lawful in essence or substance *[ḥalāl ʿain]*, it would never be permissible for anyone to eat carrion *[maita]*, or the meat of any animal not slaughtered in accordance with the ritual requirements of Islamic law.[252]

To make this point even clearer, let us consider the situation that arises when a corrupt government official *[shurṭī]* uses some of his ill-gotten money *[māl ḥarām]* to purchase lawful food *[ṭaʿām ḥalāl]*, but

[250] The basic meaning associated with the triliteral Arabic root *ḥ–l–l*, from which *ḥalāl* is one of many derivatives, is "untying." According to context , the term *ḥalāl* may need to be treated for translation purposes as: (1) a simple adjective, (2) an adjectival noun, or (3) an adjective qualifying an implicit noun. In each of these categories, the translator has several options to consider, e.g., (1) lawful, legal, licit, legitimate; allowed, allowable; permitted, permissible; admissible; (2) "that which is…" [lawful, legal, permissible, etc.]; (3) lawful conduct, permissible behavior; lawful food; lawful property, legitimate possession; etc.

[251] Abū Muḥammad Sahl ibn ʿAbdi'llāh at-Tustarī was born at Tustar (Ahwāz) ca. A.H. 200/815 C.E. He studied with Sufyān ath-Thawrī, and met Dhu 'n-Nūn al-Miṣrī (may Allah bestow His mercy upon them). His quiet life was interrupted in A.H. 261/874 C.E., when he was forced to seek refuge in Baṣra, where he died in A.H. 282/896 C.E. His influence is particularly evident in the teachings of the Sālimiyya school, which was founded by his pupil Ibn Sālim.

[252] Under certain circumstances, e.g., when a traveler is facing death from starvation, the eating of such meat is not merely permissible, but obligatory.

then goes back and cancels the deal, so that the food reverts to the possession of the original owner. In a case like this, if *ḥalāl* could only mean lawful in essence or substance *[ḥalāl ʿain]*, it would no longer be permissible for the fastidiously pious believer *[al-mutawarriʿ al-muʾmin]* to eat the meat concerned, because something has happened in the meantime to make eating it unlawful, namely, its temporary acquisition by the corrupt government official. In actual practice, however, the Muslims are unanimously agreed on the permissibility of eating this food, in spite of the fact that it came into the possession of the corrupt government official, who purchased it with his ill-gotten money, the spending of which is regarded as unlawful by all the Muslims.

It must therefore be understood that the terms *ḥalāl* [lawful] and *ḥarām* [unlawful] refer to the normal application of the sacred law *[sharʿ]*, not to the intrinsic nature *[nafs al-ʿain]* of the food, because the only food that is intrinsically lawful is the food of the Prophets *[anbiyāʾ]*, as we learn from this tradition *[ḥadīth]*:

> The Prophet (Allāh bless him and give him peace) once heard a man say: "O Allāh, grant me a means of subsistence that is absolutely lawful *[ḥalāl muṭlaq]*!"
>
> The Prophet (Allāh bless him and give him peace) then told him: "That is the sustenance of the Prophets *[rizq al-anbiyāʾ]*. You must ask Allāh to grant you a means of subsistence for which He will not punish you!"

Let us also consider how the sacred law *[sharʿ]* applies to the situation of the non-Muslim communities within the Islāmic state *[ahl adh-dhimma]*,[253] the Jews *[Yahūd]*, Christians *[Naṣārā]* and Zoroastrians *[Majūs]*, who trade in forbidden commodities *[muḥarramāt]* such as wine and pigs.

In allowing them to sell these commodities, and then collecting the tithe *[ʿushr]* from the proceeds of their sales, we are acting in accordance with the instruction handed down from [the rightly guided Caliph] ʿUmar ibn al-Khaṭṭāb (may Allāh be well pleased with him), for it was he who said:

"Leave them in charge of the business of selling [commodities unlawful to Muslims], and collect the tithe *[ʿushr]* from the proceeds of

253 The *ahl adh-dhimma* are the Jewish, Christian or Sabean subjects of an Islāmic state, who, in return for the payment of a special tax, are entitled under Islāmic law to security of their persons and their property.

their sales. And what will be done with the tithe, once it has been collected from them? Surely the Muslims will put it to good use!"

If *ḥalāl* could only mean lawful in essence or substance *[ḥalāl ʿain]*, it would not be permissible to collect such a tithe, because wine and pigs and the proceeds from their sale are all intrinsically unlawful *[ḥarām]*. It has been made lawful in practice, however, in order to provide a valuable opportunity for constructive action.

As someone put it: "Between that which is lawful *[ḥalāl]* and that which is unlawful *[ḥarām]* there is a valuable opportunity."

In order to avail himself of this valuable opportunity, the believer must grasp the sacred law *[sharʿ]* and hold it in his hand like a lamp. He must make it the criterion by which to decide what he should take for himself and what he should give to others. He must not resort to fanciful interpretations in order to get around it, and he must never depart from it completely. He must take only that which the sacred law allows him to accept, and give only that which the sacred law permits him to give, and every aspect of his behavior must come to be in conformity with the sacred law.

Whatever he consumes must be lawful according to the sacred law, but he is not obliged to go looking for sustenance that is absolutely lawful in terms of its intrinsic nature *[al-ḥalāl al-muṭlaq al-ʿain]*, since this is virtually impossible to find. It is almost entirely beyond the scope of human experience, except that Allāh may wish to confer it upon some of His saints *[awliyāʾ]* and chosen ones *[aṣfiyāʾ]*.

> And that is no great matter for Allāh. (14:20)

From the standpoint of the kind of food that is lawful for them to eat, we can distinguish three separate types of people: (1) the ordinary person who is conscientious in doing his duty *[muttaqī]*; (2) the saint *[walī]*; and (3) the spiritual deputy who is endowed with intuitive knowledge *[badal ʿārif]*.

1. In the case of the ordinary person who is conscientious in doing his duty *[muttaqī]*, that which is lawful *[ḥalāl]* is that which does not cause him to incur any liability toward his fellow creatures, and that does not render him subject to a penalty prescribed by the sacred law *[sharʿ]*.

2. In the case of the genuine saint *[walī muḥiqq]*, since he is abstinent to the point of being completely detached from the influence of the

passions *[hawā]*, his diet must be one that does not include any fancy fare. His nourishment must be strictly in keeping with his spiritual condition.

3. As for the spiritual deputy *[badal]*,[254] he is someone who is endowed with intuitive knowledge *[ʿārif]*, who is used as an instrument *[mafʿūl fīh]*, and who is devoid of self-will *[irāda]*. He is the ball of the divine decree *[kurat al-qadar]*.[255] In his case, therefore, lawful food must mean nourishment that contains no ingredient connected with personal ambition *[himma]* or self-will *[irāda]*. It is in fact received entirely through the grace of Allāh (Almighty and Glorious is He), who sustains him, guides him, and trains him by means of His all-embracing power *[qudra]*, His universal benevolence *[minna]*, and His unfailingly effective will *[mashīʾa]*, treating him like a suckling babe in the lap of his tenderhearted mother.

As long as the believer has yet to realize the full significance of the first stage, he cannot progress to the second stage, and as long as he has yet to realize the full significance of the second stage, he cannot progress to the third stage.

Just as the lawful food of the ordinary conscientious person *[muttaqī]* is of dubious legality *[shubha]* as far as the person who is free from the influence of the passions *[zāʾil al-hawā]* is concerned, the lawful food of the dispassionate individual is of dubious legality in the case of someone who is utterly devoid of self-will and personal ambition *[zāʾil al-irāda wa'l-himma]*.

[254] *Badal* is the singular of *Abdāl*. In the Sixth Discourse of Revelations of the Unseen, Shaikh ʿAbd al-Qādir (may Allāh be well pleased with him) gives the following explanation:

> Annihilation *[fanāʾ]* is the aim and object, the final destination of the journey of the saints. This was the direction sought by all previous saints and *Abdāl*: to become extinct to their own will, and let the will of the Almighty and Glorious Truth take its place, as a permanent transformation, lasting until death. That is why they came to be called *Abdāl* [lit: 'substitutes'] (may Allāh be well pleased with them all).

[255] In a footnote supplied at this point in the Damascus edition of the Arabic text, the editor suggests: "Perhaps what the author means by this is that he is absolutely deprived of self-will."

In the Third Discourse of *Revelations of the Unseen [Futūḥ al-Ghaib]*, in which he describes the condition of a person completely submitted to the will of Allāh (Almighty and Glorious is He), Shaikh ʿAbd al-Qādir al-Jīlānī (may Allāh be well pleased with him) says:

> His status comes to resemble that of a suckling babe in its nurse's arms, of a corpse in the hands of a washer of the dead, or of a ball on the receiving end of a polo-player's mallet—rolled and spun and knocked around, though inert in itself and imparting no motion to other bodies.

As the saying goes: "The bad deeds of those drawn close [to Allāh] are the good deeds of pious devotees." The lawful food of the Shaikh is therefore permissible *[mubāḥ]* for the disciple *[murīd]*, but the lawful food of the disciple is unlawful *[ḥarām]* as far as the Shaikh is concerned, on account of the purity of his spiritual state, the probity of his rank, the loftiness of his station, and his proximity to his Lord (Almighty and Glorious is He).

Some of the finer points of pious restraint *[wara']*, as illustrated by stories told about the Prophets, the saints and the righteous.

Kahmas (may Allāh bestow His mercy upon him) is reported as having said:

"I once committed a sin, and I have been shedding tears because of it for all of forty years. It all began when a brother of mine paid me a visit. I bought a grilled fish, which cost me no more than a *dānaq* [small coin], and then, when he had finished eating it, I took a chunk of plaster from the wall of a neighbor of mine, so that my guest could use it to scrub his hand clean. To my regret, I did not take the trouble to ask my neighbor's permission first."

This next story is about a man who was living in a rented house. One day, having scribbled a note on a piece of paper, he thought he might dry the ink by sprinkling it with dust from the wall of the house. It occurred to him that the house was rented from someone else, so he hesitated for a moment, but then it occurred to him that this fact was of no importance, so he went ahead and sprinkled dust on the letter. Just then, he heard a mysterious voice *[hātif]* saying: "He who now treats dust so lightly, will surely learn tomorrow [at the Resurrection] what a lengthy reckoning lies in store for him!"

People once noticed that 'Utbat al-Ghulām[256] (may Allāh bestow His mercy upon him) was dripping with perspiration in the middle of winter. When they asked him how he came to be in such a sweat, he said: "This happens to be a place where I once committed a sinful act of disobedience against my Lord." They wanted to know more about it, so he went on to explain: "It was from this wall here that I scraped a

[256] Abū 'Abdi'llāh 'Utba ibn Abbān ibn Sam'a, a celebrated ascetic of Baṣra, was nicknamed 'Utbat al-Ghulām because he was a servant *[ghulām]*, not because he was a young man (another meaning of *ghulām*). His death in A.H. 153 preceded that of his own father. He was noted for his state of profound sorrow *[ḥuzn]*, which has been compared to that of al-Ḥasan al-Baṣrī.

lump of plaster, so that a guest of mine could use it to scrub his hand clean. To my regret, I did not take the trouble to ask the owner's permission first!"

They say that Imām Aḥmad ibn Ḥanbal (may Allāh bestow His mercy upon him) once pawned a pail of his at a grocery store in Mecca. Some time later, when he was ready to redeem the pledge, the grocer brought out a couple of pails and set them in front of him. "Take whichever of the two belongs to you," said the grocer, but Imām Aḥmad replied: "It is hard for me to tell which pail is mine, so keep it, and keep the money too!" The grocer then said: "This one is yours. I only wanted to test you." "I shall not take it back," said Imām Aḥmad, as he walked away and left him holding the pail.

It is said that Rābiʿa al-ʿAdawiyya[257] (may Allāh bestow His mercy upon her) once sewed up a split in her dress by the light of a lamp belonging to the Sulṭān. As a result, she became out of touch with her heart for quite some time. When she finally recalled what had happened, she ripped her dress—and rediscovered her heart!

A person once had a dream in which he saw Sufyān ath-Thawrī (may Allāh bestow His mercy upon him) with a pair of wings, flying around the Garden of Paradise from tree to tree. "How did you achieve this state?" the dreamer asked him. "Through the practice of pious restraint *[waraʿ]*," replied Sufyān.

For sixty long years, Ḥassān ibn Abī Sinān (may Allāh bestow His mercy upon him) never slept on a comfortable couch, never ate meat containing fat, and never drank a cool drink. After he had died, he was asked by someone who saw him in a dream: "How has Allāh treated you?" "Very well," he replied, "except that I am barred from the Garden of Paradise on account of a needle I once borrowed, and which I failed to return."

A man called ʿAbd al-Wāḥid ibn Zaid had a servant who worked for him for many years, and who was a devoted worshipper [of Allāh] for no less than forty years. At the very beginning of his career, this faithful servant had worked as a measurer of corn. After he had died, he was

[257] Rābiʿa bint Ismāʾīl al-ʿAdawiyya (may Allāh bestow His mercy upon her) was born in humble circumstances. Sold into slavery as a child, she later settled in Baṣra, where she attained great renown as a remarkable saint and an effective preacher, and was highly esteemed by many of her pious contemporaries. Devoted to loving intimacy with Allah (Exalted is He), she never married. The date of her death is given as A.H. 135/752 C.E. by some authorities, and A.H. 185/801 C.E. by others. Some point to a tomb near Jerusalem as her place of burial.

asked by someone who saw him in a dream: "How has Allāh treated you?" "Very well," he replied, "except that I am barred from the Garden of Paradise, having been confronted with a heap of corn dust amounting to forty measures of grain."

As Jesus (peace be upon him) was passing by a cemetery, he called out to one of the men who lay buried there, whereupon Allāh (Exalted is He) promptly brought the man back to life. Jesus asked: "Who are you?" and he said: "I used to be a porter, carrying things for other people. One day, while I was carrying a load of wood for a certain person, I broke off a splinter and used it to pick my teeth. I have been paying the consequences ever since I died."

Concerning the ten obligations that must be discharged before pious restraint *[wara‘]* can acquire its full significance.

The penitent cannot realize the full significance of pious restraint *[wara‘]* unless he recognizes that ten things are strictly incumbent upon him:

1. The first of these obligations is to guard against using the tongue for backbiting *[ghība]*, because He has said (Exalted is He):

> And do not backbite one another. (49:12)

2. The second obligation is to avoid the tendency to harbor sinister suspicions *[sū' aẓ-ẓann]*, since He has said (Exalted is He):

> O you who believe, you must avoid a great deal of suspicion, for some suspicion is a sin. (49:12)

And the Prophet (Allāh bless him and give him peace) said:

> Beware of suspicion, for it is the most misleading source of information *[akdhab al-ḥadīth]*.

3. The third obligation is to steer well clear of mockery and ridicule *[sukhriyya]*, because He has told us (Exalted is He):

> O you who believe, one group of people should not scoff at another group of people, who may be better than they. (49:11)

4. The fourth obligation is to lower one's eyes in the presence of things that should be treated as sacred *[maḥārim]*, because He has told us (Exalted is He):

> And tell the believing men to keep their eyes downcast [and to guard their private parts]. (24:30)

5. The fifth obligation is to be true to one's word, because He has told us (Exalted is He):

> And if you give your word, you must act fairly. (6:153)

That is, you must prove that you really mean what you say.

6. The sixth obligation is to acknowledge one's dependence on the gracious favor of Allāh (Exalted is He), as a precaution against self-centered conceit, since He has told us (Exalted is He):

> It is rather that Allāh is treating you with gracious favor, inasmuch as He has guided you to faith. (49:17)

7. The seventh obligation is to spend one's wealth on that which has true value *[ḥaqq]*, and not to spend it on that which is quite worthless *[bāṭil]*, because He has told us (Exalted is He):

> And [among His faithful servants are] those who, when they spend, are neither prodigal nor parsimonious. (25:67)

In other words, they neither spend their wealth on sinful disobedience, nor withhold it from the support of worshipful obedience.

8. The eighth obligation is not to go seeking high-and-mighty status and prestige for the sake of self-aggrandizement, because He has told us (Exalted is He):

> As for that Ultimate Abode, We shall assign it to those who are neither intent on high-and-mighty status on the earth, nor on corruption. (28:83)

9. The ninth obligation is to observe the five ritual prayers *[ṣalawāt]* at the times prescribed for them each day, following the correct sequence of bowing *[rukūʿ]* and prostration *[sujūd]*, because He has told us (Exalted is He):

> Be careful to observe your prayers, and [especially] the middle prayer,[258] and stand obedient to Allāh. (2:238)

10. The tenth obligation is to stick to the course prescribed by the Sunna and the Jamāʿa,[259] since He has told us (Exalted is He):

> And this path of Mine is straight, so follow it. Do not follow other paths, lest you be separated from His path. (6:154)

[258] Usually taken to mean the *ʿaṣr* prayer (in the middle of the afternoon).

[259] The *Sunna* is the exemplary precedent *[mā sanna]* set by Allāh's Messenger (Allāh bless him and give him peace), while the *Jamāʿa* is the common practice agreed upon by his Companions during the time of the rightly guided Caliphs, Abū Bakr, ʿUmar, ʿUthmān and ʿAlī (may Allāh be well pleased with them all).

Concerning the permissibility of repenting some sins but not others.

A person may be incapable of repenting all his sins at one fell swoop, in which case it is quite permissible for him to repent some sins but not others. For instance, he may decide to repent the major sins *[kabā᾽ir]* but not the minor ones *[ṣaghā᾽ir]*, in recognition of the fact that the major sins are far more serious in the sight of Allāh, and far more likely to incur His displeasure and His wrath, whereas the minor sins have a much lower rating on the scale of gravity, since they are more readily susceptible to pardon.

It is by no means absurd for the penitent to start by repenting the most serious offenses. The time will come when faith *[īmān]* and certitude *[yaqīn]* have matured in his heart, when the luminous rays of right guidance *[hidāya]* have provided him with enlightenment, and when his inner feeling has become disposed to welcome the next stage of the penitent's progress on the return journey *[ināba]* toward Allāh (Exalted is He).

Once he has reached this stage, he will be ready to do penance for all the minor sins and barely noticeable errors, for the concealed polytheism *[shirk khafī]* and all the sins committed by the heart, and then in due course for the sinful acts of disobedience connected with various spiritual states and stations.

Whenever someone advances to a higher spiritual state and station, he always finds something there that he is obliged to deal with effectively, and something else that he is required to leave strictly alone. In other words, there is a particular commandment to be obeyed and a particular prohibition to be observed at every stage of development.

This can be learned through experience by anyone who has a real taste for this business, who sets out to follow this spiritual path *[ṭarīqa]*, and who seeks the company of those who know it well. People are therefore not measured at the very outset by a standard that can only be applied at the ultimate stage of the whole process.

> You have been sent forth on a journey that is meant to be smooth and easy for you, not on one that is meant to be difficult or even terrifying. [The path of] this religion *[dīn]* is firmly established, so advance along it in friendship, for the traveler who gets separated can neither keep on track nor stay the course.[260]

Another example of selective repentance is the case of a person who does penance for some, but not all, of the major sins *[kabā'ir]*, in recognition of the fact that some of them are more serious than others in the sight of Allāh, and that the punishment they incur is harsher and more severe. For instance, he may decide to do penance for murder *[qatl]*, robbery *[nahb]*, and all the wrongs he has committed against his fellow human beings, in recognition of the fact that human claims *[duyūn al-'ibād]* must never be left unsettled, whereas pardon is easily and swiftly obtained in matters that are entirely between him and Allāh (Exalted is He).

Or then again, he may decide to do penance for the sin of drinking intoxicating liquor *[shurb al-khamr]*, but not for having committed adultery or fornication *[zinā]*, in recognition of the fact that intoxicating liquor is the key to all that is evil *[al-khamru miftāḥu'sh-sharr]*. In the irrational state induced by intoxicating liquor, a person is liable to commit all the sins in the book. Without being consciously aware of what he is doing, he may become guilty of slander *[qadhf]*,[261] verbal abuse *[sabb]*, rejection of belief *[kufr]* in Allāh, sexual misconduct *[zinā]*, homicide *[qatl]*, and the unlawful seizure of property *[ghaṣb]*, because intoxicating liquor is the compendium of all sinful acts of disobedience; it is their mother and their point of origin.

Yet another example of selective repentance is the case of a person who does penance for a minor sin *[ṣaghīra]*, or for several minor sins *[ṣaghā'ir]*, while he is still persisting in the commission of a major sin *[kabīra]*. For instance, he may decide to do penance for backbiting *[ghība]*, or for staring at a forbidden object *[muḥarram]*, even though he is still persisting in the greater sin of drinking intoxicating liquor. In coming to such a decision, he will be influenced by the intensity of his addiction to intoxicating liquor, the passion he has developed for it, the

[260] The editor of the Arabic text (Damascus edition) has marked this paragraph as a quotation. It may be a saying of the Prophet (Allāh bless him and give him peace), or even a Divine saying *[Ḥadīth Qudsī]*.

[261] See note [153] above.

fact that drinking it has become a regular habit, and the self-induced illusion that he is using it as a medicine to cure his ailments.

It is true, of course, that the use of alcohol for medicinal purposes may sometimes be prescribed for us, but the addict's view is distorted by the devil *[shaiṭān]*, who cunningly helps him to see his addiction in a favorable light, and by the sheer force of his own appetite for liquor. He drinks it for the sake of the pleasure and enjoyment it provides, in order to banish his cares and worries, and because it is supposed to be good for one's physical health.

The more he becomes addicted to it, the more it makes him oblivious to the disastrous consequences that lie in store for him. It makes him heedless of the punishment that Allāh will eventually inflict upon him on account of his addiction. It makes him unaware of its corrupting influence on his religious values and his worldly affairs alike, because it erodes the rational faculty, the faculty that is used to balance religious and worldly interests and keep them in good array.

When we maintain the validity of repenting some of these sins but not others, we are simply acknowledging the inescapable fact that the record of every Muslim, for all practical purposes, is bound to show a combination of worshipful obedience to Allāh and sinful disobedience toward Him. Individuals differ, of course, but only in the specific details of their case histories. As for the enormity or triviality of particular sins, this is a relative question, since it all depends on the spiritual states of the people concerned, and whether they are close to Allāh or distant from Him.

The inveterate transgressor *[fāsiq]* would therefore do well to say: "If the devil *[shaiṭān]* succeeds, by means of some irresistible temptation, in coercing me to commit certain acts of sinful disobedience, there is no need for me to let go of the reins completely, to abandon all semblance of restraint, and then freely indulge in every kind of sin. Instead of simply giving up the struggle, I shall at least make the effort to single out a few sins that I could give up without too much trouble, then I shall stop committing them.

My success in dealing with some of the problems may serve as an atonement *[kaffāra]* for some of the rest. Perhaps Allāh will notice that I am afraid of offending Him by committing certain sinful acts of disobedience, that I am now refraining from them for His sake, and that I am doing battle with my lower self *[nafs]* and my devil *[shaiṭān]* in the process. If He does take notice, He will surely support my efforts and help me to succeed. Through His mercy, He may even keep me from committing any other sinful acts of disobedience!"

If the truth of the matter were not as we have stated it, no ritual prayer *[ṣalāt]* performed by an inveterate transgressor *[fāsiq]* could ever be valid, nor could there be any validity to his fasting *[ṣawm]*, his payment of the alms-due *[zakāt]*, his pilgrimage *[ḥajj]*, or any other act of worshipful obedience, since he would be told:

"You are an inveterate transgressor. You have excluded yourself from obedience to Allāh by your inveterate sinfulness *[fisq]*. You act in defiance of His commandment, so this worship *[ʿibāda]* of yours must be intended for some purpose other than the service of Allāh (Exalted is He). If you are serious in claiming that your worship is really and truly for the sake of Allāh (Almighty and Glorious is He), you must abandon your inveterate sinfulness. Obedience to Allāh must be your sole concern, so it is inconceivable that you could perform your ritual prayer *[ṣalāt]* with the intention of winning Allāh's favor, as long as you have not demonstrated your intention to win His favor by refraining from your inveterate sinfulness." This is so preposterous, of course, that it could not actually be said.

The only true analogy is the case of a person who is in debt to the tune of two dīnārs, owing one dīnār to each of two men. Although he is sufficiently solvent to be capable of repaying them both, he hands one of the two dīnārs to one of the two men, and refuses to hand over the other. He disavows his debt to the second man, even though he is well aware that the man is perfectly entitled to receive what is due to him. In a case like this, there can be no doubt that the debtor's conscience is clear of the obligation he has actually discharged, while it still bears the burden of responsibility for that which he has disavowed and refused to settle.

By the same token, a person who obeys Allāh (Exalted is He), at least as far as some of His commandments are concerned, is obedient to Him by virtue of his obedience. If he also disobeys Him by disregarding some of His prohibitions, he is disobedient toward Him by virtue of his disobedience. He is therefore a "solvent" believer *[mu'min malī']* whose faith is less than perfect. He is an obedient servant [of Allāh] by virtue of his obedience, and a disobedient and recalcitrant servant by virtue of his recalcitrance.

This is the habitual condition of someone who is still a mixer *[mukhliṭ]* as far as his religion *[dīn]* is concerned. It does not change until he reaches the stage of development where his passions *[hawā]* have ceased to be in control. He will then be acquitted of all acts of sinful disobedience, unless Allāh wishes to condemn him for them, since we have no absolute immunity *['iṣma]*.

Allāh relents toward those who repent, and He graciously bestows His mercy upon those who turn away from sin.

Traditional narratives *[akhbār]* and reports *[āthār]* on the subject of repentance *[tawba]*.[262]

It was Jābir ibn ʿAbdi'llāh[263] (may Allāh be well pleased with him and with his father) who narrated the following traditions:

Allāh's Messenger (Allāh bless him and give him peace) delivered a sermon one Friday, in the course of which he told us:

> O people, repent to Allāh before you die. Set about the performance of righteous works *[aʿmāl ṣāliḥa]* without delay, before you are too preoccupied. Reconcile whatever differences you have with your Lord, for then you will prosper. Be generous in giving alms *[ṣadaqa]*, for then you will be well provided for. Enjoin that which is right and fair *[maʿrūf]*, for then you will be granted protection, and forbid that which is wrong and unfair *[munkar]*, for then you will be enabled to achieve success.[264]

He would often say (Allāh bless him and give him peace):

> O Allāh, forgive me and relent toward me, for You are indeed the Ever-Relenting *[Tawwāb]*, the All-Compassionate *[Raḥīm]*.

The Prophet (Allāh bless him and give him peace) also said:

> When Iblīs was sent down to the earth, he said: "By Your Glory and by Your Majesty, I swear that I shall not cease to mislead the human being *[ibn Ādam]*, as long as he has a breath left in his body." The Lord then said: "By My Glory and by My Majesty, I shall not refuse to accept his repentance, as long as he has not made that gurgling sound with his final breath."

Muḥammad ibn ʿAbdi'llāh as-Sulamī (may Allāh bestow His mercy upon him) is reported as having said:

"Once, in Medina, I went and sat with a group of people who were Companions of Allāh's Messenger (Allāh bless him and give him peace). While I was sitting in their presence, one man said: 'I heard

[262] For the technical meanings of the terms *akhbār* (plural of *khabar*) and *āthār* (plural of *athar*), see notes [178] and [207] above.

[263] See note [223] above.

[264] For an extensive account of the duty to enjoin that which is right and fair *[al-amr bi'l-maʿrūf]*, and forbid that which is wrong and unfair *[an-nahy ʿani'l-munkar]*, see Vol. 1, pp. 151–70.

Allāh's Messenger (Allāh bless him and give him peace) say:

> "If anyone repents before his death, by at least half a day, Allāh will relent toward him."'

Then another man said: 'I heard Allāh's Messenger (Allāh bless him and give him peace) say:

> "If anyone repents before making the [final] gurgling sound *[ghargharal]*, Allāh will relent toward him."'"

Muḥammad ibn Muṭrif (may Allāh bestow His mercy upon him) is reported as having said: "Allāh says:

> 'Woe unto the son of Adam! He commits a sin, then he begs Me for forgiveness, and so I forgive him. Woe unto him! He promptly repeats the sin, then begs Me for forgiveness, and so I forgive him. Woe unto him! He will not give up his sin, but neither will he despair of My mercy. I call you to bear witness to the fact that I have indeed forgiven him.'"

It was Anas [ibn Mālik][265] (may Allāh be well pleased with him) who said: "After the revelation of the Qur'ānic verse *[āya]*:

> And [you are instructed] that you must beg forgiveness of your Lord, then turn to him in repentance. (11:3)[266]

Allāh's Messenger (Allāh bless him and give him peace) and his Companions would pray for forgiveness a hundred times every day, and they used to say: 'We beg forgiveness of Allāh, and we turn to him in repentance *[nastaghfiru'llāha wa natūbu ilaih]*.'"

Anas (may Allāh be well pleased with him) also reported the following tradition:

> A man once came to Allāh's Messenger (Allāh bless him and give him peace) and said: "O Messenger of Allāh, I am guilty of a sin." When the Messenger (Allāh bless him and give him peace) told him: "You must ask forgiveness of Allāh," the man said: "I do repent, but then I commit the same sin all over again."
>
> The Messenger (Allāh bless him and give him peace) then said: "However often you sin, you must always repent, so that Satan will be the one who reaches the point of sheer exhaustion." The man said: "O Prophet of Allāh, in that case my sins are likely to be very numerous," so he replied (Allāh bless him and give him peace): "Allāh's readiness to pardon is greater than your sins."

[265] Abū Ḥamza Anas ibn Mālik (d. A.H. 91–3) is one of the most prolific narrators of Prophetic tradition. His mother presented him as a servant to the Prophet (Allāh bless him and give him peace), in whose service he remained until his master died. Anas himself lived on to a very advanced age (according to various accounts, he was somewhere between 97 and 107 years old when he died).

[266] *wa ani'staghfirū Rabbakum thumma tūbū ilaihi.*

Al-Ḥasan [al-Baṣrī] (may Allāh bestow His mercy upon him) once said: "You must not entertain the wishful expectation of forgiveness without repentance *[tawba]*, nor of spiritual reward without good work *[ʿamal]*, because it is impertinent to provoke Allāh by behaving in a way that is calculated to displease Him, by neglecting the work that pleases Him, and then expecting Him to grant forgiveness. Those wishful expectations will beguile you, until His verdict on you comes into effect."

Surely you must have heard Him say (Exalted is He):

> And wishful expectations beguiled you until the ordinance of Allāh came to pass, and the Deluder deluded you concerning Allāh. (57:14)
>
> And I am indeed All-Forgiving toward anyone who repents and believes, and does righteous work, and then is rightly guided. (20:82)
>
> And My mercy embraces all things, so I shall prescribe it for those who do their duty and pay the alms-due, and those who believe in Our signs. (7:156)

The ambitious desire for Divine Mercy and the Garden of Paradise, without repentance *[tawba]* and without devotion to duty *[taqwā]*, is therefore nothing short of folly, ignorance and delusion, because repentance and devotion to duty are both clearly stipulated in these last two verses *[āyatain]* quoted from the Qurʾān.

The Prophet (Allāh bless him and give him peace) has said:

> The true believer *[muʾmin]* looks upon his sins as if he were standing at the foot of a mountain, afraid that it might topple down upon him. As for the shameless sinner *[fājir]*, he looks upon his sins as if they were merely flies that had settled on his nose, so he assumes that they will buzz off as soon as he tells them to do so.

He once said (Allāh bless him and give him peace):

> It may happen that the servant [of Allāh] commits a sin, and that the sin enables him to enter the Garden of Paradise.

When they asked him: "O Prophet of Allāh, how can it possibly enable him to enter the Garden of Paradise?" he replied:

> The sin keeps staring him in the eye, so he begs forgiveness for it. He feels remorse over it, and repents, so it actually enables him to enter the Garden of Paradise!

He has also said (Allāh bless him and give him peace):

> I have never seen a remedy that is more appropriate, or that takes effect more rapidly, than a new good deed applied to an old sin.

In the words of Allāh (Almighty and Glorious is He):

> Good deeds drive evil deeds away. This is a reminder for the mindful. (11:114)

The Prophet (Allāh bless him and give him peace) has said:

> When the servant [of Allāh] commits a sin, it takes the form of a black stain inside his heart. Then, if he repents, seeks refuge, and begs forgiveness, his heart will be cleansed of that stain. But if he does not repent, does not resort to humble entreaty, and does not beg forgiveness, sin will be added to sin, and blackness to blackness, until his heart becomes blind and he must die.

Such is the import of the words of Allāh (Exalted is He):

> No indeed; but what they have been earning has rusted upon their hearts. (83:14)

The Prophet (Allāh bless him and give him peace) has said:

> To give up a sinful error is an easier matter than trying to repent, so seize the opportunity while death is taking a nap.

Ādam ibn Ziyād (may Allāh bestow His mercy upon him) would often say: "A person like you should persuade himself to accept the idea that death has come to collect him once already, but he asked his Lord for a reprieve and He granted his request, so now he must always act in obedience to Allāh."

It has been said that Allāh (Exalted is He) once conveyed *[awḥā]* this warning to David (peace be upon him) by way of inspiration:

> Be on your guard in case I snatch you unawares, so that you encounter Me without any evidence to vindicate yourself.

A certain righteous man once entered the presence of ʿAbd al-Malik ibn Marwān,[267] who said to him: "Try making an appeal to my conscience." The following conversation then took place:

"Are you in a proper state of readiness for the advent of death, if it should come upon you?"

"No."

"Well then, are you determined to have this state of affairs transformed into a condition that would please you?"

"No."

"Do you believe that there is a dwelling place after death, in which you can ask for preferential treatment?"[268]

[267] ʿAbd al-Malik ibn Marwān was one of the tyrannical Caliphs of the Damascus-based Umayyad dynasty. He succeeded his father, Marwān ibn al-Ḥakam, in A.H. 65/685 C.E. and his reign lasted until A.H. 86/705 C.E., when he was succeeded by his son, al-Walīd ibn ʿAbd al-Malik.

[268] An allusion to the verse *[āya]* of the Qurʾān in which Allāh (Almighty and Glorious is He) has said:

> The Fire [of Hell] shall be a lodging for them; and if they ask to be treated favorably, they shall not receive favorable treatment. (41:24)

"No."

The righteous man later remarked: "I never saw such complacent attitudes adopted toward these matters by anyone in his right mind."

The Prophet (Allāh bless him and give him peace) has said:

> Remorse is a form of repentance *[an-nadam tawba]*.[269]

He has also told us (Allāh bless him and give him peace):

> When someone commits a sin, then feels remorse over it, his remorse becomes his expiation *[kaffāra]* for the sin.

Al-Ḥasan [al-Baṣrī] (may Allāh bestow His mercy upon him) once said: "There are four essential elements to repentance *[tawba]*, namely: (1) offering a prayer of supplication *[duʿāʾ]* and then making a request for forgiveness *[istighfār]* with the tongue; (2) feeling remorse *[nadam]* with the heart; (3) practicing abstinence with the limbs and organs of the physical body; (4) making a conscientious resolution never to repeat the offense."

He also said: "What is meant by sincere repentance *[tawba naṣūḥ]* is that one repents and then does not go back to committing the sin he has repented."

The Prophet (Allāh bless him and give him peace) has said:

> He who repents his sin is like someone who is guiltless of any sin. But he who begs forgiveness for his sin, and yet persists in committing it, is like someone who mocks his Lord.
>
> As for the man who says: "I beg Your forgiveness and to You I repent," then repeats his offense, then says it again, then repeats his offense, he may do this three times, but on the fourth occasion his offense will be recorded as one of the major sins *[kabāʾir]*.

It was al-Fuḍail ibn ʿIyāḍ[270] (may Allāh bestow His mercy upon him) who said: "Be your own executor *[waṣī]* and do not appoint other men to serve as your executors. How can you blame them for squandering your estate, when you have squandered it in your own lifetime?"

[269] See p. 129 above, where this same saying of the Prophet (Allāh bless him and give him peace) is quoted at the beginning of a lengthy discussion of the nature and significance of remorse *[nadam]*.

[270] Abū ʿAlī ibn al-Fuḍail ibn ʿIyāḍ at-Tālaqānī died in Mecca in A.H. 187/803 C.E. Born in Khurāsān, he is said to have been a highwayman at the beginning of his career. After his conversion he went to Kūfa, where he studied under Sufyān ath-Thawrī and became an authority on the Traditions of the Prophet (Allāh bless him and give him peace). He is famous for his bold preaching before the Caliph Hārūn ar-Rashīd, who called him "the Prince of the Muslims."

More sayings on the subject of repentance *[tawba]*.

According to Abū Umāma al-Bāhilī (may Allāh be well pleased with him), the Prophet (Allāh bless him and give him peace) once said:

> The guardian angel of the right-hand side *[ṣāḥib al-yamīn]* is in command of the guardian angel of the left-hand side *[ṣāḥib ash-shimāl]*, so if the servant [of Allāh] does a good deed, the guardian angel of the right side records ten good deeds in his credit column, and if he does a bad deed, the guardian angel of the left side is ready to record it in his debit column—but before he has time to do so, the guardian angel of the right side says: "Don't do that just yet!" He is then obliged to restrain himself for six or seven hours of the day.
>
> During that time the servant may beg forgiveness of Allāh (Exalted is He), in which case the angel will not record anything against him, or he may fail to beg forgiveness, in which case the angel will record one bad deed in his debit column.

Another version reads as follows:

> If the servant [of Allāh] commits a sin, it is not recorded against him unless and until he commits another sin. If the sins in his debit column add up to a total of five, and if he then does one good deed, five good deeds will be recorded in his favor, and those five will be set down opposite five bad deeds. At this point Iblīs (may Allāh curse him) will cry out in dismay: "How can I hope to get the better of the son of Adam? However hard I try, he renders all my effort null and void by means of a single good deed!"

According to a report transmitted by Yūnus [ibn ʿUbaidi'llāh], on the authority of al-Ḥasan (may Allāh be well pleased with him), the Prophet (Allāh bless him and give him peace) once said:

> There is not one servant [of Allāh] who does not have two angels watching over him, and the guardian angel of the right-hand side *[ṣāḥib al-yamīn]* is in command of the guardian angel of the left-hand side *[ṣāḥib ash-shimāl]*.
>
> Whenever the servant does a bad deed, the guardian angel of the left side asks his commander: "Shall I write it down?" The guardian angel of the right side responds to this by telling him: "Leave it until he has committed five bad deeds." Then, when the servant has in fact committed five bad deeds, the guardian

> angel of the left side will ask again: "Shall I write them down?" This time the guardian angel of the right side will say: "Leave it until he does a good deed." Then, when the servant has in fact performed a good deed, the guardian angel of the right side will say to his subordinate: "We have been informed that one good deed should be multiplied by ten, so let us proceed to cancel five [bad deeds] with five [good deeds], and then make sure that five of the good deeds are definitely recorded in his favor."
>
> At this point the devil *[shaiṭān]* will cry out in dismay: "When shall I ever catch up with the son of Adam?"

These traditional sayings *[aḥādīth]* are all consistent with His words (Almighty and Glorious is He):

> And I am indeed All-Forgiving toward anyone who repents and believes, and does righteous work, and then is rightly guided. (20:82)

According to ʿAlī ibn Abī Ṭālib (may Allāh ennoble his countenance): "These words were inscribed around the Heavenly Throne *[ʿArsh]* four thousand years before Adam was created: 'And I am indeed All-Forgiving toward anyone who repents and believes, and does righteous work, and then is rightly guided.'"

These traditional sayings are also in harmony with His words (Exalted is He):

> Good deeds drive evil deeds away. This is a reminder for the mindful. (11:114)

Ibn ʿAbbās (may Allāh be well pleased with him and with his father) is reported as having said: "When the servant repents, and when Allāh relents toward him, Allāh (Exalted is He) causes that servant's angelic custodians *[ḥafaẓa]* to forget the bad deeds he has committed. He causes his physical limbs and organs to forget the sinful mistakes they have made. He causes him to forget his place of residence on earth, and He causes him to forget his place of residence in heaven. So, when he comes forth on the Day of Resurrection *[Yawm al-Qiyāma]*, there will be nothing whatsoever to bear witness against him."

The Prophet (Allāh bless him and give him peace) is reported as having said:

> He who repents his sin is like someone who is guiltless of any sin.

In one version, this is followed by the words:

> ...even if he has repeated it seventy times a day.

ʿAbdu'llāh ibn Masʿūd (may Allāh be well pleased with him) once said: "If someone says: 'I beg forgiveness of Allāh the Almighty, affirming that there is no god but He, the Ever-Living, the Eternally Self-Sustaining, and I turn to Him in repentance,'[271] and if he says this three times over, He will forgive him his sins, even if they are as many as the flecks of foam upon the ocean."

Ibn Mas'ūd (may Allāh be well pleased with him) is also reported as having said: "When a person first examines his record book on the Day of Resurrection, he will see his sinful acts of disobedience inscribed in the front part, and his good deeds toward the end. But when he turns back to the early pages of the book, he will see nothing but good deeds recorded there." This is in keeping with His words (Exalted is He):

> As for them, Allāh will change their evil deeds into good deeds. (25:70)

The recipient of this favor will be the penitent upon whose repentance *[tawba]* and contrition *[ināba]* Allāh has set the seal of acceptance.

One of our worthy forefathers *[salaf]* said: "If the servant [of Allāh] repents his sins, all the sins he has committed in the past will be converted into good deeds."

This explains why Ibn Mas'ūd (may Allāh be well pleased with him) once said: "On the Day of Resurrection, some people will wish that their bad deeds were more numerous." He only said this because Allāh (Exalted is He) had spoken of transforming bad deeds into good deeds for the benefit of whomever He might choose among His servants.

According to a report transmitted on the authority of al-Ḥasan (may Allāh be well pleased with him), the Prophet (Allāh bless him and give him peace) once said:

> If one of you committed enough sins to fill the space between heaven and earth, and then repented, Allāh would relent toward him [and accept his repentance].

Such is the import of the [Divine] saying that has come down to us in the tradition *[khabar]*:

> O son of Adam, even if you came to meet Me with sins as huge as the earth itself, I would come to meet you with a correspondingly enormous measure of forgiveness.

[271] *astaghfiru'llāha'l-'Aẓīma'lladhī lā ilāha illā Huwa'l-Ḥayyu'l-Qayyūm: wa atūbu ilaih.*

A continuation of the preceding theme.

It happened one day, according to traditional reports, that ʿAbdu'llāh ibn Masʿūd (may Allāh be well pleased with him) was making his way through a certain quarter of the city of Kūfa, when he passed by a place where some dissolute types *[fussāq]* had congregated in a house belonging to one of their own kind. They were drinking intoxicating liquor, and they had with them a singer by the name of Zādhān, who was playing the lute *[ʿūd]* as he sang with a beautiful voice.

When ʿAbdu'llāh ibn Masʿūd (may Allāh be well pleased with him) heard the song Zādhān was singing, he exclaimed aloud: "What a beautiful voice that man has! If only he would use it for the recitation *[qirāʾa]* of the Book of Allāh (Exalted is He), it would be even more beautiful!" Then he wrapped his scarf around his head [to shut out the sound] and went on his way.

"Who was that?" asked Zādhān, who had heard the voice of the passerby. "That was ʿAbdu'llāh ibn Masʿūd," they told him, "the Companion of Allāh's Messenger (Allāh bless him and give him peace)." Zādhān went on to ask what he had said, so they told him: "He said: 'What a beautiful voice that man has! If only he would use it for the recitation of the Qurʾān, it would be even more beautiful!'"

As soon as Zādhān heard this, a feeling of awe invaded his heart. He rose to his feet, dashed the lute against the floor and shattered it to pieces, then rushed out in pursuit of the man whose words had touched him so profoundly. When he caught up with ʿAbdu'llāh, he put the scarf around his own neck and began to weep close beside him, so ʿAbdu'llāh embraced him, and the pair of them wept as they hugged each other. After a while, ʿAbdu'llāh (may Allāh be well pleased with him) said: "How can I fail to love someone whom Allāh loves?"

Thus it came to pass that Zādhān repented, gave up playing the lute, and stayed close to ʿAbdu'llāh until he had learned the Qurʾān. As a matter of fact, he acquired such a vast store of learning that he became an Imām in the field of religious knowledge *[ʿilm]*. Many traditional reports *[akhbār]* are prefaced by the narrator with the words: "As related by Zādhān, on the authority of ʿAbdu'llāh ibn Masʿūd (may Allāh be well pleased with him) ...," and: "As related by Zādhān, on the authority of Salmān al-Fārisī[272] (may Allāh be well pleased with him)...."

The next story is one of the tales of the Israelites *[Isrāʾīliyyāt]*:[273]

Once upon a time there lived a seductive whore, a singer who captivated people with her beauty. The door of her house was always open, and she used to sit on a couch facing the door, so that any man who happened to pass by would be sure to see her and be tempted by her charm. Before she would permit him to enter into her presence, however, he would be required to produce ten dīnārs [gold coins], or even more than that.

Now it happened one day that a pious worshipper, one of the Children of Israel, was walking past her door when he caught a glimpse of her inside the house. At the sight of her sitting on the couch, he became so infatuated with her that he got into an argument with his own lower self *[nafs]*. He eventually appealed to Allāh (Exalted is He), beseeching Him to let the feeling disappear from his heart. In spite of this, his lower self continued to respond to the temptation.

Since he could not control his lower self, he went and sold some junk he had in his possession. As soon as he had raised the necessary number of dīnārs, he presented himself at the woman's door, at which point she told him to hand the gold to an agent of hers, and made an appointment with him for a certain date and time.

When the man showed up at her house to keep the appointment, he found her beautifully made up, sitting there waiting for him on her couch. The pious worshipper went in and sat beside her on the couch, but then, just when he had stretched out his hands to touch her and was beginning to enjoy what he was doing with her, Allāh suddenly overwhelmed him with His mercy, in gracious recognition of his previous worship. He immediately found himself realizing within his heart: "Allāh (Exalted is He) can see me in this situation from His

[272] Salmān al-Fārisī [the Persian], a notable Companion of the Prophet (Allāh bless him and give him peace), is one of the most popular figures in Islāmic legends. He died ca. A.H. 35.

[273] The traditions called *Isrāʾīliyyāt* are generally transmitted on the authority of notable Jewish converts to Islām, such as Wahb ibn Munabbih and Kaʿb al-Aḥbār.

Throne on high. Here am I, engaged in something so unlawful *[ḥarām]* that all my good work has come to nothing!" His heart was stricken with dread. He began to tremble all over, and a change became noticeable in the color of his skin.

The woman looked at him and saw that he was changing color, so she said to him: "What has come over you, man?" He replied: "I am afraid of Allāh, of my Lord, so please permit me to leave." She then said to him: "Woe unto you! Many people would dearly love to experience the pleasure you have found, so what can this be that has such a weird effect upon you?" All he could say to this was: "I am really afraid of Allāh (Glorious is He, to Whom all praise is due!), and as for the money I paid to your agent, you may treat it as rightfully yours, so please permit me to leave!"

The woman responded to this by saying: "It seems as though you have never done this kind of thing before." When he said: "No, indeed I have not," she asked him: "Where are you from, and what is your name?" So he told her that he came from the village called such and such, and that his own name was so and so. At this point she finally permitted him to take his leave of her, so off he went, wailing and lamenting and weeping over himself.

As for the woman, her heart was suddenly stricken with a sense of awe, inspired by her experience with that pious worshipper, so she said inwardly to herself: "This man was committing the very first sin he had ever committed, and yet he was invaded by a fear of such intensity, while I have been sinning since the year dot. But the fact is that the Lord he fears is also my Lord, which means that my fear ought to be even more intense than his fear."

She thereupon repented to Allāh (Exalted is He), locked her door to shut people out, dressed in rags and tatters, and turned in the direction of worshipful service *[ʿibādā]*. She came to be in her worship what Allāh (Exalted is He) wished her to be, so she said inwardly to herself: "If only I could meet up with that man again, perhaps he would marry me. Then I could be with him and learn all about my religion *[dīn]* from him, and he would be a great help to me in the worshipful service of my Lord."

She therefore equipped herself to undertake a journey, carrying with her as many goods and servants as Allāh willed, and so it was that she came in due course to the village the man had mentioned. She made inquiries about him, so they informed the pious worshipper that a woman had arrived, and that she was asking about him. The pious worshipper then came out to meet her, and when the woman saw him, she tried to hide her face from his sight in case he might recognize her. But when the pious worshipper eventually saw her, recognized her face, and remembered what had happened between the pair of them, he uttered a great cry and his spirit *[rūḥ]* departed from him.

The poor woman was left to mourn her loss, and she said, speaking inwardly to herself: "I came all this way on account of him, and now he has died. I wonder if there is anyone among his close relatives who happens to be needing a wife?" As if they had heard her question, the local people told her: "He has a brother who is a righteous man *[ṣāliḥ]*, but he finds it hard to make a living, and he has no money or property at all." She responded to this news by saying: "That does not present a problem, since I have plenty of wealth for both of us." The man's brother then came forward and married her, and she eventually bore him seven sons, all of whom became Prophets *[anbiyā᾽]* among the Children of Israel.[274]

You can hardly fail to recognize the blessed grace *[baraka]* of truthfulness, obedience, and goodness of intention, when you consider how Allāh used ʿAbdu'llāh ibn Masʿūd, because he was so honest and well-intentioned, as His instrument for guiding Zādhān to the right path. This should make you realize that you cannot be instrumental in reforming the wicked until you yourself have come to be a truly righteous person *[ṣāliḥ]*, fearful of your Lord when you are alone in private, sincerely devoted to Him when you are in the company of other people, uninfluenced in your behavior by the desire to impress your fellow creatures, and affirming the Oneness of Allāh (Almighty and Glorious is He) in every aspect of your life.

Once you have reached that stage of development, you will experience an increase in your capacity for effective action and in your ability to achieve successful results. You will be shielded from the influence of the passions *[hawā]* and protected against temptation *[ighwā᾽]* in all its forms, whether it be from the devil *[shaiṭān]*, the jinn, or human beings.

[274] In a footnote to the Arabic text, the editor of the Damascus edition of *al-Ghunya* says: "This is not a valid statement concerning the Prophets *[anbiyā᾽]*. Perhaps it is one of the Israelite traditions *[Isrā᾽īliyyāt]*."

You will be kept safe from all abominations, from the morally corrupt, from heretical innovations *[bidaʿ]*, and from errors of every kind. Then, because of the positive influence you will naturally exert, the elimination of indecent behavior will be accomplished without obtrusive and self-righteous effort, and without turning that which is right and proper *[maʿrūf]* into something wrong and improper *[munkar]*, as is usually the case in our own day and age.

The typical person nowadays is unwilling to admit that he could ever do anything reprehensible, so he readily branches out into a host of abominations and terrible wickedness, such as verbal abuse, slanderous accusation *[qadhf]*,[275] assault and battery, molestation,[276] and the misappropriation of material assets. This is all due to the fact that people are so lacking in their honesty *[ṣidq]*, so deficient in their faith *[īmān]* and conviction *[yaqīn]*, and so totally dominated by their whims and passions *[ahwiya]*. Reprehensible behavior has therefore been carried to great lengths among them. The elimination of such misconduct is incumbent on them as a religious duty *[farḍ]*, which they ought to discharge by making protracted efforts to examine and correct their own faults, but they prefer to find fault with everyone but themselves. They disregard the duty that is incumbent on the individual *[farḍ ʿain]*, and attach importance only to the collective duty *[farḍ ʿala'l-kifāya]*.[277] They pay no attention to what ought to concern them, and become preoccupied with that which is no concern of theirs, ignoring the words of the Prophet (Allāh bless him and give him peace):

> Part of the excellence of a man's Islām is paying no attention to that which does not concern him.

If a person truly wishes to become an instrument for the speedy elimination of reprehensible conduct, he must make a practice of criticizing and reprimanding his own lower self *[nafs]*. He must hold it in check and wean it away from sinful acts of disobedience, from those that are inwardly concealed as well as those that are outwardly apparent.

Once he has cleansed himself of all such faults, and not a moment sooner, it will be appropriate for him to pay attention to other people. When he has reached that stage, he will be enabled to facilitate the

[275] See note [153] above.

[276] Literally, the ripping off of clothes *[takhrīq ath-thiyāb]*.

[277] See note [161] above.

elimination of reprehensible behavior by the best of all possible means, as in the case of ʿAbdu'llāh ibn Masʿūd (may Allāh be well pleased with him).[278]

Let us also consider the blessed grace *[baraka]* that was bestowed in recognition of devout service *[ʿibāda]* and truthfulness *[ṣidq]* on the part of that pious worshipper, as we recall how Allāh rescued him from the prostitute and saved him from the commission of a major sin.

> So it was, that We might turn evil and lewdness away from him; he was surely one of Our devoted servants. (12:24)

Allāh (Exalted is He) intervened between him and that harlot, giving him credit for his previous good conduct, for his honesty in private situations, and the excellent quality of his obedience in all the days and hours that had gone before.

Let us go on to consider how Allāh (Exalted is He) granted salvation to that whore, through the blessed influence of the pious worshipper, and then how his blessed influence reached his brother. Let us remember that Allāh delivered the man's brother from his life of poverty and hardship, and married him to the best of women. He enriched him and provided for him from a source he could never have imagined.[279] He caused him to be the father of seven Prophets *[anbiyāʾ]*, and He caused her to be their mother (peace be upon them all).

All that is good resides in worshipful obedience, and all that is evil lies in sinful disobedience, so away with sinful disobedience, and away with us too, if we are members of its family!

[278] As the reader will no doubt recall, ʿAbdu'llāh ibn Masʿūd (may Allāh be well pleased with him) was instrumental in reforming the conduct of Zādhān.

[279] An allusion to the promise made by Allāh (Almighty and Glorious is He), when He tells us in the Qurʾān:

> And whenever someone observes his duty to Allāh, Allāh will prepare a way out for him. And He will provide for him from sources he could never imagine. And whoever puts all his trust in Allāh, He will suffice him *[wa man yattaqi'llāha yajʿal lahu makhrajā—wa yarzuqhu min ḥaithu lā yaḥtasib: wa man yatawakkal ʿala'llāhi fa-Huwa ḥasbuh]*. (65:2,3)

Four sets of four:

The four signs that point to repentance *[tawba]*; the four signs that point to the acceptance of repentance; the four obligations owed to the penitent by other people; the four noble honors conferred on the penitent by Allāh (Exalted is He).

Four things make it possible to recognize the genuine nature of the penitent's repentance *[tawbat at-tā'ib]*, namely:

(a) The fact that he keeps his tongue from indulging in idle gossip, backbiting *[ghība]*, slander *[namīma]*, and telling lies.

(b) The fact that he does not harbor within his heart any feelings of envy or animosity toward anyone.

(c) The fact that he does not associate with evil companions, for such people would try to persuade him to abandon the resolution he has made, and their influence would make him feel confused about the validity of his firm commitment. In order to ensure that nothing of this sort can happen, he must persist in frequenting the kind of environment that will tend to increase his enthusiasm for repentance, and that will offer him plenty of incentives to carry his commitment through to completion, by strengthening his fear of failure and his hope of success.

His heart will thus be released from the knot that has kept him tied to bad habits, so he will desist from the regular practice of unlawful activities, and he will tighten the reins to prevent his lower self *[nafs]* from pursuing the desires of the flesh. As well as renouncing his sinful conduct for the immediate present, he will confirm and strengthen his determination to avoiding any repetition of it in the future.

(d) The fact that he is ready to face death, filled with remorse, seeking forgiveness for the sins he has committed in the past, and striving to obey his Lord.

2. The signs that indicate that the penitent has had his repentance accepted are also said to be four in number:

(a) The fact that he has severed all connection with immoral companions *[aṣḥāb al-fisq]*, since he now has too much self-respect to go on seeing them, and has taken instead to mingling with the righteous *[ṣāliḥīn]*.

(b) The fact that he has lost all interest in sin, and is now devoting all his energy to acts of worshipful obedience.

(c) The fact that the joy of this world has departed from his heart, and it is obvious that the sorrow of the hereafter is always in his heart.

(d) The fact that he sees no need to concern himself with that which Allāh has guaranteed to him, namely, his means of sustenance *[rizq]*, and he is therefore wholly devoted to the obedient fulfillment of whatever Allāh commands him to perform.

If these four signs are present in him, the penitent must surely be one of those of whom Allāh (Exalted is He) has said:

> Truly Allāh loves those who turn to Him repentant, and He loves those who keep themselves in purity. (2:222)

3. As for the obligations owed to the penitent by other people, these are also four in number:

(a) They must come to love him, because Allāh (Exalted is He) already loves him.

(b) They must support him with their prayer of supplication *[duʿāʾ]*, beseeching Allāh to keep him steadfast in repentance.

(c) They must not reproach him for the sins he has committed in the past, because the Prophet (Allāh bless him and give him peace) is reported as having said:

> If someone reproaches a believer *[muʾmin]* for a vile misdeed *[fāḥisha]*, he is [thereby offering himself as] an expiation for it, and Allāh (Exalted is He) is bound to make him commit that same offense himself. If someone reproaches a believer for a crime *[jarīra]*, he will not leave this world until he has committed it himself, and been disgraced because of it.

Besides, the believer does not fall into sin deliberately and on purpose, or because he is convinced that it is required of him as a religious duty! It only happens because of the enticement of the devil *[shaiṭān]*, the excessive ferocity of passionate desire, the intensity of lust, and the cumulative effect of negligence and heedlessness. Allāh (Exalted is He) has told us:

> And He has made unbelief and iniquity and disobedience detestable to you. (49:7)

In other words, He has informed us that He has made sinful disobedience hateful to the believers, so it cannot be permissible to reproach a believer for disobedience when he has repented *[tāba]* and returned to obedience *[anāba]*. Far from reproaching the penitent, his fellow believers should offer prayers on his behalf, pleading for his repentance to be confirmed, and for him to be granted support and protection.

(d) They should spend time in his company, enter into conversation with him, and single him out for special attention.

4. Allāh (Exalted is He) will also honor the penitent with four noble favors:

(a) He will rid him of every trace of sin, as if he had never sinned at all.

(b) Allāh (Exalted is He) will love him.

(c) He will protect him from Satan, who will not be allowed to have power over him.

(d) He will grant him security from fear, even before He removes him from this world, because He has said (Exalted is He):

> The angels descend upon them, saying: "Do not fear and do not grieve, but hear good tidings of the Garden [of Paradise] that you have been promised." (41:30)

Some sayings of the Shaikhs of the Spiritual Path *[Shuyūkh aṭ-Ṭarīqa]* on the subject of repentance *[tawba]*.

It was Abū ʿAlī ad-Daqqāq[280] (may Allāh bestow His mercy upon him) who said:

"Repentance has three parts or stages: *Tawba*, which is an initial stage; *ināba*, which is an intermediate stage; and *awba*, which is an ultimate stage. The term *tawba* applies to the repentance of one who repents because of the fear of punishment. The term *ināba* applies to the repentance of one who is motivated by the desire for reward or the dreadful prospect of chastisement. The term *awba* applies to the repentance of one who repents in deference to the Divine commandment, not because of the desire for reward or the fear of chastisement."

Some maintain that *tawba* is the appropriate term for the repentance of ordinary believers *[muʾminīn]*, since Allāh (Exalted is He) has said:

> And repent unto Allāh all together, O believers, for then you may be able to succeed. (24:31)[281]

They maintain that *ināba* is the appropriate term for the repentance of the saints *[awliyāʾ]* who are drawn close [to the Lord], citing the words of Allāh (Exalted is He):

> [Those who fear the All-Merciful in secret] and come with a penitently turning heart. (50:33)[282]

[280] Abū ʿAlī ad-Daqqāq (d. 1016 C.E.) was the founder of a spiritual center in Nishapur, called Khānaqāh-i Sarāwī. One of his pupils, Abu Saʿīd ibn Abi 'l-Khair of Maihana in Khurāsān, was a man of great saintliness who met and corresponded with the master-philosopher Avicenna [Ibn Sīnā]. Another was Abu 'l-Qāsim al-Qushairī, the author of an important and frequently quoted treatise entitled ar-Risālat al-Qushairiyya.

[281] *wa tūbū ila'llāhi jamīʿan ayyuha'l-muʾminūna laʿallakum tufliḥūn*. The Arabic word *tūbū* ("repent") is an imperative form of the verb *tāba*, which is derived from the same triliteral root—*t–w–b*—as the noun *tawba* ("repentance").

[282] *[man khashiya'r-Raḥmāna bi'l-ghaibi] wa jāʾa bi-qalbin munīb*. The word *munīb* ("penitently turning") is a participial adjective, from the same triliteral root—*n–w–b*—as the verbal noun *ināba* ("the act of turning [in repentance]").

As for *awba,* they maintain that this is the appropriate term for the repentance of the Prophets *[anbiyā᾽]* and Messengers *[rusul],* on the basis of their interpretation of the words of Allāh (Exalted is He):

> An excellent servant indeed [was the Prophet Job], for he was ever returning [in repentance to his Lord]! (38:44)[283]

According to al-Junaid[284] (may Allāh the Exalted bestow His mercy upon him): "Repentance *[tawba]* has three significant requirements: The penitent must feel remorse. He must make a firm resolution to refrain from any future lapse into conduct forbidden by Allāh. He must make a strenuous effort to compensate for all the wrongs he has committed."

"Repentance *[tawba],*" said Sahl ibn ʿAbdi'llāh [at-Tustarī] (may Allāh bestow His mercy upon him), "means abstaining from procrastination *[taswīf].*"[285]

Al-Junaid said: "I once heard al-Ḥārith [al-Muḥāsibī] say: 'I never say: "O Allāh, I beg You to grant me repentance." What I say instead is: "I beg You to grant me the appetite for repentance."'"

Al-Junaid also said: "I entered the presence of Sarī [as-Saqaṭī][286] (may Allāh bestow His mercy upon him) one day, and I noticed that a change had come over him, so I said to him: 'What is the matter with you?' To this he replied: 'A young man came to visit me, and he asked me about repentance *[tawba],* so I said to him: "It means that you must not forget

283 *niʿma'l-ʿabd: innahu awwāb.* The Arabic word *awwāb* ("ever returning") is an intensive adjective, or adjectival noun, derived from the same triliteral root—*᾽-w-b*—as the verbal noun *awba* ("the act of returning [in repentance]").

284 Abu 'l-Qāsim ibn Muḥammad ibn al-Junaid al-Khazzāz al-Qawārīrī an-Nihāwandī (d. A.H. 298/910 C.E.). The son of a glass merchant and nephew of Sarī as-Saqaṭī, he was a close associate of al-Muḥāsibī. Renowned for the clarity of his perception and the firmness of his self-control, he earned a reputation as the principal exponent of the "sober" school of Islāmic mysticism. His *Rasā᾽il* [Epistles] consist of letters to private individuals, and short tractates on mystical themes, some cast in the form of commentaries on Qur᾽ānic texts.

285 The Arabic verbal noun *taswīf* is derived from the particle *sawfa,* which is prefixed to a verb in order to emphasize that the action concerned will not take place until some time in the future. Sahl ibn ʿAbdi'llāh at-Tustarī (may Allāh bestow His mercy upon him) was no doubt aware of the saying of the Prophet (Allāh bless him and give him peace):

> Doomed to perdition are the procrastinators *[musawwifūn],* the people who keep saying: "We are going to repent *[sawfa natūbu].*"

286 Abu'l-Ḥasan Sarī ibn al-Mughallis as-Saqaṭī was the uncle and teacher of Junaid (may Allāh bestow His mercy on them both). Having begun his career in Baghdād as a dealer in secondhand goods, he became a pupil of Maʿrūf al-Karkhī (may Allāh bestow His mercy upon him). He died in A.H. 253/867 C.E., at the age of 98.

your sin." He contradicted me, however, for he said: "Oh no, repentance means that you do forget your sins!"' So I [al-Junaid] said: 'In my view, the truth of the matter is as the young man expressed it.'

"When Sarī asked why I took this view, I went on to say: 'Because I was once in the state of crude inadequacy *[jafā᾿]*, but then He transported me into the state of adequate sufficiency *[wafā᾿]*, so the recollection of crude inadequacy, when one is in the state of purity *[ṣafā᾿]*, is a futile exercise.' Sarī thereupon fell silent."

Sahl ibn ʿAbdi'llāh [at-Tustarī] (may Allāh bestow His mercy upon him) was another who said: "Repentance means that you must not forget your sin." But when al-Junaid (may Allāh bestow His mercy upon him) was asked about repentance, he replied: "It means that you do forget your sin."

Abū Naṣr as-Sarrāj [287] (may Allāh bestow His mercy upon him) offered the following explanation of the apparent contradiction between these two statements: "Sahl was calling attention to the spiritual states of those who are still seekers *[murīdīn]* and who therefore need to be given different signals, sometimes positive and sometimes negative. As for al-Junaid, he was referring to the repentance of those who have really experienced the truth *[muḥaqqiqīn]*, and who therefore do not remember their sins, because their hearts are so overwhelmed by the Sublime Majesty of Allāh (Exalted is He) that they are constantly devoted to the remembrance of Him."

He also said: "This is reminiscent of the occasion when Ruwaim responded to a question about repentance by saying: 'Repentance from repentance! *[at-tawba mina't-tawba]*.'"

According to Dhu'n-Nūn al-Miṣrī (may Allāh bestow His mercy upon him): "The repentance of ordinary folk is turning away from sins, while the repentance of the élite *[khawāṣṣ]* is turning away from heedless negligence *[ghafla]*."

According to Abu'l-Ḥusain an-Nūrī[288] (may Allāh bestow His mercy

[287] Abū Naṣr ʿAbdu'llāh ibn ʿAlī as-Sarrāj (may Allāh bestow His mercy upon him), who died in A.H. 378/988 C.E., is the author of a fundamental and much-quoted work entitled *Kitāb al-Lumaʿ fi't-Taṣawwuf*, of which an edition by R. A. Nicholson was published in the E. J. W. Gibb Memorial Series (Leiden–London, 1914).

[288] Abu'l-Ḥusain Aḥmad ibn Muḥammad an-Nūrī, whose family came from Khurāsān, was a native of Baghdād. He was a pupil of Sarī as-Saqaṭī and a faithful companion of al-Junaid (may Allāh bestow His mercy upon them). A leading figure in the Baghdād circle, he composed some fine poetry. He died in A.H. 295/908 C.E.

upon him): "Repentance means that you must turn away from everything apart from Allāh (Almighty and Glorious is He)."

ʿAbdu'llāh ibn Muḥammad ibn ʿAlī (may Allāh bestow His mercy upon him and upon his father and grandfather) once said: "How great is the difference between a penitent who is repenting sinful errors, a penitent who is repenting moments of heedless negligence, and a penitent who is repenting conceited pride in good deeds!"

It was Abū Bakr al-Wāsiṭī (may Allāh bestow His mercy upon him) who said: "Sincere repentance *[at-tawbat an-naṣūḥ]*[289] means that no trace of sinful disobedience remains attached to the person who is repenting, neither in private nor in public. When someone's repentance is sincere, he is not the least bit worried about anything that may lie in store for him that night or the morning after."

In his intimate communion *[munājāt]*, Yaḥyā ibn Muʿādh ar-Rāzī (may Allāh bestow His mercy upon him) used to say: "My God *[Ilāhī]*, I should not dare to say: 'I have repented and I shall not sin again,' because I am all too familiar with my own character, and I cannot guarantee the renunciation of sins, because I am all too familiar with my own weakness. Nevertheless I do say: 'I shall not sin again,' because it is always possible that I may die before I have lapsed back into sin!"

To quote another of the sayings of Dhu'n-Nūn [al-Miṣrī] (may Allāh bestow His mercy upon him):

"Seeking forgiveness without the renunciation of sin is the repentance of liars."

He also said (may Allāh bestow His mercy upon him): "The real meaning of repentance *[ḥaqīqat at-tawba]* is that the earth, for all its vast expanse, becomes so narrowly constricting for you that there is no space in it where you can feel at home, and then your own lower self *[nafs]* becomes too narrow for you, just as Allāh (Exalted is He) has informed us in His glorious Book:

> The earth, for all its vast expanse, became too narrowly constricting for them, and their own lower selves became too narrow for them, until they supposed that there could be no way to find refuge from Allāh except by turning toward Him. Then He relented toward them, so that they might repent. (9:118)"

[289] The expression is Qurʾānic in origin. Allāh (Exalted is He) has said:

> O you who believe, turn to Allāh in repentance—in sincere repentance! *[yā ayyuha'lladhīna āmanū tūbū ila'llāhi tawbatan naṣūḥā]*. (66:8)

According to Ibn ʿAṭāʾ[290] (may Allāh bestow His mercy upon him): "Repentance is actually two kinds of repentance *[at-tawba tawbatān]*. There is repentance as a return to obedience *[tawbat al-ināba]*, but there is also repentance as a positive response *[tawbat al-istijāba]*. Repentance as a return to obedience means that the servant repents [to his Lord] for fear of incurring His punishment, while repentance as a positive response means that he repents in respectful acknowledgment of His noble generosity.

Yaḥyā ibn Muʿādh ar-Rāzī (may Allāh bestow His mercy upon him) once said: "A single lapse after repentance is far worse than seventy before it."

The following story was told by Abū ʿAmr al-Anṭākī[291] (may Allāh bestow His mercy upon him):

"ʿAlī ibn ʿĪsā, the Vizier, came riding [through the streets of Baghdād] in a magnificent ceremonial parade, and some womenfrom out of town started asking: 'Who is this?' A local woman, who happened to be standing by the side of the road, then turned to them and said: 'How long will you go on asking who this is? This is a servant who has fallen from favor in the sight of Allāh, which explains why Allāh has afflicted him with the tribulation you are witnessing at this very moment.' When ʿAlī ibn ʿĪsā overheard this remark, he immediately turned around, went back to his official residence, and tendered his resignation from the office of Vizier. He then moved away to Mecca and settled in one of its outlying districts."

[290] Abu'l-ʿAbbās Aḥmad ibn Muḥammad ibn Sahl ibn ʿAṭāʾ al-Adamī was a close companion of al-Junaid (may Allāh bestow His mercy upon them both). Author of mystical verses and a prominent member of the Baghdād circle, he was put to death in A.H. 309/922 C.E.

[291] Abū ʿAmr al-Anṭākī is a saintly figure from around the time of al-Junaid (may Allāh bestow His mercy upon them).

The Fourth Discourse

Concerning the words of Allāh (Exalted is He): Surely the noblest among you in the sight of Allāh is the one of you who is most truly devout. (49:13) *[inna akrama-kum ʿinda 'llāhi atqā-kum].*

The learned scholars *[ʿulamāʾ]* hold a variety of different opinions concerning the meaning of the term *taqwā* [true devotion] and the real nature *[ḥaqīqa]* of the *muttaqī* [truly devout person]. Their views are based on the following traditional report, according to which the Prophet (Allāh bless him and give him peace) once said:

> The whole of true devotion *[taqwā]* is contained within this statement of His (Almighty and Glorious is He):
>
> | | |
> |---|---|
> | Surely Allāh commands | *inna 'llāha yaʾmuru* |
> | the implementation of justice, | *bi-'l-ʿadli wa 'l-iḥsāni wa ītāʾi* |
> | and charitable conduct, | *dhi 'l-qurbā: wa yanhā* |
> | and giving to close relatives; | *ʿani 'l-faḥshāʾi* |
> | and He forbids indecency, | *wa 'l-munkari wa 'l-baghy:* |
> | unfairness, and outrageous behavior. | *wa yaʿiẓu-kum* |
> | He appeals to your consciences, | *laʿalla-kum tadhakkarūn.* |
> | in order that you may take heed. | |
> | (16:90) | |

According to Ibn ʿAbbās (may Allāh be well pleased with him and with his father): "The truly devout person *[muttaqī]* is one who is always on his guard *[yattaqī]* against associating partners with Allāh *[shirk]*, committing the major sins *[kabāʾir]*, and being guilty of abominations and atrocities *[fawāḥish]*."

According to Ibn ʿUmar (may Allāh be well pleased with him and with his father): "True devotion *[taqwā]* means that you do not regard yourself as better than anyone else."

According to al-Ḥasan [al-Baṣrī][292] (may Allāh bestow His mercy

[292] See note 227 on p. 163 above.

upon him): "The truly devout person *[muttaqī]* is one who says about everyone he sees: 'This is someone better than me.'"

[The Caliph] ʿUmar ibn al-Khaṭṭāb (may Allāh be well pleased with him) once said to Kaʿb al-Aḥbār:[293] "Tell me what you know about true devotion *[taqwā]*." Kaʿb responded to this by asking him: "Have you ever taken a path that was riddled with spikes and thorns?" When ʿUmar said yes, he had indeed taken such a path, Kaʿb went on to ask: "So what did you do in that situation?" ʿUmar told him: "I proceeded warily and took as many precautions as I possibly could," so Kaʿb said: "That is just how it is with true devotion *[taqwā]*."

This idea was later expressed in verse, by the unknown poet who said:

You must forsake all kinds of sin, the great and the small alike,
for such is the pious duty of the righteous and devout.

You must advance as you would when treading over thorny ground,
avoiding the prickly spots and casting warily about.

Do not rule out a little sin as trivial in itself;
since mountains are made of pebbles, they can never be ruled out.

[The pious Umayyad Caliph] ʿUmar ibn ʿAbd al-ʿAzīz[294] (may Allāh bestow His mercy upon him) once said: "Pious devotion *[at-tuqā]*[295] is not a matter of fasting through the day, keeping vigil through the night, and making oneself delirious in the meantime. True devotion *[taqwā]* has more to do with abstaining from that which Allāh has declared to be unlawful, and with carrying out those duties that Allāh has declared to be strictly obligatory. Whatever sustenance Allāh may provide after that, it will be something good in addition to something good *[khair ilā khair]*."

[293] "The Rabbi Kaʿb"—whose full name was Abū Isḥāq Kaʿb ibn Mātiʿ al-Ḥimyarī—was a Jew from Yemen, who became a Muslim in the Caliphate of Abū Bakr or that of ʿUmar (may Allāh be well pleased with them). He died in A.H. 32 or 34, but he had by then acquired an enduring reputation as a revered authority on the *Isrāʾīliyāt* —the Jewish-Muslim traditions in Islām.

[294] The Umayyad dynasty became notorious for running the Empire for its own benefit as though it were its personal fief, and it was the worldly and tyrannical nature of the Umayyads, more characteristic of the pagan Age of Ignorance *[Jāhiliyya]* than of Islām, which led to their ultimate downfall. The solitary and remarkable exception was the saintly and abstemious Caliph ʿUmar ibn ʿAbd al-ʿAzīz (may Allāh bestow His mercy upon him), who reigned from A.H. 99-101/715-717 C.E. It was noted that the Caliphs Abū Bakr, ʿUmar ibn al-Khaṭṭāb and ʿAlī (may Allāh be well pleased with them) had all been bald, and so was ʿUmar ibn ʿAbd al-ʿAzīz; but after him there were no more bald Caliphs.

[295] The Arabic noun *tuqan* (pronounced *at-tuqā* when the definite article *al-* is prefixed to it) is virtually synonymous with *taqwā*.

Somebody once said to Ṭaliq ibn Ḥabīb: "Give us a concise definition of true devotion *[taqwā]*," so he responded by saying: "True devotion *[taqwā]* is acting in obedience to Allāh, in accordance with a light from Allāh, for the sake of Allāh's reward, and with a sense of shame in the presence of Allāh."

"True devotion *[taqwā]*," it has also been said, "is giving up disobedience to Allāh, in accordance with a light from Allāh, and in fear of Allāh's chastisement."

In the words of Bakr ibn ʿUbaidi'llāh (may Allāh bestow His mercy upon him): "A man cannot be truly pious *[taqī]* [296] until he has come to be pious in the way he approaches the dining room *[taqiyyu 'l-maṭʿam]*, and pious in the way he deals with anger *[taqiyyu 'l-ghaḍab]*."

To quote another of the sayings of ʿUmar ibn ʿAbd al-ʿAzīz (may Allāh bestow His mercy upon him): "The truly devout person *[muttaqī]* is subject to as much restraint as the woman who is confined to the harem *[maḥram al-ḥaram]*."

According to Shahr ibn Ḥawshab (may Allāh bestow His mercy upon him): "The truly devout person *[muttaqī]* is one who is ready to abstain from something that is quite harmless in itself, as a precaution against slipping over into something else that could be harmful."

Sufyān ath-Thawrī[297] and al-Fuḍail [ibn ʿIyāḍ][298] (may Allāh bestow His mercy upon them) both said [concerning the truly devout person]: "He is someone who loves other people to receive what he loves to receive for himself."

Al-Junaid[299] (may Allāh bestow His mercy upon him) went further than this, however, for he said:

"The truly devout person *[muttaqī]* is not someone who loves other people to receive what he loves to receive for himself. The truly devout person *[muttaqī]* is actually one who loves other people to receive more than what he loves to receive for himself. Do you know what happened to my master and teacher *[ustādhī]*, Sarī as-Saqaṭī (may Allāh bestow His mercy upon him)?[300] One day, as I recall the occasion, a friend of

[296] The Arabic adjective or adjectival noun *taqī* is virtually synonymous with the participicial form *muttaqin* (pronounced *muttaqī* when the definite article *al-* is prefixed to it).

[297] See note 238 on p. 168 above.

[298] See note 270 on p. 191 above.

[299] See note 284 on p. 205 above.

[300] See note 286 on p. 205 above.

his greeted him with 'Peace be upon you!' He promptly returned his friend's greeting, but wearing a frown as he did so, and without giving the man a cheerful smile. When I mentioned to him that I was rather puzzled by this odd behavior, he said: "According to the information I have received, when a Muslim man greets his brother with the Islāmic salutation, and his brother then returns his greeting, a hundred merciful blessings *[mi᾿a raḥma]* are shared out between the pair—ninety of them going to the more cheerful of the two, and ten to the other. So, I wanted to make sure that he would be the one to get ninety."

It was Muḥammad ibn ʿAlī at-Tirmidhī[301] (may Allāh bestow His mercy upon him) who said [concerning the truly devout person]: "He is someone who has no hostile adversary *[khaṣm]*."

According to Sarī as-Saqaṭī (may Allāh bestow His mercy upon him): "He [the truly devout person] is someone who hates his own lower self *[nafs]*."

According to ash-Shiblī[302] (may Allāh bestow His mercy upon him): "He [the truly devout person] is someone who is not wary *[lā yattaqī]* of anything less than Allāh."

In the words of the anonymous but truthful speaker: "Everything, with the sole exception of Allāh, is simply vain and futile *[bāṭil]*."

According to Muḥammad ibn Khafīf (may Allāh bestow His mercy upon him): "True devotion *[taqwā]* is the scrupulous avoidance of everything that would keep you at a distance from Allāh."

According to al-Qāsim ibn al-Qāsim (may Allāh bestow His mercy upon him), it is: "Faithful adherence to the modes of conduct prescribed by the Sacred Law *[ādāb ash-Sharīʿa]*."

According to [Sufyān] ath-Thawrī (may Allāh bestow His mercy upon him), the truly devout person *[muttaqī]* is: "He who is ever on his guard *[yattaqī]* against this world and its perils."

301 It seems reasonable to assume that this is "Tirmidhī the Wise" [al-Ḥakīm at-Tirmidhī] (d. ca. A.H. 295/908 C.E.), a contemporary of al-Junaid (may Allāh bestow His mercy upon them both). According to Trimingham, he was the first within an Islamic context to write about the Logos, for which he uses the word *Dhikr*, but his ideas fell into oblivion until resurrected by the genius of Ibn al-ʿArabī. (See: J. Spencer Trimingham, *The Sufi Orders in Islam*. Oxford University Press, 1971; pp. 4, 134 and 161.)

302 Abū Bakr ibn Jaḥdar ash-Shiblī was of Khurāsānian origin, although born in Baghdād or Samarra. The son of a court official, he rose through the ranks of the imperial service. While in Baghdād for the occasion of his investiture as Governor of Demavend, he experienced conversion. He joined the circle of al-Junaid, played a leading part in the stormy history of al-Ḥallāj, and was committed to an asylum on account of his eccentric behavior. He died in A.H. 334/946 C.E. at the age of 87. (See: A.J. Arberry, *Muslim Saints and Mystics*. London and New York: Routledge & Kegan Paul, 1966; pp.277-286.)

According to Abū Yazīd al-Bisṭāmī[303] (may Allāh bestow His mercy upon him), true devotion *[taqwā]* is: "Cautious avoidance *[tawarruʿ]* of all things that are of doubtful legality *[shubuhāt]*." He also said: "The truly devout person *[muttaqī]* is someone who, whenever he speaks, speaks for the sake of Allāh; and who, whenever he stays silent, stays silent for the sake of Allāh; and who, whenever he practices remembrance, remembers for the sake of Allāh."

It was al-Fuḍail ibn al-ʿIyāḍ (may Allāh bestow His mercy upon him) who said: "The servant [of the Lord] will not be counted as one of those who are truly devout *[muttaqīn]*—not until his enemy can feel as safe with him as his friend feels safe with him."

According to Sahl [at-Tustarī][304] (may Allāh bestow His mercy upon him): "The truly devout person *[muttaqī]* is someone who washes his hands of his personal power and strength."

To quote the words of an anonymous wise man: "True devotion *[taqwā]* means that Allāh never sees you where he has forbidden you to be, and that He never finds you absent from where He has commanded you to be."

It has been said that true devotion *[taqwā]* means: "Obediently following in the footsteps of the Prophet (Allāh bless him and give him peace)."

It has also been said to mean: "That you must always be wary *[tattaqī]*—with your heart, to guard against negligent lapses *[ghafalāt]*; with your breathing, to guard against lustful inclinations *[shahawāt]*; with your throat, to guard against pleasurable temptations *[ladhdhāt]*; and with all the limbs and organs of your physical body, to guard against bad influences *[sayyiʾāt]* of every kind—for only then will you have any hope of attaining to the Lord of the earth and the heavens."

Abu 'l-Qāsim [al-Junaid][305] (may Allāh bestow His mercy upon him) once said [concerning true devotion]: "It is excellence of moral character *[ḥusn al-khulq]*."

In the words of one of the wise: "There are three good indicators pointing to true devotion *[taqwā]* in a man, namely: An admirable

[303] See note 249 on p. 171 above.

[304] See note 251 on p. 172 above.

[305] See note 284 on p 205 above.

degree of trust [in the Lord] *[tawakkul]* in relation to what he has not yet accomplished; an admirable degree of satisfaction *[riḍā]* with what he has already achieved, and an admirable degree of patience *[ṣabr]* in accepting irrevocable loss."

As another saying has it: "The truly devout person *[muttaqī]* is someone who is warily on guard *[yattaqī]* against following the dictates of his passions *[hawā]*."

It was Mālik [ibn Dīnār][306] (may Allāh bestow His mercy upon him) who said: "Wahb ibn Kaisān informed me that one of the legal scholars *[fuqahā']* among the people of Medina once wrote to 'Abdu'llāh ibn az-Zubair[307] (may Allāh be well pleased with him and with his father): 'The people of true devotion *[ahl at-taqwā]* bear certain distinctive characteristics, by which you can identify them, namely: patience in the face of trial and tribulation *[balā']*; cheerful acceptance of destiny's decree *[qaḍā']*; gratitude in the presence of gracious favor *[na'mā']*; and humble compliance with the laws of the Qur'ān.'"

According to Maimūn ibn Mihrān (may Allāh bestow His mercy upon him): "A man will not be truly pious *[taqī]* until he has come to be far more rigorous, in calling himself to account, than any tightfisted business partner *[sharīk shaḥīḥ]* or even a despotic ruler *[sulṭān jā'ir]* would ever be."

According to Abū Turāb (may Allāh bestow His mercy upon him): "Arrayed in front of true devotion *[taqwā]* are five steep obstacles, which must be surmounted by anyone seeking to acquire it, namely: (1) the choice of severity and hardship instead of ease and comfort; (2) the choice of stalwart courage instead of meddling curiosity; (3) the choice of self-abasement instead of self-aggrandizement; (4) the choice of stern endeavor instead of recreation and leisure; and (5) the choice of death instead of life."

In the words of one of the wise: "A man cannot reach the highest level of true devotion *[taqwā]* unless he has come to the point where, if

[306] See note 246 on p. 170 above.

[307] Az-Zubair ibn al-'Awwām (may Allah be well pleased with him) was a cousin of the Prophet (Allah bless him and give him peace), and one of the earliest believers. As one of the Ten Well-Betided Ones *[al-'Ashara al-Mubashshara]*, he received the assurance of Paradise from the Prophet (Allah bless him and give him peace). He died in A.H. 36/656 C.E. One of his sons—the 'Abdu'llāh ibn az-Zubair to whom this note refers—led a revolt against the tyranny of Umayyad rule, declared himself Caliph, and seized control of Mecca before being finally defeated and slain in A.H. 73/692 C.E.

the contents of his heart were set upon a tray, and the tray was then carried around on a tour of the marketplace, he would not feel the slightest sense of embarrassment about anything that was being displayed upon it."

To quote yet another saying: "True devotion *[taqwā]* means that you must adorn your innermost being *[sirr]* for the sake of the Lord of Truth *[Ḥaqq]*, just as you adorn your external appearance for the sake of your fellow creatures *[khalq]*."

Abu 'd-Dardā'[308] (may Allāh be well pleased with him) addressed the subject in these words [of Arabic poetry]:

> The servant wishes to be granted all that he desires,
> but Allāh refuses to give—except what He wishes.
>
> "My profit and my property," says the man,
> though the finest gift he could receive is true devotion to Allāh.

According to a report transmitted on the authority of Mujāhid, Abū Sa'īd al-Khudrī[309] (may Allāh be well pleased with him) said: "A man once came to Allāh's Messenger (Allāh bless him and give him peace) and said: "O Prophet of Allāh, give me some good advice!" The Prophet (Allāh bless him and give him peace) responded to this request by telling him:

> 'You must practice true devotion *[taqwā]* to Allāh, for it is the repository of all that is good. You must engage in the sacred struggle *[jihād]*,[310] for it is the Islamic equivalent of the monastic life *[rahbāniyya]*. You must also practice the remembrance *[dhikr]* of Allāh, for it will serve as a light for your guidance.'"

Abū Hurmuz Nāfi' ibn Hurmuz (may Allāh bestow His mercy upon him) is reported as having said: "I once heard Anas [ibn Mālik][311] (may

[308] Abū 'd-Dardā' al-Khazrajī al-Anṣārī (may Allāh be well pleased with him) was a Companion of the Prophet (Allāh bless him and give him peace). Renowned for his piety and devotion, as well as for his profound knowledge of the Qur'ān, he shared with Abū Dharr Jundab ibn Junādat al-Ghifārī and Abū 'Abdi'llāh Ḥudhaifa ibn al-Yamān al-'Abasī (may Allāh be well pleased with them) the special distinction of being called *ṣāḥib sirr an-Nabī*, because of the secret knowledge imparted to them by the Prophet (Allāh bless him and give him peace). He died in A.H. 32.

[309] See note 20 on p. 81 above.

[310] The Islāmic term *jihād* [sacred struggle or holy war] is all too frequently misunderstood, especially but not only by non-Muslims. Sometimes, alas, its meaning is willfully misrepresented—by polemicists hostile to Islām, as well as by misguided zealots within the Islāmic Community itself. Fortunately for us, the works of Shaikh 'Abd al-Qādir al-Jīlānī (may Allāh be well pleased with him) contain many valuable explanations of the true significance of the term *jihād*. (For instance, see pp. 44 and 45 above.)

[311] See note 265 on p. 188 above.

Allāh be well pleased with him) say: "When someone asked [the Prophet (Allāh bless him and give him peace)]: 'O Muḥammad, who belongs to the family of Muḥammad?' he replied: 'Everyone who is truly devout *[taqī]*, for true devotion *[taqwā]* is the repository of all the virtues *[jimāʿ al-khairāt]*.'"

The real meaning of prudent conduct *[ḥaqīqat al-ittiqāʾ]* is taking precautions *[taḥarruz]*, through obedience to Allāh (Almighty and Glorious is He), in order to guard oneself against His punishment. [In a military context] one might use the expression: "So-and-so took the prudent measure of raising his shield *[ittaqā fulān bi-tursi-hi]*." The essential ingredient of true devotion *[aṣl at-taqwā]* is the taking of prudent measures against associating partners with Allāh *[ittiqāʾ ash-shirk]*. Next after that comes the taking of prudent measures against sinful acts of disobedience and things that are unmistakably bad *[ittiqāʾ al-maʿāṣī wa 's-sayyiʾāt]*. Next after that comes the taking of prudent measures against things that are merely of dubious legality *[ittiqāʾ ash-shubuhāt]*. Then, as the next priority, one must also abstain from excessive indulgence in things that are otherwise lawful and good *[faḍalāt]*.

Let us now consider the words of Allāh (Exalted is He):

O you who believe, observe your duty to Allāh, with the devotion that is truly due to Him. (3:102)	*yā ayyuha 'llādhīna āmanu 'ttaqu 'llāha ḥaqqa tuqāti-hi.*

According to the traditional Qurʾānic interpretation *[tafsīr]*, this means that the believer must obey, for then he will not disobey; that he must remember, for then he will not forget; and that he must be thankful, for then he will not be guilty of ingratitude.

It was Sahl ibn ʿAbdi'llāh [at-Tustarī][312] (may Allāh bestow His mercy upon him) who said: "There is no helper except Allāh *[lā muʿīn illa 'llāh]*. There is no guide except the Messenger of Allāh *[lā dalīl illā Rasūli 'llāh]*. There is no provision for the journey except true devotion *[lā zād illa 't-taqwā]*, and there is no proper course of action except patience in the practice thereof *[lā ʿamal illa 'ṣ-ṣabr ʿalai-hā]*."

According to al-Kinānī (may Allāh bestow His mercy upon him): "The things of this world are allocated on the basis of probationary trial *[ʿala 'l-balwā]*, while the blessings of the Garden of Paradise are

[312] See note 251 on p. 172 above.

allocated on the basis of true devotion [*ʿala 't-taqwā*]. If someone fails to establish a strong bond of true devotion [*taqwā*] and dutiful reverence [*murāqaba*] between himself and Allāh, that person will never attain to revelatory disclosure [*kashf*] and direct witnessing [*mushāhada*]."

According to [Abū 'l-Qāsim] an-Naṣrābādhī[313] (may Allāh bestow His mercy upon him): "What true devotion [*taqwā*] signifies is that the servant [of the Lord] must always be on his guard [*yattaqī*] against everything apart from Him (Exalted is He)."

To quote another of the sayings of Sahl [ibn ʿAbdi'llāh at-Tustarī] (may Allāh bestow His mercy upon him): "If a person wishes to be credited with true devotion [*taqwā*], he must give up committing sins—all sins whatsoever."

[Abū 'l-Qāsim] an-Naṣrābādhī also said: "When someone makes true devotion [*taqwā*] his constant practice, he comes to feel an ardent longing to part company with this world, because Allāh (Exalted is He) tells us:

The abode of the Hereafter is surely far better for those who practice dutiful devotion. (6:32)"	*wa la-'d-dāru 'l-ākhiratu khairun li'lladhīna yattaqūn.*

In the words of one of the wise: "If a person is really committed to true devotion [*taqwā*], Allāh will make it easy for his heart to lose interest in this world."

According to Abū ʿAbdi'llāh ar-Rūzbārī (may Allāh bestow His mercy upon him): "True devotion [*taqwā*] is the scrupulous avoidance of everything that would keep you at a distance from Allāh."[314]

According to Dhu 'n-Nūn al-Miṣrī ["the Egyptian"] [315] (may Allāh the Exalted bestow His mercy upon him): "The truly pious believer [*taqī*] is one who contaminates neither his outer being [*ẓāhir*] with acts

[313] According to al-Qushairī, Abū 'l-Qāsim Ibrāhīm an-Naṣrābādhī (d. A.H. 369/979 C.E.) is the link in the *silsila* [chain of spiritual transmission] between his own Shaikh, Abū ʿAlī ad-Daqqāq (d. A.H. 407/1016 C.E.) and Abū Bakr ibn Jaḥdar ash-Shiblī (d. A.H. 334/945–6 C.E.) (may Allāh bestow His mercy upon them all). The spelling of the name is sometimes given as Naṣrābādī, rather than Naṣrābādhī. (See: Trimingham, op. cit., p. 261).

[314] Since this definition of true devotion [*taqwā*] is precisely identical with the one attributed earlier in this Discourse (p. 213 above) to a certain Muḥammad ibn Khafīf (may Allāh bestow His mercy upon him), it may be that Abū ʿAbdi'llāh ar-Rūzbārī is another part of that same person's name.

[315] See note 163 on p. 115 above.

of stubborn defiance, nor his inner being *[bāṭin]* with negligent lapses into heedlessness, and who adopts an attitude of harmonious conformity *[ittifāq]* in his relationship with Allāh (Exalted is He)."

According to Ibn ʿAṭiyya [ad-Dārānī][316] (may Allāh the Exalted bestow His mercy upon him): "The truly devout person *[muttaqī]* has an external aspect *[ẓāhir]* and an internal aspect *[bāṭin]*. His external aspect is careful observance of the rules *[muḥāfaẓat al-ḥudūd]*, while his internal aspect is right intention *[niyya]* and sincerity *[ikhlāṣ]*."

Dhu 'n-Nūn al-Miṣrī (may Allāh the Exalted bestow His mercy upon him) also said: "There is no life worth living, except in the company of men whose hearts are always yearning for true devotion *[taqwā]*, and finding recreation in remembrance *[dhikr]*."

It was Abū Ḥafṣ [al-Ḥaddād][317] (may Allāh the Exalted bestow His mercy upon him) who said: "True devotion *[taqwā]* relates to that which is absolutely lawful *[ḥalāl maḥḍ]*—not to anything else."

According to Abu 'l-Ḥusain az-Zanjānī (may Allāh the Exalted bestow His mercy upon him): "When a person's capital consists of true devotion *[taqwā]*, tongues grow weary in attempting to describe his profit."

According to al-Wāsiṭī (may Allāh the Exalted bestow His mercy upon him): "What true devotion *[taqwā]* requires is that a person should be wary of his own piety *[an yattaqiya min taqwā]*," meaning, "of attaching undue importance to his own piety."

It is related that Ibn Sīrīn[318] (may Allāh the Exalted bestow His mercy upon him) once purchased forty jars of clarified butter. He noticed that his servant had pulled a mouse out of one of the jars, so he asked him: "From which of the jars did you remove that mouse?" "I don't know," said the servant—so Ibn Sīrīn proceeded to empty the whole lot down the drain.

We have it on good authority that one of the Imāms would never sit in the shade of a tree belonging to someone who owed him a debt. He

[316] See note 235 on p. 167 above.

[317] Abū Ḥafṣ ʿAmr ibn Salma al-Ḥaddād (d. A.H. 270/883 C.E.) is looked upon as one of the founding fathers of the Nishāpūrī school of Islamic mysticism, which is sometimes referred to as the *malāmātī* tendency. (See: Trimingham, op. cit., p. 265.)

[318] The name of Muḥammad Ibn Sīrīn is often mentioned alongside that of his contemporary, Anas ibn Mālik, who died in A.H. 91–93 (see note 265 on p. 188 above). Both are revered as reliable and prolific narrators of Prophetic tradition (may Allāh bestow His mercy upon him).

used to say: "According to the traditional report *[khabar]:*[319]

> Any loan that entails a benefit [to the lender] is a form of usury *[ribā]*."[320]

It is said that Abū Yazīd [al-Bisṭāmī][321] (may Allāh the Exalted bestow His mercy upon him) once washed an article of clothing in the presence of a companion of his, while they were out in the desert together. His companion then said: "Let us hang our clothes to dry on the walls of the vineyards," but Abū Yazīd rejected the suggestion, saying: "We must not stick pegs into people's walls!" The following exchanges then took place between the two:

"Let us hang them on the trees," said the companion.

"No," replied Abū Yazīd, "because they will cause the branches to snap."

"Well then," said the companion, "how about spreading them over the little bushes that grow around here?"

"No," Abū Yazīd objected once again. "Those little bushes serve as fodder for the riding animals, so we must not hide them from their sight."

Abū Yazīd then turned his back toward the sun, draped the wet shirt over his back, and stood quite still until one side of it had dried out. Then he turned it over and waited until the other side had dried out too.

Ibrāhīm ibn Ad'ham[322] (may Allāh the Exalted bestow His mercy upon him) is reported as having said: "I once spent the night beneath the Dome of the Rock in Jerusalem. At some point during the night, two angels came down, and one of them said to his companion: 'Who is this person here?' The second angel told him: 'Ibrāhīm ibn Ad'ham,'

[319] See note 176 on p. 130 above.

[320] The Arabic term *ribā* [usury; unjustified profit] is derived from the same triconsonantal root—*r–b–w*—as a verb meaning "to grow; to increase." As Allāh (Almighty and Glorious is He) has told us in the Qur'ān:

That which you give in usury,	*wa mā ātaitum min ribā*
so that it may grow	*li-yarbuwa*
on other people's wealth,	*fī amwāli 'n-nāsi*
does not grow at all with Allāh. (30:39)	*fa-lā yarbū ʿinda 'llāh.*

In the Fortieth Discourse of *Jalāʾ al-Khawāṭir [The Removal of Cares},* Shaikh ʿAbd al-Qādir al-Jīlānī (may Allāh be well pleased with him) issues this stern warning on the subject:

> You must not get anywhere close to transactions in which usurious interest *[ribā]* is involved, for that would amount to waging war against your Lord, and would result in the removal of blessed grace *[baraka]* from your material resources. When you make a loan, the terms of repayment should be exactly one dīnār [gold coin] for one dīnār.

[321] See note 249 on p. 171 above.

[321] See note 233 on p. 165 above.

so he said: 'That is the man whom Allāh has demoted by one degree of spiritual rank.' When his companion asked why this had happened, the angel explained: 'Because he bought some pieces of fruit in al-Baṣra, and an extra piece of the greengrocer's fruit fell on top of the pieces he had paid for.'"

Ibrāhīm then went on to say: "So I traveled back to al-Baṣra, bought some pieces of fruit from that same man, dropped one of those pieces on top of his stack of fruit, returned to Jerusalem, and went to sleep beneath the Dome of the Rock. At a certain point during the night, I suddenly became aware that two angels had descended from heaven above. One of them asked his companion: 'Who is this person here?' The second angel told him: 'Ibrāhīm ibn Ad'ham,' so he said: 'That is the man who put something back in its rightful place, and was therefore awarded a promotion in spiritual rank!'"

Concerning the standards by which true devotion *[taqwā]* is assessed at various levels of spiritual stature.

According to the view maintained by some authorities, there can be no single, all-purpose definition of true devotion *[taqwā]*, since a different standard must be applied to each of the following categories:

1. In the case of ordinary mass of people *[al-ʿāmma]*, the mark of true devotion *[taqwā]* is the renunciation of attributing partners to the Creator *[shirk bi-'l-Khāliq]*.
2. In the case of the spiritual élite *[al-khāṣṣa]*, it is detachment from the influence of the passions *[hawā]*, through the renunciation of acts of sinful disobedience *[maʿāṣī]*, and through opposition to the lower self *[nafs]* in all conditions and circumstances.
3. In the case of the élite of the spiritual élite *[khāṣṣ al-khāṣṣ]*—the category to which the saints *[awliyāʾ]* belong—it is the renunciation of self-will *[irāda]* in relation to all things, of exclusive concentration *[tajarrud]* on supererogatory acts of worship *[nawāfil al-ʿibādāt]*, of dependence on secondary causes *[asbāb]*, of reliance on anything apart from the Master *[Mawlā]*, and of clinging to any particular spiritual state *[ḥāl]* or station *[maqām]*. In all these areas, true devotion *[taqwā]* at this level requires compliance with the directly received command *[imtithāl al-amr]*, together with observance of the rules that apply to strictly obligatory religious duties *[aḥkām al-farāʾiḍ]*.
4. As for the Prophets *[Anbiyāʾ]* (blessings and peace be upon them), whatever constitutes true devotion *[taqwā]* in their case, it is a virtue peculiar to them alone. It is a mystery within a mystery *[ghaib fī ghaib]*, for it is both from Allāh and directed toward Allāh. He tells them what they must do, and He tells them what they must not do. He helps them to succeed, and He subjects them to discipline. He improves their health, and He remedies their ailments. He addresses them in words,

and He holds conversations with them. He directs them and He guides them. He gives them gifts and He cheers them up. He keeps them informed, and He enables them to see and understand.

There is no scope for the human mind *[ʿaql]* in all of this, for they are in a category far transcending ordinary humanity *[fī maʿzil ʿani 'l-bashar]*—transcending even the angels altogether—except in matters that involve the external rule of law *[al-ḥukm aẓ-ẓāhir]*, and the clear commandment issued to the Islāmic Community *[Umma]* and to the believers in general *[ʿawāmm al-muʾminīn]*. In matters of this kind, they are on an equal footing with their fellow creatures, although they are entirely distinct from them in all other respects.

It may be that some experience of this very special form of true devotion *[taqwā]* is occasionally granted to certain noble beings, such as the spiritual deputies *[abdāl]*[323] and the chosen few among the saints *[awliyāʾ]*. Their ability to express themselves invariably proves less than adequate, however, when it comes to describing that kind of experience. No clearly intelligible statement emerges, and nothing can be discerned by the faculties of hearing and sensory perception, apart from that which somehow succeeds in mastering the tongue. All that is forthcoming, therefore, is a word or a few words at most, for Allāh promptly takes control of the person concerned, restoring him to a tranquil frame of mind, stabilizing his feelings, and draping a protective covering over him. As soon as this happens, that person becomes alert to His command, takes care to guard his own tongue, and begs forgiveness of Allāh (Exalted is He) for whatever may have transpired. He will now adopt a different mode of expression, as he refines his manner of speaking with a view to making it more intelligible and comprehensible, by using terms with which people are generally familiar.

[323] See note 54 on p. 33 above.

Concerning the course of progress by which the development of true devotion *[taqwā]* is ensured.

In order of priority, the necessary stages in the development of true devotion *[taqwā]* are as follows:

1. Discharging oneself of any guilt incurred through the commission of offenses against human beings *[maẓālim al-ʿibād]*, and of any restitution due to them on account of the violation of their rights *[ḥuqūq]*.
2. Discharging oneself of any guilt incurred through the commission of sinful acts of disobedience, whether they be classed as major sins *[kabāʾir]* or merely as minor sins *[ṣāghāʾir]*.
3. Making a conscientious effort to abstain from committing the sins of the heart, for they are the mothers of all sins *[ummahāt adh-dhunūb]* and the root causes of them all. From them branch out the sins of the limbs and organs of the physical body, such as ostentatious display *[riyāʾ]*, hypocrisy *[nifāq]*, vanity *[ʿujb]*, arrogant pride *[kibr]*, cupidity *[ḥirṣ]*, avarice *[ṭamaʿ]*, fearing one's fellow creatures and pinning one's hopes on them, the pursuit of privileged status *[jāh]*, and political leadership *[riyāsa]*, and the desire to take precedence over all other human beings [lit., over the children of one's own species]. Many more items could be added to this list, but it would take a very long time to account for them all. There is only one way to acquire the necessary strength for all of this, and that is through opposing the influence the passions *[hawā]*.
4. Making a conscientious effort to abstain from the exercise of self-will *[irāda]*. This means that a person must not make any personal choice in spite of Allāh, and that he must not pursue his own plans in spite of Allāh. It means that he must not expect Him to comply with his personal preferences, and that he must not try to stipulate a particular manner and means for the provision of His sustenance. It means that he must not remonstrate with Him (Almighty and Glorious

is He) over His way of dealing with His creation, but must rather surrender everything to Him, demonstrate obedient submission *[yastaslim]* before Him, and cast himself down in abject prostration in His presence. In the Hand of His Power, he will then come to be like the suckling infant in the hand of his wet-nurse *[ẓiʾr]* and his midwife *[dāya]*, or like the corpse in the hand of the man who performs the ritual washing of the dead *[ghāsil]*. He will be stripped of his freedom of choice *[ikhtiyār]*, deprived of his power of self-will *[irāda]*, for in this lies salvation *[najāt]*—the whole of salvation.

If someone should happen to ask: "How would you describe the path that leads to that destination?" he should be told: "The path to that destination is followed by being sincere in seeking refuge with Allāh (Almighty and Glorious is He), by dedicating oneself to Him completely, by practicing constant obedience to Him—through compliance with His commandments and nonviolation of His prohibitions, by resigning oneself to acceptance of the destiny decreed by Him *[at-taslīm fī qadari-hi]*, by keeping within the limits set by Him *[ḥifẓ ḥudūdi-hi]*, and by maintaining this virtuous state of being, always and forever."

Concerning the differing views expressed by the Shaikhs on the subject of salvation *[najāt]*.

Certain differences of perspective are noticeable in the views expressed by the Shaikhs on the subject of salvation *[najāt]*. For instance, al-Junaid [324] (may Allāh the Exalted bestow His mercy upon him) once said: "There is no way for anyone to be saved, except by making an honest plea for refuge with Allāh (Almighty and Glorious is He). As Allāh (Almighty and Glorious is He) has told us:

And [Allāh also relented in mercy]	*wa ʿala 'th-thalāthati 'lladhīna*
toward the three who were	*khullifū:*
left behind, until the earth,	*ḥattā idhā ḍāqat*
became for all its vast expanse,	*ʿalai-himu 'l-arḍu*
too narrowly constricting for them,	*bi-mā raḥubat*
and their own lower selves	*wa ḍāqat ʿalai-him*
became too narrow for them,	*anfusu-hum*
until they supposed that there	*wa ẓannū*
could be no way to find refuge	*an lā maljaʾa*
from Allāh except by turning	*mina 'llāhi.*
toward Him. (9:118)"	*illā ilai-h.*

According to Ruwaim (may Allāh the Exalted bestow His mercy upon him): "There is no way for anyone to be saved, unless it be through honesty *[ṣidq]* and true devotion *[taqwā]*. As Allāh (Almighty and Glorious is He) has told us:

And Allāh delivers those	*wa yunajji 'llāhu 'lladhīna*
who have practiced true devotion	*taqaw*
in their temporary state of security.	*bi-mafāẓati-him.*
(39:61)"	

According to al-Jazīrī (may Allāh the Exalted bestow His mercy upon him): "There is no way for anyone to be saved, except by paying due respect to the fulfillment of his contractual obligation. As Allāh

[324] See note 284 on p. 205 above.

(Almighty and Glorious is He) has said [concerning those who shall gain access to the Ultimate Abode, and who shall enter the Gardens of Eden]:

[Such are] those who fulfill	*alladhīna yūfūna*
the covenant of Allāh,	*bi-ʿahdi 'llāhi*
and do not break the compact.	*wa lā yanquḍūna 'l-mīthāq.*
(13:20)"	

According to ʿAṭā'[325] (may Allāh the Exalted bestow His mercy upon him): "There is no way for anyone to be saved, except through experiencing a genuine sense of shame *[taḥqīq al-ḥayā'].* As Allāh (Exalted is He) has said:

Is he not aware	*a-lam yaʿlam*
that Allāh sees? (96:14)"	*bi-anna 'llāha yarā.*

In the words of one of the wise: "There is no way for anyone to be saved, unless it be in accordance with the Divine verdict *[ḥukm]* and the judgment long ago established *[al-qaḍā' as-sābiq]* in the foreknowledge of Allāh (Almighty and Glorious is He). As Allāh (Exalted is He) has told us [concerning those who will be far removed from the Fire of Hell]:

But as for those to whom	*inna 'lladhīna*
the reward most fair	*sabaqat*
has already gone forth from Us,	*la-hum min-na 'l-ḥusnā:*
they shall be kept far from it.	*ulā'ika ʿan-hā mubʿadūn.*
(21:101)	

It was al-Ḥasan al-Baṣrī[326] (may Allāh the Exalted bestow His mercy upon him) who said: ""There is no way for anyone to be saved, except by shunning this world and the people who are attached to it. As Allāh (Exalted is He) has told us:

The life of this world is nothing	*inna-ma 'l-ḥayātu 'd-dunyā*
but a sport and a pastime. (47:36)	*laʿibun wa lahw.*

Moreover, the Prophet (Allāh bless him and give him peace) once said:

> The love of this world is the head of every sinful error, and, for those who draw near to Allāh, there is no finer means of drawing close than the performance of the religious duties prescribed by Allāh.

[325] This is presumably ʿAṭā' as-Sulamī/as-Sulaimī (may Allāh bestow His mercy upon him), a man renowned for his extreme piety. According to some accounts, his sense of shame before Allāh (Exalted is He) was so intense that he felt unable to raise his head toward heaven. He died in A.H. 121.

[326] See note 227 on p. 163 above.

He also said:

> Since Allāh (Exalted is He) created it [this world], He has not looked at it."

Al-Ḥasan (may Allāh the Exalted bestow His mercy upon him) then went on to explain: "This means that He has not looked at it with the eye of His mercy *[raḥma]*, because it so abhorrent. It therefore constitutes the mighty screen *[al-ḥijāb al-ʿaẓīm]*, and serves to distinguish that which is pure and wholesome from that which is faulty and defective. As long as someone is still tainted by the slightest thing belonging to it, that person will not be granted access to the sweet delight of intimate conversation *[munājāt]* with Him (Glory be to Him), because it stands in opposition to Allāh, and it represents the very opposite of that which Allāh loves."

Concerning the summons issued by Allāh (Almighty and Glorious is He) to all His creatures.

Allāh (Almighty and Glorious is He) has summoned His creatures to the affirmation of His Oneness *[tawḥīd]* and to obedience toward Him. He has done so by means of the promise *[wa'd]* and the threat *[wa'īd]*, by means of attraction *[targhīb]* and intimidation *[tarhīb]*.

Thus He has cautioned and warned, instilled feelings of fear, and delivered rebukes and reprimands, in order to leave His creatures with no excuse, and to establish the evidence for the case against them, for He has told us (Almighty and Glorious is He):

[We have sent] Messengers	*rusulan mubashshirīna*
bearing good tidings, and warning,	*wa mundhirīna*
in order that mankind might have	*li-allā yakūna li-n'nāsi*
no argument against Allāh,	*'ala 'llāhi ḥujjatun*
after the Messengers. (4:165)	*ba'da 'r-rusul.*

He has also said (More Glorious is He than any other sayer):

And if We had destroyed them	*wa law annā ahlaknā-hum*
with some punishment before it,	*bi-'adhābin min qabli-hi*
they would surely have said: "Our Lord,	*la-qālū Rabba-nā*
if only You had sent us a Messenger,	*law lā arsalta ilai-nā Rasūlān*
so that we might have followed	*fa-nattabi'a*
Your signs before we were	*āyāti-ka min qabli*
humiliated and disgraced!" (20:134)	*an nadhilla wa nakhẓā.*

In another Qur'ānic verse *[āya]*, He has told us:

We never punish	*wa mā kunnā*
until We have sent	*mu'adhdhibīna*
forth a Messenger. (17:15)	*ḥattā nab'atha rasūlā.*

He has said (Exalted is He):

O mankind, now there has come	*yā ayyuha 'n-nāsu qad jā'at-kum*
to you an exhortation from your Lord,	*maw'iẓatun min Rabbi-kum*
and a healing for that	*wa shifā'un li-mā*

which is within the breasts,	*fī 'ṣ-ṣudūri*
and a guidance, and	*wa hudan*
a mercy for the believers. (10:57)	*wa raḥmatun li-'l-mu'minīn.*

For the sake of instilling fear and caution, He has said (Glorious and Exalted is He):

And Allāh warns you to beware of Him,	*wa yuḥadhdhiru-kumu 'llāhu*
and Allāh is Kind and Gentle	*Nafsah: wa 'llāhu*
with His servants. (3:30)	*Ra'ūfun bi-'l-'ibād.*

He has said (Blessed and Exalted is He):

And know that Allāh knows	*wa ''lamū anna 'llāha*
what is in your own selves,	*ya'lamu mā fī anfusi-kum*
so beware of Him. (2:235)	*fa-'ḥdharū-h.*

He has said (Magnificent is His Glory):

And know that Allāh	*wa ''lamū anna 'llāha*
is Aware of all things. (2:231)	*bi-kulli shai'in 'Alīm.*

He has said (Magnificent is His Power):

So observe your duty to Me,	*wa 'ttaqūni*
O men endowed with	*yā uli 'l-albāb.*
faculties of understanding! (2:197)	

He has said (Glory be to Him and Exalted is He):

And observe your duty to Allāh,	*wa 'ttaqu 'llāha wa ''lamū*
and know that you shall meet Him	*anna-kum mulāqū-h.*
[one day]. (2:223)	

He has said (Exalted is He):

And be on your guard against a day	*wa 'ttaqū yawman*
in which you shall	*turja'ūna*
be brought back to Allāh.	*fī-hi ila 'llāh:*
Then every soul shall be paid in full	*humma tuwaffā kullu nafsin*
for what it has earned,	*mā kasabat*
and they shall not be wronged.	*wa hum lā yuẓlamūn.*
(2:281)	

He has said (Exalted is He):

And be on your guard against a day	*wa 'ttaqū yawman*
when no soul shall give satisfaction	*lā tajzī nafsun shai'an*
on behalf of another, and no	*wa lā yuqbalu*
compensation shall be accepted of it,	*min-hā 'adlun*
nor shall any intercession	*wa lā tanfa'u-hā shafā'atun*
be of use to it, nor shall	*wa lā hum*
they be helped. (2:123)	*yunṣarūn.*

He has said (Magnificent is His Majesty):

O mankind, be careful to observe	*yā ayyuha 'n-nāsu 'ttaqū*
your duty to your Lord,	*Rabba-kum wa 'khshaw*
and dread a day when no parent	*yawman lā yajzī wālidun*
shall give satisfaction	*ʿan waladi-hi*
on his child's behalf, and no	*wa lā mawlūdun*
child shall give any satisfaction	*huwa jāzin ʿan wālidi-hi shaiʾā:*
whatsoever for his parent.	*inna waʿda 'llāhi ḥaqqun fa-lā*
Allāh's promise is true indeed,	*taghurranna-kumu*
so do not let the life of this world	*'l-ḥayātu 'd-dunyā:*
delude you, and do not let the Deceiver	*wa lā yaghurranna-kum*
deceive you in regard to Allāh.	*bi-'llāhi 'l-Gharūr.*
(31:33)	

He has said (Exalted is He):

O mankind, be careful to observe	*yā ayyuha 'n-nāsu 'ttaqū*
your duty to your Lord!	*Rabba-kum:*
The earthquake of the Hour	*inna zalzalata 's-sāʿati*
[of Doom] is a tremendous	*shaiʾun ʿaẓīm.*
thing indeed. (22:1)	

He has said (Almighty and Glorious is He):

O mankind, be careful	*yā ayyuha 'n-nāsu 'ttaqū*
to observe your duty to your Lord,	*Rabba-kumu 'lladhī*
who created you from a single soul,	*khalaqa-kum min nafsin wāḥidatin*
and from it created its mate, and from	*wa khalaqa min-hā zawja-hā*
the pair of them has scattered forth	*wa baththa min-humā*
a multitude of men and women.	*rijālan kathīran wa nisāʾā:*
And be careful to observe	*wa 'ttaqu 'llāha 'lladhī*
your duty to Allāh, whom you invoke	*tasāʾalūna*
when making claims of one another,	*bi-hi*
and to the wombs [that bore you].	*wa 'l-arḥām:*
Allāh is always Watchful over you.	*inna 'llāha kāna ʿalai-kum Raqībā.*
(4:1)	

He has said (Exalted is He):

O you who believe, be careful	*yā ayyuha 'lladhīna*
to observe your duty to Allāh,	*āmanu 'ttaqu 'llāha*
and speak words that get straight	*wa qūlū qawlan sadīdā.*
to the point. (33:70)	

He has said (Almighty and Glorious is He):

O you who believe, be careful	*yā ayyuha 'lladhīna*
to observe your duty to Allāh.	*āmanu 'ttaqu 'llāha*
And let every soul consider	*wa 'l-tanẓur nafsun*

what it has forwarded for the day ahead. And be careful to observe your duty to Allāh. Allāh is indeed Aware of what you do. (59:18)	*mā qaddamat li-ghad:* *wa 'ttaqu 'llāh:* *inna 'llāha Khabīrun* *bi-mā taʿmalūn.*

He has said (Exalted is He):

And be careful to observe your duty to Allāh; surely Allāh is terrible in retribution. (5:2)	*wa 'ttaqu 'llāh:* *inna 'llāha* *Shadīdu 'l-ʿiqāb.*

He has said (Exalted is He):

Ward off from yourselves and your families a Fire of which the fuel is men and stones. (66:6)	*qū anfusa-kum* *wa ahlī-kum nāran* *waqūdu-ha 'n-nāsu* *wa 'l-ḥijāratu.*

He has said (Almighty and Glorious is He):

What, did you suppose that We had created you for idle sport, and that you would not be returned to Us? (23:115)	*a-fa-ḥasibtum anna-mā* *khalaqnā-kum ʿabathan* *wa anna-kum* *ilai-nā lā turjaʿūn.*

He has said (Glorious and Exalted is He):

What, does the human being suppose that he shall be left to wander aimlessly? (75:36)	*a-yaḥsabu 'l-insānu* *an yutraka* *sudā.*

He has also said (Exalted is He):

What, do the people of the townships feel secure from the coming of Our wrath upon them —as a night raid while they are sound asleep? Or do the people of the townships feel secure from the coming of Our wrath upon them —in the daytime while they are at play? (7:97,98)	*a-fa-amina ahlu 'l-qurā* *an yaʾtiya-hum* *baʾsu-nā bayātan* *wa hum nāʾimūn:* *aw amina ahlu 'l-qurā* *an yaʾtiya-hum* *baʾsu-nā ḍuḥan* *wa hum yalʿabūn.*

Well then, O miserable wretch, what is your response to these Qurʾānic verses *[āyāt]*, and how do you intend to put them into practice? Have you finally stopped following the dictates of those wicked appetites of yours, which are so harmful to you in this world and the Hereafter, and which will condemn you to dwell in the abode of agony and degradation? If you end up there, you will be scorched by its fire, mangled by its serpents, bitten and stung by its scorpions and its verminous pests, eaten by its worms, beaten and flogged by its hellish guardians *[zabāniya]* [327] and custodians. You will be subjected every day to novel kinds of torment, since you will be sharing that abode with Pharaoh, Hāmān, Qārūn, and the devils.

As we mentioned at the beginning of this subsection, Allāh (Exalted is He) appeals to His creatures by means of attraction *[targhīb]* as well as intimidation *[tarhīb]*. Let us now consider some examples of the former:

He has said (Glorious and Exalted is He):

And whenever someone observes	*wa man yattaqi 'llāha*
his duty to Allāh,	*yaj'al la-hu*
Allāh will prepare a way out for him.	*makhrajā:*
And He will provide for him	*wa yarzuq-hu*
from sources he could never imagine.	*min ḥaithu lā yaḥtasib:*
And whoever puts all his trust in Allāh,	*wa man yatawakkal 'ala 'llāhi*
He will suffice him. (65:2,3)	*fa-Huwa ḥasbuh.*

He has said (Exalted is He):

And whenever someone observes	*wa man yattaqi 'llāha*
his duty to Allāh, He will acquit	*yukaffir 'an-hu*
him of his evil deeds, and He will	*sayyi'āti-hi wa yu'zim*
grant him a mighty reward. (65:5)	*la-hu ajrā.*

He has said (Exalted is He):

What has deceived you	*mā gharra-ka*
concerning your Lord,	*bi-Rabbi-ka 'l-Karīm:*
the All-Generous,	*alladhī*
who created you, then shaped you,	*khalaqa-ka*
then fashioned you in symmetry? (82:6,7)	*fa-sawwā-ka fa-'adala-k.*

He has also said (Almighty and Glorious is He):

Is not the time now ripe for	*a-lam ya'ni li'lladhīna*
the hearts of those who believe	*āmanū an takhsha'a*
to submit in all humility	*qulūbu-hum*
to the remembrance of Allāh? (57:16)	*li-dhikri 'llāhi.*

By making you feel the attraction of what He has to offer, He has invited you to seek His gracious favor, the abundance of His mercy, and the delight of His sustenance. He has invited you to seek comfort and traquillity in His presence, by embarking on the path of true devotion *[taqwā]*, sticking to it, and following it with diligent perseverance. He

[327] See note 102 on p. 73 above.

has guided you along that path in order to provide you with explanations, and to give you a clear understanding of the case [that could be made for or against you]. He has also guaranteed that you will afterwards be granted the forgiveness of sins, the remission of bad deeds, and the magnification of reward and recompense, in accordance with His words (Almighty and Glorious is He):

And whenever someone	*wa man yattaqi 'llāha*
observes his duty to Allāh,	*yukaffir ʿan-hu*
He will acquit him of his evil deeds,	*sayyiʾāti-hi*
and He will grant him a mighty reward.	*wa yuʿẓim la-hu ajrā.*
(65:5)	

Then He has aroused you from your state of delusion concerning Him, from your drowsy lack of attention to Him, from your seeming blindness to His path, and from your seeming inability to hear His Qurʾānic verses *[āyāt]*, His exhortations and His admonitions, for He has said (Exalted is He):

What has deceived you concerning	*mā gharra-ka*
your Lord, the All-Generous,	*bi-Rabbi-ka 'l-Karīm:*
who created you, then shaped you,	*alladhī khalaqa-ka*
then fashioned you in symmetry?	*fa-sawwā-ka fa-ʿadala-k.*
(82:6,7)	

He has described Himself as the All-Generous *[al-Karīm]* so that you can have no pretext for abstaining from dealing with Him, for shunning a close relationship with Him, and for paying attention to His creation rather than to Him. Then He has reminded you that it was He who created you, brought you into being from your state of nonexistence, brought you to life after you had been nothing at all, enriched you after your poverty, strengthened you after your weakness, gave you all the benefits of sight after your blindness, imparted knowledge to you after your ignorance, and guided you aright after you had gone astray.

So, what can account for your reluctance, O heedless one, to embark on the quest for His far-reaching grace and favor? What keeps you from the constant practice of obedience to Him, when such obedience would bring you honor in this world, would make you blissfully happy in the life to come, and would promote you to the highest spiritual ranks? Are you quite content with the life of this world? Have you accepted that which is inferior in exchange for that which is better? Have you preferred this world and the people who are most attached to it—and the superficial glamor that you find so charming, although it has no lasting value—instead of Paradise *[Firdaws]* on high, and companionship with the Prophets *[anbiyā᾽]*, the champions of truth *[ṣiddīqīn]* and the martyrs *[shuhadā᾽]*? Surely you must have heard His words (Almighty and Glorious is He):

> Are you content with the
> life of this world,
> rather than that of the Hereafter?
> Yet the enjoyment of the
> life of this world,
> compared with that of the Hereafter,
> is merely a trivial thing. (9:38)
>
> *a-raḍītum*
> *bi-'l-ḥayāti 'd-dunyā*
> *mina 'l-ākhira:*
> *fa-mā matā'u 'l-*
> *ḥayāti 'd-dunyā*
> *fi 'l-ākhirati*
> *illā qalīl.*

You must also have heard His words (Exalted is He):

> But you prefer the life of this world,
> although the Hereafter is better
> and more lasting. (87:16,17)
>
> *bal tu᾽thirūna 'l-ḥayāta 'd-dunyā:*
> *wa 'l-ākhiratu*
> *khairun wa abqā.*

And you must have heard His words (Exalted is He):

> Then, as for him who was insolent
> and preferred the life of this world,
> surely Hell shall be his home.
> (79:37–39)
>
> *fa-ammā man ṭaghā*
> *wa āthara 'l-ḥayāta 'd-dunyā*
> *fa-inna 'l-jaḥīma hiya 'l-ma᾽wā.*

Concerning the causes of entry into the Fire of Hell, and the causes of entry into the Garden of Paradise.

You should know that entry into the Fire of Hell is the result of unbelief *[kufr]* and the multiplication of punishment, and that the allotment of the descending levels *[darakāt]* is determined by the scale of evil deeds and evil traits of character. Entry into the Garden of Paradise, on the other hand, is the result of faith *[īmān]* and the multipication of blessed grace, while the allotment of the ascending levels *[darajāt]* is determined by the scale of righteous deeds and excellent traits of character.

You must also know that Allāh (Almighty and Glorious is He) created the Garden of Paradise and filled it with blissful comfort, as a reward for those who are worthy of it, that He created the Fire of Hell and filled it with torment, as a punishment for those who deserve it, and that He created this world and filled it with disasters as well as blessings, as an ordeal and a trial. Then, when He created His human creatures, He made the Garden of Paradise and the Fire of Hell invisible to them, so that they could not see them directly with their ordinary eyes. The blessings and disasters that exist in this world are therefore meant to serve as the model *[unmūdhaj]* of the Hereafter, and as the means by which the taste of it can be experienced.

He also created kings from among His servants here on this earth, and He conferred on them an authority that would be potent enough to instill terror in people's hearts and to control their personal inclinations. This was meant to serve as a model *[unmūdhaj]* and an allegory *[mithāl]* of His planning and management, His dominion, and the effectiveness of His command and His way of dealing with things.

He therefore provided information about all of this by way of revelation *[tanzīl]*. He described the two abodes [the abode of this world and the abode of the Hereafter], and He described His dominion *[mulk]*, His power *[qudra]*, His planning and management *[tadbīr]*, His gracious favor *[minna]*, and His works *[ṣanāʾiʿ]*. For this purpose He used the technique of coining similitudes *[amthāl]*, then He said (Exalted is He):

And as for these similitudes, We coin them for mankind, but none will grasp their meaning except those who have [the necessary] knowledge. (29:43)	*wa tilka 'l-amthālu naḍribu-hā li'n-nāsi wa mā yaʿqilu-hā illa 'l-ʿālimūn.*

Those who are well versed in the knowledge of Allāh *[al-ʿulamāʾ bi-'llāh]* are therefore qualified to understand what Allāh intends to convey by His similitudes, because a similitude is merely the depiction of something you have already witnessed with your own eyes, in order to let you see the characteristic features of that which is otherwise invisible to you. It is a device for enabling you to perceive what you cannot perceive with your ordinary eye, by causing the perceptive faculty of your heart to penetrate that which your eyesight is incapable of perceiving. Your heart can thus make sense of all the information that is being addressed to it—information about the Kingdom of Heaven *[al-Malakūt]*, information about the two abodes *[ad-dārain]*, and information about the King of kings *[Malik al-mulūk]*.

There is not a single delight or pleasure in this world that does not serve as a model for the Garden of Paradise, and as a foretaste of what will be experienced therein. Beyond all this, however, the Garden of Paradise also contains that which no eye has ever seen, of which no ear has ever heard, and the very notion of which has never occurred to any human heart.[328] If any element of this mystery were to be mentioned by name to the servants [of the Lord], the use of such a name would be to no avail, because they cannot understand its meaning here below, since they have never seen what it refers to, and it has no model in this world. The Garden of Paradise actually has no fewer than one hundred ascending levels *[darajāt]*, but He has described only three of them: one as consisting of gold, one as consisting of silver, and one as consisting of light. Then, beyond that point, there is something incomprehensible, something which human minds are quite incapable of grasping.

[328] An allusion to the Divine Saying *[Ḥadīth Qudsī]*:

I have prepared for My righteous servants that which no eye has ever seen, of which no ear has ever heard, and the very notion of which has never occurred to any human heart.

As for the agony and torment that exist in this world, these likewise constitute a model, which serves to represent the abode of punishment [in the Fire of Hell]. But then again, beyond all this, there is something that human minds are quite incapable of comprehending. In this case, that something is a whole assortment of unimaginable torments.

Whatever may lie in store for those who are condemned to the Fire of Hell, it will emerge to meet them out of His wrath, and whatever may lie in store for those who are worthy of the Garden of Paradise, it will emerge to greet them out of His mercy. For each and every one of His servants who has acquired no more than his lawful share of this world, and has thanked Him for it, He will provide a recompense in the Garden of Paradise—a recompense so great that his share of this world will seem quite tiny by comparison. By acquiring things that were not lawful to him, on the other hand, a person will deprive himself of his portion of the ascending levels *[darajāt]*, and anyone who denies their very existence will be utterly deprived of the Garden of Paradise and all that it contains.

For those who are worthy to inhabit the Garden of Paradise, there will be brides *[ʿarāʾis]* and wedding feasts *[walāʾim]* and hospitable entertainments *[ḍiyāfāt]*. The brides are for benefit of the single men *[diʿwa]*, for the very good reason that the Lord of Honor *[Rabb al-ʿIzza]* (Glory be to Him) has summoned them to the Abode of Peace *[Dār as-Salām]* in order that He may provide them with fresh new bodies and everlasting lives. The wedding feasts are for the benefit of the married partners, and the hospitable entertainments are for the reception of guests—to provide opportunities for the inhabitants of the Garden of Paradise to meet with one another, to exchange visits, and to converse in settings of intimate conviviality. They will have a gathering place in the shade of the Tree of Bliss *[Ṭūbā]*,[329] where they will meet the Messengers *[Rusul]* and visit with them, as well as enjoying occasional sessions in the company of the angels (may the peace of Allāh be upon them all).

Other amenities available to them will include market places, where they can come and select various shapes and forms, and gifts from the

329 The *Ṭūbā* tree is traditionally depicted as having its roots in Paradise, while its leaves and branches extend downwards toward the earth. According to some accounts, one of its branches will enter the mansion of each inhabitant of the Garden of Paradise, bearing flowers and ripe fruit of every imaginable kind.

All-Merciful *[ar-Raḥmān]* at the times of the ritual prayers *[ṣalawāt]*. They will have all kinds of food, drink and fruits at their disposal at every moment of the day, be it early in the morning or late at night. Their various forms of nourishment will actually be a constantly flowing stream, never cut off and never interrupted. They will receive an increase from Allāh with every day that passes, and as soon as they receive the latest increment, they will forget what they had before.

Then there is a park or recreation ground *[muntazah]* for them to enjoy. They will find it situated in the midst of charming meadows on the bank of the River of Abundance *[al-Kawthar]*.[330] Pitched on the grounds of that park are pavilions made of pearls. Each pavilion is sixty miles in length and an equal distance in width, and is made of one single pearl *[lu'lu'a]* in which no hole has been pierced. Inside those pavilions there are maidservants fragrantly perfumed, who have never been looked at by any angel, nor by any of the people of the Garden of Paradise, such as the attendants and the houries *[ḥūr]*. We know about them from the words of Allāh (Almighty and Glorious is He):

In them [are maidens] good and beautiful. (55:70)	*fī-hinna khairātun ḥisān.*

Since Allāh calls them beautiful *[ḥisān]*, who else could even attempt to describe their beauty *[ḥusn]*?! Then He goes on to say (Exalted is He)

Fair ones, cloistered in pavilions. (55:72)	*ḥūrun maqṣūrātun fi 'l-khiyām.*

For they are the select choice of the All-Merciful One *[ar-Raḥmān]*, who has chosen their beautiful forms out of all the forms in existence. They have been created from the clouds of His mercy *[raḥma]*, for when those clouds deliver rain, they send forth a shower of beautiful maidservants, in compliance with the wish of the All-Generous One *[al-Karīm]*. The light of their faces comes from the light of the Heavenly Throne *['Arsh]*. Pavilions of pearl have been pitched over them, so no one has

[330] In Vol. 1, p. 248, Shaikh 'Abd al-Qādir al-Jīlānī (may Allāh be well pleased with him) tells us that, according to the tradition *[ḥadīth]* of Anas ibn Mālik (may Allāh be well pleased with him), Allāh's Messenger (Allāh bless him and give him peace) once said:

> I was admitted to the Garden of Paradise, and—lo and behold!—there I was beside a flowing stream, flanked on both sides by pavilions made of pearls. I dipped my hand in [what looked like] water flowing by, and—lo and behold!—it was musk, of the most exquisitely fragrant kind. I said: "O Gabriel, what is this?" He replied: "This is the River of Abundance *[al-Kawthar]*, which Allāh (Exalted is He) has bestowed upon you."

seen them since the moment of their creation, for they are "cloistered in pavilions *[maqṣūrātun fi 'l-khiyām]*." To say that they have been cloistered *[quṣirna]* is a way of saying that they have been kept in confinement, so as to be accessible to their husbands alone, and to no one else in the whole of creation.

The inhabitants of the Garden of Paradise will thus lead a life of ease and comfort within palatial mansions *[quṣūr]* and in the company of their spouses. They will tarry in this state of blissful happiness as long as Allāh wills it so—until the day comes when Allāh (Almighty and Glorious is He) wishes to introduce them to a new kind of bliss *[ni'ma]* and a new form of recreation *[nuzha]*, at which point they will hear a voice calling out to them on all the ascending levels of the Gardens of Paradise *[darajāt al-Jinān]*: "O people of the Gardens of Paradise, this is the day of entertainment and happiness, relaxation and joy. You must therefore go out to your recreation ground *[muntazah]*."

In response to this call, they will sally forth on horses of pearl and sapphire, riding like the lords of their cities as they head out toward those open spaces. Then they will travel over those open spaces to those charming meadows on the bank of the River of Abundance *[al-Kawthar]*, and so Allāh will guide them to their camp sites. Every man amongst them will then dismount beside his pavilion—only to find that there is no entrance to it. The pavilion must therefore be penetrated by some means other than an ordinary doorway, and this is done when it is split open by the eye of the saintly friend *[walī]* of Allāh (Exalted is He), in order to let him know that she who is inside the pavilion has never been examined by anyone else—in fulfillment of the promise previously given by Allāh, in the abode of this world, inasmuch as He said:

In them [are maidens] good and beautiful. (55:70)	*fī-hinna* *khairātun ḥisān.*

And then He said (Exalted is He):

Fair ones, cloistered in pavilions. (55:72)	*ḥūrun maqṣūrātun fi 'l-khiyām.*

And then He went on to say:

[Fair ones] whom neither man nor jinn will have touched before them. (55:74)	*lam yaṭmith-hunna insun* *qabla-hum wa lā jānn.*

The man will then recline beside her on the couch of recreation *[sarīr an-nuzha]* inside those curtained canopies *[ḥijāl]*. Like each of the other men, he will be treated to a portion of her nuptial banquet *[walīma]*. Then, when they have sampled the main courses of the nuptial banquets, Allāh will provide them with pure wine to quench their thirst. They will derive great pleasure from the novel fruits with which Allāh supplies them on that day—from all those novel gifts, including the decorations *[ḥulā]* and the suits of clothes *[ḥulal]*, for they will be invested with the raiment of the All-Merciful One *[kiswat ar-Raḥmān]*. They will busy themselves with the maidens good and beautiful, who will satisfy their every wish and desire. Then they will move on to enjoy the delights of sitting on the marvelous carpets *[ʿabqariyyāt]*, embroidered with all kinds of decorative patterns, that grace the banks of the streams in those charming meadows. They will climb aboard the green cradle-cushions *[rafārif]* and recline upon them in comfort. All of this is foretold in His words (Exalted is He):

[There they will be] reclining on greencradle-cushions and beautiful rugs. (55:76)	*muttakiʾīna ʿalā rafrafin khuḍrin wa ʿabqariyyin ḥisān.*

When Allāh calls something beautiful, what is left for anyone else to say about it? As for the cradle-cushion *[rafraf]*, it is something that causes a person who reclines upon it to rock to and fro—as on a swing *[urjūḥa]*—to right and left, and up and down, while sharing the fun of the ride with his close companion.

When they climb aboard the cradle-cushions, Isrāfīl[331] (peace be upon him) will break into song. According to the traditional report *[khabar]* that has been handed down to us:[332]

> Of all the creatures of Allāh (Exalted is He), not one has a voice more beautiful than that of Isrāfīl (peace be upon him). So, when he breaks into song, the inhabitants of the seven heavens have their ritual prayer *[ṣalāt]* and their glorification *[tasbīḥ]* cut short.

When they climb aboard the cradle-cushions, and Isrāfīl starts singing all kinds of songs, hymning the glory and the holiness of the King Most Holy *[al-Malik al-Quddūs]*, not a single tree in the Garden of Paradise will fail to blossom, not a single screen or door will fail to

[331] Isrāfīl (peace be upon him) is the angel who is charged with the task of sounding the trumpet on the Day of Resurrection.

[332] See note 176 on p. 130 above.

tremble and burst open, not a single doorbell will fail to tinkle with its full array of chimes, and not a single thicket of gold and silver canes will fail to let the sound of his voice blow through its reeds. Those reeds will therefore play all kinds of tunes. Among all the maidens with eyes so fair *[al-ḥūr al-ʿīn]*,[333] not a single one will fail to sing her songs, and the birds will join in with their melodies. Allāh (Almighty and Glorious is He) will then tell the angels by way of inspiration: "Respond to them, and let the sound of your voices be heard by those servants of Mine who have kept their choral music *[samāʿ]* free from contamination by the woodwind instruments of Satan *[mazāmīr ash-Shaiṭān]*." The angels will promptly respond with melodies and sounds of a spiritual nature *[rūḥāniyya]*. These sounds will blend together, so as to become a single vibration. At this point Allāh (Exalted is He) will say: "Arise, O David, and stand by the leg of My throne, then celebrate My glory!" David will launch at once into the celebration of His glory, using a voice that overflows all other voices and makes them sound much sweeter.

The pleasure experienced by the people of the pavilions will thus be multiplied again and again, as they rock to and fro and swing up and down on those cradle-cushions, for they will be surrounded by all kinds of delightful sensations and songs. All of this is foretold in His words (Almighty and Glorious is He):

> [As for those who believed, and did good works], they shall be made happy in a charming meadow. (30:15)
>
> *[fa-amma 'lladhīna āmanū wa ʿamilu 'ṣ-ṣāliḥāti] fa-hum fī rawḍatin yuḥbarūn.*

It was Yaḥyā ibn Kathīr[334] (may Allāh bestow His mercy upon him) who said [in commenting on this particular Qurʾānic verse]: "The 'charming meadow' *[ar-rawḍa]* means sensual pleasure and musical entertainment *[al-ladhdha wa 's-samāʿ]*."

[333] In other words, the 'houries' of Paradise, mentioned several times in the Qurʾān. Literally, according to the Arabic lexicographers, 'women whose eyes are characterized by intense whiteness of the part that is white, and intense blackness of the part that is black,' or, more poetically, 'women with eyes resembling those of the gazelle.' Pickthall translates *wa zawwajnāhum bi-ḥūrin ʿīn* (Qurʾān 44:54): 'And We shall wed them unto fair ones with wide, lovely eyes.' (See: *The Glorious Koran*. English translation by Muhammad Marmaduke Pickthall. London: George Allen & Unwin, 1980.)

[334] Abū Zakariyāʾ Yaḥyā ibn Hāshim ibn Kathīr ibn Qais al-Ghassānī (may Allāh bestow His mercy upon him) was an expert in the tradition of the Prophet (Allāh bless him and give him peace), although some authorities have questioned his reliability. The date of his death has not been recorded, but he is known to have been a student of al-Aʿmash (d. ca. 148) and other traditionists of the same period.

Suddenly, while they are busily indulging in their sensual pleasures and enjoying their merry delight, the gateway of the King Most Holy *[al-Malik al-Quddūs]*—that is to say, the gateway of the Garden of Eden *[Jannat ʿAdn]*—will open unto them. The sound of the voices of spiritual beings *[rūḥāniyyīn]*, arrayed in ranks, will then issue forth from the Garden of Eden, vibrantly hymning the praises of the All-Generous and Nobly Exalted One *[tamājīd al-Mājid al-Karīm]* to all the ascending levels of the Gardens of Paradise *[darajāt al-Jinān]*. A wind of Eden will begin to blow, wafting forth all kinds of sweet perfume, spreading the breath of life, and fanning the gentle breeze *[nasīm]*—that is to say, the gentle breeze of nearness [to the Lord].

In the wake of this, a light will shine, and its radiance will shed a brilliant glow upon their charming meadows, their pavilions, and the banks of their rivers and streams. Every single thing that belongs to them will be filled with light. Then the Majestic One (Magnificent is His Majesty) *[al-Jalīl—jalla Jalālu-hu]* will call out to them from up above their heads:

"Peace be upon you *[as-salāmu ʿalaikum]*, My dear ones *[aḥibbāʾī]*, My saintly friends *[awliyāʾī]* and My chosen ones *[aṣfiyāʾī]*! O people of the Garden of Paradise, how did you find your recreational park *[muntazah]*? This is your special day, in lieu of the New Year's Day *[Nairūz]* of My enemies. They tried to find a special day in the world below, in order to freshen and renew for themselves the blissful happiness which they had spoiled for themselves on account of their wicked conduct and their wretched behavior. But they failed to obtain the pleasure they were seeking.

"They incurred nothing but loss, instead of what they sought to acquire immediately, in the temporal realm *[fi 'l-ʿājil]*, and they were too impatient to wait until they could obtain all this, which I had prepared in the realm of the future *[fi 'l-ājil]*, for the benefit of those who were faithfully committed to obeying Me. You turned your backs on all that they found so intensely interesting, and you refused to get involved in matters that stir up rivalry and mutual competition among people addicted to the lower world. Ah well, today they are tasting the evil consequences of that which spurred them to compete with one another in such pointless rivalry.

"How swiftly it all came to a sudden end—the sensual pleasure and the greedy satisfaction they sought in the abode of fleeting existence *[dār al-fanā']*! They have been reduced to humiliation and disgrace, whereas you have been rewarded for your patience with a Garden of Paradise, with garments of silk, with a park for recreation, and with a greeting of 'Peace!' This day is indeed your New Year's Day *[Nairūz]* and your opportunity for happy relaxation. This day is the occasion of your visit to My Abode *[Dārī]* in the Garden of Eden.

"How often I saw you during the days of your lives in the world below, on the likes of this day, busily engaged in My worship and in faithful obedience to Me! They would be luxuriating in their idle sport and games—intoxicated, bewildered, sinfully disobedient and rebellious. They would be enjoying the ephemeral vanities of the lower world, and gleefully rejoicing in the way those vanities rotated and circulated amongst them, whereas you would be vigilantly devoted to the contemplation of My Majesty *[Jalāl]*, keeping strictly within the limits set by My rules of law *[ḥudūd]*, observing the terms of My covenant *['ahd]*, and taking the utmost care to respect My rights *[ḥuqūq]*."

At this point, one of the doors of the Fires of Hell will be held open for the benefit of the inhabitants of the Gardens of Paradise. As the flames and the smoke belch forth, along with the screams and the yelling and howling of the people inside, they will view the scene from those comfortable seats of theirs. They will recognize and appreciate how bountiful are the favors that Allāh has bestowed upon them, and so they will experience an even greater measure of exultation and happiness.

As for the inhabitants of the Fire of Hell, they will gaze out from those jails and prison cells, shackled by those fetters and chains, and they will feel bitter disappointment over what has passed them by. They will stare at the faces of the inhabitants of the Gardens of Paradise, desperately imploring them to appeal on their behalf for Allāh's help, and calling out to them by their personal names, so Allāh (Blessed is His Name) will say:

See, those who are worthy of the Garden[of Paradise] are busy this day in their rejoicing, they and their spouses, reclining upon couches in the shade.	*inna aṣḥāba 'l-jannati 'l-yawma fī shughulin fākihūn: hum wa azwāju-hum fī ẓilālin 'ala 'l-arā'iki muttaki'ūn:*

There they have fruits, and they have all that they call for.	*la-hum fī-hā fākihatun wa la-hum mā yaddaʿūn:*
"Peace!"—such is the greeting from a Lord All-Compassionate.	*salām: qawlan min Rabbin Raḥīm:*
But keep yourselves apart, O you guilty ones, on this day.	*wa 'mtāzu 'l-yawma ayyuha 'l-mujrimūn:*
Did I not make a covenant with you, O you sons of Adam,	*a-lam aʿhad ilai-kum yā Banī Ādama*
that you should not worship Satan	*al-lā taʿbudu 'sh-shaiṭān:*
—surely he is an obvious enemy to you	*inna-hu la-kum ʿaduwwun mubīn:*
—and that you should worship Me?	*wa ani 'ʿbudūnī:*
This is a straight path. (36:55–61)	*hādhā ṣirāṭun mustaqīm.*

The Fire of Hell will therefore blaze all the more fiercely for them, and so their gathered throng will be dispersed and their plaintive wailing will cease. They will then be tossed toward islands in the Fire of Hell, and there, as soon as they have scrambled ashore, scorpions with stings as big as date palms will come crawling to meet them. The next thing to come rushing toward them will be a torrential stream of fire, fueled by the wrath of the All-Compelling One *[al-Jabbār]*. This flood will sweep them away and plunge them deep into the oceans of the Fires of Hell, and a herald will proclaim at the behest of Allāh (Exalted is He):

"This is your special day, the one you have been provoking Me to prepare for you by committing monstrous sins, by rebelling against Me in spite of My bountiful blessings, and by taking such gleeful delight—while still in the abode of sorrows and servitude—in what you dared to consider comparable to that which I have prepared for people faithfully committed to obeying Me. Well, those sensual pleasures are over and done with, as far as you are concerned, so now you must taste the evil consequences of the course you preferred to adopt.

"Those who have proved themselves worthy of the Garden of Paradise—from whose number you are totally excluded—are the ones who are now busily engaged in the luxurious enjoyment of wedding banquets, all kinds of fruits and an exquisite variety of gifts, the deflowering of virgin brides, the thrill of riding on the cradle-cushions *[rafārif]*, the sweet delight of listening to songs and many different types of music, My greeting of peace upon them, My kind and gentle treatment of them, and then—in addition to all this—something designed to exhaust all their previous blessings, in order to make them ready to experience their state of bliss anew, and to receive a pleasure that will greatly exceed the pleasure they have already enjoyed.

"O you who have proved yourselves worthy of the Garden of Paradise, this day has been granted to you, instead of the day of My enemies, who greeted one another [on their New Year's Day], and gave gifts to their kings and accepted gifts from them. You are the triumphantly successful ones *[al-fā'izūn]*!"[335]

Abū Huraira[336] (may Allāh be well pleased with him) is reported as having said: "A man once said to Allāh's Messenger (Allāh bless him and give him peace): 'I happen to be a man who is very fond of the sound of a beautiful voice, so tell me, is the sound of a beautiful voice to be heard in the Garden of Paradise?' He responded to this (may Allāh be well pleased with him) by saying: 'Yes indeed, by Him in whose Hand is my soul! By way of inspiration, Allāh (Almighty and Glorious is He) will instruct a tree in the Garden of Paradise to declare on His behalf: 'Listen to this, O My servants, who have been too preoccupied with My worship and My remembrance to indulge in making music with guitars *[barābiṭ]* and woodwind instruments *[mazāmīr]*!' The tree will then raise its voice to a higher pitch, producing a sound the likes of which no beings in the whole of creation have ever heard before, in order to hymn the glory of the Lord and to celebrate His holiness.'"

Abū Qallāba (may Allāh bestow His mercy upon him) is reported as having said: "A man once said to Allāh's Messenger (Allāh bless him and give him peace): 'Is there such a thing as night in the Garden of Paradise?' He responded to this (may Allāh be well pleased with him) by saying: 'Whatever can have prompted you to ask that question?' The man then said: 'I heard the statement made by Allāh (Almighty and Glorious is He) in His Book:

And in it they shall	*wa la-hum*
have their sustenance,	*rizqu-hum*
in the early morning	*fī-hā bukratan*
and in the evening. (19:62)	*wa 'ashiyyā.*

335 This is an obvious allusion to the verse *[āya]* of the Qur'ān in which Allāh (Almighty and Glorious is He) has told us:

Not equal are the inhabitants	*lā yastawī*
of the Fire of Hell and the inhabitants	*aṣḥābu 'n-nāri*
of the Garden of Paradise. The inhabitants	*wa aṣḥābu 'l-janna:*
of the Garden of Paradise—they	*aṣḥābu 'l-jannati*
are the triumphantly successful ones! (59:20)	*humu 'l-fā'izūn.*

336 See note 226 on p. 163 above.

—so I said to myself: "Night in the Garden of Paradise must fall between the early morning and the evening time."' But Allāh's Messenger (Allāh bless him and give him peace) told him: 'There is no night over there. There is never anything other than radiance and light. The forenoon *[ghuduww]* turns into the afternoon *[rawāḥ]*, and then the afternoon turns directly into the next forenoon. The inhabitants receive an exquisite variety of gifts from Allāh, at the times prescribed for the ritual prayers *[ṣalawāt]* which they used to perform in the lower world, and the angels salute them with the greeting of peace.'"

For anyone who wishes to enjoy a share in this delightful and everlasting life, it is essential to observe with care the rules and conditions of true devotion *[taqwā]*, as they are set forth in His words (Almighty and Glorious is He):

It is not piety, that you turn your	*laisa 'l-birra an tuwallū wujūha-kum*
faces to the East and to the West.	*qibala 'l-mashriqi wa 'l-maghribi*
True piety is [the piety of]	*wa lākinna 'l-birra*
one who believes	*man āmana*
in Allāh and the Last Day	*bi-'llāhi wa 'l-yawmi 'l-ākhiri*
and the angels and the Book	*wa 'l-malā'ikati wa 'l-kitābi*
and the Prophets;	*wa 'n-nabiyyīn:*
one who gives his wealth,	*wa āta 'l-māla ʿalā*
for love of Him,	*ḥubbi-hi*
to kinsfolk and to orphans	*dhawi 'l-qurbā*
and the needy	*wa 'l-yatāmā*
and the wayfarer	*wa 'l-masākīna*
and to those who beg,	*wa 'bna 's-sabīli*
and to set slaves free;	*wa 's-sā'ilīna wa fi 'r-riqāb:*
one who duly performs the	*wa aqāma 'ṣ-ṣalāta*
ritual prayer, and pays the alms-due.	*wa āta 'z-zakāh:*
[It is the piety of those] those who fulfill	*wa 'l-mūfūna*
their covenant when they have	*bi-ʿahdi-him*
committed themselves to a covenant,	*idhā ʿāhadū:*
and who are patient in tribulation	*wa 'ṣ-ṣābirīna fi 'l-ba'sā'i*
and adversity and in time of stress.	*wa 'ḍ-ḍarrā'i wa ḥīna 'l-ba's:*
Such are they who are sincere.	*ulā'ika 'lladhīna ṣadaqū:*
Such are the truly devout. (2:177)	*ulā'ika humu 'l-muttaqūn.*

It is also incumbent upon such a person to ensure that the prescribed penalties and reparations of Islām are duly put into effect.

Ḥudhaifa ibn al-Yamān[337] (may Allāh be well pleased with him) is

[337] Abū ʿAbdi'llāh Ḥudhaifa ibn [the son of] al-Yamān al-ʿAbasī (may Allāh be well pleased with them both) was among the earliest to embrace Islām, and he came to be one of the most distinguished of all the Companions of the Prophet (Allāh bless him and give him peace). He was famous for his dedication to an abstinent way of life. Together with Abū 'd-Dardā' and Abū Dharr (may Allāh be well pleased with them both), he was one of those Companions who were called *ṣāḥib sirr an-Nabī*, because of the secret knowledge imparted to them by the Prophet (Allāh bless him and give him peace). He died in A.H. 36.

reported as having said, in an interpretative commentary *[tafsīr]* on His words (Exalted is He):

O you who believe,	*yā ayyuha 'lladhīna*
come into [the religion of] peace,	*āmanu 'dkhulū*
each and every one of you. (2:208):	*fi 's-silmi kāffa.*

"Islām consists of eight portions: (1) The ritual prayer *[ṣalāt]* is a portion, (2) the alms-due *[zakāt]* is a portion, (3) fasting *[ṣiyām]* is a portion, (4) the Pilgrimage *[Ḥajj]* is a portion, (5) the Lesser Pilgrimage or Visitation *[ʿUmra]* is a portion,[338] (6) the sacred struggle or holy war *[jihād]*[339] is a portion, (7) enjoining what is right and fair *[al-amr bi-'l-maʿrūf]* is a portion, and (8) forbidding what is wrong and unfair *[an-nahy ʿani 'l-munkar]* is a portion.[340] What a terrible failure is he who has no portion at all!"

According to a report transmitted by ʿAṣim, i.e., ʿAṣim the Cross-Eyed *[al-Aḥwal]*, on the authority of Anas ibn Mālik[341] (may Allāh be well pleased with him), the Prophet (Allāh bless him and give him peace) once said:

> The likeness of Islām is that of a firm and sturdy tree: Belief in Allāh *[al-īmān bi-'llāh]* is its root. The five daily ritual prayers *[ṣalawāt]* are its forks. The fast *[ṣiyām]* of Ramaḍān is its bark. The Pilgrimage *[Ḥajj]* and the Visitation *[ʿUmra]* are its sap. The minor ablution *[wuḍūʾ]* and the major ablution *[ghusl]* to remove defilement are its supply of water. The reverential treatment of one's parents *[birr al-wālidain]* and respect for the bond of kinship *[ṣilat ar-raḥim]* are its branches. The scrupulous avoidance of things forbidden by Allāh *[al-kaff ʿan maḥārimi 'llāh]* makes up its foliage. Righteous deeds *[aʿmāl ṣāliḥa]* are its fruit, and the remembrance of Allāh *[dhikru 'llāh]* makes up its veins.

Then he went on to say (Allāh bless him and give him peace):

> Just as a tree can neither flourish nor develop properly unless it bears green leaves, Islām cannot develop properly except through the scrupulous avoidance of things forbidden by Allāh, and through the doing of righteous deeds.

[338] For the extensive treatment given by Shaikh ʿAbd al-Qādir al-Jīlānī (may Allāh be well pleased with him) to each of the first five of these "portions of Islām," the reader is referred to the relevant chapters and subsections in Vol. 1.

[339] See note 310 on p. 215 above.

[340] The seventh and eighth of these "portions of Islām" are of considerable importance to anyone seeking for a better understanding of the varied manifestations of "political activism" in the contemporary Muslim world. In an earlier volume of the present work, Shaikh ʿAbd al-Qādir al-Jīlānī (may Allāh be well pleased with him) has devoted an entire—and highly illuminating—chapter to the subject of *al-amr bi-'l-maʿrūf wa 'n-nahy ʿani 'l-munkar* [the duty to enjoin what is right and fair and to forbid what is wrong and unfair]. (See: Vol. 1, pp. 151–70.)

[341] See note 265 on p. 188 above.

Concerning the nature of the Fire of Hell and what Allāh has prepared therein for its inhabitants, and the nature of the Garden of Paradise and what Allāh has prepared therein for its inhabitants.

Abū Huraira[342] (may Allāh be well pleased with him) is reported as having said: "Allāh's Messenger (Allāh bless him and give him peace) once said:

> 'When the Day of Resurrection *[Yawm al-Qiyāma]* has finally arrived, and all creatures have been gathered together on a single piece of high ground "for a Day of which there is no doubt *[li-Yawmin lā raiba fīh]*,"[343] a black shadow will envelop them, and the darkness will be so intense that they will not be able to see one another. The assembled creatures will all be standing on the balls of their feet [as they try to peer upwards], even though the distance between them and their Lord (Almighty and Glorious is He) will still be that of a journey that normally takes seventy years to complete.'

"He then went on to say (Allāh bless him and give him peace):

> 'While they are in that situation, the Creator *[al-Khāliq]* (Blessed and Exalted is He) will suddenly make Himself manifest to the angels. The earth will at once become radiant with the light of its Lord, and the darkness will vanish away. All those creatures will thus be enveloped by the light of their Lord, while the angels are circling around the Heavenly Throne *[ʿArsh]*, hymning the praise of their Lord and celebrating His holiness.'

[342] See note 226 on p. 163 above.

[343] An allusion to the words of Allāh (Almighty and Glorious is He):

Our Lord, You are the One who shall gather mankind together for a Day of which there is no doubt. Allāh does not fail to keep the tryst. (3:9)	*Rabba-nā inna-ka Jāmiʿu 'n-nāsi li-yawmin lā raiba fī-h: inna 'llāha lā yukhlifu 'l-mīʿād.*
How [will it be with them] when We have brought them all together for a Day of which there is no doubt, when every soul shall be paid in full for what it has earned, and they shall not be wronged? (3:25)	*fa-kaifa idhā jamaʿnā-hum li-yawmin lā raiba fīh: wa wuffiyat kullu nafsin mā kasabat wa hum lā yuẓlamūn.*

"He then continued (Allāh bless him and give him peace):

'While those creatures are all standing there in rows, with each religious community *[umma]* lined up in a separate area, the record sheets *[ṣuḥuf]* and the balance *[mīzān]* will suddenly be brought to the fore. The record sheets will be laid in the scale, while the balance is held suspended by the hand of one of the angels, and they will sometimes cause it to rise up high, and at other times to sink down low.'

"To this he added (Allāh bless him and give him peace):

'While they are in that state, lo and behold, the screen will suddenly be removed from Garden of Paradise, which will then be brought nearer. A wind will blow forth from inside it, and the Muslims will discover that it has a fragrant aroma like musk, even though the distance between them and the Garden of Paradise is still that of a journey that normally takes five hundred years to complete.

'The lid will then be removed from Hell *[Jahannam]*, and a wind will blow forth from it, together with a terrible cloud of smoke. The wicked sinners will thus discover that it has a stinking aroma, even though the distance between them and Hell is still that of a journey that normally takes five hundred years to complete.

'Hell will then be brought closer, dragged along by means of an enormous chain, to which it has been firmly tied. Nineteen keepers, chosen from among the angels, will be tugging at that chain, and each of those keepers will be accompanied by seventy thousand other angels, serving as his assistants. While each of the nineteen keepers, together with his assistants, takes a turn at dragging Hell along, the other keepers, together with their assistants, will be walking to the right and left of it, and following up behind it. Each and every angel amongst them will hold in his hand a grappling hook made of iron. They will shout and bellow as they goad Hell along, but its slow progress will be made to the accompaniment of moaning and sighing, staggering and stumbling, clouds of gloom and smoke, rattling and clanking noises, and a towering inferno stoked by the fury of its rage against its own inhabitants. Thus they will eventually install it in a position midway between the Garden of Paradise and the place where the resurrected creatures are kept standing *[al-mawqif]*.

'At this point, Hell will lift its gaze. As soon as it spies the creatures assembled there, it will bolt toward them in order to devour them. Its keepers will have to pull on its chains to hold it in check, for if it were left to its own devices, it would pounce upon every believer *[mu'min]* and unbeliever *[kāfir]* without distinction. Once it sees that it has been effectively restrained from attacking the assembled throng of creatures, it will simmer and boil with an intensity that can hardly be distinguished from the most furious kind of rage. Then it will heave another sigh, and the resurrected creatures will hear the sound of the gnashing of its teeth. This will cause their hearts to shudder and tremble with alarm. They will fly into a state of panic, their eyes will glaze over, and their hearts will end up in their throats.'"

According to another report, somebody once said: "O Prophet of Allāh, describe Hell to us!" He responded to this (Allāh bless him and give him peace) by saying:

> Very well. Like this earth in magnitude. Seventy degrees of longitude. Dark black. It has seven heads, and each of its heads has thirty doors. The length of each of its doors is equal to the distance of a journey that would take three nights. Its upper lip protrudes against its nose, while it trails its lower lip on the ground. In each of its nostrils there is a shackle and and enormous chain, which is held in the grasp of seventy thousand angels, all of them rough, stern, their teeth grimly gritted, their eyes like live coals, and their colors like the flames of fire. While their nostrils give vent to lofty columns of flame and smoke, they stand at the ready, prepared at all times to receive and carry out the command of the All-Compelling One *[al-Jabbār]* (Blessed and Exalted is He).

Then the Prophet (Allāh bless him and give him peace) went on to say:

> There will come a moment when Hell *[Jahannam]* asks its Lord (Almighty and Glorious is He) for permission to perform an act of worshipful prostration *[sujūd]*. He will give it permission to do so, and Hell will thereupon adopt an attitude of prostration for as long as Allāh wills. Then the All-Compelling One *[al-Jabbār]* (Almighty and Glorious is He) will say: "Now raise your head!"

He continued (Allāh bless him and give him peace):

> Hell will raise its head at once, saying: "Praise be to Allāh, who has made me the instrument by which He exacts retribution from those who disobey Him, and has not made anything in the whole of His creation an instrument by which to exact retribution from me!"

To this he added (Allāh bless him and give him peace):

> Then Hell will say, over and over again, with a tongue that is fluent *[ṭaliq]* and eloquent *[dhaliq]* and smooth *[saliq]*: "Praise be to Allāh *[al-ḥamdu li'llāh]*!" For as long as Allāh wills, it will go on repeating this declaration of praise, in a loud voice peculiar to itself alone.
>
> Then Hell will heave a deep sigh, which will so affect those who hear it that not a single one of them will fail to sink down on his knees—not one angel brought near to the Lord *[mal'ak muqarrab]*, not one Prophet sent as a Messenger *[nabī mursal]*, and not one of those resurrected creatures who are present at the place of standing *[al-mawqif]*.
>
> Then Hell will heave a second deep sigh, and not a single eye that still has a drop of moisture in it will fail to shed a tear.
>
> Then Hell will heave a third deep sigh, and even if those who hear that sigh—be they human beings or jinn—were each endowed with the merit of seventy-two Prophets, they would surely be moved to embrace her as a man embraces a woman *[la-wāqa'ū-hā]*.[344]

[344] In Arabic, the words *Jahannam* [Hell], *an-Nār* [the Fire of Hell], *al-Janna* [the Garden of Paradise], *ad-dunyā* [this world] and *al-ākhira* [the hereafter] are all grammatically feminine. This makes it easy for an Arabic speaker or writer to personify them as female beings, if he wishes to represent them as characters in a parable, rather than as abstract entities.

Then Hell will heave a fourth deep sigh, and nothing that is capable of speech will fail to have its speech arrested. The only exceptions will be Gabriel, Michael, and [Abraham] the Bosom Friend *[Khalīl]* of the All-Merciful One *[ar-Raḥmān]* (Almighty and Glorious is He), each one of whom will say, as they cling to the Heavenly Throne *[ʿArsh]*: "My own soul, my own soul *[nafsī, nafsī]*—that is all I beg You to spare!"

The Prophet (Allāh bless him and give him peace) continued:

Then Hell will send forth a shower of sparks, as numerous as the stars. Each spark will be like an enormous cloud arising in the West, and that shower of sparks will fall upon the heads of the assembled creatures.

He went on to say (Allāh bless him and give him peace):

Then the Bridge *[Ṣirāṭ]* will be erected over Hell. Seven hundred arches will be made ready to support it, and the distance between each pair of arches will be that of a journey taking seventy years.[345] The dimensions of the Bridge *[Ṣirāṭ]* will be as follows: from the first platform down to the second platform, the distance of a journey taking five hundred years; from the second down to the third, the distance of a journey taking five hundred years; from the third down to the fourth, the same distance again; from the fourth down to the fifth, the same distance again; from the fifth down to the sixth, the same distance again; and from the sixth down to the seventh, likewise. This seventh platform will be the widest of them all, the hottest of them all, the most deeply concave of them all, the most varied of them all [in its range of torments], and the most fiery of them all—by a factor of seventy.

As for the lowest platform, its flames will rise up past the Bridge on the right side and the left, as they soar into the sky to a distance of three miles. Each platform will be hotter, more thickly littered with live coals, and beset with more varied kinds of torment than the one above it—by a factor of seventy.

Upon each platform there will be an ocean, rivers, mountains and trees. The height of each of those mountains, as it towers up into the sky, will be equal to the distance of a journey taking seventy thousand years. There will be seventy such mountains on each platform, and on each mountain there will be seventy thousand separate hills. On each of those separate hills there will be seventy thousand thorny trees *[shajara ḍarīʿ]*.[346] Each of those trees will have seventy branches, and there will be seventy serpents and seventy scorpions lurking on each of its branches. Each of those serpents will be three miles in length, and as for the scorpions, they will resemble huge Bactrian camels. Seventy thousand pieces of fruit will be dangling from each of those trees, and each piece of fruit will have the shape of a devil's head. Inside almost every one of those pieces of fruit there will be seventy worms, and each of those worms will be exceedingly long. Some pieces of fruit will not contain worms, but they will have thorns inside them instead.

The Prophet (Allāh bless him and give him peace) also used to say:

Hell *[Jahannam]* has seven entrances, and each of those entrances has seventy valleys. The depth of each of those valleys is the distance of a journey taking

[345] ***Author's note:*** According to one version of this report, there will be seven arches [rather than seven hundred].

[346] See note 168 on p. 125 above.

seventy years. Each of those valleys has seventy thousand branches, and in each of its branches there are seventy thousand caves. In each of those caves there are seventy thousand crevices, and each of its crevices extends to the distance of a journey taking seventy years. Seventy thousand snakes are lurking inside each of those crevices, and there are seventy thousand scorpions inside the jaws of each of those snakes. Each of those scorpions has seventy thousand spinal columns, and each of its spinal columns contains a flask of poison. Neither the unbeliever *[kāfir]* nor the hypocrite *[munāfiq]* will reach his final destination without experiencing all this to the full.

He also said (Allāh bless him and give him peace):

While the assembled creatures are down on their knees, and Hell is prancing about like a camel in heat, a herald will issue a proclamation in a very loud voice. The Prophets *[anbiyā᾽]*, the champions of truth *[ṣiddiqūn]*, the martyrs *[shuhadā᾽]* and the righteous *[ṣāliḥūn]* will thereupon spring to their feet. Then they will offer a proposal, to the effect that wrongs should be set right. Then they will offer a second proposal, the effect of which will be that the disembodied spirits *[arwāḥ]* and the physical bodies *[ajsād]* engage in mutual debate, and that the physical bodies win the argument against the disembodied spirits. Then they will offer a third proposal to Allāh, as a result of which the record sheets *[ṣuḥuf]* will fly up into the air—and fall into the hands of the people assembled at the place of Resurrection. One person will have his record given to him in his right hand, another will have his record given to him in his left hand, and yet another will have his record given to him behind his back.

As for those who receive their records with their right hands, they will be granted a light from the Light of their Lord, and the angels will congratulate them on their mark of honor. They will then pass over the Bridge *[Ṣirāṭ]*, through the mercy of their Lord, and proceed to enter their Gardens of Paradise. Their guardians will be waiting to meet them at the gates of their Gardens of Paradise, ready to present them with their garments and their riding mounts, and to equip them with all the finery that will suit them best.

They will then disperse to their respective dwellings, and gleefully make tracks toward their palatial mansions, where they will enter into the company of their spouses. They will see sights that their tongues could never have described, that their eyes have never beheld, and the very idea of which has never occurred to their hearts. They will eat and drink, and put on their fine new clothes and ornaments. They will then embrace their spouses, to the utmost extent of which they are capable.

Then they will offer praise to their Creator *[Khāliq]*, who has banished their sorrow from them, replaced their sense of anxiety with a feeling of security, and made their reckoning an easy matter for them to undergo. Then they will express their gratitude for all that their Lord has bestowed upon them. They will say: "Praise be to Allāh *[al-ḥamdu li'llāh]*, who has guided us to this, for we could not have guided ourselves, if Allāh had not guided us." They will be highly delighted when they recognize the provisions they have obtained from their life in this lower world, for they were people of conviction *[mūqinīn]*, people of faith *[mu᾽minīn]*, believers in the truth *[muṣaddiqīn]*, people whose fears and hopes and longings were focused on their Lord. That is the criterion by which the saved obtain salvation *[naja 'n-nājūn]*, and by which the unbelievers are doomed to perdition *[halaka 'l-kāfirūn]*.

As for those who receive their records with their left hands or from behind their backs, their faces will be darkly stained, the fair color of their eyes will be altered, a brand will be stamped on the tips of their noses, their bodies will be bloated, and their skins will turn coarse and rough. They will cry out in woeful distress, when they look at their records and see their sins with their own eyes. Whatever the nature of the sins they committed in the past, be they minor or major offenses, they will find them every single one of them substantiated in their records.

They will therefore be dejected in their feelings, and their thoughts will be filled with foreboding. Their alarm will be intense, and great will be their anxiety. Their heads will be bowed, their eyes downcast, and their necks bent low. They may try to steal a glance at the Fire of Hell that awaits them, but once they have looked, it will be impossible for them to withdraw their gaze from the sight, because they have laid their eyes upon something that is enormous, huge, horrifying, momentous, overwhelming, distressing, terrible, dreadful, tragic, repulsive, disturbing to the feelings and tear-provoking to the eyes.

They will thus acknowledge their servitude to their Lord. They will confess their sins, and they will experience their confession as a scorching fire, a shameful disgrace, a sorrowful affliction, a painful agony, a compulsory obligation, and an extremely distasteful necessity.

He then went on to say (Allāh bless him and give him peace):

While the people are down on their knees, confessing their sins in the presence of their Lord (Almighty and Glorious is He), their eyes will be so obscured that they cannot see clearly, their feelings will be so downcast that they cannot think rationally, and their limbs will be trembling so violently that they cannot produce articulate speech. Their bonds of kinship will be severed, so that they cannot connect with one another. There will therefore be no family ties to link them together on that day, and they will not be responsible for one another. They will be stricken with such personal loss that they cannot recuperate. They may beg for a second chance, but their pleading will go unanswered. They will have to acknowledge the truth of that which they used to dismiss as false, for now they are thirsty and unable to quench their thirst, hungry and unable to satisfy their hunger, naked and unable to clothe their nakedness, defeated and unable to triumph. They are stricken with grief and deprivation, having lost themselves and their families, their goods and their profits.

He also said (Allāh bless him and give him peace):

While the people are in this conditon, Allāh (Exalted is He) will suddenly command the keepers of Hell *[Jahannam]* to make their exit from it, together with their assistants, and to bring with them all their tools and instruments, such as chains, shackles and grappling hooks. They will thereupon emerge from Hell and take up a position outside it, while they wait to see what further orders they will be given.

He continued (Allāh bless him and give him peace):

When the wretched people notice that the keepers have come out from Hell, and when they set eyes upon their fetters and their gear, they will start biting their own hands. They will eat their fingernails, then cry out in distress as their blood comes gushing forth. Their feet will shake and stumble, and they will despair of anything good. Then Allāh (Exalted is He) will give the order: "Seize them and tie them up, then roast them on the blazing Fire *[Jaḥīm]*, then bind them securely in chains!"

He went on to say (Allāh bless him and give him peace):

Whenever Allāh wishes to cast a group of people into those layers [of Hell], He summons their keepers and says to them: "Seize these people!" Seventy angels immediately rush toward each individual member of the group concerned. They tighten their bonds, putting heavy shackles on their necks and fixing chains through their noses. This causes them to be throttled, and their spinal columns are also broken to pieces, since their forelocks are bent over behind their backs and tied to their feet.

He also said (Allāh bless him and give him peace):

Once they have been subjected to this treatment, their eyes will become glazed, their jugular veins will be inflated, the flesh of their necks will be scorched, and their blood vessels will be stripped bare. The heat of the shackles will burn into their heads, causing their brains to boil. Their brains will then spill out onto their outer layers of skin and trickle down to their feet. This will cause their outer layers of skin to peel off, and the fleshy parts beneath to turn green, as the pus flows out of them.

When the shackles are placed on their necks, they will fill the whole area between their shoulders and their ears. Their fleshy parts will therefore be scorched, their lips will be hacked to pieces, their teeth will be exposed like fangs, and their tongues will stick out as they utter noises and screams. Those shackles will gleam with the glow of soaring flames, the heat of which will flow through their veins like blood, leaving them hollow. Since the flames of the Fire of Hell will also be flowing through them, the heat of those shackles will reach their hearts. Detached from their strings, their hearts will move up till they reach their throats, and this will intensify their strangulation. Their voices will be cut off completely, and their outer layers of skin will totally disappear.

Then, while they are in this condition, Allāh (Exalted is He) will command the keepers of Hell *[Jahannam]* to provide them with clothing. They will dress them at once in shirts and pants. These garments will be extremely dark black in color, reeking with the stench of decay, rough and coarse to the touch, and ablaze from the intensity of their heat. If they were set down on the mountains of the earth, they would cause them to melt away.

He continued (Allāh bless him and give him peace):

Then Allāh (Almighty and Glorious is He) will say to the keepers of Hell *[Jahannam]*: "Herd them away to their dwelling places!" They will thereupon produce another set of chains, longer and coarser than those in which the people had already been firmly secured. Each of the angels will then take one of those chains and use it to bind all the members of one of the religious communities *[umma mina 'l-umam]* together. Then he will place the end of the chain over his shoulder and turn his back on them. Then he will set off with them, dragging them along with their faces on the ground.

In the rear of each religious community there will be a team of seventy thousand angels, prodding its members with goading irons until they drive them to Hell, at the brink of which they will bring them to a halt.

He went on to say (Allāh bless him and give him peace):

At this point the angels will say to them: "This is the Fire of Hell, the reality of which you were in the habit of denying. Is this mere sorcery, or can you not see? Now you must roast in it, so you may or may not have the patience to endure, but that will not make the slightest difference as far as you are concerned. You are simply being repaid for what you used to do."

He also said (Allāh bless him and give him peace):

As soon as they have been brought to a halt at the brink of Hell, its gates will be opened to admit them and its covering will be removed to expose its contents. Its Fire will blaze and burst forth in flames, and a terrible cloud of smoke will then emerge from it, together with a hail of sparks, as numerous as the stars in the sky. These sparks will fly up high into the sky, to the distance of a journey taking seventy years. Then all of this will come back down, to fall on the heads of the people in chains. The hair on their heads will thus be consumed by fire, and their skulls will be cracked and shattered.

He continued (Allāh bless him and give him peace):

Then Hell will scream in the loudest voice it can muster: "Come here to me, O people of the Fire, come here to me! By the Might and Glory of my Lord, I shall most certainly inflict retribution upon you!" Then it will say: "Praise be to Allāh, who has made me angry on account of His anger, and who is using me to inflict retribution upon His enemies. My Lord, add heat to my heat, and add strength to my strength!"

He went on to say (Allāh bless him and give him peace):

Yet another set of angels will then come forth from Hell, and each one among them will approach one of the religious communities *[umma mina 'l-umam]*. He will pick up the members of that community at his leisure, and then topple them facedown into Hell. This means that they will land on their heads—eventually, since they will go on falling for the distance of a journey taking seventy years, before they reach the peaks of the mountains of Hell.

To this he added (Allāh bless him and give him peace):

Even when they finally reach the peaks of the mountains of Hell, they will not alight upon those peaks until each and every individual amongst them has had his skin stripped and replaced no less than seventy times.

He also said (Allāh bless him and give him peace):

> The first meal they get to eat on those mountain peaks will be a meal consisting of the fruit called *az-zaqqūm*,[347] the heat of which is outwardly apparent, the bitterness of which is extremely intense, and the thorns of which are very many. While they are chewing that meal of theirs, the angels will suddenly come upon them, beating them with their goading irons till their bones are smashed to pieces. Then the angels will grab hold of them by their legs and fling them into Hell, so that they plunge headfirst for the distance of a journey taking seventy years, before landing on the outlying ridges of the mountains of Hell.

To this he added (Allāh bless him and give him peace):

> They will not alight upon those outlying ridges, however, until each and every individual amongst them has had his skin stripped and replaced no less than seventy times.

He also said (Allāh bless him and give him peace):

> That meal of theirs will be stuck in their mouths, for they will find it impossible to swallow and stomach. The food will thus combine with the heart to form a lump in the area of the gullet, causing a choking sensation. Each and every individual amongst them will then appeal for help in the form of something to drink. It will suddenly become apparent to them that, within those mountain ridges, there are river valleys streaming into Hell, so they will set off walking until they reach them, at which point they will bend down over them and attempt to drink the liquid they contain.

He continued (Allāh bless him and give him peace):

> The result of this will be that the skin is stripped from their faces, to be carried away in the current. They will find that it is actually impossible to drink from those streams, and so they will turn around and try to move away from them. The angels will be catching up with them, however, while they are still bending over those springs, and they will flog them till their bones are smashed to pieces. Then they will grab hold of them by their legs and fling them into Hell, so that they plunge headfirst for the distance of a journey taking one hundred and forty years, through blazing flames and a terrible cloud of smoke, before landing in those river valleys.

To this he added (Allāh bless him and give him peace):

> They will not alight upon those river valleys, however, until each and every individual amongst them has had his skin stripped and replaced no less than seventy times.

He went on to say (Allāh bless him and give him peace):

> The ultimate destination of the liquid that flows from those mountain springs is down in those river valleys. They will try to drink from it, but only to find that it is the fluid of Hell's inferno *[mā' al-Jaḥīm]*. It will not settle in their stomachs until Allāh has stripped and replaced the skin of each and every individual amongst them no less than seventy times.

[347] See note 167 on p. 125 above.

To this he added (Allāh bless him and give him peace):

> As soon as some of that liquid has settled in their bellies, their intestines will be cut to pieces, which will then come out through their buttocks. The rest of it will flow through their viens, causing their fleshy parts to melt and their bones to crack. The angels will soon catch up with them, to beat them with their goading irons on their faces, their backsides and their heads. Each goading iron of theirs has three hundred and sixty cutting edges, so when they are used to strike people on their heads, their skulls are smashed in and their spinal columns are shattered to bits. Then they are dragged into the Fire of Hell, lying flat upon their faces, until they find themselves right in the middle of its blazing inferno. The Fire will then consume their outer layers of skin, and burn its way into their ears. Its flames will thus emerge through their nostrils and their ribs, while the pus oozes out of their bodies. Their eyes will pop out of their sockets, to dangle down over their cheeks.
>
> After all this, they will be joined together with those devils *[shayāṭīn]* of theirs, the ones they used to obey, and with those deities *[āliha]* of theirs, to whom they used to appeal for help. They will be thrown into places that are narrow and cramped, so they will cry out in their woe and distress, until their possessions are produced—only to be heated in their own fire, then used to brand them on their foreheads and their sides, then pressed down on their backs so that they come out through their bellies.
>
> They have earned this treatment, for they are the friends of Hell *[awliyā' Jahannam]* and the associates of the devils and the stones *[quranā' ash-shayāṭīn wa 'l-ḥijāra]*. They piled up their sins like mountains, in order to make sure that their punishment would be very severe indeed. The height of one such mountain of sins is equal to the distance of a month-long journey, while its width is that of a five-day march, its thickness is that of a five-night trek, and its peak is like that of al-Aqra', which is a mountain in the remotest part of Syria. In the face of that mountain there are thirty-two sharp teeth, some of which stick out from its head, while some of them appear beneath the bottom of its beard. Its nose is like an enormous hill. As for the length and coarseness of the hair on its head, it resembles the cedar tree, and the sheer abundance of it is like all the thickets of this world. Its upper lip is contracting, while the lower one is ninety cubits *[dhirā']* in length.[348] The length of its hand is equal to the distance of a ten-day journey, and the thickness of it is equal to that of a single day's march. Its thighs are like a couple of metal plates, and the thickness of its skin is forty cubits on its arm. The length of its leg is equivalent to the distance of a five-night journey, while the thickness of it is equal to that of a single day's march. Each pupil of its eyes resembles Ḥirā', which is a mountain near Mecca. When tar is poured over its head, the fire inside it glows more brightly, for it can only add to its inflammation.

According to one traditional report, the Prophet (Allāh bless him and give him peace) used to say:

> By the One who holds my soul in His hand, if a man were to emerge from the Fire of Hell—dragging a chain, with his hands shackled to his neck, with

[348] As a unit of length, the Arabic term *dhirā'*—like the medieval English cubit—is based on the length of the forearm from the elbow to the tip of the middle finger. While it is usually equal to about 18 inches, it sometimes signifies a length of 21 inches or even more.

> shackles on his neck and iron fetters on his legs—and if his fellow creatures were then to catch sight of him, they would certainly flee from him and run as far away from him as they possibly could.

The traditional report continues:

> Due to the intensity of the heat of the Fire of Hell, its grievous affliction, the varied range of its torment, and the narrowness of its dwelling places, the fleshy parts of its inhabitants will turn green, their bones will split and crack, their brains will boil and pour down over their outer layers of skin. As their skin is burned away, their limbs will be cut off at the joints. Then, as the pus oozes out from their dismembered limbs, their bodies will come to be riddled with maggots and worms. Those maggots and worms will soon grow so fat that they come to resemble the wild ass. They will also develop claws, and those claws of theirs will be just like the talons of vultures and eagles. They will burrow into the areas between the outer skin and the flesh of their victims, and rip them to shreds. They will give out a moaning sound in the process, and they will scurry to and fro, just as a frightened wild animal scurries to and fro. They will eat their victims' flesh and drink their blood, for they have no other form of food and drink.
>
> The angels will come and seize those people, then drag them along with their faces down on the live coals and stones, which stick out from the ground as if they were teeth. They will keep dragging them along until they reach the ocean of Hell *[Jahannam]*. This means covering the distance of a journey taking seventy years, so they will not reach it until all their joints are broken, nor without having their skins stripped and replaced no fewer than seventy thousand times each day. When the angels finally bring them to their destination, they will hand them over to the keepers of the ocean of Hell, who will immediately grab them by their legs and shove them into it. No one knows the depth of that ocean, except the One who created it.

According to some accounts, the following description is recorded in one of the books of the Torah *[asfār at-Tawrāh]:*

> The ocean of this world, by comparison with the ocean of Hell, is like a small well on the shore of the ocean of this world. So, when they are thrown into it, and experience the first touch of the torment it has to offer, they will say to one another: "As it seems now, the torment inflicted upon us before this was actually a form of gentle clemency."

The traditional report continues:

> They will sink down once, before rising again to the surface. Then the ocean will boil, as it plunges them down to a depth of seventy fathoms. The distance of each fathom will be equivalent to the distance of the East from the West. Then the angels will herd them together with their goading irons, beating them with these sharp rods and driving them back down to the very bottom of the ocean, to the distance of a journey taking seventy years. Their only food and drink will be what the ocean provides, so they will rise back up from its lowest depth, covering the distance of a journey taking one hundred and forty years.

> On reaching the surface, one of them will wish to pause for breath, so the angels will approach him with their goading irons, rushing toward him in order to give him a beating. This time, however, he will remember that, if he raises his head, seventy thousand goading irons will be aimed at that head of his. Since none of them ever misses its target, they will send him back down to a depth of seventy fathoms, each fathom being equivalent to the distance of the East from the West.

The traditional report continues further:

> They will stay in the ocean of Hell for as long as Allāh wills that this state of affairs should last. In the meantime, their flesh and bones will be eaten away, so that only their spirits survive. They will eventually be struck by a wave that rolls them along for seventy years, then casts them ashore on one of the beaches of the ocean of Hell. On that beach there are seventy thousand caves, and deep inside each cave there are seventy thousand crevices. Each of those crevices extends as far as a journey lasting seventy years, and lurking deep inside each crevice there are seventy thousand snakes. The length of each of those snakes is seventy cubits, and each of those snakes has seventy sharp fangs. Within each of those fangs there is a flask of poison, and lurking inside the jaws of each of those snakes there are a thousand scorpions. Each of those scorpions has seventy vertebrae, and in each of those veretbrae there is a flask of poison.

The traditional report goes on to tell us:

> Once their spirits have finally come ashore from that ocean of Hell, and have found their way into those caves, they will be provided with new bodies and new skins. Then they will be shackled in iron, at which point those serpents and scorpions will come out and attack them. Each and every individual amongst them will find that he has seventy thousand snakes and seventy thousand scorpions clinging to him. They will have no choice but to endure this onslaught with patience. Then the snakes and scorpions will climb up to their knees, and they will again have no choice but to endure the onslaught with patience. Then the snakes and scorpions will climb up to their chests, so they will yet again endure with patience. Then the snakes and scorpions will climb up to their collarbones, and patient endurance will once again be their only response. Then the snakes and scorpions will climb up higher still, attaching themselves to their noses, their lips, their teeth and their ears. At this point they will begin to panic, but they have nowhere to turn for refuge, except by running away into Hell, so into Hell they will tumble. As for the serpents, meanwhile, they will be chewing their flesh and sucking their blood, and as for the scorpions, they will be stinging them so hard that their fleshy parts will drop off piece by piece, and their limbs will be cut off at the joints. Even when they have tumbled into the Fire of Hell, it will take seventy years for the Fire to burn them clear of the poison injected into their systems by all those serpents and scorpions.

The traditional report continues:

> Then the Fire of Hell will burn them for seventy years, at the end of which time they will be equipped with new skins, different from the skins they had before. Then they will beg to be supplied with food, so the angels will bring them a

> special meal, ironically called "the wedding feast *[al-walīma]*," which is actually as dry and as hard as iron. They will attempt to chew it, but they will find it quite impossible to eat the slightest morsel of it, so they will spit it out of their mouths. They will then set about devouring their own hands, as the only way to satisfy the extreme intensity of their hunger. They will begin by eating their fingertips and their palms. Once they have eaten those, they will start on their forearms and eat them too, as far as their elbows. Then they will start on their elbows, and go on eating all the way up to their shoulders, until only the tips of their shoulders are left uneaten. If they could get their mouths to reach any part of their bodies after that, they would certainly eat that part as well! After they have done all this to their bodies, however, they will be suspended from the tree called *az-zaqqūm*,[349] by means of iron flesh-hooks attached to their Achilles' tendons *[ʿarāqīb]*.

The traditional report continues further:

> Seventy thousand of them will be suspended from a single branch, with their heads hanging downward, yet this will not cause the branch to bend. Then the blazing inferno will be ignited beneath them, and the heat of the Fire of Hell will rise to scorch their faces. This will go on for a period of seventy years, so that their bodies will melt away and only their spirits will survive intact.
>
> Then they will be supplied with fresh skins and new bodies. But then they will be suspended once again, this time by their fingertips, with the flames of the Fire of Hell beneath them. Those flames will rise and penetrate inside them through their buttocks, consuming their hearts before eventually emerging from their noses, their mouths and their ears. This process will also go on for a period of seventy years, so that their bones and their flesh will melt away and only their spirits will survive intact.
>
> Then they will be granted a brief respite, while they are supplied with fresh skins and new bodies. But then they will be suspended once again, this time by their eyes, for the same length of time and with similar consequences.
>
> They will not cease to be tormented in this fashion, until there is not one joint in their bodies by which they have yet to be suspended, and not a single hair on their heads by which they have yet to be left dangling. Even though death approaches them from every joint in their bodies, they will not turn into lifeless corpses, while yet another ghastly torment is lying in wait behind them. Finally, when this particular form of punishment has been inflicted on them in every detail, the angels will bring them down from the branch of the tree. They will then take each and every individual amongst them off to his dwelling place, shackled with a chain and dragged along with his face to the ground.

The traditional report goes on to tell us:

> The dimensions of their dwelling places in Hell will be commensurate with their wicked deeds. One of them, for instance, will be assigned to a lodging the length of which is equal to a month-long journey, and the width of which is similar. A fire will be ignited in it, and no one else will share it with him. Another of them, meanwhile, will be assigned to a lodging of which both the

[349] See note 167 on p. 125 above.

length and width correspond to a journey of only twenty-nine nights. Yet others will be assigned to progressively smaller and narrower lodgings, till the point is reached where one of them is given a lodging that measures the equivalent of a one-day journey in both length and width.

The torments inflicted on them will match the size of their lodgings, so they will be in several different postures while receiving their punishment. One of them will take his punishment while standing on his head. One of them will take his punishment in a sitting position. One of them will take his punishment while squatting down on his knees. One of them will take his punishment while standing on his legs. One of them will take his punishment while sprawled out flat on his belly. In each of these lodgings, the breathing space available to the occupants will be narrower than the tip of a spear.

The height of the fire inside the various lodgings will also vary. In one case, the fire will reach up to the ankles of the occupant. One of them will be in fire up to his knees. One of them will be in fire up to his waist. One of them will be in fire up to his navel. One of them will be in fire up to his collar bone. One of them will be completely immersed in a flood of fire, which will sometimes lift him up to the surface, and sometimes spin him around, as it plunges him down into its depths to the distance of a month-long journey.

Once they have settled into their dwelling places, they will all link up with their comrades, and weep until their tears run dry. Then they will shed tears of blood, to the point where ships could be launched in the current of their tears.

The traditional report continues:

They will have one day to spend together in the pit of the blazing inferno, after which there will never be another opportunity for them to congregate. When Allāh gives permission on that day, a herald will cry out in the pit of the blazing inferno, and his voice will be heard by those at the very top and those at the very bottom, by those who are nearest to the center and those who are at the farthest edge. This is what is called the Gathering *[al-Ḥashr]*. The herald will say: "O people of the Fire of Hell, assemble together!" In response to this summons, they will all assemble together in the pit of the blazing inferno of Hell *[al-Jaḥīm]*, accompanied by the tormenting angels *[zabāniya]*.[350]

The traditional report goes on to tell us:

The people of the Fire of Hell will then start arguing with one another. Those who used to be despised will say to those who were scornful: "We used to be your followers in the world below,[351]

So will you be of any help to us at all in the face of Allāh's punishment?" (14:21)	*fa-hal antum mughnūna ʿan-nā min ʿadhābi 'llāhi min shaiʾ.*

[350] See note 102 on p. 73 above.

[351] A slightly paraphrased version of the Qurʾānic verse *[āya]*:

Then the weak will say to those who were proud: "We used to be your followers." (14:21)	*fa-qāla 'ḍ-ḍuʿafāʾu li'lladhīna 'stakbarū: innā kunnā la-kum tabaʿan.*

Those who were proud will say:

"Every one of us is in it; indeed, Allāh has already passed judgment on His servants." (40:48)	*innā kullun fī-hā* *inna 'llāha qad ḥakama* *baina 'l-'ibād.*

Those who were proud will also say to those who used to be despised: "You may turn to us for help, but for you there is no word of welcome here!" Those who used to be despised will then say to those who were proud:

"No, you are the ones for whom there is no word of welcome! You prepared this for us in advance, and how evil is the outcome!" (38:60)	*bal antum* *lā marḥaban bi-kum:* *antum qaddamtumū-hu la-nā:* *fa-bi'sa 'l-qarār.*

Those who used to be despised will take exception to hearing this from those who were proud, and they will say:

Our Lord, whoever did prepare this for us, be sure to give him a double portionof torment in the Fire of Hell! (38:61)	*Rabba-nā man qaddama* *la-nā hādhā fa-zid-hu* *'adhāban ḍi'fan fi 'n-nār.*

In response to this, those who were proud will say:

"If Allāh had guided us aright, we would surely have guided you aright." (14:21)	*law hadā-na 'llāhu* *la-hadainā-kum.*

Those who used to be despised will then say to those who were proud: "Not so! [You were only interested in your] scheming by night and day, when you were instructing us to disbelieve in Allāh, and to set up rivals in competition with Him. (34:33). This means that we are untainted by you, and that we are innocent of the things you invited us to do in the lower world."

The traditional report continues:

Then all of them will turn toward the devils *[shayāṭīn]* who are their fellow inmates, and the latter will tell them: "We led you into error, as we tempted you and lured you away from the right path." Eventually, when they have finished saying what they have to say on this subject, Satan himself *[ash-Shaiṭān]* will proclaim, in a high-pitched voice peculiar to him:

"Allāh surely promised you a promise of truth (14:22), and Allāh summoned you, but you did not respond to His call, and you did not believe that His promise was true.

"I made you a promise, too, but then I let you down, for I had no authority over you, except that I called to you and you obeyed me. So do not lay the blame on me, but blame yourselves. I cannot come to your aid, nor can you be of any assistance to me (14:22), for I am quite ungrateful, on this day, for the fact that you rendered worshipful service to me, instead of to Allāh."

The traditional report continues, citing the words of Allāh (Almighty and Glorious is He):

And then a herald in between them	*fa-adhdhana mu'adhdhinun*

will cry out: "The curse of Allāh
is on the evildoers!" (7:44)

baina-hum an laʿnatu ʾllāhi
ʿala ʾẓ-ẓālimīn.

Then the traditional report goes on to tell us:

At this point, those who used to be despised will curse those who were proud, and those who were proud will curse those who used to be despised. All of them will curse the devils who are their fellow inmates, and their fellow inmates will curse them in return. Then they will say to those fellow inmates of theirs: "If only we were separated from you by the distance that separates the two horizons from each other—for you are evil companions[352] for us today, just as you were evil ministers *[wuzarāʾ]* for us in the lower world."

When it finally dawns on them that they are all lumped together in a single congregation, they will start saying to one another: "Come on! Let us go and look for the custodians of this place. Perhaps they will intercede on our behalf in the presence of their Lord, so that He may relieve us of the torment for a day."[353]

The traditional report continues further:

In spite of this, however, they will continue to suffer torment. The keepers of Hell will stay out of their reach for as long as seventy years, and then, when they eventually come around to them, they will say:

"Did your Messengers not come
to you with clear proofs?" (40:50)

a-wa-lam taku taʾtī-kum
rusulu-kum bi-ʾl-bayyināt.

"Yes indeed,"[354] they will all respond together, whereupon the keepers of Hell will say:

"Then make your plea,
although the pleading
of the unbelievers is in vain."
(40:50)

fa-ʾdʿū:
wa mā duʿāʾu ʾl-kāfirīna
illā fī ḍalāl.

Then, according to the same traditional report:

When they see that the keepers of Hell will not do them any good, they will turn to the angel Mālik[355] with their next appeal for help, as they cry:

"O Mālik, let your Lord make an end of us! (43:77) Let Him finally put us to death!"

[352] Up to this point, the sentence beginning "If only..." is almost identical—except that the pronouns and one noun are in the plural instead of the singular—with the Qurʾānic verse *[āya]* in which Allāh (Exalted is He) has told us:

Till, when he comes to Us, he says:
"If only I were separated from you
by the distance that separates
the two horizons from each other—
for you are an evil companion." (43:38)

ḥattā idhā jāʾa-nā qāla
yā laita
bainī wa baina-ka
buʿdu ʾl-mashriqaini:
fa-biʾsa ʾl-qarīn.

[353] *yukhaffif ʿan-nā yawman mina ʾl-ʿadhāb.* This last phrase in the sentence is a direct quotation from the Qurʾān (40:49).

[354] The response "Yes indeed *[balā]*!" is a quotation from the same verse *[āya]* of the Qurʾān (40:50).

[355] The literal meaning of the Arabic word *mālik* is 'someone in authority; an owner or possessor.' Mālik is the name of the angel who presides over Hell, superintending the torments inflicted on its occupants.

Mālik will keep them waiting for as long as it would take to travel the world, withholding his answer and declining to give them any response. Then, when he finally condescends to address them, it will be to say:

"You will have to linger on (43:77) for many aeons of time, before He finally puts you to death."

When they see that Mālik will not do them any good, they will address their appeal for help directly to their Lord. To Him they will say:

"Our Lord, bring us forth out of it!	*Rabba-nā akhrij-nā min-hā*
Then, if we revert,	*fa-in ʿudnā*
we shall be evildoers indeed."	*fa-innā ẓālimūn.*
(23:107)	

—That is to say, "if we revert to our former habit of disobeying You."

Then, as the traditional report goes on to tell us:

The All-Compelling One *[al-Jabbār]* (Glory be to Him and Exalted is He) will keep them waiting for as long as seventy years. During all that time, He will neither respond to their request nor provide them with any benefit. Then, when He finally does reply to them in His own words, He will reduce them to the status of dogs, for He will say:

"Slink away into it,	*[qāla] 'khsaʾū fī-hā*
and do not speak to Me." (23:108)	*wa lā tukallimūn.*

The traditional report continues further:

When they see that their Lord will not bestow His mercy on them, and that He will not grant them any favor, they will say to one another, referring to their torment:

"It is all the same for us whether	*sawāʾun ʿalai-nā*
we writhe in agony, or whether we	*a-jaziʿnā*
patiently endure;	*am ṣabarnā*
we have no place of refuge. (14:21)	*mā la-nā min maḥīṣ.*
Now we have no intercessors,	*fa-mā la-nā min shāfiʿīn:*
nor any loyal friend.	*wa lā ṣadīqin*
If only we could have	*ḥamīm:*
another turn [on earth],	*fa-law anna la-nā karratan*
so that we might be numbered	*fa-nakūna*
among the believers!" (26:100–102)	*mina 'l-muʾminīn.*

The traditional report recounts what will happen to them next:

Then, as the angels are taking them away to their dwelling places, their feet will slip and stumble. Any argument they try to make will be refuted, and they will see what their Lord (Almighty and Glorious is He) has in store for them. They will lose all hope of His mercy, and their sense of despair will throw them into a state of terrible distress. A profound awareness of shame and degradation will descend upon them, so they will sadly bemoan the loss of all the opportunities they squandered in the course of their worldly lives.

> As well as having their own heavy burdens loaded on their necks, they will also have to carry the burdens of those who used to be their followers and attendants, without the slightest reduction in those burdens of theirs. Their torments will be more numerous than the specks of dust on the earth and the drops of water in the oceans. They will be accompanied by some of the guardians of Hell *[zabāniya]*,[356] whose orders are abrupt, whose manner of speaking is harsh and crude, whose bodies are as prodigious as the lightning in the sky, whose faces are like live coals, whose eyes are like flames, whose coloring is dark and gloomy, whose teeth and nails are like the horns of cattle. The goading irons they hold in their hands are long, heavy and fiercely hot; if they used them to strike the mountains, the mountains would be split asunder by the force of the blow, then crumble like rotten old bones. The guardians of Hell will use these instruments to beat the sinners who have disobeyed their Lord, so those sinners will have every reason to shed tears of blood, once their ordinary tears have run dry. They may plead with their tormentors, but their pleas will go unanswered. They may weep and sob for mercy, but the *zabāniya* will show them no compassion. They may beg for a drink of cold water, but the only liquid they get from the guardians of Hell will be a kind of pus that roasts their faces.

According to the same traditional report, the Prophet (Allāh bless him and give him peace) used to say:

> An enormous cloud will gather each day, then drift over the people of the Fire of Hell. The flashes of lightning from it will dazzle their eyes, its thunder will crash down on their backs, and it will cast a gloom so dense that they cannot even see their hellish guardians. Then the cloud will proclaim, in its own peculiar booming voice: "O people of the Fire of Hell, would you not like me to give you a shower of rain?" They will all respond in chorus: "Shower us with cold water!" But the cloud will subject them for an hour to a hail of stones, which will fall on their heads and smash their skulls to pieces. Then it will rain upon them for another hour, this time with streams of boiling water, live coals in great abundance, smokeless flames of fire, and sharp hooks of iron. Then, for the next hour, it will shower them with snakes, scorpions, maggots and worms, and filthy slime.

The traditional report continues:

> Whenever it rains in Hell *[Jahannam]*, the ocean of Hell becomes full to overflowing, so its depths begin to surge in waves and it heaves in a mighty rage. It leaves neither shore nor mountain in Hell uncovered by its rising tide, and so it submerges all the people of the Fire, although they do not die.

The traditional report continues further:

> The torments of Hell *[Jahannam]* will thus become worse and worse for those disobedient sinners, as conditions there become more and more extreme in every respect. Since they have incurred the retribution of their Lord, those who are doomed to reside there must suffer increasing degrees of harshness, heat, wailing and moaning, fire and smoke, darkness and gloom, stress and strain, poisonous fumes, boiling water, blazing and scorching flames, and every kind of agony.

[356] See note 102 on p. 73 above.

Let us therefore take refuge from it with Allāh—and from the deeds that lead to it, as well as from the companionship of its people! O Allāh, our Lord and its Lord, do not cause us to arrive within its confines! Do not place its shackles upon our necks! Do not clothe us with its garments! Do not feed us with its bitter fruit called *az-zaqqūm*,[357] and do not make us drink its boiling liquid! Do not put its keepers in charge of us! Do not treat us as fuel for its fire! By Your mercy, enable us instead to cross safely over its Bridge *[Ṣirāṭ]*, and deflect its sparks and flames away from us, in order that You may deliver us, through Your mercy, from it and from its smoke, and from its grief and its torment. Āmīn, O Lord of All the Worlds!

The Prophet (Allāh bless him and give him peace) also used to say:

> If even the least impressive door of Hell were to be opened in the West, it would cause the mountains of the East to evaporate, just as drops of rain evaporate in the heat of the sun. If even a single spark from Hell were to fly out and fall in the West, while a man was in the East, his brain would boil and spill out over his body.
>
> Among all the inhabitants of the Fire of Hell, those who suffer the mildest torment are men who are forced to wear shoes made of fire, which emerges through their ears and their noses, and which causes their brains to boil. Next come those who are hurled down onto one of the rocks of Hell, so that they bounce off it, just as a grain of corn bounces out of a hot frying pan, and each time they fall off one rock they land upon another.

This means that all the inhabitants of the Fire of Hell are made to suffer torments commensurate with the wickedness of their respective deeds. Let us therefore take refuge with Allāh from their deeds and their destination!

The Prophet (Allāh bless him and give him peace) has told us:

> As for the torment inflicted on those who do not protect their private parts, they will be suspended by their genital organs for as long as they lived in this world, so that their physical bodies will disintegrate completely and only their spirits will survive intact. Then they will be released, to be equipped with new bodies and fresh skins. Then they will be tormented all over again. Every individual amongst them will be flogged by seventy thousand angels, for a period corresponding to his lifetime in this world, so that their physical bodies will disintegrate completely and only their spirits will survive intact. Such will be their punishment.
>
> As for the torment inflicted on the thief, he will be dismembered limb by limb, then put together again. That will be the extent of his punishment, except that each individual among the class of thieves will also be assaulted by seventy thousand angels, armed with large razor blades.

[357] See note 167 on p. 125 above.

> As for the torment inflicted on those who give false witness, they will be suspended by their tongues. Then each individual amongst them will be flogged by seventy thousand angels, so that their physical bodies will disintegrate completely and only their spirits will survive intact.
>
> As for the torment inflicted on those who attribute partners to Allāh *[al-mushrikīn]*, they will be lodged in the cavern of Hell, which will then be sealed to keep them from escaping. Inside that cavern, they will find themselves in the midst of snakes, scorpions, many live coals, and fierce flames and smoke. Every hour, each individual amongst them will have his skin stripped and renewed no fewer than seventy thousand times.
>
> As for the torment inflicted on cruel and arrogant tyrants, they will be placed in coffins made of fire. Then locks will be fastened to keep them inside, and the coffins will be deposited in the lowest tier of the Fire of Hell. Every hour, each individual amongst them will be subjected to ninety-nine different kinds of torment. Each of them will have his skin stripped and renewed a thousand times every day. Such will be their punishment.

According to the traditional report, the Prophet (Allāh bless him and give him peace) went on to say:

> As for those who are guilty of the betrayal of trust, they will bring their trickery with them. Then they will be thrown into the ocean of Hell *[Jahannam]*. To ensure that they go down all the way to the very bottom of it—the depth of which is known to none but the One who created it—they will then be told: "You must dive down deep, in order to get rid of your fraudulent deceit!"
>
> On hearing this, they will dive as deep as Allāh wills. Then they will return to the surface, sticking their heads out as they gasp for breath. At this point, however, each one of them will be assailed immediately by seventy thousand angels, each of them armed with a goading prong made of iron, ready to be swung against his head. Such will be their punishment forever.

According to the same traditional report, the Prophet (Allāh bless him and give him peace) also used to say:

> Allāh has condemned the people of the Fire of Hell to remain in it for aeons *[aḥqāb]*. While I do not know how many those aeons will be, I can tell you that a single aeon *[ḥuqb]* is a period of eighty thousand years, and that a year is three hundred and sixty days. In the context of Hell, however, one day is the equivalent of a thousand years by your reckoning.

Woe, therefore, to the people of the Fire of Hell! Woe to those faces—those faces that used to regard the heat of the sun as more than they could bear—at the time when the Fire is scorching them! Woe to those heads—those heads that used to regard an ordinary headache as more than they could bear—at the time when Hell's boiling water *[ḥamīm]* is being poured on top of them! Woe to those eyes—those eyes that used to regard ophthalmia *[ramad]* as more than they could bear—

at the time when they are losing their color and glazing over within the Fire of Hell! Woe to those ears—those ears that used to take such delight in listening to gossip and scandal—at the time when the flames are flaring out of them! Woe to those noses—those noses that used to twitch in discomfort at the smell of decaying corpses—at the time when they are having to inhale the Fire of Hell! Woe to those necks—those necks that used to regard the slightest ache or pain as more than they could bear—at the time when shackles are being fastened to them! Woe to those skins—those skins that used to regard coarse clothing material as more than they could bear—at the time when they are being clad in garments made from a fiery material that is coarse indeed to the touch, that gives off a stinking odor, and that is smoldering with fire! Woe to those bellies—those bellies that used to regard an ordinary stomach-ache as more than they could bear—at the time when the bitter fruit called *az-zaqqūm*,[358] combined with boiling water, is entering inside them and cutting their intestines to pieces! Woe to those feet—those feet that used to regard the slightest soreness as more than they could bear—at the time when they are being forced to wear shoes made of fire!

Woe to the people of the Fire of Hell, in all their varied torments! O Allāh, by virtue of this stupendous knowledge, and of Your universal grace and favor, do not cause us to be numbered among its inhabitants!

[358] See note 167 on p. 125 above.

On crossing the bridge of Hell and entering the Garden of Paradise, as explained by the Prophet (Allāh bless him and give him peace) in a traditional report that has been handed down to us on the authority of Abū Huraira (may Allāh be well pleased with him).

According to Abū Huraira[359] (may Allāh be well pleased with him), Allāh's Messenger (Allāh bless him and give him peace) used to say:

The bridge of Hell *[jisr Jahannam]* has seven arches. The distance between each pair of arches is equal to that of a journey taking seventy years, while the width of the bridge is like the sharp edge of a sword. The first group of people will cross over it as quickly as it takes to blink an eye. The second group, at the speed of a brief flash of lightning. The third group, at the speed of a violent gust of wind. The fourth group, at the speed of birds. The fifth group, at the speed of horses. The sixth group, at the speed of a man in a hurry. As for the seventh group, they will cross over it at an ordinary walking pace.

When all seven groups have crossed over, one man will still be waiting, which means that he will be the very last to cross that bridge. "Cross over!" he will be told, so he will set his two feet upon it, but one of them will slip. Then he will straddle the bridge and try crawling along it on his knees, but the Fire of Hell will lick at his hair and his skin as he does so.

He will continue to wriggle along on his belly, for his other foot will slip, leaving him with one hand holding fast, while the other hand dangles loose. The Fire of Hell will attack him in that position, so he will suppose that he has no chance of escaping from its clutches. Nevertheless, he will continue to wriggle along on his belly, until he finally succeeds in getting beyond its reach. As soon as he is clear of it, he will look at it and say: "Blessed be the One who has delivered me from you! I cannot imagine that my Lord has ever given anyone, in ancient or modern times, the likes of what He has given me! He did indeed deliver me from you, after I had seen you and met you face to face!"

One of the angels will then approach him, take him by the hand, and lead him to a pond in front of the entrance to the Garden of Paradise. The angel will say to him: "Bathe yourself in this pond, and drink from it."

[359] See note 226 on p. 163 above.

> He will thereupon bathe himself in the pond, and take a drink from it. As he does so, the sweet aroma of the people of the Garden of Paradise will keep wafting toward him, and he will catch glimpses of their many colors. Then the angel will lead him away and make him stand at the entrance to the Garden of Paradise, saying to him: "Stand here and wait, until you receive permission from your Lord (Almighty and Glorious is He)."
>
> While he is standing at the entrance to the Garden of Paradise, he will catch sight of the occupants of the Fire of Hell. He will also hear them howling like dogs, so he will weep as he pleads: "O my Lord, turn my face away from the people of the Fire of Hell. I shall never ask You, O my Lord, for any other favor!"
>
> That same angel will then come to him from the presence of the Lord of All the Worlds (Almighty and Glorious is He). The angel will move his face away from the Fire of Hell, and turn it around toward the Garden of Paradise.

From the same traditional report, transmitted on the authority of Abū Huraira (may Allāh be well pleased with him), we learn that Allāh's Messenger (Allāh bless him and give him peace) went on to say:

> The spot where that man is obliged to stand and wait will be no more than a footstep away from the entrance to the Garden of Paradise, so he will find himself looking directly at the door of the Garden of Paradise. As he surveys its width, he will discover that the two side-posts of the door of the Garden of Paradise are very far apart—so far apart, in fact, that even the swiftest of birds would take forty years to fly from one of them to the other.
>
> That man will then make a request of his Lord (Almighty and Glorious is He), to whom he will say: "O my Lord, You have indeed treated me with the utmost kindness. You have delivered me from the Fire of Hell, and You have averted my face from the inhabitants of the Fire of Hell and turned it toward the Garden of Paradise. Between me and the door of the Garden of Paradise there is now but a single footstep, so I beg You, O my Lord, through Your Might and Glory, to let me enter the door! I shall not ask You for anything other than this. But do place a screen between me and the inhabitants of the Fire of Hell, so that I cannot hear the dreadful hissing sound it constantly emits, and so that I cannot see its occupants.
>
> That same angel will then come to him again from the presence of the Lord of All the Worlds (Almighty and Glorious is He). "O son of Adam," the angel will say, "you are so untrue to your word! Did you not insist that you would not ask for anything else?"
>
> The man will respond to this reproach by swearing: "No, by the Might and Glory of the Lord, I shall not ask for anything else!" The angel will thereupon take him by the hand and cause him to enter the door. Then the angel will fly away, returning to the presence of the Lord of All the Worlds (Almighty and Glorious is He).

The Prophet (Allāh bless him and give him peace) continued:

> Now that he is inside the Garden of Paradise, that man will look to his right and to his left, as well as to his front, scanning an area that extends to the distance

of a whole year's journey, yet he will not see anyone there. In all that space, he will see nothing but trees and fruit, and the nearest tree will be just one footstep away from the spot on which he is standing.

As he looks at that tree, he will notice that its trunk is of gold and its branches of bright silver, that its leaves are like the finest ornaments any human being ever saw, that its fruits are creamier than butter and sweeter than honey, and that its aroma is more fragrant than musk.

That man will be utterly bewildered by all the sights he sees. He will therefore say: "O my Lord, You have delivered me from Hell *[Jahannam]* and allowed me to enter the door of the Garden of Paradise, so You have treated me with the utmost kindness. The distance between me and this tree is merely that of a single footstep; I shall ask You for nothing else, apart from permission to take that one step!"

That same angel will thereupon come to him and say: "You are so untrue to your word, O son of Adam! Did you not insist that you would not ask for anything more?" So what do you mean by making this extra request, and what has become of the solemn oath you swore? Do you not feel any sense of shame?"

The angel will thereupon take him by the hand and transport him to the least imposing of all the dwellings assigned to him. To his amazement, he will find this to be a palatial mansion, built of pearls, that stretches before him to the distance of a full year's journey.

As soon as he arrives there, however, and surveys the scene in front of him, he will find himself looking at another dwelling place, at which point that pearly mansion—along with everything else that is now behind him—will seem to him like no more than a dream. Once he has seen it, he will be unable to control himself, so he will say: "O my Lord, I am asking You to grant me this dwelling, and I shall not ask You for anything else!"

One of the angels will thereupon come to him and say: "O son of Adam, did you not commit yourself to the solemn oath you swore by your Lord? You are so untrue to your word, O son of Adam! Nevertheless, the dwelling is yours." As soon as he arrives there, however, and surveys the scene in front of him, he will find himself looking at yet another dwelling place, at which point the previous one will seem to him like no more than a dream. So he will say: "O my Lord, I am asking You to grant me this dwelling!"

That same angel will thereupon come to him and say: "O son of Adam, what is the matter with you? Do you never fulfill a solemn vow? Did you not insist that you would not ask for anything else?" Nevertheless, the angel will not reproach him too severely, because it will be quite obvious to him that the poor man is almost beside himself through being exposed to such marvels and wonders. So the angel will tell him: "It is yours!"

The Prophet (Allāh bless him and give him peace) continued:

At this point, yet another dwelling place will suddenly appear in front of him, and those he saw previously will seem to him like no more than a dream. He will therefore be left flabbergasted, too dumbfounded to express himself in coherent speech.

Allāh's Messenger (Allāh bless him and give him peace) will then say to him: "What is the matter with you now? Have you no request to make of your Lord?"

Recovering his power of speech, the man will reply: "O my master, may Allāh bless you *[yā sayyidī, ṣalla 'llāhu ʿalaik]*! By Allāh, I have already given my oath to the Lord of Might and Glory *[Rabb al-ʿIzza]* on so many occasions that I now feel afraid of Him. I have asked Him for so much that I now feel a sense of shame."

At this point, the Lord of Might and Glory (Magnificent is His Majesty) will say to the man: "Will it please you if I gather the whole world—from the day when I created it till the day when I caused it to be no more—and put it all together for your sake, then multiply it ten times over for your benefit?"

That man will respond to this by saying: "O my Lord, can You be making fun of me, when You are the Lord of All the Worlds?" The Lord of Might and Glory (Majestic and Exalted is He) will then say to the man: "I am indeed Capable of doing it, so ask Me for whatever you wish!"

At this point, the man will say: "O my Lord, allow me to join the company of human beings!"

An angel will thereupon come and take him by the hand, then walk with him into the Garden of Paradise, until something becomes apparent to him—something the like of which he has never seen. At the sight of this apparition, he will immediately prostrate himself, saying in his posture of prostration: "My Lord (Almighty and Glorious is He) has manifested Himself to me!" The angel will then say to him: "Lift up your head. This is your dwelling place, although it is only the least of your dwellings."

The man will then say: "If Allāh (Almighty and Glorious is He) had not made me close my eyes, they would have been completely dazzled by the radiant light of this palatial mansion."

While the man is proceeding to make himself at home in that palatial mansion, another man will come to meet him. At the sight of this person's face and clothing, he will be rendered speechless with astonishment, thinking that his visitor must be an angel. The newcomer will approach him, saying: "Peace be upon you, and Allāh's mercy and blessings *[as-salāmu ʿalaik—wa raḥmatu 'llāhi wa barakātuh]*! This is just the right moment for you to arrive here!" The first man will return his greeting of peace, then ask him: "Who are you, O servant of Allāh?" The other will reply: "I am a steward *[qahramān]* at your service. I have been appointed to manage this particular household, but you also have at your disposal a thousand other stewards like me, each of them in charge of one of your palatial mansions." You have a thousand palatial mansions in your possession, each with a staff of one thousand servants, as well as wives from among the brides of Paradise with those lovely eyes of theirs *[al-ḥūr al-ʿīn]*.[360]

On entering that palatial mansion of his, the man will discover that it has a dome, which has been carved out of a single pearl. He will find that there are seventy apartments inside the hollow interior of the dome, with seventy rooms inside each apartment. On closer inspection, he will notice that each room has

[360] See note 333 on p. 241 above.

> seventy doors, and that each of those doors is equipped with its own dome of pearls. When he enters those domes, he will be the very first person to open them, since they have never been opened previously by any of Allāh's creatures.
>
> At a certain point during his tour of the hollow interior of that great dome, lo and behold, he will suddenly find himself inside a dome that has been carved out of a precious red stone. It is seventy cubits in height, and has seventy doors. Each of those doors leads through to a precious stone, of similar height and likewise equipped with seventy doors. None of the precious stones is of the same color as the one next to it. Inside each of the precious stones there are spouses, bridal thrones *[manāṣṣ]*, and raised couches.
>
> On entering the jeweled dome, the man will find a wife waiting there to receive him—one of the brides of Paradise with those lovely eyes of theirs *[al-ḥūr al-ʿīn]*. She will greet him at once with the Islāmic salutation, and he will give her the greeting of peace in return, but then he will stand rooted to the spot, too stunned to say another word. To put him at his ease, she will therefore say to him: "This is just the right time for you to visit us. I am your wife!"
>
> When he looks into her face, the man will see his own face in hers, just as one of you might look at your face in the mirror, and see the reflection of its handsome features, its beauty and its fair complexion. She is decked out with seventy articles of clothing, each of them adorned with seventy colors, of which no two are alike. When looking at her from behind, he can see the calf of her leg. Whenever he moves to view her from a different angle, she becomes seventy times more beautiful in his eyes, for she is a mirror to him, and he is a mirror to her.

From the same traditional report, transmitted on the authority of Abū Huraira (may Allāh be well pleased with him), we learn that Allāh's Messenger (Allāh bless him and give him peace) went on to say:

> Each of those palatial mansions will be equipped with three hundred and sixty doors, and each of those three hundred and sixty doors will be surmounted by a dome made from a pearl, a sapphire, and some other kind of gem. None of those domes will be of the same color as the one next to it. When the owner surveys the area that stretches into the distance behind his palatial mansion, he will be viewing his own estate as far as his eye can see. When he sets out on a journey into that area, he will travel through his own estate for a hundred years, making a thorough inspection of everything he comes across along the way.
>
> Whenever he takes up residence in one of his palatial mansions, the angels will come in to visit him through each and every gate, bearing the greeting of peace *[salām]* and bringing him gifts from the presence of the Lord of All the Worlds. Not one of those angels will come without bringing a set of gifts, and those gifts will always be different from the presents brought by any other angel. Every day, and all day long, the angels will come to salute him with the greeting of peace, and they will come bearing gifts. The proof of this is recorded in the Book of Allāh (Almighty and Glorious is He), for He tells us:

And the angels will enter unto them by every gate, [saluting them with]:	*wa 'l-malā'ikatu yadkhulūna ʿalai-him min kulli bāb:*

"Peace be upon you, because you persevered with patience." Fair indeed is the Ultimate Abode! (13:23,24)	*salāmun ʿalai-kum bi-mā ṣabartum fa-niʿma ʿuqba 'd-dār.*

He has also told us (Exalted is He):

And there they shall have their sustenance in the early morning and in the evening. (19:62)	*wa la-hum rizqu-hum fī-hā bukratan wa ʿashiyyā.*

According to Abū Huraira (may Allāh be well pleased with him), the Prophet (Allāh bless him and give him peace) also used to say:

> This man will be referred to as "that poor fellow" by the other inhabitants of the Garden of Paradise, on account of the superiority of their dwelling places over his, in spite of the fact that the "poor fellow" will have eighty thousand servants to wait on him at mealtimes! Whenever he feels an appetite for food, those servants will respond to his need by setting up one of the tables they keep ready for use on such occasions. The top slab of each of those tables is made from a red sapphire or ruby *[yāqūta ḥamrāʾ]*, set in a yellow sapphire or topaz *[yāqūta ṣafrāʾ]*, with a rim of pearls, sapphires and chrysolite or peridot *[zabarjad]*.[361] The legs of each table are made from pearls, and they have a circumference of twenty miles.
>
> As soon as this table has been set up, seventy different kinds of food will be laid out upon it, all for him to choose from. Eighty servants will be standing in front of him, ready to wait upon him. Each of those servants will be holding a plate of food and a glass containing something to drink. The food on each plate will be quite different from that on any other plate, and the drink in each glass will be quite different from that in any other glass. He will find the first to be just as tasty as the last, and he will find the last to be just as delicious as the first. He will compare them one with another, and he will not fail to sample each and every kind of food and drink.
>
> As far as the servants are concerned, every single one of them will be given his fair share of that food and drink, once it has been removed from the master's presence. Besides, there will not be a single one of them who does not have seventy-two wives from among the brides of Paradise with those lovely eyes of theirs *[al-ḥūr al-ʿīn]*,[362] as well as two human wives *[ādamiyyatān]*. Each of those wives will have a palatial mansion, built from a green sapphire set inside a red one. There will be seventy thousand door panels in each of those palatial mansions, and each door panel will have its own dome, carved out of a pearl.
>
> Among all those wives, there will not be a single one who is not wearing seventy thousand articles of clothing, with seventy thousand colors in each article of clothing, and none of those articles of clothing will resemble any other. Among all those wives, furthermore, there will not be a single one who does not have a thousand maidservants in front of her, standing ready to attend to her needs, as well as seventy thousand maidservants to wait upon her in her private sitting room. Among all those maidservants, there will not be a single one whom she

361 See note 81 on p. 61 above.

362 See note 333 on p. 241 above.

does not keep actively employed in attending to her needs. Whenever a meal has been prepared for her, seventy thousand maidservants will stand in front of her, each of them holding a plate of food and a glass containing something to drink, and none of these offerings will be like any other.

The man may find himself longing to see a brother of his, someone he used to love for the sake of Allāh (Almighty and Glorious is He) during his life in the world below. Prompted by concern for his brother's welfare, and fearing that he may have perished, the man will say: "I wish I knew what my brother So-and-So has been doing!" Allāh (Almighty and Glorious is He) will be fully aware of what is in his heart, so He will instruct his angels by way of inspiration: "Convey this servant of Mine to his brother!" One of the angels will thereupon bring him a thoroughbred riding camel, saddled and padded with blankets of light.

The Prophet (Allāh bless him and give him peace) continued:

The angel will salute him with the greeting of peace, so he will greet him with peace *[as-salām]* in return. Then the angel will tell him: "Get up and mount this camel! Away you go to find your brother!"

The man will then proceed to mount the camel, and so he will set out on a journey through the Garden of Paradise. The distance he has to travel would take a thousand years on this earth, but he will cover it in less time than one of you would take to mount a thoroughbred camel and ride it for just one league *[farsakh]*.[363]

Nothing will happen to him until he reaches the home of his brother. He will thereupon salute him with the greeting of peace, and his brother will greet him with peace *[as-salām]* in return, as he assures him that he is a very welcome guest. He will then say: "Where have you been, O my brother? I have been so concerned about about you!"

Each of them will thereupon embrace the other, then both of them will say: "Praise be to Allāh, the One who has brought us together again!" The pair of them will go on praising Allāh (Almighty and Glorious is He) in the most beautiful voices ever heard by any human being.

At this point, Allāh (Almighty and Glorious is He) will say to them: "O you two servants of Mine, this is not the time for serious work. This is rather the time for cheerful greetings and requests, so put your requests to Me, and I shall grant you both whatever you wish." In response to this offer, the pair of them will say: "O Lord, allow us to be together in this station [of Paradise]!"

Allāh (Almighty and Glorious is He) will therefore cause that station [of Paradise] to be the place where they can settle down and make themselves at home *[majlis]*, in a tent encased in pearls and sapphires. Their wives will also be given a similar dwelling place, and so they will all proceed to drink, eat, and enjoy themselves.

As soon as one of the men in the Garden of Paradise has taken a morsel of food and put it in his mouth, it may occur to him that he actually fancies a different

[363] The *farsakh* [parasang, or league] is three miles of the Hāshimī measure, i.e. thirty bow-shots reckoning the bow-shot as four hundred cubits, or sixty bow-shots reckoning the bow shot as two hundred cubits. (See E.W. Lane, *Arabic-English Lexicon*, art. *F–R–S–KH*.)

kind of food. If this should happen, the morsel concerned would immediately change into whatever he really wanted to eat!

According to the same traditional report, transmitted on the authority of Abū Huraira (may Allāh be well pleased with him), somebody once asked: "O Messenger of Allāh, what makes up the ground of the Garden of Paradise?" To this he replied (Allāh bless him and give him peace):

> Its ground is a kind of marble or alabaster slab *[rukhāma]* consisting of smooth silver, and its dust consists of musk. Its hills are of saffron, and its walls are made of pearls and sapphires, as well as of gold and silver. The outside of the walls can be seen from the area inside them, and their interior is likewise visible from their exterior. In the whole of the Garden of Paradise, there is not one palatial mansion of which the exterior is not visible from the interior, and the interior from the exterior.
>
> In the whole of the Garden of Paradise, furthermore, there will not be one man who is not dressed in a waist-wrapper *[izār]*, an upper-body shawl *[ridā']*, and other garments, not one of which has been cut, and not one of which has been sewn. Nor will there be one man among them who is not wearing a crown, hollowed out of a large pearl, and studded with with smaller pearls, sapphires, and chrysolite or peridot *[zabarjad]*.[364] He will have two plaited strands *[ḍafīratān]* of gold in his hair, and around his neck he will wear a collar of gold, encased in pearls and green sapphires. On the wrist of each and every man amongst them there will be three bracelets: a bracelet of gold, a bracelet of silver, and a bracelet of pearl. Beneath their crowns there will be diadems of pearls and sapphires. Over those garments of theirs they will be wearing fine silk brocade *[sundus]*, and over that fine silk brocade there will also be thick silk brocade interwoven with gold *[istabraq]*, as well as plain green silk.
>
> As for the cushions on which the people of the Garden of Paradise will be reclining in the greatest comfort, their inner surfaces consist of thick silk brocade interwoven with gold *[istabraq]*, and their outer surfaces of beautiful multicolored carpeting *['abqarī]*. The cushions are laid on raised couches, made of red sapphire, and these have pearls as their supports. Each and every one of those raised couches has a thousand decorative patterns, with seventy colors to each pattern, and no two patterns are alike. Seventy thousand rugs are spread out in front of each of those raised couches, with seventy colors to each rug, and not one of those rugs bears any resemblance to the one beside it. To the right of each of those raised couches there are seventy thousand pedestals, with an equal number to the left, and not one of those pedestals is similar to any other.

According to Abū Huraira (may Allāh be well pleased with him), the Prophet (Allāh bless him and give him peace) also used to say:

> The people of the Garden of Paradise in their entirety, the loftiest of them and the lowliest of them in spiritual rank, will be of the same physical height as Adam, and the physical height of Adam (peace be upon him) is sixty cubits

[364] See note 81 on p. 61 above.

[dhirāʿ].[365] They will all be youthful, devoid of bodily and facial hair, anointed with kohl[366] and lined with charcoal around the eyes—they and their womenfolk to exactly to same extent.

When they have received all the special treatment thus far described, a herald will utter a proclamation within the Garden of Paradise. Raising his voice so that it can be heard by those at the loftiest and the lowliest levels, by those who are nearest to him, and by those who are farthest away, the herald will cry: "O people of the Garden of Paradise, are you pleased with your dwelling places?" To this they will all reply in chorus: "Yes, by Allāh! Our Lord has now caused us to dwell in the dwelling place of dignity and honor. We have no desire for any change of location, nor do we wish for any substitute instead of it. We are well pleased with our Lord as a neighbor! O Allāh, our Lord, we have listened to Your herald, and we have given him an honest reply. O Allāh, our Lord, we yearned to look upon Your countenance, and You showed it to us for that, as You surely knew, would be the most excellent part of our reward."

The Prophet (Allāh bless him and give him peace) continued:

At this point, Allāh (Almighty and Glorious is He) will give an order to the particular Garden of Paradise in which He has His dwelling *[manzil]* and His seat *[majlis]*. He will tell that Garden, the name of which is the Abode of Peace *[Dār as-Salām]*: "Gather up all your finery and make yourself really beautiful! Make yourself ready for the visit of My servants!" She will listen intently to her Lord, and will obey Him even before the word of command has been completely expressed. She will immediately gather up all her finery, and make herself ready to receive the visitors of Allāh (Exalted is He), whereupon Allāh (Exalted is He) will give the order to one of the angels: "Invite My servants to come and visit Me!"

That angel will promptly set forth from the presence of the All-Merciful One *[ar-Raḥmān]*, in order to proclaim this invitation at the top of his voice. In a deliciously sweet and drawn out voice, peculiar to himself alone, the angel will say: "O people of the Garden of Paradise! O saintly friends *[awliyāʾ]* of Allāh! Come visit your Lord!"

The sound of the angel's voice will thus be heard by the loftiest and the lowliest of the inhabitants of the Garden of Paradise, so all of them will mount up on riding beasts, whether they be she-camels or plain old nags. Keeping to the shady side, they will ride toward hills of white musk and yellow saffron. Then, when they reach the entrance [to the Abode of Peace], they will utter a special form of salutation. In expressing this salutation *[taslīm]* of theirs, they will say: "Peace be upon us from our Lord *[as-salāmu ʿalai-nā min Rabbi-nā]*!" Then they will seek permission to enter, and permission will be granted to them, so they will move straight ahead and go in through the gate.

At this point, a wind will blow forth from beneath the Heavenly Throne, the name of it being The Whirlwind *[al-Muthīra]*. It will pulverize the hills of musk and saffron, filling the people's collars and sleeves with dust, and heaping dust

365 See note 348 on p. 257 above.

366 Kohl (from the Arabic word *kuḥl*) is a powder, usually a preparation of pulverized antimony, used for darkening the edges of the eyelids.

on their heads and over their clothes. Thus they will enter [the Abode of Peace]. As they look toward the Throne *['Arsh]* of their Lord and His Footstool *[Kursī]*, they will see a bright light beaming at them, but without His making Himself clearly manifest to them, so they will say: "Glory be to You, our Lord Most Holy *[Subḥāna-ka Rabba-nā Quddūs]*, Lord of the Angels and of the Spirit *[Rabb al-Malā'ikati wa 'r-Rūḥ]*. Blessed and Exalted are You *[tabārakta wa ta'ālait]*! Allow us to see, so that we may look upon Your countenance!"

In response to this plea, Allāh (Almighty and Glorious is He) will give the order to the veils, which are made of light: "Remove yourselves!" Without interruption, one veil after another will thereupon withdraw itself, until seventy veils have withdrawn themselves—each veil being seventy times more intensely radiant than its predecessor—at which point the Lord of Might and Glory (Almighty and Majestic is He) will manifest Himself to them in perfect clarity. They will at once fall down in abject prostration before Him, to remain in that posture for as long as Allāh wills. While they are still prostrating themselves, they will say: "Glory be to You! To You be the praise and the glorification *[tasbīḥ]* for ever and ever! You have delivered us from the Fire of Hell, and You have caused us to enter the Garden of Paradise. Good indeed is the abode! We are utterly and completely content with You, so be well pleased with us!"

Allāh (Blessed and Exalted is He) will respond to this by saying: "I am indeed well pleased with you, to the fullest extent. But this is not the appropriate time for serious work. This is rather the time for refreshment and blissful happiness, so ask of Me and I shall grant your requests, and make your wishes known to Me, for then I shall give you even more."

Thus they will make their dearest wishes known, although they will do so without having to say a word. They will all have the same wish in common, namely that He should allow them to keep what He has given them on a permanent basis. He will therefore say to them (Exalted is He): "I shall indeed allow you to keep what I have given you on a permanent basis, and the same applies to all the extra blessings I have bestowed upon you!"

On hearing this promise from their Lord, they will raise their heads at once, as they utter the affirmation of the Supreme Greatness of Allāh *[at-takbīr]*.[367] They will be not be capable, however, of raising their eyes directly toward their Lord (Almighty and Glorious is He), due to the extreme intensity of the Light of the Lord of Might and Glory *[Nūr Rabb al-'Izza]*. (By the way, that reception room *[majlis]* is called the East Wing of the Dome of the Throne of the Lord of All the Worlds *[Sharqī Qubbat 'Arsh Rabb al-'Ālamīn]*.) The Lord of Might and Glory will say to them: "Welcome, O My servants, My neighbors, My chosen ones, My dear ones, My saintly friends *[awliyā'ī]*, the best I have among all My creatures, and My obedient people!"

Pulpits of light will suddenly appear in front of the Throne of the Lord of Might and Glory; beneath those pulpits, chairs of light; beneath those chairs, cushions; beneath those cushions, padded quilts; and beneath those padded quilts, carpets.

[367] That is to say, they will exclaim: "*Allāhu Akbar* [Allāh is Supremely Great!]"

The Lord of Might and Glory will then say to them: "Come, seat yourselves according to your honor and nobility." So the Messengers *[Rusul]* will come forward and seat themselves upon those pulpits, while the Prophets *[Anbiyā']* come forward and seat themselves upon those chairs, and the righteous *[ṣāliḥūn]* come forward and seat themselves upon those carpets. Tables of light will then be set up for their benefit, each table being adorned with seventy different colors, and crowned with an array of pearls and sapphires.

The Prophet (Allāh bless him and give him peace) went on to say:

The Lord of Might and Glory will then say to His helpers *[ḥafada]*: "Give them cooked food to eat!" Seventy thousand dishes, made from pearls and sapphires, will at once be set out for them on each and every table, with each and every dish containing seventy different kinds of cooked food.

The Lord of Might and Glory will then say to them: "Eat up, O My servants!" So they will eat as much of all that as Allāh wills. They will say to one another: "The food we are enjoying today is so special! The meals we used to eat, at home with our families, seem like nothing but a dream by comparison!"

The Lord of Might and Glory will then say to His helpers *[ḥafada]*: "Now give My servants something to quench their thirst!" Obedient to His command, the helpers will at once provide the servants of their Lord with a thirst-quenching beverage, and they will drink from it, saying to one another as they do so: "By comparison with the drink we can now enjoy, what we used to drink seems like nothing but a dream!"

The Lord of Might and Glory will then say to His helpers *[ḥafada]*: "You have supplied them with cooked food, and you have given them plenty to drink, so now you must provide them with fruit for their dessert!" Obedient to His command, the helpers will at once provide the servants of their Lord with fruit for their dessert. While eating it, they will say to one another: "By comparison with what we are now enjoying for dessert, the fruit we used to eat seems like nothing but a dream!"

The Lord of Might and Glory will then say to His helpers *[ḥafada]*: "You have supplied them with cooked food, you have given them plenty to drink, and you have provided them with fruit for their dessert, so now you must equip them with fine clothes and adornments." Obedient to His command, the helpers will at once produce fine clothes and adornments for the servants of their Lord to wear. As they are dressing themselves up in them, they will say to one another: "By comparison with all this finery, our previous clothing and adornments seem like nothing but a dream!"

Then, while they are still sitting in their seats, Allāh (Almighty and Glorious is He) will send forth, from beneath His Throne, a wind that is called The Whirlwind *[al-Muthīra]*. As it blows toward them with a cloud of musk and camphor—whiter than snow—from beneath the Throne, this wind will deposit a gentle dust upon their robes and their heads, as well as inside their collars and sleeves, fragrantly perfuming them in the process. The tables will then be removed from their presence, along with whatever is left of the food spread out upon them.

At this point, the Lord of Might and Glory will say to them: "Ask of Me now, for I shall grant your requests, and make your wishes known to Me, for I shall give you even more!" They will all respond to this together, saying in chorus: "O Allāh, our Lord, what we ask of You is that You should be well pleased with us!" So He will say (Almighty and Glorious is He): "I have indeed already come to be well pleased with you, O My servants!"

The Prophet (Allāh bless him and give him peace) continued further:

On hearing these words of acceptance from their Lord, they will at once bow down in abject prostration before Him, proclaiming His Glory and His Supreme Greatness *[bi-'t-tasbīḥ wa 't-takbīr]*[368] as they do so. The Lord of Might and Glory will then say to them: "O My servants, lift up your heads! This is not the appropriate time for serious work. This is rather the time for refreshment and blissful happiness."

They will therefore lift up their heads, with their faces glowing from the Light of their Lord. The Lord of Might and Glory (Almighty and Majestic is He) will then say to them: "Now depart to your dwellings!" They will thereupon go forth from the presence of their Lord. Then their youthful attendants will come to meet them, bringing their riding beasts.

Thus each and every one amongst them will mount his she-camel or his plain old nag, and seventy thousand youthful attendants will mount up beside him, on the same kind of animal as the one he is riding. If any of them wishes to make his way home separately, he will set off accordingly, then the rest of them will travel together, until one of their number approaches the palatial mansion that represents his destination.

As soon as one of them reaches his own palatial mansion, and enters the presence of his wife, she will arise to greet him and bid him welcome. She will say to him: "You have come back home to me, O my darling! You have come back home to me—and with so much more than you had, when I saw you leave on your trip! You have grown more handsome than ever. You have acquired an even greater radiance and beauty. You are wearing splendid new clothes, a fresh perfume, and so much finery!"

At this point, an angel will issue a proclamation from the presence of the All-Merciful One *[ar-Raḥmān]* (Almighty and Glorious is He), crying out in a very loud voice: "O people of the Garden of Paradise, that is how it will always be for you, as your state of bliss is constantly renewed for your benefit!"

[In the words of Allāh (Almighty and Glorious is He)]:

And the angels will enter unto them	*wa'l-malā'ikatu yadkhulūna*
by every gate, [saluting them with]:	*'alai-him min kulli bāb:*
"Peace be upon you, because	*salāmun 'alai-kum*
you persevered with patience."	*bi-mā ṣabartum*
Fair indeed is the Ultimate Abode!	*fa-ni'ma 'uqba 'd-dār.*
(13:23,24)	

Your Lord will surely pronounce the greeting of peace upon you, and you will be provided with many kinds of food and drink, as well as clothing and finery.

[368] That is to say, they will exclaim: "*Subḥāna 'llāh* [Glory be to Allāh!]" and: "*Allāhu Akbar* [Allāh is Supremely Great!]"

According to Abū Huraira (may Allāh be well pleased with him), the Prophet (Allāh bless him and give him peace) also used to say:

> In the Garden of Paradise there are one hundred ascending stages *[mi'a daraja]*. Between each two stages there is a commanding officer *[amīr]*, who is viewed by the inhabitants as worthy of respect, and as fit to exercise authority.
>
> The Garden of Paradise contains mountains of white musk and yellow saffron, the effects of which are highly beneficial to the inhabitants. When they eat their food, the gas they expel from their stomachs is even more fragrant than musk. When they drink their pure wine, their skins simply perspire. They do not evacuate their bowels, nor do they urinate. They do not spit, nor do they blow their noses. They do not fall sick, nor do they suffer from headaches.

According to Abū Huraira (may Allāh be well pleased with him), the Prophet (Allāh bless him and give him peace) also used to say:

> The people of the Garden of Paradise, the loftiest and the lowliest of them alike, spend their time as follows: They start the day by reclining in comfort for two hours, then they indulge for two hours in friendly competition *[wa yatafāḍalūna]*.[369] After praising their Creator *[Khāliq]* for the next four hours, they spend two hours visiting with one another.
>
> There are times of night and day in the Garden of Paradise, and there is darkness. Its nighttime is far brighter, however, than any daytime. The day has seventy parts.
>
> As for the least well endowed of all the people of the Garden of Paradise, he is still someone who—if all of mankind and the jinn came to visit him at once—would have enough chairs, cushions, quilts and rugs for his guests to sit and recline upon, as well as enough tables, dishes, servants, food and drink to entertain them satisfactorily, if not to the same extent as the next man above him.
>
> As for the trees in the Garden of Paradise, their trunks are mostly of gold, although some are of silver, some of sapphire, and some of chrysolite or peridot *[zabarjad]*.[370] Their palm boughs *[sa'af]* are constituted from the same range of materials. Their leaves are like the most beautiful articles of clothing anyone has ever seen, while their fruits are more creamy than butter and sweeter than honey. The height of each of those trees is equal to the distance of a journey taking five hundred years, while its thickness at the base of the trunk is equal to the distance of a seventy-year journey.
>
> Whenever any man amongst the inhabitants of the Garden of Paradise happens to raise his eyes, he will find himself looking at the far end of a branch of one of the trees, and at the fruits with which it is laden. He will notice that every tree bears seventy thousand types of fruit, yet no kind has quite the same taste

[369] At this point in the Damascus edition of the Arabic text of *al-Ghunya*, the editor inserts the following footnote:

> "As for the use of the expression *wa yatafāḍalūna* in this context, the meaning of it needs to be investigated. It would also be advisable to check the wording of the *ḥadīth* for correctness."

[370] See note 81 on p. 61 above.

and flavor as any other. If he feels a desire to sample one of those many varieties, the branch that carries the particular fruit he fancies will bend down toward him—from the distance of a journey taking five hundred years, or fifty years, or less than that—so that he may pick the fruit with his hand, if he wishes to do so. If it is not convenient for him to pick it with his hand, he has only to open his mouth, for the fruit will simply drop into his open mouth. As soon as any item is harvested from those fruit trees, Allāh will immediately create something even finer and tastier to take its place. Then, once the man has picked all the fruit he needs to satisfy his appetite, the bough will return to its previous position.

There is one tree that does not bear fruit. It is laden instead with spathes or envelopes *[akmām]* containing unembroidered silk, articles of clothing, silk brocade *[sundus]*, ornaments, and fine carpets *[ʿabqarī]*. There is also one tree amongst them that bears spathes containing musk and camphor.

According to Abū Huraira (may Allāh be well pleased with him), the Prophet (Allāh bless him and give him peace) also used to say:

The people of the Garden of Paradise will behold their Lord every Friday [the Day of Congregational Prayer].

If a diadem *[iklīl]* from the Garden of Paradise were ever to be sent down from heaven above, the light of the sun would disappear.

There are certain palatial mansions in the Garden of Paradise, each of which has four streams inside it: water from a spring, milk from a spring, wine from a spring, and honey from a spring. If someone drinks any part of this, the taste it leaves behind will prove to be the flavor of musk *[ṣāra khitāmu-hu miskan]*.[371]

They will not drink anything from it until it has been blended in a mixture from the fountains of the Garden of Paradise, one of which is known as *az-Zanjabīl* [Ginger],[372] another as *Tasnīm*,[373] and the other as *Kāfūr* [Camphor].[374] Those who are brought near [to the Lord] will drink a pure wine concocted from all of these.

[371] An allusion to the verse *[āya]* of the Qurʾān in which Allāh (Almighty and Glorious is He) has told us, with reference to a pure wine given to the righteous to drink in the Garden of Paradise:

Its end result shall be the taste of musk. (83:26) *khitāmu-hu misk.*

[372] This statement attributed to the Prophet (Allāh bless him and give him peace) lends support to the view of those authorities who take *Zanjabīl* to be another name for *Salsabīl*, the fountain from which the wine of Paradise is drawn. As we read in the Qurʾān:

And therein they shall be given to drink	*wa yusqawna fī-hā*
a cup whose mixture is *zanjabīl*,	*kaʾsan kāna mizāju-hā zanjabīlā:*
a spring therein, named *Salsabīl*. (76:17,18)	*ʿainan fī-hā tusammā Salsabīlā.*

Some commentators understand this to mean that the wine of the fountain will have the aromatic flavor of ginger. According to the classical Arabic lexicographers, *zanjabīl* [ginger; the root of the ginger plant] "has a property that is warming, digestive, lenitive in a small degree, strengthening to the venereal faculty, clearing to the phlegm, sharpening to the intellect, and exhilarating." (See: E.W. Lane, *Arabic-English Lexicon*, art. Z–N–J–B–L.)

Were it not for the fact that Allāh has passed judgment amongst them, to the effect that they must hand the goblet around from one to another, they would never let it leave their mouths.

In the course to paying visits to one another, the people of the Garden of Paradise will cover the distance of a journey taking a hundred thousand years, and even more than that. Nevertheless, when they return from visiting their brethren, they will find their way home more directly than one of you could get back to his house.

When the people of the Garden of Paradise have seen their Lord (Almighty and Glorious is He), and are ready to set out for home, every man amongst them will be given a green pomegranate *[rummāna]* containing seventy seeds. Each seed will have seventy colors, and no seed will be of quite the same sort as any other. Then, as they make their departure from the presence of their Lord (Almighty and Glorious is He), they will pass through the markets of the Garden of Paradise. There will be no business of buying and selling in progress in those markets, but they will be well stocked with ornamental goods, articles of clothing, silk brocade *[sundus]*, thick silk brocade interwoven with gold *[istabraq]*, unembroidered silk, decorative items of gold and jewelry *[zukhruf]*, fine carpets *[ʿabqarī]* woven from pearls and sapphires, and diadems suspended on display. They will therefore take from those markets as many of these varied goods as they can carry with them, and yet the markets will not have their stocks diminished by as much as a single item.

The markets of the Garden of Paradise will also contain dummy figures, similar in form to the most handsome human beings in existence. The forehead of each of these dummy figures will be marked with the inscription: "If anyone wishes to have the same good looks as mine, Allāh will cause that person to become just as handsome as my shape and form." If anyone responds to this by wishing that his own face could be just as good looking as that of the dummy figure, Allāh will promptly fulfill that person's wish.

373 This fountain is mentioned in the Qurʾān, in connection with the pure wine referred to in note 371 above:

And its mixture is from *Tasnīm*, a fountain at which those brought near [to the Lord] do drink. (83:27,28)	*wa mizāju-hu min Tasnīm:* *ʿainan yashrabu* *bi-ha 'l-muqarrabūn.*

As an ordinary verbal noun, the Arabic word *tasnīm* means "raising something into the shape of a camel's hump *[sanām]*." According to the classical lexicographers, the fountain is called *Tasnīm* because it flows above the elevated chambers and pavilions of Paradise. (See: E.W. Lane, *Arabic-English Lexicon*, art. *S–N–M*.)

374 The fountain called *Kāfūr* [Camphor] is also mentioned in the Qurʾān, where Allāh (Almighty and Glorious is He) has told us:

Surely the pious shall drink of a cup whose mixture is camphor, a fountain at which the servants of Allāh do drink. (76:5,6)	*inna 'l-abrāra yashrabūna* *min kaʾsin kāna mizāju-hā* *kāfūrā: ʿainan* *yashrabu bi-hā ʿibādu 'llāhi.*

As in the case of *Zanjabīl* [Ginger], referred to in note 372 above, the statement here attributed to the Prophet (Allāh bless him and give him peace) lends support to the view of those authorities who take *Kāfūr* [Camphor] to be the actual name of the fountain. According to some, however, notably including the distinguished commentator al-Baiḍāwī, the meaning of the Qurʾānic verse *[āya]* is that the wine of Paradise will be mixed with camphor *[kāfūr]* because of its agreeable coolness and aroma.

Then they will depart for their own dwelling places, and their servants will promptly line up in rows to meet them, standing to attention in order to bid them welcome and greet them with the salutation of peace. Each of them will engage in cheerful conversation with the companion who is traveling with him, until the good news of his arrival reaches his wife. She will then be so transported by joy that she will set out toward him. She will meet him at his door with a welcoming greeting and the salutation of peace. She will give him a hug and he will embrace her, and so they will go inside together, locked in a mutual embrace.

If any woman from among the womenfolk of the Garden of Paradise ever happened to come into view, no angel brought near [to the Lord] nor any Prophet sent as a Messenger *[Nabī Mursal]* who caught sight of her would fail to be enchanted by her beauty.

The last draught to be drunk by the people of the Garden of Paradise in the wake of their meal is a beverage called "pure and plentiful" *[ṭahūr dihāq]*. As soon as a draught of it has been drunk, their food and drink will be fully digested. It will cause the contents of their bellies to acquire a fragrance like that of musk. Their belching and burping will also have the scent of musk, and there will be no pain or discomfort in their bellies. When they drink, they will stimulate a healthy appetite for the meal, so this will always be their regular practice.

The riding animals of the people of the Garden of Paradise are created from white sapphire.

The Prophet (Allāh bless him and give him peace) also used to say:

There are three Gardens of Paradise: [The one known simply as] the Garden *[al-Janna]*; [The Garden of] Eden *[ʿAdn]*; and The Abode of Peace *[Dār as-Salām]*. [The one known simply as] the Garden *[al-Janna]* is smaller than the Garden of Eden *[Jannat ʿAdn]* by a factor of seven hundred million.

As for the palatial mansions of the Garden, their exterior is of gold, while their interior consists of chrysolite or peridot *[zabarjad]*.[375] Their turrets are made from red rubies, and their balconies are constructed by an arrangement of strung pearls.

The man among the people of the Garden of Paradise will enjoy reclining next to his wife for a single session lasting seven hundred years, during the whole of which time he will never once move away from her side. Then his other wife will call out to him from a palatial mansion that is even more beautiful, saying: "O my brother [in faith], the time has now come for you to let us have our turn with you!" So the man will say: "Who are you?" and she will reply: "I am part of that [consolation] to which Allāh (Almighty and Glorious is He) is referring when He says:

So no soul knows what comfort is kept secretly in store for them, as a reward for what they used to do. (32:17)	*fa-lā taʿlamu nafsun mā ukhfiya la-hum min qurrati aʿyun: jazāʾan bi-mā kānū yaʿmalūn.*

[375] See note 81 on p. 61 above.

He will therefore move over to join her, and he will continue to reside with her for a period of seven hundred years, eating and drinking in her company and having sexual intercourse with her throughout that time.

In the Garden of Paradise there is a tree, in the shade of which a rider can travel for seven hundred years without ever passing beyond it. Streams flow beneath that tree, and whole cities are built upon each of its many branches. The length of each of those cities is ten thousand miles, and the distance between each city and the next is like the distance between the East and the West. The springs of the Fountain of Paradise *[Salsabīl]* flow from those palatial mansions toward those cities. A single leaf from that tree is enough to provide shade for an enormously large community.

When a man from among the people of the Garden of Paradise enters the presence of his wife, she will say: "By the One who has so generously honored me with you, I swear that nothing in the Garden of Paradise is more dear to me than you are!" Of course, the man will also tell his wife that he feels the same way about her.

The Prophet (Allāh bless him and give him peace) also used to say:

In the Garden of Paradise there are things that defy all efforts to describe them, of which no conception can be formed by the hearts of the learned, of which nothing can be heard by the ears of the attentive, and in it there are things that have never been seen by the eyes of created beings.

Allāh (Almighty and Glorious is He) will cause those who love one another for His sake to alight in the Garden of Eden *[Jannat ʿAdn]*, where He will settle them upon a pillar made from a single red ruby, the thickness of which is equal to the distance of a journey taking seventy thousand years. From this vantage point, overlooking seventy thousand residential areas, each area having a palatial mansion, they will survey the inhabitants of the Garden. Marked in light upon their foreheads, they will bear an inscription that reads: "These are they who love one another for the sake of Allāh *[hāʾulāʾi 'l-mutaḥābbūna fi 'llāh]*."

If one of them happens to gaze from his palace toward the inhabitants of the Garden, the radiance of his face will fill the mansions of the inhabitants of the Garden with light, just as the sun illuminates the houses of the people of the earth. The inhabitants of the Garden will then look upon his face, and they will say to one another as they do so: "This must be one of those who love one another for the sake of Allāh (Almighty and Glorious is He). See how his face is like the moon on the night when it is full!"

The handsomeness of the true specimen of manhood *[rajul]*, in contrast to the handsomeness of the manservant *[khādim]* among the people of the Garden of Paradise, is like [the brilliance of] the moon on the night when it is full, in contrast to [the fainter brilliance of] the stars.

As for the womenfolk of the Garden of Paradise, they mark the end of their meal by singing in delightfully sweet and drawn-out voices: "We are the women who are everlasting, so we shall never die. We are the women who are safe and sound, so we shall never be afraid. We are the women who are satisfied, so we shall never be discontented. We are the women who are forever young, so we shall never grow senile and decrepit. We are the women who are always clothed, so we shall never go naked. We are the women who are good, the women who are beautiful, the wives of a truly noble people."

As for the birds of the Garden of Paradise, each of them has seventy thousand feathers. Each of those feathers has a different color, quite unlike that of any other. The size of each bird amongst them is a mile in width by a mile in length. Whenever the true believer *[mu'min]* desires them to provide him with something to satisfy his appetite, he has only to fetch a bird and place it inside the bowl from which he intends to eat. The bird will then flap its wings and, as it rises, seventy kinds of food will fall from it into the bowl—such as cooked fare and all sorts of other tasty morsels. The flavor of this food is more delicious than honeydew, its tenderness is softer than butter, and its whiteness is whiter than buttermilk. As soon as he has eaten some of it, the bird will flap its wings again and fly away, without shedding a single feather in the process.

So that they can always enjoy this kind of service, their birds and their riding animals are carefully tended in the pastures of the Garden of Paradise surrounding their palatial mansions.

Allāh (Exalted is He) will give the people of the Garden of Paradise signet rings of gold for them to wear, these being the signet rings of eternal life. Then He will give them signet rings made of sapphire and pearls. That will be when they visit Him in the Abode of Peace *[Dār as-Salām]*.

When the people of the Garden of Paradise go to visit their Lord, they will eat and drink and thoroughly enjoy themselves.

Allāh's Messenger (Allāh bless him and give him peace) also said:

The Lord of Might and Glory *[Rabb al-'Izza]* (Almighty and Majestic is He) will say: "O David, extol Me with your beautiful voice!" David will then extol Him for as long as Allāh (Exalted is He) wishes this celebration of His praise to continue, so that nothing in the Garden of Paradise will miss the opportunity to hear the beauty of his voice and its delightful sweetness. Then the Lord of Might and Glory (Almighty and Majestic is He) will present them with fine clothing and adornments. Then they will depart to rejoin their wives.

Every man among the people of the Garden of Paradise has access to the benefits provided by a tree called the Tree of Bliss *[Ṭūbā]*.[376] Whenever one of them wishes to dress himself up in clothes of extremely high quality, he has only to make his way to the Tree of Bliss *[Ṭūbā]*, the spathes or envelopes *[akmām]* of which will at once be opened up for him. These wardrobes are of six different kinds, each one of them containing seventy types of clothing. No article of clothing has the same color as any other, nor is any garment tailored from the same fabric as another. He may therefore take his pick, selecting whichever of these items he wishes to wear.

The following message is inscribed on the wives of the people of the Garden of Paradise—on the area between the throat and the breast of every woman amongst them: "You are my dearly beloved, and I am your dearly beloved *[anta*

[376] See note 329 on p. 237 above.

ḥabībī wa ana ḥabībatu-ka]. There is no one who could ever be a match for you, and no one who could ever take your place. For you there is no malice or deceit within my heart." The man will therefore stare at the area between his wife's throat and breast, and he will see right through to the innermost core of her being *[sawād kabidi-hā]*, beyond her flesh and bones, for his innermost core is a mirror to her, and her innermost core is a mirror to him. This penetration will not do her any damage, however, except in the sense that the sapphire is 'damaged' by having a string threaded through it!

The whiteness of these ladies is like the whiteness of coral pearls, and their pure clarity is like the pure clarity of sapphires. As Allāh (Almighty and Glorious is He) has told us:

> It is as if they were sapphires and coral pearls. (55:58)
>
> *ka-anna-hunna 'l-yāqūtu wa 'l-marjān.*

When the people of the Garden of Paradise go riding, their mounts will be fine she-camels and plain workhorses. The hoof of one of these she-camels will make contact with the ground at the farthest point within its range of vision. In the case of that plain workhorse, the touchdown point for its hoof will also be at the farthest spot within its range of sight. These animals have been created from pearls and sapphires. The magnitude of every riding beast amongst them is seventy miles [from nose to tail]. The reins and bridles of the fine she-camels, and also those of the plain workhorses, are cords of pearls and chrysolite or peridot *[zabarjad]*.[377]

377 See note 81 on p. 61 above.

Concerning the words of Allāh (Almighty and Glorious is He), in which He has given us the following description of the people of the Garden of Paradise:

Allāh has therefore warded off
from them the evil of that day,
and He has made them find
cheerfulness and joy.

fa-waqā-humu ʾllāhu
sharra dhālika ʾl-yawmi
wa laqqā-hum naḍratan
wa surūrā.

And He has granted them,
as a reward for all that they endured,
a Garden [of Paradise] and silk attire.

wa jazā-hum
bi-mā ṣabarū
jannatan wa ḥarīrā.

Reclining therein upon couches,
they will experience there neither
[the fierce heat of] a sun
nor bitter cold.

muttakiʾīna fī-hā ʿala ʾl-ʿarāʾik:
lā yarawna fī-hā
shamsan
wa lā zamharīrā.

And close upon them
is the shade thereof,
while its clustered fruits
bow down low.

wa dāniyatan ʿalai-him
ẓilālu-hā:
wa dhullilat
quṭūfu-hā tadhlīlā.

And goblets of silver
are brought around
for them, and vessels
as clear as crystal,

wa yuṭāfu ʿalai-him
bi-āniyatin min
fiḍḍatin wa akwābin
kānat qawārīrā.

Crystal-clear vessels made of silver,
which they have measured exactly
to the measure [of their own deeds].

qawārīran min fiḍḍatin
qaddarū-hā
taqdīrā.

And in it their thirst is quenched
with a cup the mixture of which is
zanjabīl [ginger],

wa yusqawna fī-hā
kaʾsan kāna mizāju-hā
zanjabīlā—

A fountain therein, named *Salsabīl.*

ʿainan fī-hā tusammā Salsabīlā.

And waiting on them are
immortal youths
whom, if you could see them,
you would take for scattered pearls.

wa yaṭūfu ʿalai-him
wildānun mukhalldaūn:
idhā raʾaita-hum
ḥasibta-hum luʾluʾan manthūrā.

And when you see, there you will see a state of bliss and a high estate.	*wa idhā ra'aita thamma* *ra'aita na'īman wa mulkan kabīrā.*
Their raiment will be fine green silk and gold brocade. They will be adorned with bracelets of silver, their Lord will slake their thirst with a pure drink.	*'āliya-hum thiyābu* *sundusin khuḍrun* *wa istabraq: wa ḥullū asāwira* *min fiḍḍa: wa saqā-hum* *Rabbu-andhum* *sharāban ṭahūrā.*
[And it will be said unto them]: "Behold, this is a reward for you. Your endeavor [upon earth] has found acceptance." (76:11–22)	 *inna hādhā kāna la-kum jazā'an* *wa kāna sa'yu-kum* *mashkūrā.*

As for His words (Almighty and Glorious is He):

Allāh has therefore warded off from them the evil of that day... (76:11)	*fa-waqā-humu 'llāhu* *sharra dhālika 'l-yawmi...*

—what He means is that, on the Day of Resurrection *[Yawm al-Qiyāma]*, He will spare them from having to experience the awful intensity of the Reckoning *[Ḥisāb]* and the dread terror of Hell *[Jahannam]*.

[As we know from traditional accounts, attributed to the Prophet (Allāh bless him and give him peace) and transmitted on the authority of Abū Huraira (may Allāh be well pleased with him):][378]

When Hell is brought forth upon the parade grounds of the Resurrection *['araṣāt al-Qiyāma]*, it will be led there by nineteen keepers from among the angels. Each and every one of those keepers will be accompanied by seventy thousand other angels, serving as his assistants, all of them rough, stern, their teeth grimly gritted, their eyes like live coals, and their colors like the flames of fire. While their nostrils give vent to lofty columns of flame and smoke, they stand at the ready, prepared at all times to receive and carry out the command of the All-Compelling One *[al-Jabbār]* (Blessed and Exalted is He).

Each keeper and his assistants will thus drag Hell along by means of a shackle and an enormous chain, sometimes walking to the right of it, sometimes to the left of it, and sometimes following up behind it. Each and every angel amongst them will hold in his hand a grappling hook made of iron. They will shout and bellow as they goad Hell along, but its slow progress will be made to the accompaniment of moaning and sighing, staggering and stumbling, clouds of gloom and smoke, rattling

[378] See pp. 248–68 above.

and clanking noises, and a towering inferno stoked by the fury of its rage against its own inhabitants. Thus they will eventually install it in a position midway between the Garden of Paradise and the place where the resurrected creatures are kept standing *[al-mawqif]*.

At this point, Hell will lift its gaze. As soon as it spies the creatures assembled there, it will bolt toward them in order to devour them. Its keepers will have to pull on its chains to hold it in check, for if it were left to its own devices, it would pounce upon every believer *[muʾmin]* and unbeliever *[kāfir]* without distinction. Once it sees that it has been effectively restrained from attacking the assembled throng of creatures, it will simmer and boil with an intensity that can hardly be distinguished from the most furious kind of rage. Then it will heave another sigh, and the resurrected creatures will hear the sound of the gnashing of its teeth. This will cause their hearts to shudder and tremble with alarm. They will fly into a state of panic, their eyes will glaze over, and their hearts will end up in their throats.

Then Hell will heave a deep sigh, which will so affect those who hear it that not a single one of them will fail to sink down on his knees—not one angel brought near to the Lord *[malʾak muqarrab]*, not one Prophet sent as a Messenger *[Nabī Mursal]*, and not one of those resurrected creatures who are present at the place of standing *[al-mawqif]*.

Then Hell will heave a second deep sigh, and not a single eye that still has a drop of moisture in it will fail to shed a tear.

Then Hell will heave a third deep sigh, and even if those who hear that sigh—be they human beings or jinn—were each endowed with the merit of seventy-two Prophets, they would surely suppose that they must be embracing her as a man embraces a woman *[la-ẓannū anna-hum muwāqiʿū-hā]*,[379] and that they could not possibly escape from her embrace.[380]

Then Hell will heave a fourth deep sigh, and nothing that is capable of speech will fail to have its speech arrested. The only exceptions will

[379] In a previous subsection of this Discourse, where this account of Hell's appearance at the Resurrection is attributed to the Prophet (Allāh bless him and give him peace), the wording is slightly different at this point. In the passage translated on page 250 above, the Arabic text reads *la-wāqaʿū-hā* [they would surely be moved to embrace her as a man embraces a woman], instead of *la-ẓannū anna-hum muwāqiʿū-hā* [they would surely suppose that they must be embracing her as a man embraces a woman]. The additional phrase at the end of the paragraph—about the impossibility of escape—occurs only in this second version of the report.

[380] See note 344 on p. 250 above.

be Gabriel, Michael, and [Abraham] the Bosom Friend *[Khalīl]* of the All-Merciful One *[ar-Raḥmān]* (Almighty and Glorious is He), each one of whom will say, as they cling to the Heavenly Throne *[ʿArsh]*: "My own soul, my own soul *[nafsī, nafsī]*—that is all I beg You to spare!"

Then Hell will send forth a shower of sparks, as numerous as the stars. Each spark will be like an enormous cloud arising in the West, and that shower of sparks will fall upon the heads of the assembled creatures.

This, then, is the shower of sparks *[sharar]* which Allāh will ward off from the true believers *[muʾminīn]* who faithfully discharge their solemn vow, and who are in dread of His chastisement, fearing that it might be inflicted upon them. For Allāh (Exalted is He) will surely protect all those who are committed to the affirmation of His Oneness and to faith *[ahl at-tawḥīd wa 'l-īmān]*—as He will protect all those who remain faithful to the example set by His Messenger *[ahl as-Sunna]*—from the evil *[sharr]* of that day.[381] He will cause them to experience His mercy. He will make their final reckoning easy for them to undergo. He will cause them to enter His Garden of Paradise, and He will grant them everlasting life therein, for all eternity, through His loving grace.

As for the unbelievers *[kāfirīn]*, on the other hand, and those who are guilty of attributing partners to Him and of worshipping idols *[ahl ash-shirk wa 'l-awthān]*, He will cause them to suffer evil upon evil, fear upon fear, and torment upon torment. For He will cause them to enter Hell *[Jahannam]*, and He will make them live therein forever, for all eternity.

Then He has told us (Almighty and Glorious is He):

> And He has made them find cheerfulness and joy. (76:11) — *wa laqqā-hum naḍratan wa surūrā.*

Cheerfulness *[naḍra]* shows in people's faces,[382] while joy *[surūr]* is felt

[381] For a full understanding of the commentary devoted by the author (may Allāh be well pleased with him) to the Qurʾānic verse *[āya]*:

> Allāh has therefore warded off from them the evil of that day. (76:11) — *fa-waqā-humu 'llāhu sharra dhālika 'l-yawmi.*

—it is important to be aware that the Arabic word *sharar* [(a shower of) sparks] is derived from the same triconsonantal root—*sh-r-r*—as the word *sharr* [evil].

[382] The word *naḍra* [cheerfulness; cheerful radiance] also occurs in one other verse *[āya]* of the Qurʾān, where the context clearly confirms this comment by the author (may Allāh be well pleased with him):

> You will recognize in their faces the cheerful radiance of bliss. (83:24) — *taʿrifu fī wujūhi-him naḍrata 'n-naʿīm.*

In its fullest sense, according to the classical Arabic lexicographers, the expression *naḍrata 'n-naʿīm* signifies: "the beauty and brightness of aspect characteristic of blissful enjoyment" or "of a plentiful and pleasant and easy state of existence"—or "the brightness, or glistening, and moisture upon the skin that is characteristic thereof." (See E.W. Lane, *Arabic-English Lexicon*, art. *N–Ḍ–R*.)

within their hearts.[383] What is alluded to here is the following experience:

As soon as the true believer *[mu᾿min]* has emerged from his grave or tomb on the Day of Resurrection *[Yawm al-Qiyāma]*, he will look straight ahead of himself. There, lo and behold, he will see a human being whose face is like the sun, and who is laughing merrily. This person will be dressed in white robes, and on his head there will be a crown.

The newly resurrected believer will gaze at the unusual individual, until the latter draws near to him and says: "Peace be upon you, O saintly friend of Allāh *[salāmun ʿalaik, yā waliyya 'llāh]*!" He will respond to this greeting by saying: "And upon you be peace *[wa ʿalaika 's-salām]*! Who are you, O servant of Allāh? Are you one of the angels *[mal᾿ak mina 'l-malā᾿ika]*?" To this the other will reply: "No, by Allāh!" The following questions and answers will then be exchanged between the pair:

"Are you one of the Prophets *[nabī mina 'l-anbiyā᾿]*?"

"No, by Allāh!"

"Are you one of those drawn near [to the Lord] *[mina 'l-muqarrabīn]*?"

"No, by Allāh!"

"Well then, who are you?"

"I am your own righteous conduct *[ʿamal ṣāliḥ]*. I have come to greet you with the good news of your admission to the Garden of Paradise and salvation from the Fire of Hell."

"O servant of Allāh, do you really know that for a fact, so that you can confidently give me such glad tidings?

"Yes!"

Once this assurance has been given, the conversation will continue as follows:

"Well then, what do you want from me?"

"Climb up on my shoulders and use me as your means of transport."

"Glory be to Allāh *[Subḥāna 'llāh]*! It cannot be right and proper for the likes of you to be ridden as a means of transport!

"Oh yes, it is entirely appropriate, considering how long I rode about on your shoulders in the realm of the lower world. So now I am begging you, for the sake of Allāh's countenance, to mount up and ride upon me."

The newly resurrected believer will thereupon agree to mount and ride upon the embodiment of his own righteous conduct, at which point

[383] It is significant to note that the word *surūr* [joy, happiness, gladness] is derived from the same triconsonantal root—*s–r–r*—as the term *sirr* [secret; the hidden recesses of the innermost being].

the latter will say to him: "Do not be afraid! I shall be your escort to the Garden of Paradise."

This will make him feel happy, and his happiness *[faraḥ]* will become apparent in his face, so much so that it will soon be glistening and sparkling with delight. Radiant light *[nūr]* will be visible in his face, while joy *[surūr]* is felt within his heart, for this is in accordance with the words of Allāh (Almighty and Glorious is He):

And He has made them find cheerfulness and joy. (76:11)	*wa laqqā-hum naḍratan wa surūrā.*

As far as the unbeliever *[kāfir]* is concerned, as soon as he has emerged from his grave or tomb, he will also look straight ahead of himself. There, lo and behold, he will see a swarthy, blue-eyed man with an ugly face, swarthier than the pitch blackness of the tomb on a dark and gloomy night. The man will be dressed in black robes. His canine teeth will scratch the ground, and, as he treads upon it, his footsteps will produce a rumbling noise like thunder. The stench he gives off will be worse than that of a rotting corpse.

The unbeliever, though wishing he could turn his face away from him, will say: "Who are you, O servant of Allāh?" To this the ugly figure will reply: "O enemy of Allāh, come here to me, come here to me! You belong to me, and I belong to you this day." The following exchanges will then take place between the pair:

"Woe unto you! Are you a devil *[shaiṭān]*?"

"No, by Allāh, but I am your own wicked conduct *[ʿamal ṭāliḥ]*!"

"Well then, what do you want from me?"

"I propose to mount upon your shoulders and use you as my means of transport!"

"I implore you, by Allāh, to grant me a bit of leeway here, since you would be exposing me to disgrace in the sight of all my fellow creatures!"

"By Allāh, there is no way out of your predicament, considering how long you rode about on me [in the realm of the lower world], so today I am going to mount up and ride upon you!"

The embodiment of his wicked conduct *[ʿamal ṭāliḥ]* will thereupon proceed to use the newly resurrected unbeliever as his means of transport, for this is in accordance with the words of Allāh (Almighty and Glorious is He):

And they shall be carrying their burdens on their backs. O how evil	*wa hum yaḥmilūna awzāra-hum ʿalā ẓuhūri-him:*

are the loads they have to bear! (6:31)	*a-lā sā'a mā yazirūn.*

Then Allāh (Almighty and Glorious is He) has made mention of His saintly friends *[awliyā']*, for He has told us:

And He has granted them, as a reward (76:12)	*wa jazā-hum*

That is to say, in addition to the good tidings [of cheerfulness and joy].

for all that they have endured, (76:12)	*bi-mā ṣabarū*

That is to say, for their patient endurance in the face of trials and tribulations, in the performance of commandments and the avoidance of prohibitions, and in submissive acceptance of the decree of destiny *[qadar]*.

a Garden [of Paradise] and silk [attire]. (76:12)	*jannatan wa ḥarīrā.*

As far as the Garden of Paradise is concerned, they will lead a life of ease and comfort therein. As for the silk, they will use it as the material for the clothes they wear.

Next, Allāh (Almighty and Glorious is He) has told us:

[They will be] reclining therein... (76:13)	*muttaki'īna fī-hā*

That is to say, in the Garden of Paradise.

upon [raised and canopied] couches. (76:13)	*'ala 'l-arā'ik.*

That is to say, upon raised couches *[surur]* with canopies *[ḥijāl]*, i.e., curtains *[sutur]*, draped over them.[384]

They will experience there neither a sun nor bitter cold. (76:13)	*lā yarawna fī-hā shamsan wa lā zamharīrā.*

That is to say, they will not be afflicted by the heat of the sun, nor by the bitter cold of severe frost, because there is neither winter nor summer in the Garden of Paradise.

[384] According to the classical Arabic lexicographers, the term *arīka* (of which *arā'ik* is the plural form) denotes: "a raised couch *[sarīr]* in a *ḥajala*, which is a tent, or pavilion, or chamber, adorned with cloths or curtains." According to one authority, the *arīka* is so named because it was originally made of the wood of the thorny trees termed *arāk*, from which the sticks traditionally used for cleaning the teeth are also made. (See E.W. Lane, *Arabic-English Lexicon*, art. *'–R–K.*)

Then Allāh (Almighty and Glorious is He) has told us:

And close upon them is the shade thereof, while its clustered fruits bow down low. (76:14)	*wa dāniyatan ʿalai-him ẓilālu-hā: wa dhullilat quṭūfu-hā tadhlīlā.*

That is to say, the shade of the trees [is close upon them]. What is alluded to here is the following state of affairs:

The inhabitants of the Garden of Paradise may eat of its fruits while they are standing up, if they so wish, or while they are sitting down, if they so wish, or even, if they so wish, while they are sleeping. Whenever they want to enjoy some fruit, the clusters will bow down close enough to them for one of them to stand up and take his pick. Such is the explanation of His words (Almighty and Glorious is He):

while its clustered fruits bow down low. (76:14)	*wa dhullilat quṭūfu-hā tadhlīlā.*

Then He has told us (Almighty and Glorious is He):

And flasks of silver are brought around for them, and vessels. (76:15)	*wa yuṭāfu ʿalai-him bi-āniyatin min fiḍḍatin wa akwābin.*

These vessels *[akwāb]* are actually mugs or tankards *[kīzān]*, except that they have round tops[385] and are not equipped with handles. He has also said (Almighty and Glorious is He):

[Those vessels] are crystal beakers, crystal beakers made of silver. (76:15–16)	*kānat qawārīrā qawārīran min fiḍḍatin.*

In other words, the vessels concerned are of the type called *qawārīr* [beakers normally made of crystal, in the sense of clear, colorless glass of the highest quality], but in this case they are made of silver. The explanation of the seeming paradox is simply this: Whereas the *qawārīr* of this lower world are made of earthly material, the *qawārīr* of the Garden of Paradise are made of silver.

Allāh (Almighty and Glorious is He) has then added these words to His description of the vessels:

They have measured them in exact proportion. (76:16)	*qaddarū-hā taqdīrā.*

That is to say, the vessels *[akwāb]* have been measured to match the proportions of the flask *[inā᾿]*, and the flask has been measured to fit the

[385] The roundness of their tops is referred to as a way of indicating that these vessels *[akwāb]* have no spouts. (See E.W. Lane, *Arabic-English Lexicon*, art. *K–W–B* and art. *K–W–Z*.)

palm of the servant in charge of dispensing the people's drink. This has been done to ensure that exactly the right amount is always poured. Not a drop will be left in the flask, and not a drop too much will be poured, since all the elements involved have been measured to correspond exactly. Such is the import of His words (Exalted is He):

They have measured them in exact proportion. (76:16)	*qaddarū-hā taqdīrā.*

He has also told us (Exalted is He):

And in it their thirst is quenched with a cup. (76:17)	*wa yusqawna fī-hā ka'san.*

That is to say, their thirst is quenched with a [cup of] wine *[khamr]*, since no receptacle that does not contain wine can be called a [wine] cup *[ka's]*![386]

He has also told us (Exalted is He):

The mixture of it is ginger. (76:17)	*kāna mizāju-hā zanjabīlā.*

That is to say, the whole of it has had ginger *[zanjabīl]* mixed in with it. Then Allāh (Almighty and Glorious is He) has spoken of:

A fountain therein, named *Salsabīl*. (76:18)	*'ainan fī-hā tusammā Salsabīlā.*

This fountain flows toward them from the Garden of Eden *[Jannat 'Adn]*,[387] for it passes through every Garden, then returns to its source. It touches every part of the Garden of Paradise.

He has also told us (Exalted is He):

And waiting on them are immortal youths. (76:19)	*wa yaṭūfu 'alai-him wildānun mukhalladūn.*

These youths are the attendants *[ghilmān]* who will never become white-haired with age. Since they have been granted immortal youth, they will never attain the age of puberty, let alone grow old. Speaking of these ever-youthful attendants, Allāh (Almighty and Glorious is He) has told us:

If you could see them, you would take for scattered pearls. (76:19)	*idhā ra'aita-hum ḥasibta-hum lu'lu'an manthūrā.*

[386] According to the classical Arabic lexicographers, the term *ka's*, which usually means "a drinking-cup; a cup containing wine; a cup full of wine," may sometimes signify "wine" itself. When a cup does not contain wine, however, it is called *qadaḥ* instead of *ka's*. (See: E.W. Lane, *Arabic-English Lexicon*, art. *K–'–S*.)

[387] That is to say, according to the Arabic lexicographers, "the Garden of Perpetual Abode." (See: E.W. Lane, *Arabic-English Lexicon*, art. *'–D–N*.)

That is to say, they would seem like pearls on account of their handsome appearance and the whiteness of their complexion, and like scattered pearls on account of their great number. In other words, they would seem like scattered pearls too numerous for anyone to count them all.

Then Allāh (Almighty and Glorious is He) has told us:

And when you see, there... (76:20)	*wa idhā ra'aita thamma...*

That is to say, over there in the Garden of Paradise.

You will see a state of bliss and a vast estate. (76:20)	*ra'aita na'īman* *wa mulkan kabīrā.*

What this signifies in detail is as follows: Any man, who is numbered among the inhabitants of the Garden of Paradise, will be the owner of a palace. Within that palace there will be seventy palatial mansions. Inside every mansion there will be seventy apartments. Every apartment will be constructed from a hollowed pearl, the height of which extends skyward to the distance of a league *[farsakh]*,[388] while its width and length are a league by a league. It will be equipped with four thousand door panels made of gold.

Inside that apartment there will be a thronelike raised couch *[sarīr]*, embroidered with threads of pearl and sapphire on the right side and the left, respectively. There will also be four thousand footstools made of gold, with supporting legs of red ruby. That thronelike raised couch will have seventy cushions spread upon its surface, every cushion of a different color. The owner will be reclining there on his left side, clad in seventy articles of clothing tailored from silk brocade. The garment closest to his body will be made of white silk, and on his forehead he will wear a diadem *[iklīl]*, embedded with chrysolite or peridot *[zabarjad]*,[389] sapphires, and various kinds of jewels, every jewel being of a different color. Upon his head he will wear a crown of gold, with seventy corners to it, and on every corner a pearl as wide as the entire distance between the East and the West. On his wrist he will carry three bracelets: a bracelet of gold, a bracelet of silver, and a bracelet of pearl. On his fingers and toes he will be wearing rings of gold and silver, studded with various kinds of precious stones.

[388] See note 68 on p. 48 above.

[389] See note 81 on p. 61 above.

On duty in his presence there will be ten thousand ever-youthful attendants, who will never reach adulthood, let alone become white-haired with age.

A table made from a single red ruby will also be set in front of him, the size of its top being a mile in width by a mile in length. Laid out upon that table will be seventy thousand kitchen utensils made of gold and silver, and in each of those bowls and dishes there will be no fewer than seventy different kinds of food. Then, as soon as he has picked out some tasty morsel with his hand, it may occur to him that he would actually prefer another, in which case the taste and texture of the morsel concerned will immediately be transformed, so that it turns into the one he really fancies.

Youthful attendants *[ghilmān]* will be ready to wait upon him at table, holding drinking vessels of silver in their hands, as well as flasks of silver from which to pour his drink. They will have both wine and water with them. He will thus be able to eat as much of all the various dishes as forty men could ordinarily consume, for as soon as he has had his fill of a particular kind of food, they will give him a draught of whichever drink he happens to prefer, and he will then relieve his indigestion by burping and belching.

Allāh (Almighty and Glorious is He) will grant him access to a thousand different ways of experiencing an appetite.[390] The man will go on drinking till he breaks out in a sweat, then, once he has started to perspire, Allāh will make him aware of the existence of a thousand separate entrances to the appetite for food and drink. Through those entrances, birds resembling enormous thoroughbred she-camels will fly into his presence, alighting to form a row in front of him. Each bird will then proceed to offer a description of itself, in a charmingly melodious voice, more delightful by far than any singing to be heard in this lower world. It will say: "O saintly friend of Allāh *[yā waliyya 'llāh]*, eat me up, for I have been raised and cared for in such and such an aviary in the pastures of the Garden of Paradise, and I am accustomed to drinking

[390] Literally, "Allāh (Almighty and Glorious is He) will open up *[yaftaḥu]* for him a thousand doors or gates of appetite." The verb *yaftaḥu* is derived from the triliteral root *f–t–ḥ*, which conveys the basic idea of "openness". For a full account of many important ramifications of this Arabic root, see the Translator's Introduction to *The Sublime Revelation [al-Fatḥ ar-Rabbānī]*, another volume in the Al-Baz series of English translations of the works of Shaikh ʿAbd al-Qādir al-Jīlānī (may Allāh be well pleased with him).

from such and such a fountain." The birds will go on appealing to him in those beautiful voices of theirs, until he eventually looks up and fixes his gaze on one bird in particular—the one with the most compelling voice, as well as the most attractive self-description—and feels the desire to make a meal of it. Allāh (Almighty and Glorious is He) is well aware, of course, of the liking for it that has now become lodged in the heart of His servant. That bird will therefore come at once and alight upon the table—part of it cut into strips, salted and dried *[qadīd]*, part of it broiled, grilled or roasted *[shawī]*, and all of it whiter than snow and sweeter than honey. The man will then proceed to eat until he has had his fill of it, until his appetite has been fully satisfied. At this point the bird will become a bird again, just as it was before, and it will fly out through the very door by which it entered.

As for the man, he will be reclining all the while "upon raised and canopied couches *[ʿala 'l-arāʾiki]*,"[391] and his wife will be right there beside him, turning her face toward his. He will see his own face reflected in hers, on account of the pure clarity and whiteness of her complexion. Whenever he wishes to have sexual intercourse with her, he will give her a longing look, yet he will feel too shy to invite her in explicit terms. She will be well aware, however, of what her husband wants from her, so she will make him a frank proposal, saying: "By my father and my mother, I urge you to raise your head and look at me directly, for you belong to me this day, and I belong to you!" He will respond to this by making love to her with all the strength and vigor of a hundred ancient heroes *[miʾa rajul min al-awwalīn]*, and with all the passionate desire of forty stalwart men. When he approaches her sexually, he will discover that she is a virgin. He will not let his attention stray from her for one moment, during a period of forty days. Then, when he finally reaches the point of exhaustion, he will notice that the aroma of musk is emanating from her, and this will serve to increase still further the love he feels for her as a wife. As an inhabitant of the Garden of Paradise, he will have four thousand and eighty wives like her, and each wife will have seventy menservants and maidservants.

391 An allusion to the verse *[āya]* of the Qurʾān (76:13) discussed by the author (may Allāh be well pleased with him) on p. 294 above. (See also note 384 above).

From another traditional report, this one transmitted on the authority of ʿAlī ibn Abī Ṭālib (may Allāh be well pleased with him), we learn that the Prophet (Allāh bless him and give him peace) once said:

> If a maidservant or a manservant [belonging to the inhabitants of the Garden of Paradise] were ever to emerge into this lower world, all the people of this world would surely engage in mortal combat over her or him, until they were all extinct. And if the maidens of Paradise, with eyes so fair *[al-ḥūr al-ʿīn]*,[392] were ever to let their locks of hair trail down upon the earth, the light of the sun would be extinguished, because of their vastly brighter radiance.

Someone once asked: "O Messenger of Allāh, how great is the contrast [in the Garden of Paradise] between the manservant *[khādim]*, on the one hand, and the man who is served as a master *[makhdūm]*, on the other?" To this he replied (Allāh bless him and give him peace):

> By the One in whose Hand my soul is held, the distinction [in the Garden of Paradise] between the manservant *[khādim]*, on the one hand, and the man who is served as a master *[makhdūm]*, on the other, is like the stars that are almost too faint to be visible, in contrast to the moon at the halfway point [i.e., in the middle of the month, when it is at the full].[393]

Let us now resume our description of the state of bliss enjoyed by that inhabitant of the Garden of Paradise:

While he is sitting there upon his thronelike couch *[sarīr]*, lo and behold, Allāh (Almighty and Glorious is He) will send him an angel, bearing seventy fine articles of clothing, each of a different kind. These gifts will be tucked out of sight between the two fingers of the angel, who will also be conveying the salutation of peace and contentment. On reaching the door of the man's abode, the angel will come to a halt, saying to the doorkeeper: "Permit me to enter the presence of Allāh's saintly friend *[walī]*, for I come to him as the Messenger of the Lord of All the Worlds." The doorkeeper will say in response: "By Allāh, I do not possess the authority to converse with him directly. Nevertheless, I shall mention you to my immediate superiors among the doorkeeping

[392] See note 333 on p. 241 above.

[393] From the general context of this passage, it seems safe to assume that the contrast referred to here—first by the anonymous questioner and then by the Prophet (Allāh bless him and give him peace)—is one that exists in the Garden of Paradise, although this is not explicitly stated in either case. To confirm the assumption, we may adduce the rather similar traditional report (cited on p. 285 above) from which we learn, on the authority of Abū Huraira (may Allāh be well pleased with him), that the Prophet (Allāh bless him and give him peace) also used to say:

> The handsomeness of the true specimen of manhood *[rajul]*, in contrast to the handsomeness of the manservant *[khādim]* among the people of the Garden of Paradise, is like [the brilliance of] the moon on the night when it is full, in contrast to [the fainter brilliance of] the stars.

staff." They will then refer the matter from one to another in turn, until the information finally reaches him, after passing through seventy doors. The last in the chain of doorkeepers will tell him: "O saintly friend of Allāh *[yā waliyya 'llāh]*, the Messenger of the Lord of All the Worlds is waiting at the outside door." He will then grant permission for the messenger to enter into his presence, so the angel will come inside and say: "Peace be upon you, O saintly friend of Allāh *[as-salāmu ʿalaik, yā waliyya 'llāh]*! The Lord of Might and Glory (Almighty and Majestic is He) extends to you the greeting of peace, and He is well-pleased with you." On hearing this news, but for the fact that Allāh (Almighty and Glorious is He) has not condemned him to death, the man would die of sheer happiness.

Such is the import of His words (Exalted is He):

And greater yet [is the promise of] good pleasure from Allāh; that is the mighty triumph. (9:72)	*wa riḍwānun mina 'llāhi akbar: dhālika huwa 'l-fawzu 'l-ʿaẓīm.*

Such is likewise the import of His words (Exalted is He):

And when you see. (76:21)	*wa idhā ra'aita.*

By this He means: "And when you, O Muḥammad, see."

There you will see a state of bliss... (76:21)	*thamma ra'aita naʿīman...*

That is to say, over there you will see the state of bliss in which he finds himself.

and a high estate. (76:21)	*wa mulkan kabīrā.*

He must be endowed with a high estate indeed, when the Messenger of Allāh, the Lord of All the Worlds, may not enter his presence without permission!

Then Allāh (Glorious and Exalted is He) has told us:

Upon them will be green garments of fine silk and thick brocade. (76:21)	*ʿāliya-hum thiyābu sundusin khuḍrun wa istabraq.*

That is to say, their outer garments will consist of silk brocade *[dībāj]*.[394] By using the expression "upon them *[ʿāliya-hum]*," He has simply allowed for the unstated but obvious fact that the undergarment,

394 According to the classical Arabic lexicographers, the term *istabraq* is properly applied to thick *dībāj* [silk brocade], or, more precisely, to "closely woven, thick, beautiful *dībāj* [silk brocade] interwoven with gold." (See E.W. Lane, *Arabic-English Lexicon*, art. *B–R–Q* and art. *D–B–J*.)

the one right next to the person's skin, will consist of plain white silk.[395]

Then He has told us (Exalted is He):

They will also be adorned with bracelets of silver. (76:21)	*wa ḥullū asāwira min fiḍḍa.*

In another verse *[āya]*, from a different chapter *[sūra]* of the Qur᾿an, we also read:

They will be adorned therein with bracelets of gold and of pearls. (22:23)	*yuḥallawna fī-hā min asāwira min dhahabin wa lu᾿lu᾿ā.*

This means that there must be three types of bracelets altogether.

Then Allāh (Almighty and Glorious is He) has told us:

And their Lord will slake their thirst with a pure drink. (76:21)	*wa saqā-hum Rabbu-hum sharāban ṭahūrā.*

In order to grasp the full significance of these words, one needs to be aware of the following scenario:

At the entrance to the Garden of Paradise there stands a tree, from whose trunk two fountains gush forth. So, whenever a man succeeds in crossing the Bridge over Hell *[aṣ-Ṣirāṭ]*, and in reaching these two fountains, he will plunge into one of the springs in order to bathe himself therein. He will thus acquire an aroma that is even more delightful than musk. His physical height will now be seventy cubits *[dhirāʿ]*,[396] matching the stature of Adam (peace be upon him).[397]

All the people of the Garden of Paradise, the men and the women alike, will be of exactly the same age on the birthday of Jesus (peace be upon him), when each and every one of them will become a permanent thirty-three-year-old person. The young boy will grow older in a hurry, until he becomes a thirty-three-year-old adult, while the gray-haired elder will quickly shed his aged condition and revert to the age of thirty-three. All of them, the men and the women alike, will be endowed with the same good looks as Joseph, the son of Jacob (peace be upon them both).

[395] In the context of the English translation alone, the expression "upon them" would hardly call for an explanation. In the original Arabic, however, the expression *ʿāliya-hum*, as a quite uncommon synonym for the familiar *ʿalai-him*, does seem to suggest a nuance in need of interpretation.

[396] See note 348 on p. 257 above.

[397] According to one traditional report, cited earlier in this Discourse (p. 276 above), the physical height of Adam (peace be upon him) was sixty cubits, rather than seventy.

As well as bathing himself in one of the two fountains, the man will drink from the other, thereby expelling all unworthy feelings from inside his breast, whether they be spite and malice, anxiety and worry, jealousy and envy, or grief and sorrow. For, by means of that water, Allāh (Almighty and Glorious is He) will bring his heart into the open. He will thus emerge with his heart in the same condition as the heart of Job *[Ayyūb]*, and with his tongue transformed into one that can speak the Arabic language as fluently as the tongue of Muḥammad (may Allāh bless them both, and may He grant them peace).

The man and his companions will then press on beyond the two fountains, until they come to the gateway itself, at which point the guardians of the Garden of Paradise will say to them: "Have you been through the process of purification?" They will all say yes, so the guardians will say: "Enter, to dwell herein forever!" By greeting them with the good news of eternal residence, before the actual moment of entry *[bi 'l-khulūd qabla 'd-dukhūl]*, they intend to assure them that they will never have to leave.

As soon as someone goes in through the entrance to the Garden of Paradise, he will be accompanied by the two angels who were always with him in the realm of the lower world, these being none other than the Noble Recorders *[al-Kirām al-Kātibīn]*.[398] At that very same moment, lo and behold, he will notice the presence of another angel, this one accompanied by a thoroughbred she-camel, created from a single green corundum *[yāqūṭa khaḍrā']*. Its bridle and reins appear to be made from a red ruby *[yāqūṭa ḥamrā']*. As for the saddle on its back, the front and rear portions both consist of pearls and sapphires, while its main surface is of gold and silver. This angel will also bring with him seventy fine articles of clothing and other adornments [including a crown], so the man will try them on, as well as setting the crown upon his head.

The angel, who will also be accompanied by ten thousand youthful attendants, resembling hidden pearls, will then say to the man: "O saintly friend of Allāh *[yā waliyya 'llāh]*, you must mount up and ride, for

[398] These guardian angels are mentioned in the Qur'ān:

And yet over you there are watchers,	*wa inna 'alai-kum la-ḥāfiẓīn:*
Noble Recorders, who know	*Kirāman Kātibīn:*
whatever you do. (82:10–12)	*ya'lamūna mā taf'alūn.*

According to the traditional commentaries, every human being is constantly supervised by two of these guardian angels, one on the right hand to record the person's good deeds, and one on the left to record the bad deeds committed.

this wondrous thoroughbred she-camel belongs to you, as do others just like her." He will thereupon adopt her as his means of transport, availing himself of the fact that she has a pair of wings, and that the range of her every stride extends to the farthest point in sight.

Riding along on the back of his fabulous thoroughbred she-camel, with ten thousand youthful attendants ever on duty in his presence, and still accompanied by the two angels who were always with him in this lower world, the man will now keep traveling until he reaches his palatial mansions, and makes himself at home in them.

Then Allāh (Glorious and Exalted is He) has told us [that it will be said unto them]:

"Behold, this... *inna hādhā*

In other words, all this that has been described for your benefit, in this form *[ṣūra]* and in this chapter *[sūra]* of the Qurʾān...[399]

is a reward for you. *kāna la-kum jazāʾan*

That is to say, it is a reward for those deeds of yours that deserve to be well recompensed.

And your endeavor [upon earth]... *wa kāna saʿyu-kum...*

That is to say, your work *[ʿamal]*...

has found acceptance." (76:22) *mashkūrā.*

In other words, Allāh (Almighty and Glorious is He) has acknowledged the merit of your deeds, and He has therefore rewarded you with the Garden of Paradise.

This brings us to the end of the Fourth Discourse.

Praise be to Allāh, the Lord of All the Worlds!
[al-ḥamdu li'llāhi Rabbi 'l-ʿālamīn].

[399] From a linguist's point of view, it is interesting to note the decidedly unusual occurrence—directly side by side in the original Arabic sentence—of the two words *ṣūra* [form] and *sūra* [chapter of the Qurʾān]. (In the Arabic script, the difference in pronunciation—and consequently in meaning—is clearly indicated by spelling the former with the initial letter *ṣād*, and the latter with the initial letter *sīn*.)

Appendix to the First Discourse[411]

Concerning the episode of the original "Satanic Verses"

In view of the crucial importance of this historical episode, from which Shaikh ʿAbd al-Qādir (may Allāh be well pleased with him) has drawn the extremely valuable lessons contained in the First Discourse of this Chapter of al-Ghunya, it seems desirable to supply the reader with the full account provided in the Sīra [Biography] of the Prophet (Allāh bless him and give him peace), as reported by the celebrated historian Abū Jaʿfar Muḥammad ibn Jarīr aṭ-Ṭabarī (d. A.H. 310/923 C.E.):[412]

The following account was related to me by Yaʿqūb ibn Ibrāhīm, who heard the report from Ibn ʿUlayya, on the authority of Muḥammad ibn Isḥāq, who heard it from Saʿīd ibn Minā, the freedman *[mawlā]* of Abu'l-Bakhtarī:

Allāh's Messenger (Allāh bless him and give him peace) was met by al-Walīd ibn al-Mughīra, al-ʿĀṣ ibn Wāʾil [as-Sahmī], al-Aswad ibn al-Muṭṭalib ibn Asad ibn ʿAbd al-ʿUzzā, and Umayya ibn Khalaf—all men of good repute among their own people.[413] They said: "O Muḥammad, come now, let us worship what you worship, and you worship what we worship. Let us all get together in this matter. If what you worship is better than what we worship, we can participate in it with you and take our share of it, and if what we worship is better than what you worship, you can participate in it with us and take your share of it."

[411] Supplied by the translator for the benefit of readers who may not be familiar with the historical background.

[412] The version supplied in this Appendix is a translation from the Arabic text of *Taʾrīkh aṭ-Ṭabarī*, published by Al-ʿAlamī Library, Beirut, Lebanon, A.H. 1403/1984 C.E.; vol. 2, pp. 75–7.

[413] According to some traditional reports, the Prophet (Allāh bless him and give him peace) was making a circumambulation of the Kaʿba when this meeting took place.

So Allāh (Almighty and Glorious is He) sent down this revelation concerning them:

> Say: "O you unbelievers, I do not worship what you worship, nor are you worshipping what I worship. I will not worship what you have worshipped, neither will you worship what I worship. You have your religion and I have mine!" (109:1–6)

In other words, if you will only worship Allāh (Almighty and Glorious is He) on condition that I worship what you worship, I have no need of you at all. You can have your religion, all of it, and I have mine.

Now Allāh's Messenger (Allāh bless him and give him peace) was earnestly concerned about the welfare of his people *[ḥarīṣ ʿalā ṣalāḥ qawmih]*, wishing to draw them close if only he could find a way of doing so. It has been mentioned that he longed for a way to attract them, and the course he adopted was as follows, according to what Ibn Ḥamīd told me that Salama said Muḥammad ibn Isḥāq told him, as reported from Yazīd ibn Ziyād of Medina on the authority of Muḥammad ibn Kaʿb al-Quraẓī:

When Allāh's Messenger (Allāh bless him and give him peace) saw that his people were turning their backs on him, and he was pained by their alienation from what he had brought them from Allāh (Almighty and Glorious is He), he felt a longing *[tamannā]* that there might come to him from Allāh (Almighty and Glorious is He) a message that would reconcile his people to him. Because of his love for his people and his earnest concern for their welfare, it would delight him if the obstacle that made his task so difficult could be removed; so he reflected on the prospect and longed for it, and it was very dear to him.

It was then that Allāh (Almighty and Glorious is He) sent down the revelation:

> By the Star when it sets, your comrade is not astray, neither does he err; nor does he speak out of caprice.... (53:1–3)

and when the Prophet (Allāh bless him and give him peace) reached His words:

> Have you thought of *al-Lāt* and *al-ʿUzzā*—and *Manāt* the third, the other? (53:19–20)

and while he was reflecting upon it, and desiring to bring it [the reconciliation he so longed for] to his people, Satan inserted upon his tongue: "These are the exalted *Gharānīq*,[417] whose intercession is approved."[418]

When [the people of the tribe of] Quraish heard this, they were delighted and greatly pleased at the way in which he spoke of their gods, and they listened to him; while the believers were firmly convinced that what their Prophet (Allāh bless him and give him peace) had brought them from their Lord (Almighty and Glorious is He) was true, not suspecting a mistake or a vain desire or a slip. When he reached the prostration [mentioned in the last verse of the Sūra] and the end of the Sūra in which he prostrated himself, the Muslims prostrated themselves when their Prophet (Allāh bless him and give him peace) bowed down in prostration, confirming what he had brought and obeying his command.

The idolatrous polytheists of Quraish and others who were in the mosque also prostrated themselves when they heard the mention of their gods, so that everyone in the mosque, believer and unbeliever alike, bowed down in prostration, except al-Walīd ibn al-Mughīra, who was an old man who could not do so, and who therefore took a handful of dust from the valley and bent over it.

Then the people dispersed, and Quraish went out, delighted at what had been said about their gods, saying: "Muḥammad has spoken of our gods in splendid fashion. He alleged in what he recited that they are the exalted *Gharānīq* whose intercession is approved."

The news reached the companions of the Prophet (Allāh bless him and give him peace) who were in Abyssinia. It was being reported that Quraish had accepted Islām, so some men started to return while others remained behind.

Then Gabriel (peace be upon him) came to Allāh's Messenger (Allāh bless him and give him peace) and said: "What have you done, O Muḥammad? You have recited to these people something I did not bring you from Allāh (Almighty and Glorious is He), and you have said what He did not say to you."

[417] See note [8] above.

[418] *tilka'l-gharānīqu'l-ʿulyā—ʿindaha'sh-shafāʿatu turtaḍā*. Another traditionally accepted reading—*turtajā* ('to be hoped for')—is the one adopted by Shaikh ʿAbd al-Qādir (may Allāh be well pleased with him). See p. 4 above.

Allāh's Messenger (Allāh bless him and give him peace) was bitterly grieved and was greatly in fear of Allāh (Almighty and Glorious is He). So Allāh (Almighty and Glorious is He) sent down [a revelation], for He was merciful to him, comforting him and making light of the affair and telling him that every Prophet and Messenger before him had experienced the kind of longing he had felt, and had wanted what he wanted, and that Satan had interjected something into their desires, just as he had on his tongue.

So Allāh (Almighty and Glorious is He) annulled what Satan had suggested, and Allāh (Almighty and Glorious is He) established His verses *[āyāt]*. That is to say, He assured him that he was just like the [earlier] Prophets and Messengers. Then Allāh (Almighty and Glorious is He) sent down the revelation:

> We have not sent a Messenger or a Prophet before you without it happening that, when he experienced a longing, Satan cast suggestions into his longing. But Allāh will annul what Satan has suggested. Then Allāh will establish His revelations—surely Allāh is All-Knowing, All-Wise. (22:52)[419]

Thus Allāh (Almighty and Glorious is He) relieved His Prophet's grief, and made him feel safe from his fears; and He annulled what Satan had suggested in the above-mentioned words about their gods, by His revelation (Almighty and Glorious is He):

> Are yours the males and His the females? That would indeed be an unfair division! They are nothing but names which you and your fathers have given them, for which Allāh has sent down no authority. They follow nothing but surmise and that which they themselves desire. And yet guidance from their Lord has come to them! Or shall man have whatever he fancies?
>
> But to Allāh belongs the Last and the First. How many an angel there is in the heavens whose intercession is of no avail, except after Allāh gives leave to whomever He wills and is well pleased. (53:21–26)

In other words, how can the intercession of their gods avail with Him (Almighty and Glorious is He)?

When the annulment of what Satan had put upon the tongue of the Prophet (Allāh bless him and give him peace) came from Allāh (Almighty and Glorious is He), Quraish said: "Muḥammad has repented of what he said about the position of your gods in relation to

[419] Also clearly relevant here is the immediately following verse *[āya]* of the Qur'ān:

> That He may make that which Satan suggested a temptation to those whose hearts are diseased and hardened. (22:53)

Allāh (Almighty and Glorious is He); he has altered it and brought something else." Now these two sentences which Satan had put upon the tongue of Allāh's Messenger (Allāh bless him and give him peace) were in the mouth of every polytheistic idolater *[mushrik]*, and they became more violently hostile to the Muslims and the followers of the Messenger (Allāh bless him and give him peace).

As for those companions of Allāh's Messenger (Allāh bless him and give him peace) who had left Abyssinia—having heard that the people of Mecca had accepted Islām, when they prostrated themselves along with Allāh's Messenger (Allāh bless him and give him peace)—they were informed when they approached Mecca that the report was false. So none came into the town without the promise of protection or in secrecy.

Among those who did come into Mecca and stayed there until the Prophet (Allāh bless him and give him peace) migrated to Medina, and who were present with him at the time of [the Battle of] Badr, were (from the tribe of Banī ʿAbd Shams ibn ʿAbd Manāf ibn Quṣayy): ʿUthmān ibn ʿAffān ibn Abi'l-ʿĀṣ ibn Umayya with his wife Ruqayya,[421] the daughter of Allāh's Messenger (Allāh bless him and give him peace), and Abū Ḥudhaifa ibn ʿUtba ibn Rabīʿa ibn ʿAbd Shams with his wife Sahla, the daughter of Suhail, and a number of others, thirty-three men all told.[422]

[421] After the death of the lady Ruqayya (may Allāh be well pleased with her), which occurred during the Battle of Badr, ʿUthmān ibn ʿAffān married her sister Umm Kulthūm (may Allāh be well pleased with him and with her). He thus came to be known by the epithet Dhu'n-Nūrain [He of the Two Lights].

[422] A parallel tradition—reported on the authority of Muḥammad ibn Kaʿb al-Quraẓī and Muḥammad ibn Qays—is also given by aṭ-Ṭabarī (in the immediately following passages of the work cited in note [412] above).

Concerning the Author, Shaikh ʿAbd al-Qādir al-Jīlānī

A Brief Introduction by the Translator[1]

The Author's Names and Titles

A rich store of information about the author of *Sufficient Provision for Seekers of the Path of Truth* is conveniently available, to those familiar with the religious and spiritual tradition of Islām, in his names, his surnames, and the many titles conferred upon him by his devoted followers. It is not unusual for these to take up several lines in an Arabic manuscript, but let us start with the short form of the author's name as it appears on the cover and title page of this book: *Shaikh ʿAbd al-Qādir al-Jīlānī*.

Shaikh: A term applied throughout the Islamic world to respected persons of recognized seniority in learning, experience and wisdom. Its basic meaning in Arabic is "an elder; a man over fifty years of age." (The spellings *Sheikh* and *Shaykh* may also be encountered in English-language publications.)

ʿAbd al-Qādir: This is the author's personal name, meaning "Servant [or Slave] of the All-Powerful." (The form *ʿAbdul Qādir*, which the reader may come across elsewhere, is simply an alternative translitera-tion of the Arabic spelling.) It has always been a common practice, in the Muslim community, to give a male child a name in which *ʿAbd* is prefixed to one of the Names of Allāh.

[1] Reproduced for the convenience of the reader, with slight modifications from the version printed on pp. xiii-xix of: Shaikh ʿAbd al-Qādir. *Revelations of the Unseen (Futūḥ al-Ghaib)*. Translated from the Arabic by Muhtar Holland. Houston, Texas: Al-Baz Publishing, Inc., 1992.

al-Jīlānī: A surname ending in *-ī* will often indicate the bearer's place of birth. Shaikh ʿAbd al-Qādir was born in the Iranian district of Gīlān, south of the Caspian Sea, in A.H. 470/1077-8 C.E. (In some texts, the Persian spelling *Gīlānī* is used instead of the arabicized form al-Jīlānī. The abbreviated form *al-Jīlī*, which may also be encountered, should not be confused with the surname of the venerable ʿAbd al-Karīm al-Jīlī, author of the celebrated work al-Insān al-Kāmil, who came from Jīl in the district of Baghdād.)

Let us now consider a slightly longer version of the Shaikh's name, as it occurs near the beginning of *Al-Fatḥ ar-Rabbānī [The Sublime Revelation]: Sayyidunā 'sh-Shaikh Muḥyi'd-Dīn Abū Muḥammad ʿAbd al-Qādir (Raḍiya'llāhu ʿanh).*

Sayyidunā 'sh-Shaikh: "Our Master, the Shaikh." A writer who regards himself as a Qādirī, a devoted follower of Shaikh ʿAbd al-Qādir, will generally refer to the latter as *Sayyidunā* [our Master], or *Sayyidī* [my Master].

Muḥyi'd-Dīn: "Reviver of the Religion." It is widely acknowledged by historians, non-Muslim as well as Muslim, that Shaikh ʿAbd al-Qādir displayed great courage in reaffirming the traditional teachings of Islām, in an era when sectarianism was rife, and when materialistic and rationalistic tendencies were predominant in all sections of society. In matters of Islamic jurisprudence *[fiqh]* and theology *[kalām]*, he adhered quite strictly to the highly "orthodox" school of Imām Aḥmad ibn Ḥanbal.

Abū Muḥammad: "Father of Muḥammad." In the Arabic system of nomenclature, a man's surnames usually include the name of his first-born son, with the prefix *Abū* [Father of—].

Raḍiya'llāhu ʿanh: "May Allāh be well pleased with him!" This benediction is the one customarily pronounced—and spelled out in writing—after mentioning the name of a Companion of the Prophet (Allāh bless him and give him peace). The preference for this particular invocation is yet another mark of the extraordinary status held by Shaikh ʿAbd al-Qādir in the eyes of his devoted followers.

Finally, we must note some important elements contained within this even longer version: *al-Ghawth al-Aʿẓam Sulṭān al-Awliyāʾ Sayyidunā 'sh-Shaikh Muḥyi'd-Dīn ʿAbd al-Qādir al-Jīlānī al-Ḥasanī al-Ḥusainī (Raḍiya'llāhu ʿanh)*.

al-Ghawth al-Aʿẓam: "The Supreme Helper" (or, "The Mightiest Succor"). *Ghawth* is an Arabic word meaning: (1) A cry for aid or succor. (2) Aid, help, succor; deliverance from adversity. (3) The chief of the Saints, who is empowered by Allāh to bring succor to suffering humanity, in response to His creatures' cry for help in times of extreme adversity.

Sulṭān al-Awliyāʾ: "The Sultan of the Saints." This reinforces the preceding title, emphasizing the supremacy of the *Ghawth* above all other orders of sanctity.

al-Ḥasanī al-Ḥusainī: "The descendant of both al-Ḥasan and al-Ḥusain, the grandsons of the Prophet (Allāh bless him and give him peace)." To quote the Turkish author, Shaikh Muzaffer Ozak Efendi (may Allāh bestow His mercy upon him): "The lineage of Shaikh ʿAbd al-Qādir is known as the Chain of Gold, since both his parents were descendants of the Messenger (Allāh bless him and give him peace). His noble father, ʿAbdullāh, traced his descent by way of Imām Ḥasan, while his revered mother, Umm al-Khair, traced hers through Imām Ḥusain."

As for the many other surnames, titles and honorific appellations that have been conferred upon Shaikh ʿAbd al-Qādir al-Jīlānī, it may suffice at this point to mention *al-Bāz al-Ashhab* [The Gray Falcon].

The Author's Life in Baghdād

Through the mists of legend surrounding the life of Shaikh ʿAbd al-Qādir al-Jīlānī, it is possible to discern the outlines of the following biographical sketch:

In A.H. 488, at the age of eighteen, he left his native province to become a student in the great capital city of Baghdād, the hub of political, commercial and cultural activity, and the center of religious learning in the world of Islām. After studying traditional sciences under such teachers as the prominent Ḥanbalī jurist *[faqīh]*, Abū Sa'd 'Alī al-Mukharrimī, he encountered a more spiritually oriented instructor in the saintly person of Abu'l-Khair Ḥammād ad-Dabbās. Then, instead of embarking on his own professorial career, he abandoned the city and spent twenty-five years as a wanderer in the desert regions of 'Irāq.

He was over fifty years old by the time he returned to Baghdād, in A.H. 521/1127 C.E., and began to preach in public. His hearers were profoundly affected by the style and content of his lectures, and his reputation grew and spread through all sections of society. He moved into the school *[madrasa]* belonging to his old teacher al-Mukharrimī, but the premises eventually proved inadequate. In A.H. 528, pious donations were applied to the construction of a residence and guesthouse *[ribāṭ]*, capable of housing the Shaikh and his large family, as well as providing accommodation for his pupils and space for those who came from far and wide to attend his regular sessions *[majālis]*.

He lived to a ripe old age, and continued his work until his very last breath, as we know from the accounts of his final moments recorded in the Addendum to Revelations of the Unseen.

In the words of Shaikh Muzaffer Ozak Efendi: "The venerable 'Abd al-Qādir al-Jīlānī passed on to the Realm of Divine Beauty in A.H. 561/1166 C.E., and his blessed mausoleum in Baghdād is still a place of pious visitation. He is noted for his extraordinary spiritual experiences and exploits, as well as his memorable sayings and wise teachings. It is rightly said of him that 'he was born in love, grew in perfection, and met his Lord in the perfection of love.' May the All-Glorious Lord bring us in contact with his lofty spiritual influence!"

The Author's Literary Works

***Al-Fatḥ ar-Rabbānī* [The Sublime Revelation].** A collection of sixty-two discourses delivered by Shaikh 'Abd al-Qādir in the years A.H. 545-546/1150-1152 C.E. Arabic text published by Dār al-Albāb, Damascus, n.d. Arabic text with Urdu translation: Madīna Publishing Co., Karachi, 1989. Translated from the Arabic by Muhtar Holland. Houston, Texas: Al-Baz Publishing, Inc., 1992.

Even a non-Muslim scholar like D.S. Margoliouth was so favorably impressed by the content and style of *Al-Fatḥ ar-Rabbānī* that he wrote:[2] "The sermons included in [this work] are some of the very best in Muslim literature: the spirit which they breathe is one of charity and philanthropy: the preacher would like to 'close the gates of Hell and open those of Paradise to all mankind.' He employs Ṣūfī technicalities very rarely, and none that would occasion the ordinary reader much difficulty...."

***Malfūẓāt* [Utterances].** A loosely organized compilation of talks and sayings by Shaikh ʿAbd al-Qādir, almost equal in total length to Revelations of the Unseen. Frequently treated as a kind of appendix or supplement to manuscript and printed versions of *Al-Fatḥ ar-Rabbānī*. Translated from the Arabic by Muhtar Holland. Houston, Texas: Al-Baz Publishing, Inc., 1992.

***Futūḥ al-Ghaib* [Revelations of the Unseen].** A collection of seventy-eight discourses. The Arabic text, edited by Muḥammad Sālim al-Bawwāb, has been published by Dār al-Albāb, Damascus, 1986. German translation: W. Braune. *Die Futūḥ al-Gaib des ʿAbd al-Qādir*. Berlin and Leipzig: Walter de Gruyter & Co., 1933. English translations: (1) M. Aftab-ud-Din Ahmad. *Futuh Al-Ghaib [The Revelations of the Unseen]*. Lahore, Pakistan: Sh. Muhammad Ashraf. Repr. 1986. (2) Shaikh ʿAbd al-Qādir al-Jīlānī. *Revelations of the Unseen (Futūḥ al-Ghaib)*. Translated from the Arabic by Muhtar Holland. Houston, Texas: Al-Baz Publishing, Inc., 1992.

***Jalāʾ al-Khawāṭir* [The Removal of Cares].** A collection of forty-five discourses by Shaikh ʿAbd al-Qādir. Arabic text with Urdu translation published by Maktaba Nabawiyya, Lahore, n.d. Translated from the Arabic by Muhtar Holland. Ft. Lauderdale, Florida: Al-Baz Publishing, Inc., 1997.

[2] In his article "ʿAbd al-Ḳādir" in *Encyclopaedia of Islam* (also printed in *Shorter Encyclopaedia of Islam*. Leiden, Netherlands: E.J. Brill, 1961).

Sirr al-Asrār **[The Secret of Secrets].** A short work, divided into twenty-four chapters, in which "the realities within our faith and our path are divulged." English translation: *The Secret of Secrets by Ḥaḍrat ʿAbd al-Qādir al-Jīlānī*, interpreted by Shaykh Tosun Bayrak al-Jerrahi al-Halveti. Cambridge, England: The Islamic Texts Society, 1992.

Al-Ghunya li-ṭālibī ṭarīq al-ḥaqq **[Sufficient Provision for Seekers of the Path of Truth].** Arabic text published in two parts by Dār al-Albāb, Damascus, n.d., 192 pp. + 200 pp. Translated from the Arabic (in 5 vols.) by Muhtar Holland. Hollywood, Florida: Al-Baz Publishing, Inc., 1997.

Other works attributed to Shaikh ʿAbd al-Qādir include short treatises on some of the Divine Names; litanies *[awrād/aḥzāb]*; prayers and supplications *[daʿawāt/munājāt]*; mystical poems *[qaṣāʾid]*.

May Allāh forgive our mistakes and failings, and may He bestow His blessings upon all connected with our project—especially our gracious readers! Āmīn.

Muhtar Holland

About the Translator

Muhtar Holland was born in 1935, in the ancient city of Durham in the North East of England. This statement may be considered anachronistic, however, since he did not bear the name Muhtar until 1969, when he was moved—by powerful experiences in the *latihan kejiwaan* of Subud—to embrace the religion of Islām.*

At the age of four, according to an entry in his father's diary, he said to a man who asked his name: "I'm a stranger to myself." During his years at school, he was drawn most strongly to the study of languages, which seemed to offer signposts to guide the stranger on his "Journey Home," apart from their practical usefulness to one who loved to spend his vacations traveling—at first on a bicycle—through foreign lands. Serious courses in Latin, Greek, French, Spanish and Danish, with additional smatterings of Anglo-Saxon, Italian, German and Dutch. Travels in France, Germany, Belgium, Holland and Denmark. Then a State Scholarship and up to Balliol College, Oxford, for a degree course centered on the study of Arabic and Turkish. Travels in Turkey and Syria. Then National Service in the Royal Navy, with most of the two years spent on an intensive course in the Russian language.

In the years since graduation from Oxford and Her Majesty's Senior Service, Mr. Holland has held academic posts at the University of Toronto, Canada; at the School of Oriental and African Studies in the University of London, England (with a five-month leave to study Islamic Law in Cairo, Egypt); and at the Universiti Kebangsaan in Kuala Lumpur, Malaysia (followed by a six-month sojourn in Indonesia). He also worked as Senior Research Fellow at the Islamic Foundation in Leicester, England, and as Director of the Nūr al-Islām Translation Center in Valley Cottage, New York.

* The name Muhtar was received at that time from Bapak Muhammad Subuh Sumohadiwidjojo, of Wisma Subud, Jakarta, in response to a request for a suitable Muslim name. In strict academic transliteration from the Arabic, the spelling would be *Mukhtār*. The form *Muchtar* is probably more common in Indonesia than *Muhtar*, which happens to coincide with the modern Turkish spelling of the name.

His freelance activities have mostly been devoted to writing and translating in various parts of the world, including Scotland and California. He made his Pilgrimage *[Ḥajj]* to Mecca in 1980.

Published works include the following:

Al-Ghazālī. *On the Duties of Brotherhood.* Translated from the Classical Arabic by Muhtar Holland. London: Latimer New Dimensions, 1975. New York: Overlook Press, 1977. Repr. 1980 and 1993.

Sheikh Muzaffer Ozak al-Jerrahi. *The Unveiling of Love.* Translated from the Turkish by Muhtar Holland. New York: Inner Traditions, 1981. Westport, Ct.: Pir Publications, 1990.

Ibn Taymīya. *Public Duties in Islām.* Translated from the Arabic by Muhtar Holland. Leicester, England: Islamic Foundation, 1982.

Hasan Shushud. *Masters of Wisdom of Central Asia.* Translated from the Turkish by Muhtar Holland. Ellingstring, England: Coombe Springs Press, 1983.

Al-Ghazālī. *Inner Dimensions of Islamic Worship.* Translated from the Arabic by Muhtar Holland. Leicester, England: Islamic Foundation, 1983.

Sheikh Muzaffer Ozak al-Jerrahi. *Irshād.* Translated [from the Turkish] with an Introduction by Muhtar Holland. Warwick, New York: Amity House, 1988. Westport, Ct.: Pir Publications, 1990.

Sheikh Muzaffer Ozak al-Jerrahi. *Blessed Virgin Mary.* Translation from the Original Turkish by Muhtar Holland. Westport, Ct.: Pir Publications, 1991.

Sheikh Muzaffer Ozak al-Jerrahi. *The Garden of Dervishes.* Translation from the Original Turkish by Muhtar Holland. Westport, Ct.: Pir Publications, 1991.

Sheikh Muzaffer Ozak al-Jerrahi. *Adornment of Hearts.* Translation from the Original Turkish by Muhtar Holland and Sixtina Friedrich. Westport, Ct.: Pir Publications, 1991.

Sheikh Muzaffer Ozak al-Jerrahi. *Ashki's Divan.* Translation from the Original Turkish by Muhtar Holland and Sixtina Friedrich. Westport, Ct.: Pir Publications, 1991.

Shaikh ʿAbd al-Qādir al-Jīlānī. *Revelations of the Unseen (Futūḥ al-Ghaib).* Translated from the Arabic by Muhtar Holland. Houston, Texas: Al-Baz Publishing, Inc., 1992

Shaikh ʿAbd al-Qādir al-Jīlānī. *The Sublime Revelation (al-Fatḥ ar-Rabbānī).* Translated from the Arabic by Muhtar Holland. Houston, Texas: Al-Baz Publishing, Inc., 1992

Shaikh ʿAbd al-Qādir al-Jīlānī. *Utterances (Malfūẓāt).* Translated from the Arabic by Muhtar Holland. Houston, Texas: Al-Baz Publishing, Inc., 1992

Shaikh ʿAbd al-Qādir al-Jīlānī. *The Removal of Cares (Jalāʾ al-Khawāṭir).* Translated from the Arabic by Muhtar Holland. Ft. Lauderdale, Florida: Al-Baz Publishing, Inc., 1997

Subject Index, Volume Two

BOOKS PUBLISHED BY AL-BAZ PUBLISHING INCLUDE:

1. **Revelations of the Unseen** (*Futūḥ al-Ghaib*) ($19.00)
   78 Discourses by Shaikh ʿAbd al-Qādir al-Jīlānī
2. **The Sublime Revelation** (*Al-Fatḥ ar-Rabbānī*) ($29.00)
   62 Discourses by Shaikh ʿAbd al-Qādir al-Jīlānī
3. **Utterances of Shaikh ʿAbd al-Qādir** (*Malfūẓāt*) ($16.00)
4. **The Removal of Cares** (*Jalāʾ al-Khawāṭir*) ($25.00)
   45 Discourses by Shaikh ʿAbd al-Qādir al-Jīlānī
5. **Sufficient Provision for Seekers of the Path of Truth**
   (*Al-Ghunya li-Ṭālibī Ṭarīq al-Ḥaqq*) ($110.00)
   by Shaikh ʿAbd al-Qādir al-Jīlānī (may Allāh be well pleased with him)
   This encyclopedic work is a complete resource on the inner and outer aspects of Islām. The translation has been published in 5 volumes. 1738 pages. Translated by Muhtar Holland.

Books scheduled for publication in 1997 include:

1. **Concerning the Affirmation of Divine Oneness**
   (*Risālat at-Tawḥīd*)
   by Shaikh Walī Raslān ad-Dimashqī (d. A.H. 695)
   This is a Risāla on *shirk khafī* (hidden *shirk*). *Shirk* is associating partners with Allāh. Also in the book is a commentary by Shaikh Zakariyyāʾ al-Anṣārī called "*Kitāb Fatḥ ar-Raḥmān*." Also in the book is a commentary on the commentary by Shaikh ʿAlī ibn ʿAṭiyya ʿAlawān al-Ḥamawī (d. A.H. 936) called "*Sharḥ Fatḥ ar-Raḥmān*." This is a very important book. Translated by Muhtar Holland.
2. **The Proper Conduct of Marriage in Islām** (*Ādāb an-Nikāḥ*)
   by Imām al-Ghazālī
   This is Book 12 of *Iḥyā ʿUlūm ad-Dīn*. Translated by Muhtar Holland.

3. **Fifteen Letters**
(*Khamsata ʿAshara Maktūban* otherwise known as *Maktūbāt*)
Fifteen letters by Shaikh ʿAbd al-Qādir al-Jīlānī to one of his disciples. Originally written in Persian, they were translated into Arabic by ʿAlī Ḥusāmu'd-dīn al-Muttaqī (the Devout). Translated by Muhtar Holland.

4. **Necklaces of Gems** (*Qalāʾid al-Jawāhir*)
by Shaikh Muḥammad ibn Yaḥyā at-Tādifī
A Biography of Shaikh ʿAbd al-Qādir al-Jīlānī (may Allāh be well pleased with him), on the Marvelous Exploits of the Crown of the Saints, the Treasure-trove of the Pure, the Sulṭān of the *Awliyāʾ*, the Sublime *Quṭb*, Shaikh Muḥyi'd-dīn ʿAbd al-Qādir al-Jīlānī. Translated by Muhtar Holland.

To order contact: Al-Baz Publishing, Inc.
4401 Sheridan Street, Suite 226
Hollywood, Florida 33021

Phone: (954) 964-5227
Fax: (954) 981-7304
E-mail: albaz@bellsouth.net *or*
ruslan@herald.infi.net